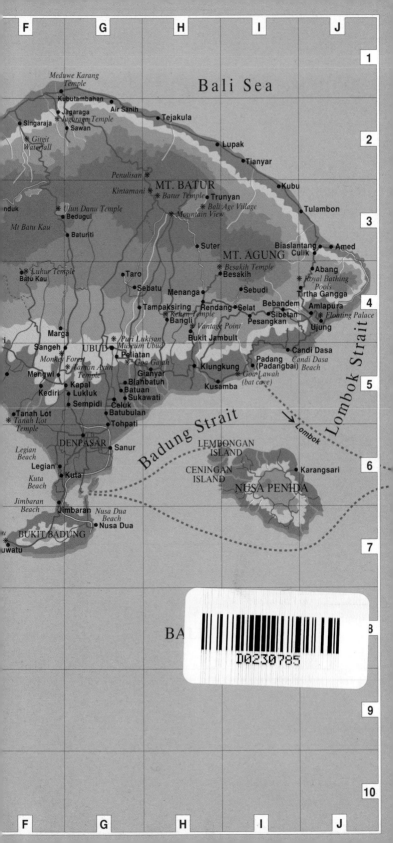

Over the last thousand years, the
Balinese have transformed the
landscape of their island, terracing
hillsides and digging canals to irrigate
the land, enabling them to grow rice.

All the young men in a village perform the "monkey dance", which has its roots in the *sanghyang* trance dances of Bali. Their chants, reminiscent of the chattering of monkeys, simulate the sounds of a *gamelan* orchestra.

A cremation ceremony, one of the most complex Balinese rituals, may last for days. At the heart of Balinese Hinduism is the belief in the cycle of life, death, and rebirth. ●53. The soul can only be freed and reincarnated when the body is destroyed and returned to the elements of earth, fire, water, air, and ether.

EVERYMAN GUIDES
PUBLISHED BY DAVID CAMPBELL PUBLISHERS LTD, LONDON

BALI – ISBN 1-85715-862-8

© 1996 David Campbell Publishers Ltd
© 1995 Editions Nouveaux-Loisirs, a subsidiary of Gallimard, Paris

NUMEROUS SPECIALISTS AND ACADEMICS
HAVE CONTRIBUTED TO THIS GUIDE:

EDITORS: Debbie Guthrie Haer,
Juliette Morillot, Irene Toh

LAYOUT: Tan Tat Ghee, Tan Seok Lui
PRODUCTION: Edmund Lam
MAPS: Bruce Granquist, Tan Seok Lui

AUTHORS:
NATURE: Tony and Jane Whitten, Lyn and
Cody Shwaiko, Steve Lansing
HISTORY: Adrian Vickers
ART AND TRADITIONS: Kati Basset,
Jean Couteau, Diana Darling, Thomas M.
Hunter, Jr., Wayan Aryati Hunter,
A.G. Roberts
ARCHITECTURE: MadeWijaya,
Bruce Granquist
BALI AS SEEN BY PAINTERS: Lorne Blair
BALI AS SEEN BY WRITERS: Adrian Vickers,
Thomas M. Hunter, Jr.
PRACTICAL INFORMATION: Diana Darling,
Donna van Wely
GLOSSARY: Caren Zilber

ITINERARIES:
Lorne Blair, Diana Darling
CELUK JEWELERS: Lyn and Cody Shwaiko
BALI MUSEUM: Bron and Garrett Solyom

ILLUSTRATORS:
NATURE: Anuar Bin Abdul Rahim,
Kathryn Blomfield, Tan Siew Beng
ARCHITECTURE: Bruce Granquist
ART AND TRADITIONS: Anuar Bin Abdul
Rahim, Kathryn Blomfield, Made Berata
PRACTICAL INFORMATION:
Heather Thompson, Kathryn Blomfield

PHOTOGRAPHY: Rio Helmi
ADDITIONAL PHOTOGRAPHY: Lorne Blair,
Diana Darling, Kati Basset, Lawrence Lim,
Guido Alberto Rossi, and others.

ARCHIVAL PHOTOGRAPHS/DOCUMENTALISTS:
John Falconer, Leo Haks

SPECIAL THANKS TO:
YUKO NAUMANN, SUTEJA NEKA, WAYAN
WARTINI, AGUNG RAI, IDA ANAK AGUNG
GDE AGUNG, ANAK AGUNG ALIT ARDI,
COKORDE PUTRA SUKAWATI, MICHEL
PICARD, NEVILLE ROSENGREN, MUSEUM
PURI LUKISAN, CHRIS CARLISLE, SEAN
FOLEY, AND THE INDONESIAN TOURIST
PROMOTION BOARD.

THIS BOOK IS DEDICATED TO THE MEMORY
OF LORNE BLAIR (1946–95)

PRINTED IN ITALY BY EDITORIALE LIBRARIA.

EVERYMAN GUIDES
79 Berwick Street
London W1V 3PF

BALI

EVERYMAN GUIDES

CONTENTS

11

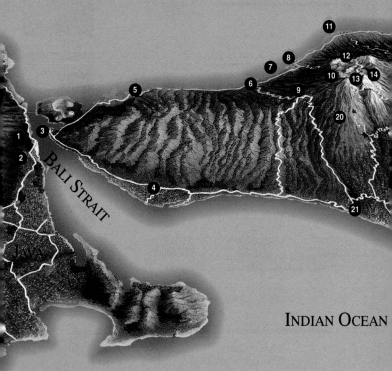

1. Ketapang   2. Banyuwangi   3. Gilimanuk   4. Negara   5. Pura Pulaki   6. Seririt   7. Lovina   8. Singaraja   9. Pupuan   10. Lake Tamblingan   11. Kubutambahan   12. Lake Buyan   13. Puri Candi Kuning

27. Culik   28. Pura Luhur Uluwatu   29. Airport   30. Kuta Beach   31. Denpasar   32. Gianyar   33. Klungkung   34. Padang Bai   35. Candi Dasa   36. Amlapura   37. Sanur   38. Serangan Island   39. Nusa Dua

JAVA SEA

JAVA

BALI STRAIT

INDIAN OCEAN

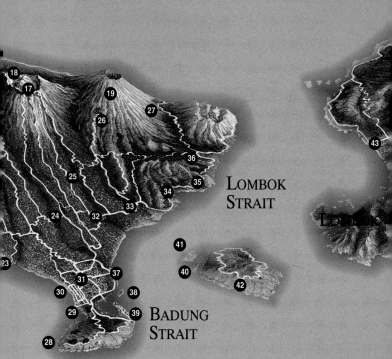

LOMBOK
STRAIT

LOMBOK

BADUNG
STRAIT

HOW TO USE THIS GUIDE

The symbols at the top of each page refer to the different parts of the guide.

■ NATURAL ENVIRONMENT
● UNDERSTANDING BALI
▲ ITINERARIES
◆ PRACTICAL INFORMATION

The itinerary map shows the main points of interest along the way and is intended to help you find your bearings.

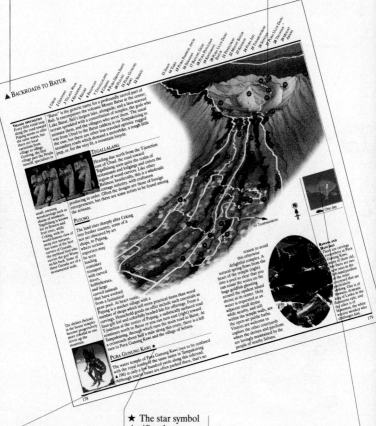

▲ BACKROADS TO BATUR

VILLAGE SPECIALTIES
Every little retail stop along the road toward Pujung seems to offer the same wares, but there are local variations from village to village: the first, Goalong, has long turned specializes in

"Batur" is the generic name for a profoundly sacred part of Bali. It encompasses the volcano, Mount Batur at the center, Lake Batur, Bali's largest lake, alongside, and a lava-scarred terrain sprinkled with a constellation of temples, the gods who way from Ubud to the Batur caldera is via Tampaksiring up the east, but there are other less-traveled options: rugged country roads which demand a motorbike, a tough little jeep, or, for the very fit, a mountain bicycle.

TEGALLALANG

Heading due north from the T-junction east of Ubud, the road toward Tegallalang soon enters the realm of restaurants and lodging and enters the region of wood-carvers. Like other Balinese handicrafts, this is a wholesale cottage industry, with craftsmen producing to order. Often the designs are those of foreign entrepreneurs, but there are some artists to be found among the artisans.

small, attaining woodcarvings such as chains of monkeys. Tegallalang is known for its fine and, at Ceking, with its world-famous view of the rice terraces. One of Goalong's best carvers of Garuda carries the god who on his back. Some of these Garuda are of monumental scale.

PUJUNG

The land rises sharply after Ceking into lusher country, some of it not yet obscured by art shops, to Pujung, where serious carvers may be seen loading container transport with carved doors, hobbyhorses, and large carved animals that have evolved from a fantastical gene pool. Pujung is a market village with a number of shops which sell more practical items than wood carvings. Household goods on offer include such essentials as faux-gilt foil and colorfully beaded lids for offerings. From a T-junction in the center of Pujung you can turn east (right) toward Tampaksiring, through which runs the main road to Batur. At a crossroads about half a mile along this route, there is a left turn to Pura Gunung Kawi and the village of Sebatu.

The shrines (below) in the house become progressively more colorful as one drives up the mountain.

PURA GUNUNG KAWI ★

The water temple of Pura Gunung Kawi (not to be confused with the royal tombs of the same name in Tampaksiring ▲ 196) is only a few hundred yards along this sideroad. Although tourist buses are often parked there, that's no

reason to avoid this otherwise delightful complex. A natural spring flows from the heart of the temple (right) into a pool so clear that you can count the scales on the huge goldfish ghosting around the opulent island shrine at its center. Holy water is respected as an adjacent small shrine within the temple walls, the open-air public baths. Visitors are welcome to explore the other courtyards where the shrines and pavilions are lovingly maintained by the people of nearby Sebatu.

RANWA AND HANUMAN
There are carvings everywhere at Pura Gunung Kawi. Many of them are old, but there are two new ones in the food pavilion of the inner courtyard that are particularly striking. One is of Rawana, demonic king of Lanka in the Ramayana epic, and the other is about Hanuman, the white warrior monkey who challenges him.

178   179
One day
TO TAMPAKSIRING

12 JASAN · 13 GOALONG · 14 PURA PUSEH, APUH · 15 GALANG · 16 RUJALI · 17 BANTING GEDE · 18 PIGADAGAN · 19 TEGALLALANG · 20 SEGA · 21 TAPAKAN · 22 KANWA · 23 ULER BATUR · 24 PURA LATI · 25 KEBON · 26 PURA GUNUNG · 27 PENAMPANAN · 28 PUJUNG · 29 PURA ULUN DANU · 30 MOUNT · 31 BATUR

■●▲◆
The symbols alongside a title or within the text itself provide cross-references to a theme or place dealt with elsewhere in the the guide.

★ The star symbol signifies that a particular site has been singled out by the editors for its special beauty, atmosphere, or cultural interest.

The mini-map locates the particular itinerary within the wider area covered by the guide.

---

mountain.

continues north to Batur or you can turn east (right) toward Tampaksiring, through which runs the main road to Batur. At a crossroads about half a mile along this route, there is a left turn to Pura Gunung Kawi and the village of Sebatu.

PURA GUNUNG KAWI ★

The water temple of Pura Gunung Kawi (not to be confused with the royal tombs of the same name in Tampaksiring ▲ 196) is only a few hundred yards along this sideroad. Although tourist buses are often parked there, that's no

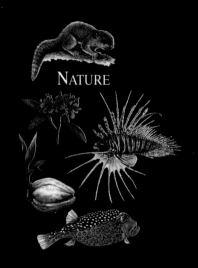

NATURE

Rainfall is the major climatic variable in Bali and differs markedly across the island. Dry seasons range from a few days to eight or nine months with corresponding major variations in vegetation: torrid lowland rain forest; periodically dry forest where some deciduous trees react to the lack of water by losing their leaves; and yellow and brown savanna vegetation in some coastal areas. On the mountain slopes, trees are characteristically adorned with garlands of light green lichen.

■ LOWLAND RAIN FOREST

Lowland rain forests are justly admired for their enormous trees and climbers, their rare wildlife, their many and varied types of plants, and their close-knit ecological relationships.

■ SAVANNA

The remaining savanna of Bali is reminiscent of the plains of east Africa, with large, umbrella-shaped and thorny acacia trees, dry and cracked soil, herds of grazing animals, and colorful birds.

FIG TREES

Fig trees are regarded as keystone species in rain forests because they provide food for a variety of animals such as monkeys, bats, squirrels, pigeons, hornbills, and barbets. Some fig trees have fruit on their branches; others on their trunks.

LONTAR PALM

Savannas often have large numbers of lontar palms ■ 23 towering above other vegetation. The trunk is similar to the coconut's, but the leaves are like a many-fingered palm. It bears black nuts, which contain pleasant-tasting flesh and water. These are sometimes sold on the roadside in Bali.

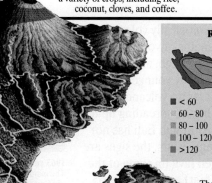

CULTIVATED LAND
Sun, rain, and fertile volcanic soil combine to make most of Bali ideal for cultivation. The uncolored area of the map below represents land where the natural vegetation has been extensively modified to grow a variety of crops, including rice, coconut, cloves, and coffee.

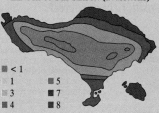

RAINFALL (IN INCHES)

- ■ < 60
- ■ 60 – 80
- ■ 80 – 100
- ■ 100 – 120
- ■ >120

RAINFALL
The rainy season in Bali lasts from approximately November to March, bringing weak northwesterly winds and sultry conditions. Rainfall varies from more than 120 inches on the southern slopes of Mount Agung and Mount Batu Karu to less than 60 inches along the northern coast, the peninsula, and southern Nusa Penida.

■ **MONTANE FOREST**
Above about 5000 feet, tree height decreases with elevation until the trees form a gnarled, elfin forest where every trunk and bough is covered with a blanket of moss and lichen. In drier areas, the dominant tree is the she-oak or casuarina, with needle-like leaves ■ *19*.

■ **DECIDUOUS FOREST**
Almost all of the remaining deciduous forest on Bali is in very rugged country, where rivers are few and far between.

LENGTH OF DRY SEASON (IN MONTHS)

- ■ < 1
- ■ 1   ■ 5
- ■ 3   ■ 7
- ■ 4   ■ 8

DRY SEASON
The dry season, generally from April to October, is marked by strong southeasterly winds from the cool Australian interior. As shown above, the length of the dry season increases as one moves away from the island's interior.

HOMALIUM TOMENTOSUM
A typical tree of the deciduous forest, *Homalium tomentosum* can grow up to 115 feet tall and 3 feet in diameter. The red timber of these trees tends to split and is not very durable.

SAWO KECIK
Found in deciduous forests, the sawo kecik is a medium-sized tree, the timber of which is much sought after for carving. The fruit are quite tasty and are popular during their short season.

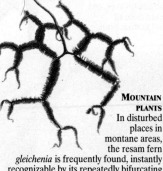

MOUNTAIN PLANTS
In disturbed places in montane areas, the resam fern *gleichenia* is frequently found, instantly recognizable by its repeatedly bifurcating fronds. Long ago the stout old stems were cut and fashioned into writing pens, and the stems in general have been used to make matting, rope, partition walls, pouches, and other goods. The young leaves are used in medicines.

Virtually all of Bali is geologically volcanic. The western hills are the remains of volcanos from more than one million years ago, and the peaks to their east are progressively younger. These are classified as basaltic strato volcanos, and the lava they spew is quite liquid, spreading up to a half a mile in an hour. Although Bali has not had an eruption for twenty years, the signs are still present in the barren lava on some of the slopes of Agung (9950 feet) and Batur (5665 feet). Volcanos rule every facet of Bali's geology: they create the island's landforms, regenerate its soils, and help produce the downpours which sustain the island's agriculture. In acknowledgment of the pervasive role volcanos play in their lives, the Balinese consider them sacred.

1963 ERUPTION
The major eruption of Mount Agung in early 1963 reduced its height from 10,370 feet to 9950 feet, and the smothering hot ash, the lava, and the ensuing mudflows killed more than 1000 people.

FORK-TAILED SWIFT
Coming from Siberia in winter, these birds can be seen swooping over the open mountain tops, mouths agape, catching the aerial plankton of small insects.

RICHARD'S PIPIT
This species is widespread in the open grassy areas. Although more frequently seen in the lowlands, it can also be found in open areas on the high mountains.

JAVANESE RHODODENDRON
The Javanese rhododendron is found throughout Bali, growing on trees as well as among stones and rocks next to small streams, on lava streams, screes, and even close to sulphurous vents.

SENDUDUK
This flower is one of the most showy plants of the mountains. It can also be seen in scrubby areas, even along roadsides.

VOLCANO WITHIN A VOLCANO
In Indonesia secondary volcanos, such as Mount Batur, commonly develop inside calderas. This bird's-eye view shows the Batur caldera and its secondary volcano today. The original volcano destroyed during the caldera-forming event is gradually being rebuilt in the form of Mount Batur.

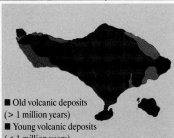

■ Old volcanic deposits
(> 1 million years)
■ Young volcanic deposits
(< 1 million years)
■ Recent lava fields ■ Tertiary limestone
■ Loose sands and gravels ■ Alluvial plains

GEOLOGY OF BALI
Although primarily volcanic, the geology of Bali also includes areas of land formed by ancient coral reefs which were pushed out of the sea. The Prapat Agung peninsula in the northwest, the Bukit in the south, and Nusa Penida were formed in this way.

VOLCANO FERN
Some of the hardiest plants in the hot and dry conditions experienced on the slopes of volcanos are thick-bladed ferns such as the volcano fern (*Selliguea*).

CASUARINA TREES
The most characteristic tree of volcano slopes is the casuarina (above). Looking rather like a pine it can easily be distinguished by its pendulous "needles", which are made up of short sections (right).

1. FIRST MOUNT BATUR
Mount Batur was once taller than present-day Mount Agung. About 30,000 years ago, molten rock created by the subduction of the Indo-Australian Plate beneath the Eurasian Plate worked its way through fissures in the earth toward Batur's surface.

2. THE ERUPTION
In a cataclysmic eruption of lava and ash, the magma chamber beneath the volcano emptied rapidly.

3. SUMMIT DISAPPEARS
The top of the volcano did not blow apart but began to sink in a series of big blocks into the empty magma chamber.

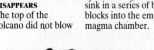

4. CHILD VOLCANO FORMS
Some 10,000 years after the caldera-forming eruption, another eruption formed the secondary volcano. Part of the caldera began to fill with water and formed Lake Batur. The secondary volcano, like the first, is known as a composite volcano, where eruptions of ash, cinder, and rock fragments alternate or combine with lava flows, building a cone. Multiple cones may form a large volcanic edifice that could one day experience another large caldera-forming eruption.

EDELWEISS
The most famous Indonesian mountain plant, the edelweiss, is one of the first plants to colonize new volcanic deposits. Pilgrims climbing Mount Agung believe that this white-felted plant is a gift from heaven, and take small (or large) pieces down the mountain as souvenirs.

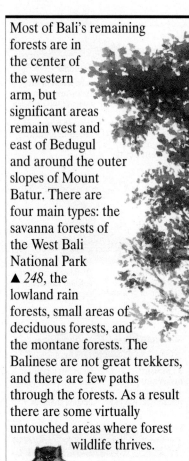

Most of Bali's remaining forests are in the center of the western arm, but significant areas remain west and east of Bedugul and around the outer slopes of Mount Batur. There are four main types: the savanna forests of the West Bali National Park ▲ *248*, the lowland rain forests, small areas of deciduous forests, and the montane forests. The Balinese are not great trekkers, and there are few paths through the forests. As a result there are some virtually untouched areas where forest wildlife thrives.

BLACK GIANT SQUIRREL
The largest squirrel in Asia, it can be nearly 30 inches long. It is a shy animal of the high canopy, capable of spectacular leaps between trees.

TIGER
The last Bali tiger was shot in 1937, although there is an unconfirmed record of villagers finding a tiger's corpse in 1963. Extensive surveys since then have revealed no further signs of the animal.

PARADISE TREE SNAKE
This beautiful snake grows to about 4 feet. It is mildly poisonous and feeds on small birds and mammals.

MACAQUES
Long-tailed macaques are commonly seen along roadsides near forests and near some of the temples. They can be vicious when stealing food from unwary human visitors.

WILD BANTENG
Only a handful of wild banteng now survives in Bali's westernmost forests. They are more or less indistinguishable from the domestic Bali cattle.

FOREST SNAIL
Bali has a number of interesting snails. *Asperitas waandersiana* is restricted to Bali and east Java. The form shown above is found only in remnant forests and other damp places on Nusa Penida.

WREATHED HORNBILL
In the depths of the remote western forests, loud swishing wing beats announce the presence of Bali's largest bird, the wreathed hornbill. They generally fly in pairs as they search the tree tops for ripe fruit.

BALI STARLING
The star of Bali's wildlife is the exquisite Bali starling, which lives in the savanna and deciduous forests of the northwest. The trade in caged birds has driven this lovely bird to the edge of extinction. It is still critically endangered (only about fifty survive in the wild) but conservation efforts have improved its prospects ▲ *250*.

GREATER RACQUET-TAILED DRONGO
The unusual tail of the greater racquet-tailed drongo distinguishes it from all other birds. It is found in forested areas, while some of its lesser adorned relatives may be seen around Bali cattle, waiting for the beasts to stir up insects in the pasture.

BLACK LEAF MONKEY
Bali's black leaf monkey may be found in all the forests but it is far from common. Its young have bright orange fur for the first few months.

PINK-NECKED PIGEON

EMERALD DOVE
The emerald dove and pink-necked pigeon are difficult to see among the green leaves of the canopy. The best place to look for them is in fruiting fig trees.

CHESTNUT-BREASTED MALKOHAS
At home in the highland forest and scrub, these birds are surprisingly hard to see because they skulk around, preferring to jump and clamber rather than fly.

Coconut plantations, particularly common in west Bali, also cover the southern foothills below the high forest ridges. Many of Bali's coconut trees are coming to the end of their productive lives, and in some areas the common tall varieties are being replaced by dwarf hybrids, which fruit when the trunk is only about 6 feet tall. Coconut trees are ubiquitous in villages, where they are equally important for secular and religious life.

COCONUT PALMS
Every 210 days, a year in the local calendar, the Balinese make special offerings to the coconut tree, which provides raw material for a multitude of items used in everyday life. Farmers pray for a plentiful harvest, then sprinkle the tree and offerings with holy water. A productive tree provides from fifty to a hundred mature nuts annually for about fifty years.

COCONUT HUSK
The husk is the source of coir, used in making mats and ropes. The hard inner layer of the coconut is used to make charcoal filters and trinkets such as buttons.

COCONUT ROOTS
Even the roots of the coconut tree are valued for use in medicine.

COCONUT LEAVES
Hats, fans, and baskets are just a few of the items made from the leaves of the coconut palm. In Bali, the leaves are also woven into offerings and temple decorations.

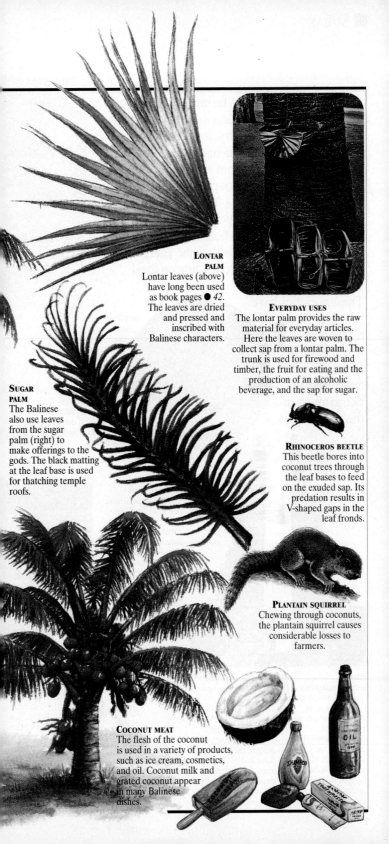

LONTAR PALM
Lontar leaves (above) have long been used as book pages ● 42. The leaves are dried and pressed and inscribed with Balinese characters.

EVERYDAY USES
The lontar palm provides the raw material for everyday articles. Here the leaves are woven to collect sap from a lontar palm. The trunk is used for firewood and timber, the fruit for eating and the production of an alcoholic beverage, and the sap for sugar.

SUGAR PALM
The Balinese also use leaves from the sugar palm (right) to make offerings to the gods. The black matting at the leaf base is used for thatching temple roofs.

RHINOCEROS BEETLE
This beetle bores into coconut trees through the leaf bases to feed on the exuded sap. Its predation results in V-shaped gaps in the leaf fronds.

PLANTAIN SQUIRREL
Chewing through coconuts, the plantain squirrel causes considerable losses to farmers.

COCONUT MEAT
The flesh of the coconut is used in a variety of products, such as ice cream, cosmetics, and oil. Coconut milk and grated coconut appear in many Balinese dishes.

Generations of Balinese farmers have changed the island's landscape, clearing forests, digging irrigation canals, and terracing hillsides so that they could grow their life-sustaining rice. This elaborate irrigation system was made possible by the coordination of cooperatives known as *subak*. All farmers whose fields are fed by the same source, such as a spring or a canal, belong to an individual *subak*. There are more than a thousand *subak* in Bali, with some villages having more than one, depending on local drainage patterns ◆ *304*.

These societies have provided the framework which has made Bali one of the most efficient rice growers in the archipelago.

SUBAK TEMPLES
Paralleling the physical system of terraces and irrigation works, the Balinese have also constructed intricate networks of shrines and temples dedicated to the goddess of the lake (who lives in Lake Batur); the rice goddess; the earth mother, and other agricultural deities.

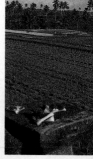

RICE GODDESS
The Balinese believe rice is a gift of the gods, part of an all-encompassing life force of which humans partake. The first fruits from each harvest are given back to the gods, and complex ceremonies and festivals accompany every stage of growth in the life of the rice plant.

SUBAK RESPONSIBILITIES
Subak are democratic organizations in which members meet regularly to coordinate plantings, to control the distribution of irrigation water, and to plan the building and maintenance of weirs and canals, as well as to organize ritual offerings and *subak* temple festivals. Because most of Bali's 150 rivers and streams flow within deep-cut gorges, the Balinese have had to dig tunnels, some more than a mile long, to divert water to their rice fields.

JAVAN MUNIA
Birds, especially the Javan munia, which feed in large flocks, can devastate an unguarded rice field. Plastic bags and flags help protect ripening rice from these pests.

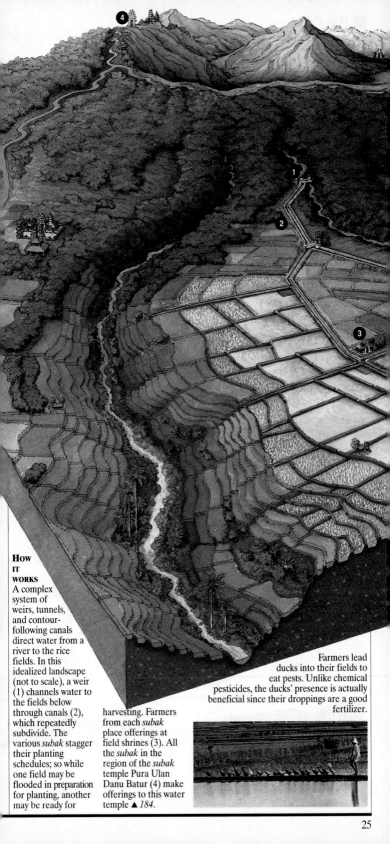

How IT WORKS

A complex system of weirs, tunnels, and contour-following canals direct water from a river to the rice fields. In this idealized landscape (not to scale), a weir (1) channels water to the fields below through canals (2), which repeatedly subdivide. The various *subak* stagger their planting schedules; so while one field may be flooded in preparation for planting, another may be ready for harvesting. Farmers from each *subak* place offerings at field shrines (3). All the *subak* in the region of the *subak* temple Pura Ulan Danu Batur (4) make offerings to this water temple ▲ 184.

Farmers lead ducks into their fields to eat pests. Unlike chemical pesticides, the ducks' presence is actually beneficial since their droppings are a good fertilizer.

■ BALI'S COAST

Flocks of frigate birds fly high above Kuta beach. They look like angular kites, their wings barely moving.

More than sun and sand await the visitor to Bali's beautiful coast. Kuta, with its pounding waves for surfing, Sanur, with its protecting reef for a quiet family swim, Uluwatu, with its fascinating rock pools, and Benoa Bay's mangrove forest all host a world of creatures, large and small, whose habitat is the shallow waters of the island's coast.

KUTA
The beach that runs along Tuban, Kuta, Legian, and Seminyak has no offshore reef and is full of energy, with large waves pounding onto a gently sloping beach. The sea creatures here have to be either good swimmers or good burrowers. The *Donax* shells (right) and sand dollars (below) are found just below the surface of the fine sand.

DONAX SHELLS

BUBBLER CRABS
Bubbler crabs live below the sand's surface. They rebuild their burrows twice each day, leaving circles of sand "bubbles" around the entrance (above).

DOVE SHELL
Along Sanur beach at low tide the most common seashell to be found is the variable dove shell.

Eucheuma algae (above), which is boiled as a vegetable, clings to the rocks around Uluwatu.

SAND DOLLARS

ULUWATU
The dramatic temple at Uluwatu ▲ 278 is flanked on both sides by steep cliffs and sandy bays (below). It is possible to walk down to the northerly bay, where the local people gather a wide range of foods from the rocks and coral.

TURBAN SHELL

OCTOPUS

LOBSTER

ULUWATU BEACH
At Uluwatu, people with hooked sticks search the flat reef at low tide looking for turban shells, whose meat makes a tasty meal. The octopus and lobster are also popular finds.

SANUR BEACH

Sanur is protected from the force of the ocean waves by a coral reef ranging from 300 to 3000 feet offshore, so the waves on the shore are rather small and gentle. Out in the meadows of sea grass (1) are brittle stars (2), starfish (3), sea cucumbers (4), hermit crabs (5), free-living *Fungia* corals (6), and sea urchins (7). Waders, such as the common sandpiper, search for food among the bountiful life at the sea's edge.

PERIWINKLE

FIDDLER CRAB

MANGROVE FISH

In creeks running through Benoa Bay's mangrove forest some two dozen species of fish can be found, including the pipefish and small puffer fish.

PUFFER FISH

PIPEFISH

BARNACLES

COCKLES

BENOA BAY

This bay is fringed by the last mangrove forest on Bali. At low tide the soil surface is teeming with fiddler crabs. Periwinkles and barnacles cover the roots of *Rhizophora* trees. In the sandy mud in front of the mangroves, cockles are much sought after as food.

At the edge of Benoa Bay, mudskippers graze on the surface of the mud and can survive out of the water for minutes on end.

RHIZOPHORA

MUDSKIPPERS

SONNERATIA

TREES OF THE MANGROVE

There are two main types of mangrove trees in Benoa: *Rhizophora*, with stilt roots propping up the main trunk and *Sonneratia*, with pointed aerial roots penetrating the soil surface from the cable root beneath. Since the soil is generally waterlogged, both these devices allow air to be absorbed into the trees' roots.

■ NUSA PENIDA'S MARINE LIFE

The rare sulfur crested cockatoo is found only on Nusa Penida, not on Bali itself.

Nusa Penida ▲ *280* is an arid limestone island in the strait that separates Bali and Lombok. The island straddles the Wallace Line, named after Sir Alfred Wallace, the first person to recognize the break in the types of fauna that occur to the east of Bali and Borneo. Nusa Penida, though quite close to Bali, is a curious blend of both areas. There is marine life found here that is not found elsewhere in Bali. Nusa Penida is surrounded by fierce currents which surge up to five knots and create dangerous whirlpools. The resultant oxygenation, combined with the nurturing tropical sun, provides conditions for the growth of plankton and the consequent cornucopia of marine life.

BOMMIES
Dome-shaped colonies, some with more than ten coral varieties, can grow up to 10 feet or higher. Known as "bommies", they are some of the oldest forms of animal life, some taking a thousand years to grow.

OCEANIC SUNFISH
Nusa Penida is the only place in Bali where the oceanic sun fish (*mola mola*) is regularly sighted. It can span almost 7 feet between its dorsal and ventral fins, and because of its size may take the unwary diver by surprise. However, the sunfish has a slow and gentle nature, often allowing divers to come close enough to stroke it.

MANTA RAYS
The rich waters of the Nusa Penida channel attract these plankton feeders throughout the year. Although spotted in other waters around Bali, Nusa Penida is the only place where the huge manta rays (*Manta alfredi*) are regularly seen. They can grow to a span of 23 feet and can weigh more than 2800 pounds.

JUVENILE BATFISH
Schools of these fish parade the reef edge.

MOORISH IDOL
This fish is easily recognizable and common among the reefs.

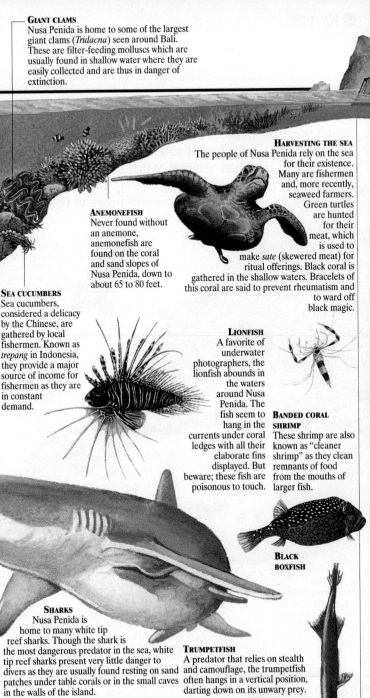

GIANT CLAMS
Nusa Penida is home to some of the largest giant clams (*Tridacna*) seen around Bali. These are filter-feeding molluscs which are usually found in shallow water where they are easily collected and are thus in danger of extinction.

ANEMONEFISH
Never found without an anemone, anemonefish are found on the coral and sand slopes of Nusa Penida, down to about 65 to 80 feet.

HARVESTING THE SEA
The people of Nusa Penida rely on the sea for their existence. Many are fishermen and, more recently, seaweed farmers. Green turtles are hunted for their meat, which is used to make *sate* (skewered meat) for ritual offerings. Black coral is gathered in the shallow waters. Bracelets of this coral are said to prevent rheumatism and to ward off black magic.

SEA CUCUMBERS
Sea cucumbers, considered a delicacy by the Chinese, are gathered by local fishermen. Known as *trepang* in Indonesia, they provide a major source of income for fishermen as they are in constant demand.

LIONFISH
A favorite of underwater photographers, the lionfish abounds in the waters around Nusa Penida. The fish seem to hang in the currents under coral ledges with all their elaborate fins displayed. But beware; these fish are poisonous to touch.

BANDED CORAL SHRIMP
These shrimp are also known as "cleaner shrimp" as they clean remnants of food from the mouths of larger fish.

BLACK BOXFISH

SHARKS
Nusa Penida is home to many white tip reef sharks. Though the shark is the most dangerous predator in the sea, white tip reef sharks present very little danger to divers as they are usually found resting on sand patches under table corals or in the small caves in the walls of the island.

TRUMPETFISH
A predator that relies on stealth and camouflage, the trumpetfish often hangs in a vertical position, darting down on its unwary prey.

MORAY EEL
A nocturnal predator, the moray eel (above) hides in holes and crevices by day. Though usually docile, its teeth inspire a healthy respect in most divers.

EMPEROR ANGELFISH

BALI RASBORA
This is the only endemic fish on the island of Bali and is restricted to Lake Bratan and some southern rivers.

Central Bali is scoured by rivers, which are fed directly by both rainfall in the central highlands of Bali and by springs from the hillsides. The Balinese make offerings at the springs to ensure the flow of water through the elaborate irrigation system ■ *24* that sustains the island's rice crops. Rafting trips are a wonderful way to see some of the wilder parts of Bali and its rivers ◆ *308*.

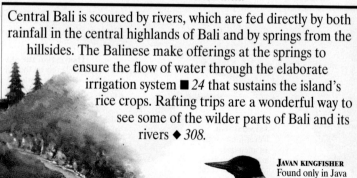

JAVAN KINGFISHER
Found only in Java and Bali, this bird can be seen along the river gorges or perched on poles in rice fields.

WATER STICK
The water stick insect spends most of its life among plants or stones. It preys on small fish and tadpoles.

RIVER CRAB
The common river crab in Bali's rivers probably breeds in the estuaries, and the young migrate upstream.

GOBY
The most attractive fish native to Bali is the elegant goby, which is found in stony rivers. The sucking fins on its chest allow it to climb up rapids and weirs.

SNAKEHEAD
This swift, torpedo-shaped fish is the largest predator in the rivers. The male jealously guards the eggs laid by the female. These fish, which can grow up to 3 feet long, have been known to attack young children.

TILAPIA
Originally from Africa, this fish has been so widely introduced that it can now be found in most lakes and rivers.

PRAWN
There are a number of prawn species in the lowland rivers. Some are quite tolerant of poor water quality.

GUPPY
The guppy, originally from Trinidad, can be found in almost every lake, river, canal, and rice field on the island. The female (above) is rather dull and much larger than the attractive male.

boundary designated by the 19th
century naturalist Alfred Russel
Wallace, to differentiate the flora &
fauna of the Sunda Shelf from the
Sahul Shelf, to which Australia bel
earliest fossil remains of hominids
found in Java, and are between 1.7
Bali was still joined to Java as part
known as the Sunda Shelf, and Pal
in Bali indicate hominid presence with
years ago rice-growing people with
and speaking Austronesian langu

> "THROUGH THE CENTURIES, CIVILIZATION UPON CIVILIZATION FROM ALL DIRECTIONS HAS SETTLED ON THE ISLANDS OVER THE ANCIENT MEGALITHIC CULTURES OF THE ABORIGINES..."
>
> MIGUEL COVARRUBIAS, *ISLAND OF BALI*, 1937

MEGALITHS AND SARCOPHAGI. These Austronesian peoples moved eastward into the Melanesian and Polynesian islands some 2000 years ago, taking with them practices such as pork eating, betel chewing, ship-centered cultural images, and forms of kinship and ritual that show ties with early Balinese culture. In Bali remnants of this early culture still exist, in the form of standing stones, stone seats, and stone altars, and in stepped temples. The burial system suggests the

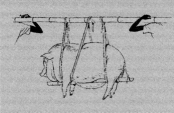

existence of a stratified society, people buried in sarcophagi probably being of higher status. Grave goods, including heart-shaped axes, glass, and carnelian beads, have also been recovered, though many sarcophagi were robbed of their contents. Some sarcophagi were oval in shape, others took more elaborate forms (below, left), with human heads and zoo-anthropomorphic figures carved on them. The site of Gilimanuk ▲ *249* in west Bali has proved important.

BRONZE AGE BALI. The early Balinese also acquired the art of metallurgy which spread from South China and Vietnam sometime between the 8th and 3rd centuries BC. This culture is known as Dongson after a site in Vietnam, and its highly developed techniques of casting from molds produced pieces with elaborate spiral motifs and distinctive anthropomorphic figures. Decorated mold fragments have been found at Manuaba in Bali, an indication that these drums were of local manufacture, unlike many of the other Dongson drums found in Indonesia, which may have been made elsewhere. The raw materials for bronze, copper, and tin are not found in Bali, so the early Balinese must have traded with other cultures to obtain them. The most famous Balinese example is the "Moon of Pejeng", a huge waisted drum the height of a man, which is kept in a temple in Pejeng, central Bali ▲ *194*. It is the largest example in Southeast Asia. According to legend, the drum was the wheel from the chariot of the goddess of the moon (though some legends say it was her earplug) and it fell to earth, where it was caught in a tree. Whatever its source, modern metallurgists marvel at its size, design, and tone.

*2500–2001 BC
Trade routes spread from the eastern Mediterranean through Europe.*

*2000 BC
Settlement of Melanesia by immigrants from Indonesia begins.*

*1500–1001 BC
Silk fabrics in China.*

*566–486 BC
Buddha.*

Section of a bronze kettledrum (below).

A bronze instrument (above), probably from the Dongson culture.

*488–221 BC
Warring States period in China.*

*112 BC
Opening of Silk Road across Central Asia linking China to West.*

33

10TH CENTURY

200
Indian epic poems:
Mahabharata *and*
Ramayana.

914
*First inscriptions
recording a Hindu
kingdom in Bali.*

905
*Javanese kings launch
expedition against
Bali.*

INDIANIZED KINGDOMS IN BALI. When Balinese rulers first began to leave inscriptions for posterity they did so in the forms and languages which had been brought from India. Thus the Sanur pillar ▲ *275* of AD 914, which records the reign of Sri Kesari, was written in a combination of Indian and Balinese scripts and languages. Possibly contemporary with the Sanur pillar, but developing into the late 11th century, is the religious complex of Goa Gajah ▲ *190*, situated near the site of Bali's ancient capital of Bedulu. Goa Gajah encapsulates the classical mixture of Hinduism and Buddhism in ancient Bali, with a cave for meditation containing a set of three *lingga,* or phalluses, of Siwa, a holy bathing place and a sculpture of the Buddhist deity Hariti. At that time Bali began to take on a unique Hindu-Buddhist identity.

RELATIONS WITH JAVA. Bali's Hindu-Buddhism was mediated by the larger island of Java, where rich and powerful states which used Indian models were established from about the 8th century. From at least the 10th century onward ascendant rulers in east Java strove to demonstrate their power through expeditions against Bali. Relations also went the other way. In the 10th century the marriage between a queen from Bali's ruling Warmmadewa dynasty and her consort Udayana produced the great king of east Java, Airlangga (left). These rulers and their families left many inscriptions, and a number of portrait statues depicting god-kings, such as those found in a famous temple at Penulisan, may represent them. A brother or nephew of Airlangga, Anak Wungsu, is commemorated in a series of 11th-century royal tombs at "Poet's Mountain", Gunung Kawi, in central Bali. These tombs ▲ *196* consist of commemorative shrines carved into solid rock.

12TH CENTURY

960
*Establishment of Sung
dynasty in China.*

1041
*Airlangga rules east
Java.*

1066
*Norman conquest of
England.*

EAST JAVA'S RULE IN BALI. In the 12th century the link with east Java was continued when the Jaya dynasty, with its famous kings Jayasakti (1146–50) and Jayapangus (1178–81), ruled Bali. Jayasakti is recorded in one inscription as having been sent to rule Bali by his father, the ruler of the kingdom of Kadiri in east Java and a descendant of Airlangga. With the establishment of this dynasty the circle of Javanese-Balinese interrelations was complete. From this period many of the classic works of ancient Indonesian literature, the Indian-style poems known as *kekawin,* began to be written and circulated more widely in Bali.

MAJAPAHIT BALI. The powerful King Kertanegara of Java practiced a form of Hindu-Buddhist tantric religion at home

Illustrated Balinese manuscript of one of the Majapahit kings.

and combined this with political expansion abroad. He launched a major expedition to Sumatra, and another in 1284 to conquer Bali's kingdom based at Bedulu. After Kertanegara's demise, Java's new kingdom was Majapahit, the center of an empire whose influence stretched from the Malay peninsula to the eastern islands of what is now Indonesia. Majapahit bequeathed to Bali the basis of many of the features of its present civilization: the styles of royal rule and ritual, the accoutrements of kingship, the principles of caste, art styles, and temple architecture (right). With the gradual disintegration of Majapahit in the 15th century, and the ascendancy of Islam, Javanese ties with Bali were lessened. Many Javanese moved to Bali, taking with them the symbols of the Majapahit courts, for example, the kris ▲ 150.

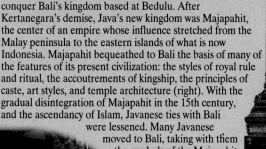

MAJAPAHIT TO GELGEL. Certain transformations took place in Bali however. In the courtly *gambuh* dance-drama (left) the palace hierarchies of ancient Java were given form, while in Balinese *babad*, or dynastic genealogies, the important families of Bali traced their ancestry to Javanese ancestors. One of the strongest tangible links was through ancestral krises, the most potent being those given by the rulers of Majapahit to those sent to rule at the capital of Samprangan (near present-day Gianyar). It did not remain the capital for long, and the kingdom was moved to Gelgel. The stories of these ancestors are still performed in the masked *topeng* dance-drama.

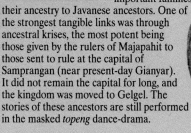

1131
Jaya dynasty, of Javanese descent, rule Bali.

1206
Mongols under Genghis Khan begin conquest of Asia.

1284
King Kertanegara of east Java conquers Bali.

1343
Conquest of Bali by Javanese kingdom of Majapahit.

1350
Golden age of Majapahit Empire in Java.

1492
Christopher Columbus' expedition to the Americas.

16TH CENTURY

GELGEL, WATURENGGONG, AND NIRARTHA. The kingdom of Gelgel came into its own, according to Balinese traditions, under King Waturenggong. Gelgel is presented as ruling not only the whole of the island of Bali, but also parts of east Java and the island of Lombok. Gelgel's greatness is attributed to Bali's prime spiritual figure, the priest Nirartha, traditionally considered the first Brahman to come to Bali from Java. The Siwa-worshiping Brahmans of Bali regard him as their ancestor, and many of the present religious institutions of Bali are attributed to him. As well as establishing the present forms of high priestly rituals and priest-ordered caste ● 48, Nirartha is supposed to have founded a succession of Bali's most important temples, ending with the temple at Uluwatu ▲ 278, on the tip of the Bukit peninsula.

c. 1550
Golden age of Gelgel under King Waturenggong and his priest, Nirartha.

1588
Defeat of Spanish Armada.

1597
First Dutch expedition lands in Bali.

● ENDURING KINGDOMS IN COLONIAL SEAS

This upside-down map of Bali, in which north is at the bottom of the image, was originally published in 1598 and was redrawn by the Dutch artist W. O. J. Nieuwenkamp.

1639–46
War with Javanese kingdom of Mataram over east Java.

c. 1650
End of kingdom of Gelgel.

c. 1660
Rise of north Balinese kingdom of Buleleng.

Royal children of Raja of Buleleng, 1870's (right).

1694
Establishment of kingdom of Klungkung as successor to Gelgel.

1711
Rise of central Balinese kingdom of Mengwi.

1740
Kingdom of Karangasem consolidates its rule of island of Lombok.

1768
Karangasem rules north and west Bali.

1771
Kingdom of Mengwi loses control of Blambangan in east Java.

1789
French Revolution.

1793
Rise of kingdom of Gianyar.

17TH CENTURY

THE NEW KINGDOMS. Kingdoms in Southeast Asia were dynamic collections of different interests. As quickly as strong kings were able to bring different groups together as expressions of a divine will, other rulers were able to establish separate power bases and present themselves as manifestations of other divine wills. So too in Bali. Various lords with local power bases were able to maintain themselves autonomously while still being part of Gelgel. Sometimes, as in the case of Gusti Batan Jeruk, Minister of Gelgel, they rebelled and their rebellions led to the prototypes of new kingdoms being established. The greatest of these rebellions saw the kings of Gelgel thrown out of their palace by the Chief Minister, Gusti Maruti, to wander through a set of shifting alliances and furious wars until their descendants could establish a new kingdom at Klungkung, a few miles north of Gelgel.

EUROPEAN PRESENCE AND THE SLAVE TRADE. The stimulus for lords to change their status came from a new source of wealth, slaves. The overall picture of Bali remained the same: a kingdom of high status, with many powerful lords arranged around it. But when Klung-kung became the

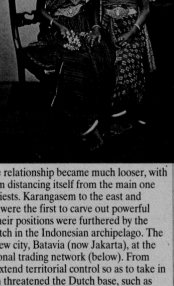

new high kingdom the relationship became much looser, with each separate kingdom distancing itself from the main one and finding its own priests. Karangasem to the east and Buleleng to the north were the first to carve out powerful separate identities. Their positions were furthered by the ascendance of the Dutch in the Indonesian archipelago. The Dutch established a new city, Batavia (now Jakarta), at the center of an international trading network (below). From there they sought to extend territorial control so as to take in those kingdoms which threatened the Dutch base, such as Mataram on Java, or which contradicted Dutch trading interests, such as Makassar on Sulawesi. Bali benefited initially from this new situation because the Dutch provided a ready market for slaves and new

"IT SEEMS DIFFICULT TO RECONCILE THE SOFT-MANNERED, PEACE-LOVING BALINESE WE KNOW WITH THE INTRIGUE AND VIOLENCE OF THEIR TURBULENT PAST."

MIGUEL COVARRUBIAS, *ISLAND OF BALI*, 1937

opportunities for Balinese rulers to assert their power elsewhere, as did the kings of Mengwi in east Java and the kings of Karangasem in Lombok. The period from the fall of Gelgel in the mid-17th century until the expansion of Dutch colonial territory at the end of the 18th century saw a more fluid situation in Bali, with kingdoms rising and falling, warring and making alliances at a rapid rate.

1800
Rise of kingdom of Bangli.

1814
British expedition against north Bali.

19TH CENTURY

19TH-CENTURY KINGDOMS. At the end of the 18th century the identities of the kingdoms of Bali became more fixed: Klungkung, Karangasem, Buleleng, Jembrana, Tabanan, Mengwi, Badung, Gianyar, and Bangli, the last two being the newest. Even when one kingdom took over others these separate entities were maintained. The slave trade dried up as the colonial powers consolidated and changed their moral and economic needs, and Bali went through a difficult period after Mount Tambora on Sumbawa erupted in 1815 and buried parts of Bali in a foot of ash. But by the middle of the 19th century Tambora's ash had become the basis of rich rice crops, and Bali's independence made it an important trading center, particularly with Singapore, to which Hindu Bali could supply pigs, and from which it could receive Indian cloth, weapons, and opium to trade on.

Opium den.

1825–30
Java War against the Dutch.

1846
First Dutch war on North Bali unresolved.

COLONIAL WARS. As Europe started to turn its interests from profitable colonies to fully controlled empires, the Dutch began to expand their interests throughout the Indonesian archipelago. By the middle of the 19th century a prosperous

1848
Balinese defeat second Dutch attack.

1849
Dutch conquest of north and west Bali.

1894
Dutch conquest of Lombok.

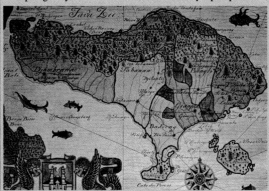

1905 map of Bali drawn by W. O. J. Nieuwenkamp.

MADS LANGE
Acting as an agent between local lords and imperial powers, a few European merchants prospered along with Bali and Lombok in the 1820's and 1830's. One of the most famous of these "country traders" was Mads Lange ▲ *276*, who had a powerful patron in the lord of Kesiman. His fortunes waned however when the Dutch wars of 1846–9 brought Bali's prosperity to an end.

and independent Bali was an irritation. Between 1846 and 1849 the Dutch waged three wars in an attempt to take control of north Bali. Only at the end of the third of those wars were they successful, and then only because other Balinese kings had sought to use Dutch military intervention for their own ends. Between 1849 and 1894 the Dutch got no further. They spent this time consolidating their rule in the north, fighting resisting lords and establishing coffee plantations. The wars of the rajas between 1884 and 1894, involving nearly all the kingdoms of Bali, including those in Lombok, gave the Dutch their chance. In 1894 they defeated the Balinese kings of Lombok and their residency on Bali was extended to the eastern island.

20TH CENTURY

The Raja of Buleleng commits suicide with his subjects during the Dutch invasion.

1895–1900
Kingdoms of Gianyar and Karangasem cede power to the Dutch.

1898
The United States takes over Philippines from the Spanish.

1902
Boer War ends. Orange Free State becomes British Crown Colony.

1903
Coronation durbar in Delhi for King Edward VI.

1904
Russo-Japanese War breaks out.

1906
Puputan in Badung. Dutch take over Badung and Tabanan kingdoms.

ENDING THE KINGDOMS. The imperative to tidy up the map and bring all the islands of what is now Indonesia under Dutch control saw the Dutch launch a ruthless set of military and diplomatic campaigns in the late 19th and early 20th centuries. Bali fell into the net of a new rational and bureaucratic style of colonialism in that push. After the Karangasem kingdoms in Lombok fell to the Dutch in 1894, this east Balinese kingdom began to make more and more concessions to the Dutch. Likewise the kingdom of Gianyar, worsted in a series of power plays in central Bali, was convinced by the king-making lord of Ubud to make peace with the Dutch. Between 1895 and 1900 Karangasem and Gianyar ceded their sovereignty to the Dutch and benefited by not being stripped of all the signs of their power. Not so the other kingdoms of south Bali. They stubbornly stood against the Dutch, and were ruthlessly finished off in what they considered "endings", *puputans*. In 1906 the Dutch landed in what is now the northern end of the resort of Sanur, marched through nearby Kesiman and then on to the palaces of Badung. These rulers with all their followers and families, over 1000 people in all, dressed in white, had the rites of the dead applied to them, and marched out to be cut down by the relentless gunfire of the Dutch. Armed as the Balinese were with only krises, spears and shields, the military technology of the Dutch rapidly cut a bloody swath through their ranks. Those who did not die immediately were dispatched to the heaven of the god Wisnu by their followers, while many of the kings' women stabbed themselves to death in the palace. The scene was repeated on a smaller scale in Klungkung in 1908 in a move that marked the end of independent Bali. The great palaces of Denpasar and Klungkung were razed in an arrogant show of power.

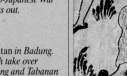

TAKEOVER AND RESISTANCE. The military conquests of 1849 to 1908 were really first steps in a much more complex process of colonial control. The Dutch sent their bureaucratic "managers" to survey the island, describe it and then see where it was amenable to change. They expended vast resources training people in the knowledge of the island they wanted to control. By the early

In this 1847 map by ethnographer W. R. van Hoevell, Bali is shown as an appendage to Java.

20th century the Dutch had defined and categorized Balinese "caste", "religion", and "society" in their own terms. The net effect was to freeze one set of hierarchical distinctions and to make hypothetical models binding on those who had never believed in them. Dutch interpretations of "traditional" duties involved forcing the Balinese to do slave labor, the infamous *kerja rodi*. Resistance to slavery and to unrealistic caste categorizations were met with force and bureaucratic regulations. The Balinese were expected to suffer in silence, to fit the colonial image of docile natives.

COLONIAL TOURISM. Guilt, a policy of being seen to be preserving "native" culture, and the need for new sources of revenue combined to produce a colonial policy of making Bali a tourist destination. Bali in the early 20th century went through a series of disasters: an earthquake and the eruption of Mount Batur in 1917 destroyed many temples and palaces and took many lives; the worldwide influenza epidemic of that time killed thousands; new taxes and the loss of traditional forms of patronage meant great hardship for most Balinese; and then the Great Depression topped off this privation. Simultaneous with these conditions was the development of the image of Bali as the ultimate tourist destination, culturally rich, with smiling people, an island of dances and temples to attract the wealthy of the world, and one with which most of the Dutch civil servants posted there also fell in love.

THE COMING OF THE JAPANESE. As Dutch rule became entrenched over the whole of the archipelago, all those who were part of the Netherlands East Indies – Balinese, Javanese, Sumatrans, and members of a hundred other ethnic groups – came to feel a common bond. The most obvious thing that they had in common was the experience of colonialism, but 2000 years of trade and contact via great kingdoms such as Majapahit meant that the feeling of a common heritage could easily be linked by skillful leaders to a desire to become a nation. A number of Balinese intellectuals joined colleagues from other islands in support of a nationalist movement, but any political action was harshly repressed by the Dutch. It was thus only in 1942, when the Japanese swept Europe's agents of empire out of Asia, that desires for independence could come to fruition.

The Japanese came promising a "Greater East Asian Co-Prosperity Sphere", and for a while their rule looked more attractive than that of the Dutch. However even those who had welcomed them as liberators came to feel either the harsh repression of the military police or the privation of the later war years as all the essentials of life were sucked up by the Japanese war machine. Resentment of the Japanese was only surpassed by expectations of freedom: the Dutch, it was felt, should not be allowed to return whatever happened.

1907
English and French agree on independence for Thailand.

1908
Puputan in Klungkung, Bali. Dutch take over Klungkung and Bangli kingdoms and establish rule in Bali.

1926–7
Communist Party uprising in Java and Sumatra.

1930
Ho Chi Minh founds Indochina Communist Party.

1932
A coup ends absolute monarchical rule in Thailand.

1933
Hitler seizes power in Germany.

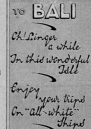

This advertisement by the KPM shipping line was one of many that encouraged travelers to come to Bali.

REVOLUTION AND INDEPENDENCE. Sukarno, the man brought back from political exile by the Japanese to gain popular support, was part Balinese. His relations with the Japanese were always ambivalent, and in Bali he had a large amount of popular support. When he declared a Republic of Indonesia after the bombing of Hiroshima the Balinese quickly organized to take Japanese weaponry and oppose any Dutch return. There were still many Balinese, especially those from the higher castes who had done well under the Dutch, who were anti-independence, and much of the struggle on Bali was against other Balinese, a portent of darker times to come. For most of the Indonesian Revolution of 1945–9 the main

struggles took place on Java. Balinese supporters of the Republic joined the fighting there after Bali's main guerrilla leader, Ngurah Rai, was killed in a heroic last stand against Dutch forces at the end of 1946. One group of Balinese leaders joined in the Dutch-sponsored "State of Eastern Indonesia", and at one time its prime minister was the prince of Gianyar, Ida Anak Agung Gde Agung. However the prince (later Foreign Minister of the Republic) turned the tables on the Dutch by bringing the government of the State down in protest against Dutch military action against the Republic on Java, and thus hastened the gaining of independence.

TURMOIL AND PRESIDENTIAL PATRONAGE.
The new Republic of Indonesia had its enemies within and without. Under the rule of its first president, Sukarno (right), cabinets rose and fell at a rapid rate, and pro-Dutch, Islamic, and military groups attempted coups, assassinations, and separatist rebellions. Bali remained loyal to Sukarno, but the island was wracked by revenge killings and criminal activities. Bali, because of Sukarno's fondness for the place, occupied a special place in the Republic. During this era the image of Bali as the island of dancers and artists was restored. Sukarno went further; he encouraged tourism to the island and initiated the construction of the first of the big hotels there, the Bali Beach, with Japanese war reparation money. The attempt to get tourism going foundered on the political chaos of the time, and it and Bali's economy and social conditions were not helped by a catastrophic eruption of Bali's largest volcano, Mount Agung, in 1963.

POLITICAL CONFLICT AND THE NEW ORDER. The great majority of Balinese may have been Sukarnoists, but the rest of their politics was a case for disagreement. Balinese society became sharply polarized; most members of the high-caste elite were supported by the Indonesian Nationalist Party (PNI), and the peasant farmers and others who rejected the caste system found support in the Indonesian Communist Party (PKI). When the conflict came to a head, the results were beyond the belief of any observers. On Bali whole villages were

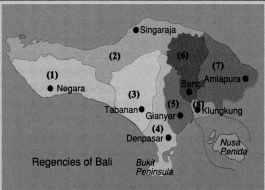

Regencies of Bali

destroyed, friend killed friend, brother killed brother, and innocent bystanders were swept up in the slaughter which followed an abortive coup in Jakarta in 1965, blamed on the Communists. Estimates put the number who died on Bali at between 80,000 and 100,000 as the PKI was totally destroyed by the PNI. Out of the conflict a group of crack Javanese military officers eventually gained control of the Republic. Sukarno was discredited both because of leftist leanings and because his lavish lifestyle was linked to the devastated economic state of the nation. In 1967 Sukarno officially handed over power to the key military officer whose actions had led to the establishment of a "New Order" to replace the old. The new president was a less flamboyant Javanese who had risen quietly through various campaigns to become President Suharto (right).

KIRAB REMAJA NASIONAL III 1993

1978
Ida Bagus Mantra, Brahman religious scholar and educationalist, becomes governor of Bali.

DEVELOPMENT AND THE NEW TOURIST ERA.
The birth of the "New Order" with its goal of development coincided with the flourishing of international tourism. The hippies who trailed from Amsterdam to Darwin brought a new era for Bali. Ironically Sukarno's dreams of making Bali a tourist mecca were fulfilled by Suharto's government, and the hippies who spread the fame of the island's artists, rites and landscapes. Most Balinese view the period from the late 1970's to the end of the 1980's as something of a boom time, culturally and in terms of tourism. A Balinese governor replaced a Javanese one, and under him patronage of the arts and international attention ensured that the arts continued to receive the national recognition they had had under Sukarno. At the same time tourism assured Bali of a key economic role in Indonesia, as the tourist sector almost overtook agriculture in Bali's regional economy and brought many subsidiary industries, such as finance and garment manufacturing, to the island. The recession of the early 1990's saw Bali's spurt of growth slow down as the Balinese debate the island's future direction.

1987
Ida Bagus Oka succeeds Ida Bagus Mantra as governor of Bali.

● THE BALINESE LANGUAGE

SPOKEN LANGUAGE

LONTAR LEAVES
Strips of lontar palm leaves carry the literature of many Old Javanese and Balinese manuscripts ■ 23. The leaves are bound by a string running through holes pierced in the side or center of the leaves. Writers would use an iron stylus to inscribe their words, then blacken the lines with soot.

ILLUSTRATED MANUSCRIPTS
Several anonymous works survive in illustrated manuscripts from the late 19th and early 20th centuries.

Nearly all Balinese speak the national language of Indonesia, Bahasa Indonesia, a language Indonesian nationalists developed from the Malay language. The Balinese language is a completely different language from Bahasa Indonesia, although both are part of the Austronesian family of languages. The Balinese language has many levels; although each of the levels uses the same basic linguistic structure and many common nouns, the vocabulary for each level varies. This is particularly true of verbs connected with human activities and body parts. When referring to eating, for example, one would ask "Have you eaten?" by saying to a member of the higher castes *"Ratu sampun marayunan,"* but to a person of low status, the same question is *"cai suba madaar"*. The Balinese caste system requires that different vocabularies be used according to differences in rank. This means that a low caste person uses the formal high Balinese words in speaking to a person of a higher caste, while the latter will answer using the low vocabulary; you speak "up" to a person of higher status, who speaks "down" to you. As caste distinctions loosen, people prefer to use a respectful version of high Balinese among people they do not know or in formal situations, while still speaking low or common Balinese among family and friends. ● 90. Since Bahasa Indonesia is taught in schools and used as the lingua franca of commerce and government, its use has had a democratizing effect, unifying the scattered islands of the country and blurring the once distinct levels of Balinese speech.

SINGING LANGUAGE
The flowery language of poems and love stories written in Kawi is meant to be sung or recited, not read silently.

LITERARY LANGUAGES

In literature and in the theater, the language varies with the genre. In the sacred chantings of the high priests, the language is a form of Sanskrit, the language of the gods, and thus the most suitable form with which to call them. Dramas whose stories about Rama (left) and the Pandawa brothers come from Indian epics use the language of poetry called Kawi, sometimes called Old Javanese since it was the ancient literary language of Java. Kawi actually describes a number of related languages that are forms of Javanese or Javanese Balinese. In one dramatic performance many languages may be used. In the shadow plays ● 58, for example, the heroes and gods speak Old Javanese, the clowns and servants translate for the audience in Balinese, while the puppeteer may sing from time to time in other forms of Kawi.

ARTS AND TRADITIONS

Bali-Hinduism dominates the everyday lives of most Balinese. The religion is a combination of elements from the Indian Shivaite and Buddhist traditions with older beliefs and practices originating from the archipelagic world of Indonesia. Here, ancestors are deified, as are the fundamental forces of nature ● *46*. The resulting blend continues to be antidogmatic, changing as it absorbs aspects of the various religious systems that are brought to the island.

TEMPLES
Temples are the meeting points of humans and gods. There are temples for almost all aspects of Balinese life, including those for ancestors, rice fields, and the village ● *96*. At temple anniversaries, the gods descend from the mountains to take their seats in the shrines where they will be welcomed with offerings (right).

GESTURES OF PRAYER
Hands at the level of the brow indicate a prayer addressed to the gods and deified ancestors. Hands with fingers down symbolize an invocation to the demons. In between is the human salutation.

PROCESSIONS
Palanquins carry the gods around in a procession for visits to neighboring temples and for cleansing ceremonies. Offerings are presented to the visiting gods.

<blockquote>
"I HAVE, MYSELF, NEVER KNOWN A BALINESE WHO TOOK CEREMONIAL REQUIREMENTS, EVEN VERY MINOR ONES, LIGHTLY."

CLIFFORD GEERTZ, *NEGARA*, 1980
</blockquote>

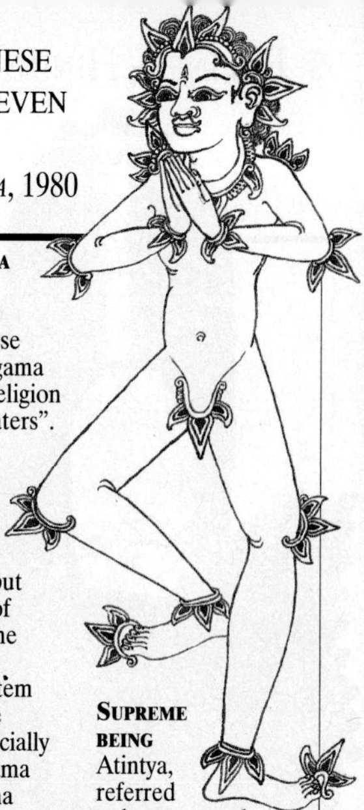

AGAMA TIRTHA

One of the oldest names for the Balinese religion is "Agama Tirtha", or "religion of the holy waters". The name demonstrates not only the sign of water as a tool of purification, but also the role of irrigation in the overall socio-ecological system ■ 24. Now the religion is officially known as Agama Hindu Dharma Indonesia.

SUPREME BEING

Atintya, referred to by most modern Balinese as Sang Hyang Widhi Wasa, has gained importance in recent years because he falls in line with religious beliefs that revolve around a single god, of whom all other gods are manifestations. He is also often associated with the sun god.

COSMIC HARMONY

Rituals seek to maintain cosmic harmony among the three levels of the Hindu universe: that of the gods above the mountain peaks, the demons below the earth and sea, and the human world in between ● 98.

● BALINESE HINDU PANTHEON

The Hindu pantheon is an encyclopedia of mutable powers. Its manifestations in Bali are embedded in deep traditions of animism and the veneration of ancestors. Rather than being "characters", the Hindu gods are experienced as abstractions associated with natural forces: Wisnu with rain and nurturing, and Brahma with creativity, fire, and volcanos. Although Balinese Hinduism is currently undergoing a reformation to bring it into the mainstream of classical Hinduism, the Balinese pantheon still includes sacred powers specific to Bali, usually under the generic term *bhatara*, or god. Here we discuss some of the more prevalent gods, a few among many on this "island of the gods".

THE SUPREME GOD
Sang Hyang Widhi Wasa is the "One Supreme Unknowable God". He is represented (above) as Atintya, a being in meditation surrounded by flames. Although Bali-Hinduism is essentially monotheistic, the average Balinese does not pray or make offerings directly to Sang Hyang Widhi, but to the manifestations of this deity.

DEIFIED ANCESTORS
The most intimate gods are the deified ancestors. The relationship between a Balinese and his ancestors is at once reverent and practical. The souls of the dead can be absorbed into heaven only by the purification rites of the living. In return, the ancestors bestow blessings and sometimes advice through trance mediums. *Bhatara kawitan* is the term for the original clan ancestor.

ANCIENT KINGS
Ancient kings are also influential deities, and sometimes manifest themselves during their temples' anniversary celebration with varying degrees of dignity, from an aroma of roses or the preternatural skill of dancing children to violent trance and the inexplicable falling of dishes.

TRIMURTI
The godhead is more generally expressed as the Trimurti, or Hindu trinity. The Trimurti is made up of Brahma, the creator; Wisnu, the preserver, and Siwa, the destroyer.

46

"O, SARASWATI, PRAISE TO YOU WHO ARE THE GIVER OF BLESSINGS, YOU WHO HAVE THE FORM OF DESIRE. WE WILL HOPE TO MAKE A SUCCESSFUL BEGINNING; MAY WE HAVE THE POWER TO SUCCEED."

MANTRA APPEARING AT BEGINNING OF BALINESE TEXTS

GODS RESIDING IN NATURE

Of all the gods residing in nature, the most powerful are those associated with the mountains, lakes, and the sea. The god of Mount Agung, Ida Bhatara Gunung Agung, is honored at Besakih and at *meru* (pagoda shrines) in temples islandwide. Ida Bhatari Dewi Ulun Danu Batur is the goddess of Lake Batur, and her temple is on the edge of Batur crater (above). The sea is a place of danger and of purification. The Balinese do not refer to a god of the sea but to *segara,* which means "sea".

SARASWATI

Saraswati, consort of Brahma, is the goddess of knowledge, wisdom, and the arts. She is usually depicted as a beautiful, richly dressed woman riding a goose. Her anniversary falls on the last day of the 210-day Balinese calendar, when offerings are made to books, and reading and writing are not allowed.

DEWI SRI

The beloved goddess of rice, Dewi Sri (above) is the anima of a rice cult of particular beauty. Her shrines in the rice fields are simple structures of virgin bamboo ● 78. Her realm includes granaries and the rice basket, and she is honored in a number of different cyclical rituals, including the daily offerings set out after cooking. *Dewa* are male spirits, and *Dewi* are female, though the Balinese say that the gods embody both sexes.

BHATARI DURGA

Bhatari Durga is the consort of Siwa in her ferocious aspect. She rules over demons, ghosts, and witches. Her most famous manifestation in Bali is Rangda, the queen of the witches in the *Calonarang* dance drama ▲ 148.

47

● TYPES OF PRIESTS

Priests, the most respected members of Balinese society, help guide the actions of the people to ensure harmony in the Bali-Hindu universe. The three basic levels are the high priests, or *pedanda*; the temple priests, or *pemangku*; and the mediums or healers, called *balian*.

BALIAN
Balian are the mediums for the gods and ancestors. The gods speak through a *balian taksu*, who is called into a trance. The *balian* is consulted for a variety of reasons, such as to discover who is reincarnated, the cause of an illness, and to locate the place now occupied by a soul.

TWICE-BORN
After years of study with another high priest, a Brahman is ordained a *pedanda* in a ritual ceremony where he symbolically dies, is cremated and reborn as a pure man. Male priests are consecrated with their wives (above); thus a wife may take over her husband's position at his death.

PRIEST'S PARAPHERNALIA

To prepare the holy water the *pedanda* requires a variety of instruments, the most important of which are a wand for sprinkling holy water (1), a lamp (2), a prayer bell (3), and a stand for the holy water (4).

PEDANDA DUTIES

All *pedanda* must be of the Brahman caste, but not all Brahmana become *pedanda*. *Pedanda*, who are not bound to specific temples, officiate at rituals for those bound to them by kinship or tradition.

Their primary tasks are making the most potent holy water for big temple festivals, and directing the rituals of life and death ● *52*, such as tooth filings and cremations. They use holy hand gestures, *mudras*, and *mantra* for making the holy water.

PEDANDA BUDA AND SIWA

Among the several types of *pedanda*, the most common are the *pedanda Siwa*. There is a small minority of *pedanda Buda*. They follow either Shivaite or Buddhist traditions, with their own specific literature and rituals. Some rituals require *pedanda* of both types to perform side by side (above).

PEMANGKU

Pemangku, always dressed in white, can come from any caste other than Brahman. They consecrate offerings, make holy water, and preside over temple ceremonies. The most important *pemangku* are those attached to the village temples, but there are also *pemangku* for irrigation temples, family temples, and others, sometimes up to a dozen or more in a village.

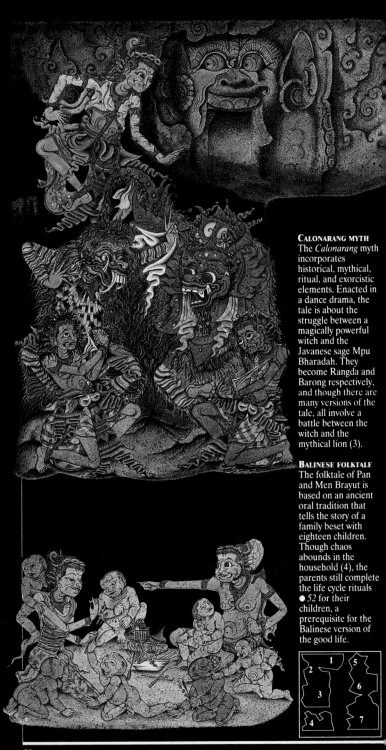

CALONARANG MYTH
The *Calonarang* myth incorporates historical, mythical, ritual, and exorcistic elements. Enacted in a dance drama, the tale is about the struggle between a magically powerful witch and the Javanese sage Mpu Bharadah. They become Rangda and Barong respectively, and though there are many versions of the tale, all involve a battle between the witch and the mythical lion (3).

BALINESE FOLKTALE
The folktale of Pan and Men Brayut is based on an ancient oral tradition that tells the story of a family beset with eighteen children. Though chaos abounds in the household (4), the parents still complete the life cycle rituals ● 52 for their children, a prerequisite for the Balinese version of the good life.

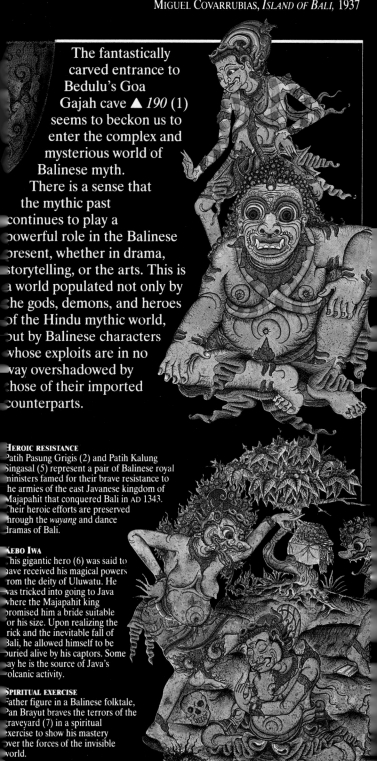

"... THE PRIMITIVE BALINESE MADE OF THEIR ISLAND A MAGIC WORLD POPULATED BY GODS, HUMAN BEINGS, AND DEMONS..."

MIGUEL COVARRUBIAS, *ISLAND OF BALI*, 1937

The fantastically carved entrance to Bedulu's Goa Gajah cave ▲ 190 (1) seems to beckon us to enter the complex and mysterious world of Balinese myth.

There is a sense that the mythic past continues to play a powerful role in the Balinese present, whether in drama, storytelling, or the arts. This is a world populated not only by the gods, demons, and heroes of the Hindu mythic world, but by Balinese characters whose exploits are in no way overshadowed by those of their imported counterparts.

HEROIC RESISTANCE

Patih Pasung Grigis (2) and Patih Kalung Singasal (5) represent a pair of Balinese royal ministers famed for their brave resistance to the armies of the east Javanese kingdom of Majapahit that conquered Bali in AD 1343. Their heroic efforts are preserved through the *wayang* and dance dramas of Bali.

KEBO IWA

This gigantic hero (6) was said to have received his magical powers from the deity of Uluwatu. He was tricked into going to Java where the Majapahit king promised him a bride suitable for his size. Upon realizing the trick and the inevitable fall of Bali, he allowed himself to be buried alive by his captors. Some say he is the source of Java's volcanic activity.

SPIRITUAL EXERCISE

Father figure in a Balinese folktale, Pan Brayut braves the terrors of the graveyard (7) in a spiritual exercise to show his mastery over the forces of the invisible world.

In the eyes of the Hindu-Balinese, existence is a continuous cycle of life, death, and rebirth, until one attains *moksa*, when the body becomes one with the macrocosm. Rituals at various stages of life on earth ensure that the individual progresses toward this desired state.

REINCARNATION
Everything has its beginning far above the highest mountain, where since earliest time souls have originated and where the souls of the deified ancestors dwell. If an ancestor's soul is still subject to desire – it is hungry, as people say – it will come to earth as an incarnating "shadow". Its rebirth occurs within the same lineage, and grandchildren might bear their incarnating grandfather's soul.

INFANT GODS
The baby, which embodies the soul of a reincarnating ancestor, is said to be an infant god or *dewa*, until it is 42 days old. It is carried about on a family member's hip as it is not allowed to touch the impure soil until it is 105 days old. Its first birthday is celebrated 210 days after birth, a year in the Balinese calendar ● *82*, and the mother makes a temple offering to announce the child's arrival in the village.

TOOTH FILING
The ceremony of tooth filing, meant to overcome the elements of man's bestiality, occurs after a child reaches puberty. The pointed canine teeth are considered animalistic, and all six upper front teeth are filed even. Because of the expense of this ceremony, a number of families may join in a mass tooth filing to share costs (above).

MARRIAGE
Full adulthood begins after marriage (above). During the ceremony, offerings are addressed to the demonic forces, who have to be placated before proper sexual desire is exercised. To show knowledge of domestic duties, a bride and bridegroom may simulate activities such as weaving or washing during the ceremony.

CREMATION TOWER

A cremation is the most important rite of passage that a family can perform for its loved ones. The body may be buried until a cremation can be arranged, then it is hoisted up an elaborate stairway to a decorated tower (right) supported on a bamboo substructure. The tower is a symbolic representation of the universe, with the upper tiers symbolizing the various heavens where the soul is heading.

SARCOPHAGUS

In a joyous procession, the cremation tower is transported to the grounds where the body is placed in an animal-shaped sarcophagus. The sarcophagus is the dead's vehicle to the mountain of the soul's origin. Pots of holy water are poured over the corpse, then it and the tower and other cremation paraphernalia are consumed by fire.

COLLECTING THE ASHES

After the body is burned, the ashes are collected, ground finely, and offered to the sea. All physical remains having been restored to the five elements, the soul is now freed to journey through purgatory and, if need be, taken to hell to be tortured and eventually cleansed.

RETURNING HOME

In a final ceremony that may be held years later, the soul is called back from the sea and after several cleansing rituals, taken to the mountain temple and released to return to its heavenly abode. It has become a deified ancestor, and is worshiped at a special shrine.

Offerings made of palm leaf, flowers, and foodstuffs are an art form associated with every ritual occasion in Bali. The Balinese belief in the forces of the invisible world dictates that offerings be created with a spirit of thankfulness and loving attention to detail. The Balinese seem never to tire of producing these colorful and highly symbolic, ephemeral creations for every ritual, from the simplest daily household offerings to gods, demons, and ancestors to massive ceremonies such as the Panca Wali Krama held at Pura Besakih to purify and bring blessings upon the entire world.

GEBOGAN

Gebogan (right) are towering offerings constructed around the base of a banana trunk. Prepared by the women of the household, they are presented to the deities at temple birthdays. Typically, the first layer is composed of fruits, followed by layers of rice cakes in many shapes and colors. The next layer is a *canang sari* offering or *cili*, and the top an exuberant arrangement of flowers.

SARAD

Elaborate offerings made of dyed rice dough arranged against a framework of bamboo and cloth symbolize the form and content of the Balinese mythic world. *Sarad* (above) will typically include representations of Bedawang Nala and Naga Basuki, the cosmic turtle and dragon who provide support for the physical world. Another popular subject is Boma, son of the earth goddess, a fearsome but protective figure who represents all living things growing from the earth.

POROSAN

The colors of the *porosan* – red for areca nut, green for betel leaf, and white for lime – represent Brahma, Wisnu, and Siwa, the three gods of the Hindu Trimurti.

LAMAK

A small temporary shrine of bamboo called a *sanggah cucuk* is always found beneath a *penjor*. Small offerings to the deities are placed here for as long as the *penjor* is in use. This shrine is often "clothed" in a symbolic garment called a *lamak* (right). The colorful runners made of plaited palm leaf often contain images of prosperity and fertility like the Cili, an ancient symbol of both human and wet rice life cycles.

PENJOR

A *penjor* is an offering in the form of a tall, decorated bamboo pole whose gracefully curving upper end is said to resemble both the tail of the Barong, symbol of goodness, and the peak of the sacred mountain, Mount Agung. *Penjor* are placed in front of each Balinese household for the Galungan holiday ◆ *300* and are also used in conjunction with important temple ceremonies and life-cycle rituals. Hanging from the end of every *penjor* are beautifully plaited palm leaf creations called *sampian*.

KWANGEN

The *kwangen* (left) is a small, triangular offering containing flowers, a small betel quid and often Chinese coins. *Kwangen* are used in the Balinese form of prayer called *muspa* (to pray with flowers). The Chinese coins in a *kwangen* are said to represent human action, purified in the act of worship.

GAYAH

While most offerings are constructed by women, elaborate offerings made of meat are fashioned by men for use on major ritual occasions. The *gayah* or *sate gede* (right) is said to represent the animal kingdom, the complement to the kingdom of plant life so often represented in offerings made by women. Creations such as these represent the Balinese notion that offerings symbolize the "entire contents of the world".

CANANG SARI

Canang sari offerings (above) differ in form and function depending on locality but in general are said to embody the essence or *sari* of human prosperity, a kind of repayment to the forces of the invisible world for their gifts to human society. Typically, *canang sari* offerings contain flowers, leaves, liquid fragrance, and a symbolic betel quid.

55

An *odalan* celebrates the gods coming to the annual commemoration of the founding of their temple. The people renew their ties with the gods and also reinforce their bonds with each other during the elaborate preparations and ceremonies of the *odalan*. As the *odalan* date varies from one temple to another, the visitor usually has an opportunity to see one.

PRAYER
Prayers are followed by the blessing of the believers through the sprinkling of holy water and the application of blessed rice on their foreheads.

PROCESSION RITUALS
Processions have different ritualistic functions: to guide the invited gods, to collect water for the symbolic bathing of the gods, and to present each family's offering (below) to be blessed by the temple priest. The gods are invited to enjoy the essence of the offerings, artistic performances, and the various ceremonies.

GREETING THE GODS
Dancers circle the temple's central shrine three times, moving only to the right, which symbolizes ascent of the sacred mountain. This ritual is repeated around a shrine in front of the temple where the invisible deities' followers are greeted.

DANCE
FOR THE DEITIES
In ancient ritual dances,
some masculine and warlike, the
others feminine and graceful (above), devotees
welcome the gods. If the dances are to the evil
spirits of the ground, the dancers pour alcohol as a
sacrifice to the earth. Then a temple priest makes
offerings to dispel the evil influence once the spirits
have been drawn to the site.

CARNIVAL
A social as well as religious affair,
the *odalan* celebration gives the
temple a carnival atmosphere with
food and toy stalls, games
of chance ● *94*, dances,
and night-long
drama
performances. At
the end of the
odalan, the priests
politely invite the
deities to leave
after what they
hope has been a
pleasing visit.

TRANCES
Trance patterns differ
from one
place to
another.
If planned,
trances are considered
living proof of the
presence of gods or
other spirits.
Sometimes unplanned
trances occur, possibly
as the manifestation of
a dissatisfied god or
spirit. As mediums,
trancers can transmit a
god's suggestions, for
example a modification
to a ritual or the
addition of a new one.

BLOOD SACRIFICE
Cockfights ● *95*,
permitted at ritual
ceremonies such as
odalan, are a blood
sacrifice to purify and
appease the spirits of
the earth. Offerings
made to the evil
forces are not
consumed, but the
devotees do take
home their own
offerings to the gods.
Collective offerings
stay in the temple.

Wayang kulit, shadow puppet theater, is Bali's most complex, sacred art form. It is a traditional medium of moral and spiritual instruction, and it is also wonderfully entertaining. The physical principles are simple: an oil lamp is hung behind a screen of stretched cloth, and in the space between them, shadows are produced by flat, leather puppets. To carry this out is very difficult. A single puppeteer, *dalang*, manipulates all the puppets, often several at a time, speaking for them in a myriad of voices and in several different languages, while conducting a small ensemble of *gamelan* musicians as well. The plays themselves are a long series of interludes created by the *dalang* around an episode from classical literary texts.

DALANG IN PRAYER
The *dalang* is director-performer, puppet-maker, literary arbiter, musician, comic and priest. Before he performs, he conducts the rite of *pasupati* (the awakening of magical powers) for the puppets and himself. During a performance, he is said to incarnate the god Siwa.

PUPPET-MAKING
The puppets are made from stiffly tanned hide mounted on handles of horn or bone, each cut out in its characteristic shape and pierced with a fine lace-like pattern that allows the lamplight to reveal details of face and dress. The arms joined at the shoulders are manipulated with great expressiveness. Although hidden by the screen, the puppets are beautifully painted on both sides in honor of their sacred status.

GENDER WAYANG
The magical work of *wayang kulit* is greatly assisted by its music, which is considered to be difficult to play. The compositions of the small *gamelan* ensemble called *gender wayang* are dazzlingly complicated and played at lightning speed.

"THE FANTASTIC ADVENTURES OF THE LITTLE LEATHER PUPPETS HAVE A POWERFUL HOLD ON THE IMAGINATION OF YOUNG AND OLD ALIKE..."

MIGUEL COVARRUBIAS,
ISLAND OF BALI, 1937

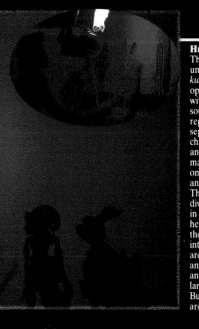

HEROES AND VILLAINS

The grand theme underlying all *wayang kulit* is the struggle of opposing forces within the human soul. This is represented by the separation of characters into heroes and villains, who make their entrances on the *dalang*'s right and left respectively. There is a further division of characters in some plays. The heroes and villains of the Hindu epics who introduce the story are equally exalted and speak in the ancient literary language Kawi ● *42*. But their speeches are interpreted into high Balinese by servant-clowns, or *punakawan*. The *punakawan* then discuss the dramatic adventure in common Balinese, and it is through them that the *dalang* propels the drama and reveals the meaning to the audience.

RAKSASA

The ritual force of *wayang kulit* comes from the powers captured in those puppets that represent supernatural energies. Demons (right and below), or *raksasa*, are invoked and allowed to express themselves under th wily control of the *dalang*.

KAYONAN

The *kayonan* (above) symbolizes the holy mountain, the tree of life, and the *dalang*, who embraces left and right. It opens and closes a performance, which may last six hours or more.

BHATARA GURU

Bhatara Guru (above), or Siwa, may descend in the magical play of *wayang kulit*, the only performing art in Bali in which the Hindu gods are represented.

Balinese *wayang kulit* owes its form to its Javanese precedents, but over the past four hundred years it has evolved its own unique puppets, music, and ritual.

The Balinese puppets, for example, are smaller and more naturalistic than those of the Javanese, which are more stylistic because Islam forbids portrayal of the human form. Balinese performances, which often begin late at night, are usually an offering that completes a ritual or major event in the community. The great Indian epics, the *Mahabharata* and *Ramayana,* provide most of the characters of the *wayang kulit* theater, but serve as only a thematic sketch for the plot of the actual plays created by the Balinese puppeteer (*dalang*)● 58.

INNOVATIONS
A few innovative *dalang* have devised original *wayang kulit.* Wayan Wija of Sukawati has created a *wayang Tantri,* complete with an entire set of puppets telling the cycle of Tantri stories, which seem to come from the same source as Aesop's fables and *A Thousand and One Nights.*

WIBISANA
Brother of the wicked king Rawana, who kidnaps Sita in the *Ramayana*, Wibisana (left) disagrees with Rawana's action and rebels. The king's other brother, Kumbakarna, also disagrees but remains loyal. A *dalang* may take this episode to explore moral problems of great subtlety.

BIMA
Bima (below), the fiery man of action, is one of the five Pandawa brothers, the heroes of the *Mahabharata*. Each of the brothers represents some aspect of the human ideal. Through mortal contest with their cousins, the Kurawas, the Pandawas' attributes are transmuted into virtues. For example, Bima's ferocity becomes true courage.

RANGDA
Wayang kulit stories are based not only on Indic-Hindu literature but also on old tales of Javanese or Balinese origin. One of these is the exorcistic *Calonarang* story, which features Rangda (right), queen of the witches.

DELEM AND SANGUT
The *punakawan* (servant-interpreters) of the villains are the uncouth and arrogant Delem (above) and his weasel-like sidekick, Sangut (far right). Through these two, a *dalang*'s comic improvisations may go to otherwise unspeakable extremes.

MERDAH AND SANGUT
The fun begins when the *punakawan* of the heroes and the villains are left alone to discuss things in common Balinese.

TWALEN AND MERDAH
Beloved Twalen (right) and his son Merdah (above, center) are the *punakawan* of the heroes. With his droll eye, gravelly voice and love of food, Twalen is the most popular of the *wayang kulit* characters. He also has a magical aspect; he is a shaman, and it is said that he is older than time, a son of the supreme god Sang Hyang Widhi Wasa ● *46*.

Bali is world renowned for its profusion of musical activities and the variety of its instrumental ensembles called *gamelan* ● 64 as well as its vocal forms. Traditionally, however, no one in Bali plays music as pure concert, or only for pleasure, because music has above all a socio-religious function, as the accompaniment for rituals, dance, and drama during the innumerable religious ceremonies.

GAMELAN GAMBANG
Like other kinds of archaic sacred ensembles, *gamelan gambang* is heptatonic and its repertoire is inspired by singing literature. Its strange xylophones provide the most complex interlocking counterpoint.

ARJA OPERA
In the classical "opera" *arja* (left), still similar to the old court drama *gambuh* ● 66, actors have to be excellent singers, dancers, clowns, or tragedians, all at the same time.

MARCHING BANDS
Music can be mobile in Bali, where religious processions are usually accompanied by a marching band. The martial music, *beleganjur*, is played with drums, big cymbals, and gongs of all sizes. A favorite with young people, new rhythmic variations are created yearly.

> "MUSIC IS UBIQUITOUS IN BALI; ITS ABUNDANCE IS FAR OUT OF PROPORTION TO THE DIMENSIONS OF THE ISLAND."
>
> MICHAEL TENZER, *BALINESE MUSIC*, 1991

COURTLY GAMELAN
Rarely seen today, *gamelan semar pegulingan* (right) was the favorite of the palaces. Its repertoire is derived from one of the oldest orchestras, *gamelan gambuh* ● *66*. The refined melodies of *gamelan gambuh*'s deep-voiced bamboo flutes have been simplified to fit melodic bronze percussions. The closely related *gamelan pelegongan* accompanies the *legong* dances ● *70* and classical theater.

THE VOCAL GAMELAN
The human voice replaces instruments in *cak,* the vocal *gamelan* in which the chorus imitates the sounds of the *gamelan* percussions. Inspired by earlier trance dances, *cak* is more well-known in the form of the modern *kecak,* which accompanies a choreography of the epic *Ramayana.*

GAMELAN JEGOG
Music styles vary regionally. Western Bali, for example, has developed its own distinctive music, dominated by the use of bamboo, which grows to enormous sizes there. A special form of gamelan called *jegog* uses only gigantic bamboo tubes and trunks (left). The sound is impressive, and a competition among *gamelan jegog* ensembles creates a cacophonic chorus.

THE MUSICIANS
In spite of the complexity and high quality of Balinese music, most musicians are not professionals. Their participation is just one of many contributions of the "citizen" to the community, similar to those of church choir members elsewhere. They learn by rote and imitation, without musical scores.

● GAMELAN

 The instrumental ensembles known as *gamelan* are predominant in Balinese music. Each village owns at least one *gamelan,* if not a dozen. There are some twenty-five types of all sizes, in metal or bamboo, comprising mostly percussion instruments such as gongs, drums, metallophones, or xylophones. But each *gamelan* orchestra, with its own specific tuning, is a single entity – like a single instrument played by a group. So the instruments from one *gamelan* cannot be exchanged with another. This ensures the integrity of each *gamelan* as a single instrumental corps.

BLESSING THE GAMELAN
Everything in the Balinese world has a spirit which must be kept alive with offerings. So after manufacture, the *gamelan* is purified and a sacrificial offering is made to ask the spirit of the *gamelan* to return. Before each performance, offerings are made to ask for the spirit's kindness.

GAMELAN FOUNDRY
Bronze *gamelan* are made by metalsmiths called *pande gong*, traditionally belonging to the *Pande* clan. Experts in tuning, they understand much better than the musicians themselves the different musical scales, which range from four to seven notes, but are mostly pentatonic.

BALINESE STYLE
The Balinese style is best expressed in the ornamental figuration often called *kotekan*. In this interlocking counterpoint, the notes of a sole melodic or rhythmic line are shared among the associated parts, often at astonishing tempos. This extraordinary coordination reflects the collective mind and interdependence of individuals that characterize Balinese society.

GONG KEBYAR

When classical *gamelan* such as *gong gede* passed from the fading aristocracy into the hands of the villagers, most of the *gamelan* instruments were recast to become the popular *gong kebyar*, a multi-purpose big *gamelan* born around 1915. Freed from the ritual restrictions in temples and palaces, the *kebyar's* rhapsodic, virtuoso style . revolutionized the Balinese music world. Pure music, then pure dance, finally blossomed.

SECRET BEHIND THE SOUND

Pairs of metallophones are intentionally tuned with a slight difference of pitch between instruments of the same pair. When the same tone is struck simultaneously on the two instruments, the result is the vibrating, tremolo resonance characteristic of the big Balinese *gamelan*. Unlike Western music, there is no agreed norm for tuning.

GAMELAN ANGKLUNG

The old bronze *gamelan angklung* is common throughout Bali. Its sweet repertoire for rituals, especially funerals, uses only four notes. But some ensembles have added keys to the tiny metallophones

KEBYAR HEGEMONY

Created for the *kebyar* style, the *gamelan gong kebyar* borrows elements of the repertoires of all kinds of *gamelan* and appropriates their functions in ritual and drama accompaniment. In return, *kebyar* style influences other kinds of *gamelan.* Archaic rhythmic accompaniment with bamboo tubes, called *kepyak* (above), used in the old *gamelan joged bumbung,* has been replaced in modern *gamelan joged bumbung* by common drums and cymbals borrowed from the *gong kebyar.*

to play *kebyar* music and other secular pentatonic pieces. The word *angklung* originally referred to bamboo rattles like those shown in the 1950's photo to the right, but the rattles are rarely seen in Bali today.

● GAMBUH AND WAYANG WONG

Gambuh, the oldest known dance drama on Bali, is considered the forebear of the classical dances and dance dramas inspired by Javanese literature. Its legacy of archetypal characters, their individual interpretative styles, musical themes, and stage production have influenced many other dances, including *wayang wong* and *legong* ● 70. Very few active village *gambuh* troupes remain, though efforts are being made to return the dance form to the popularity it enjoyed during the heyday of the royal families when performances accompanied princely ceremonies or temple celebrations.

PRINCESS AND CONDONG
Galuh (above left), the good princess character in Balinese drama, and her *condong*, the archetype of the good attendant and confidante, feature in the *gambuh* stories. In each episode, Prince Panji loses and finds his beloved princess. Until the 1920's, male actors also played the female roles in Balinese classical dramas.

PRINCE PANJI
The *gambuh* dramas are primarily based on the *Malat* Hindu-Javanese tales about wars and rivalries between the little east Javanese kingdoms under the Majapahit empire. Prince Panji is the archetype of the refined prince, war hero, and fine dancer, while Majapahit is still a symbol of Indonesian state greatness.

MILITARY ACTION
The dance drama's dramatic action is rooted in the social and military hierarchy of the Javanese court of the Majapahit era, thus preserving the ideals and manners of 14th century Java and Bali. Balinese classical dramas still use the Old Javanese literary language.

GAMELAN GAMBUH
Yard-long flutes, two-stringed *rebab*, drums, and old Javanese percussion instruments form the *gamelan gambuh*. Later classical *gamelan* have borrowed its melodic themes and adapted them to metallophones.

In the masked drama *wayang wong*, human performers take on the roles played by the shadow puppets of *wayang kulit* ● 58, and their movements are inspired by the two-dimensional style of the puppets. The rare presentations of *wayang wong* are mainly ceremonial, occurring at the *odalan* festivals ● 56 of temples where the masks are kept. Devotees perform the dance as an offering to the gods.

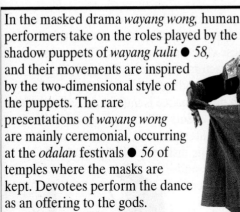

RAMA
Prince Rama (right) is a model of gentleness and an incarnation of the Hindu god Vishnu. Traditionally, a *wayang wong* performance shows only one episode in his many adventures.

RAWANA
King of the evil giants, Rawana (above) kidnaps Sita, Rama's loyal wife. As in every Balinese drama, *wayang wong* displays the victorious battle of good over evil.

TWALEN
Every kind of Balinese classical drama uses the servant characters inherited from the shadow puppet theaters. They serve as mediators between the aristocratic characters and the public. *Wayang* dramas use two pairs of servants, one to serve the good, the other to serve the evil side. Twalen (right) is the oldest servant of the good King Rama.

MONKEY ARMIES
An army of monkeys led by the white monkey Hanuman helps Rama defeat evil. Each monkey has a name, its own headdress, and dancing style. The actor who portrays Hanuman must display a variety of skills, including those of dancer, acrobat, and mimic.

BARONG KEDINGKLING
This itinerant *Ramayana* seems to be an archaic form of *wayang wong* with exorcistic functions. Formerly, troupes went from house to house dispensing blessings and healing while the small monkeys shook the fruit trees (right) to ensure their fertility.

An ancient and still popular masked dance drama, *topeng* draws its inspiration from the *babad* literature, historico-mythical chronicles of the Balinese clans and kingdoms. The masks represent archetypal characters and invoke the symbolic presence of ancestral spirits, lending special authority to the genealogical tales. Each performance is individualized and often interweaves local issues and events with an ancient tale. Whether performed as a ritual or as entertainment, *topeng* is a tool for communicating history, philosophy, moral standards, and government messages.

PERFORMANCE OFFERINGS
Before a performance, the dancer makes offerings to the spirit of the masks. Sacrificial offerings are also made on the stage, asking the low spirits not to disturb the performance. Balinese artists also pray to obtain *taksu*, the divine inspiration for a charismatic performance.

TOPENG PAJEGAN
Topeng pajegan, or "*topeng* solo", where only one dancer plays all the characters, is used only in ritual. The drama ends with the appearance of the Sidha Karya (above), who blesses special offerings and gives a little money taken in these offerings to a child from the audience.

TOPENG DALEM
This extremely refined king character (right) enters dancing, then mimes a speech which his servant translates into Balinese. In *prembon*, a more recent drama which blends *topeng* masked characters with *arja* opera, the Dalem role and some of the other characters are unmasked in order to be able to sing.

FULL-MASKED CHARACTERS
Topeng Keras, a minister, and Topeng Tua, an elder statesman, are two of the aristocratic characters introduced in dancing before the actual story beings. They usually do not take part in the drama.

TOPENG TUA

TOPENG KERAS

SERVANTS
As is the tradition in Balinese theater, the comical court servants, or *punakawan*, are key players of the performance. Half-masked, they not only tell the audience what their noble masters have to say but also bring Balinese literature and philosophy within reach of the general public. They serve as directors, controlling the players' entrances and exits, even improvising when a player is not ready.

THE BONDRES
A parade of *bondres*, or commoner clown characters, brings elements of the present into the story by poking fun at the faults of the lower classes and portraying idiosyncrasies of local villagers. In this way, the audience is instructed and disciplined by the example of the servants correcting the *bondres*.

With its highly disciplined body movements and intricate pattern of synchronized steps, the *legong*, classical dance of the princely courts, is a very abstract dance drama, almost pure dance. Two identically dressed *legong* dancers and a similarly dressed *condong*, or servant, play all the roles in the story. There are several *legong* dances, depending on the story chosen from the *Malat* Hindu-Javanese literature.

SYNCHRONIZED MOVEMENTS
The two *legong* dancers mirror each other's movements, snapping their necks from side to side, flashing their eyes and fans. Their sharp, accurate movements correspond with the highly intricate patterns of the energetic music.

PRINCE'S PROPERTY
The *legong* was formerly associated with palaces. *Legong* dancers were chosen among the most attractive young villagers and were the prince's property. Some later became the prince's concubines.

IBU RENENG
Renowned teacher of the *legong*, Ibu Reneng (left and below) died in 1993. She remembered her own tears of frustration as a child determined to master the dance movements perfectly. Before her death, she expressed concern that today's performances for tourists lacked the technical perfection and the spirit of the dances done for rituals.

CHILD DANCERS
Training begins at age five and performances begin between the ages of eight and twelve. Traditionally, the *legong* dancers retired once their menstrual cycles began as they were then considered no longer pure.

"AS THE ARCHETYPE OF THE DELICATE AND FEMININE, THE *LEGONG* IS THE FINEST OF BALINESE DANCES."

MIGUEL COVARRUBIAS, *ISLAND OF BALI*, 1937

THE STORY
There were many stories for *legong* dances, of which eight are still known. The most common is the story of King Lasem's kidnapping of a princess. Upon hearing that the princess' brother is on his way to rescue her, Lasem plans to meet and kill him. On the way, Lasem is attacked by a bird, played by the former *condong* (right). Mad with anger, Lasem kills the bird.

CONDONG
The court attendant, or *condong* (below), opens with a lively dance of her own before the actual play begins. In the midst of her swaying movements, she picks up two fans, which she later passes to the *legong* dancers. The *condong* role is difficult and requires a very energetic temperament.

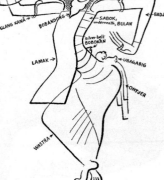

SUMPANG
UDENG
KIPAS
PETITIS
KARAROKÉ
GEGEMPOLAN
BERKAPAT
RONRONAN
SUBANG
SESIMPING
GLANG KANA
BOBANDONG
SABOK, underneath, BULAN
BADJU
Silver belt BOBOKAN
LAMAK
UBAGABIG
TONTJER
WASTRA

THE COSTUME
The dancers are richly dressed in leather painted gold. Each wears a headdress with frangipani blossoms and enormous ear plugs of gold. Layers of cloth are wrapped around the chest of the performer, a traditional style of dress for brides and classical dancers.

● SCULPTURE

Most contemporary Balinese sculpture is the product of a marriage between the 9th-century Hindu-Buddhist style and the ancient island animist vision. In spite of all the religious and political upheavals, sculpture has changed little over time in terms of themes and iconography; the demon figure carved on the lintel of the entrance to the Goa Gajah cave ● *190* centuries ago is very similar to the Boma head (above) carved above temple entrances today. But new and bigger markets for Balinese sculpture have resulted in a growing trend for sculpture with non-religious themes.

MODERN SCULPTURE
Wayan Cemul of Ubud, one of the most modern of sculptors working in stone, draws his inspiration from the pre-Hindu time of megaliths.

CHINESE INFLUENCE
Although Indian influence predominates in the iconography of stone carving, a Chinese influence permeates much of wood carving. The technique of painting wood is Chinese, as are some of the characters, particularly the winged lions and the *barong* masks.

POSTWAR SCULPTOR
I.B. Tilem of Mas, the son of I.B. Nyana, was the most important of the postwar sculptors. Tilem's sculpture (above) exhibits an ingenious use of the void created by the natural rot of wood.

PURPOSEFUL PLACEMENT

Spiritual scenes of divine birds enliven the upper section of a building (right), a position near the gods, while hideous, infernal scenes of carved animals appear in relief on the lower section of temple walls, nearer the evil ground spirits.

CLASSICAL SCULPTURES

The religious and symbolic purpose of a piece of classical Balinese sculpture determines the type and style of materials used and the ultimate placement of the piece. Guardian statues of demons (left) are set at the entrance to a temple, an area considered impure.

ANIMIST FORMS

Ancient animist forms have always survived in Bali alongside the elaborate Indian and Chinese imports, as seen in the work of prewar sculptors Cokot and Nyana. In primitive style, Cokot transferred the demonic and animal world to huge trunks (right), expressing the strong Balinese feeling for nature and the fear of the supernatural.

I. B. Nyana was master of the elongated style which developed in the 1930's. He later turned instead to a shortening of characters, as shown in this phallic statue of two girls (above).

One of the most popular exported crafts, Balinese painting today reflects not only its roots in the artistic traditions of the Hindu-Javanese who migrated to Bali from east Java in the 14th and 15th centuries, but also the influence of Western artists living in Bali during the 1920's and 1930's, who encouraged Balinese artists to expand their horizons. The arrival in the 1920's of artists Walter Spies ● *112* and Rudolf Bonnet ▲ *166* changed the course of Balinese painting by introducing secular themes and new materials. They helped form Pita Maha ▲ *162,* a group that encourages the arts.

PENGOSEKAN STYLE
Painters in the village of Pengosekan ▲ *174* developed their own painting style. Paying systematic attention to nature, they used a variety of animal and natural themes, often with a close-up perspective as shown in the painting (above) by Ketut Gelgel.

KAMASAN STYLE
The dominant influence of Balinese painting came from the eastern Javanese kingdom of Majapahit, where iconography was based on the puppet play versions of Indian epic literature. This style, found in stone on some east Javanese temples, has evolved into the traditional painting of the Javanized kingdoms of Bali as seen in the ceilings (right) of the Kerta Gosa in Klungkung. The classical *"wayang style"* is still practiced in nearby Kamasan.

RELIGIOUS CONTENT
Before the arrival of the Europeans, paintings and drawings always served a religious purpose and had religious content. The painted stories taught myths and reinforced rituals. Thus, a cremation sarcophagus (left) was decorated with drawings of the punishment of hell.

> "THE BIRTH OF INDIVIDUALISM RESCUED BALINESE PAINTING FROM ITS LATENT STATE AND PLACED IT ON THE SAME LEVEL AS THE EMANCIPATED SCULPTURE..."
>
> MIGUEL COVARRUBIAS, *ISLAND OF BALI*, 1937

I GUSTI NYOMAN LEMPAD
Balinese artists developed their own individual styles using materials introduced by the Westerners. Lempad, a traditional architect and sculptor, began to draw on discovering European drawing paper.

YOUNG ARTISTS STYLE
In the late 1950's, Dutch painter Arie Smit ● *115* fired a creative outburst in painting by distributing colors and canvases to children. He helped found a "naive" school in Penestanan called "Young Artists" ▲ *172*, exemplified by scenes (right) of daily life done in strong, simple colors inside a more or less sophisticated set of drawing outlines.

INTERNATIONAL PAINTERS
Bali has some contemporary international painters, such as Made Wianta, whose work (left), although abstract, follows the basic structures of Balinese painting with its repetition of pattern and emphasis on contour and warm colors.

VILLAGE TRADITIONS
Today painting in Bali is more village-based. Training may be village-wide, with the same patterns used by everyone and with artists learning from each other. But the basic style is changeless, with a "clutter" concept of space, the predominance of lines, and repetition.

The Balinese have a genius for making tools from plants. Although plastic, glass, and metal are replacing natural materials for many domestic objects, there are many others whose ideal material is woven leaves and tree fibers. Basketry has myriad uses in everyday Balinese life; it may be a quick and simple plaiting of palm leaves for an improvised wall, or a finely crafted basket. The raw materials are native plants: bamboo ● *78*, rattan, and the leaves of pandanus and various palms ■ *22*. The transitory nature of these materials makes them especially appropriate for ritual use, which requires that the implements be *sukla*, not previously used.

BASKETS AND RICE
Because rice is by nature sacred, the objects associated with it also have ritual uses. The rough weave of the bamboo tray, or *niyu*, is ideal for winnowing rice. The *niyu* also serves as a tray for daily offerings.

STACKED SOKS
The *sok* is a square basket of woven bamboo, usually with a lid, and comes in numerous sizes from miniature to huge. It is the Balinese alternative to cupboards and drawers, and stores anything from onions to offerings.

RICE BASKET
The *sok asi* (rice basket) is used to store fresh steamed rice and is also used for certain kinds of offerings.

KUKUSAN
The conical *kukusan* is used for steaming rice. A simple kind of holy water can be made by tossing water onto the kitchen roof and catching it with the *kukusan*. The water that drips through is sprinkled on the hair for purification.

FIGHTING COCKS
Like racehorses, cocks must be stabled to ensure special care and training for cockfights ● 95. Bell-shaped baskets or *guwungan* (above) are easy to move and the cocks can enjoy the morning sun and shady grass in the afternoon. The bottom of the cage can be removed to allow the cocks to dig down in a patch of sand. The *kisa* (above), used for transporting cocks to a cockfight, is much more restrictive.

WEAVING WALLS
Kelabang (right) is a quickly available building material made by plaiting the leaves of a palm branch. Because it comes from such a lofty source, *kelabang* is appropriate for the ceilings and walls of temporary ritual structures and for use in the rice fields to enclose seedlings.

WEDDING RITUAL
The high point of Balinese wedding rituals, at least from the point of view of the guests, is when a small mat of fresh

TO MARKET, TO MARKET
Pigs go to market in body cages woven from bamboo strips.

plaited leaves is held up. The bride secures one corner with her left hand, and the bridegroom pierces it three times with his kris: first gently with just the tip, then more deliberately, then confidently to the hilt, amid noisy cheers from the crowd.

Bamboo is as elegant and versatile as the Balinese themselves. This tree-sized grass grows abundantly throughout the island, and the Balinese use it with special flair in architecture and to make domestic tools, musical instruments, and many ritual objects.

FRIEND TO THE ENVIRONMENT

Bamboo conserves Bali's topsoil by reinforcing its steep river ravines. It also provides an ecologically friendly alternative to timber for construction, furniture, and *objets d'éstime.*

SEMAT

Women use long wisps of bamboo known as *semat* in the making of offerings. The *semat,* pinched off by the thumbnail as the women work, pins together complex confections of fresh leaves.

BUILDING WITH BAMBOO

Traditional architecture takes full advantage of bamboo's unique lightness and strength as a building material for posts, roof beams, and rafters. The principle supports are placed with respect to the direction of growth. Bamboo's cellular composition, with its hard skin and long, vertical internal structure, make it easy to split lengthwise for weaving *bedeg* slats. In the fog-soaked mountains of Bali, roofs of bamboo shingles are still in use.

TEMPORARY SHRINES

The cyclical nature of Balinese ceremonies often requires "virgin" shrines. Bamboo, freshly available and ready to use, is the natural choice of material.

BASKETS

The ubiquitous bamboo basket has myriad uses ranging from steaming to storage ● 76.

TAPPING TUAK

The simple, precarious one-poled ladder (right) is used to tap a beer of fermented palm sap called *tuak*.

Bamboo containers (left) come in all shapes and sizes.

HOLY WATER

Hollow lengths of bamboo (right) are used to transport holy water. The Balinese concept of purity requires that containers be uncontaminated by prior use.

PENJOR

These festooned poles of bamboo, called *penjor*, are offered to the gods when they go abroad on high holy days. *Penjor* are often decorated with the produce of the land, bundles of rice, cakes, fruit, and *sampian* offerings ● 55.

MUSICAL INSTRUMENTS

Instruments of bamboo register the natural loveliness of the original material. The archaic music of the *gambuh* theater ● 66 resounds through huge flutes (below) with a mournful, ancestral wind. The sacred *gamelan gambang* ● 62 has bamboo keys.

KNIVES

Knives cut from green bamboo can be razor sharp. They are used not only for ritual slaughter but also by traditional midwives for severing the umbilical cord.

Balinese medical theory is grounded in the cosmology of magic. Although traditional plant remedies are being eclipsed by the swifter, more vigorous Western medications, many Balinese still consult a traditional healer, or shaman, as a parallel precaution. The island's flora-pharmacopoeia is used in three ways: as *boreh*, plants ground to a paste and applied externally; *loloh*, a drink; and *simbuh*, chewed up with raw rice and blown forcefully onto the affected area.

MASSAGE
The aim of traditional massage is to restore the balance between body and soul. It also keeps the limbs supple and the skin soft. Skillful massage healers are also adept at realigning dislocated joints and exorcizing "chronic fatigue syndrome", but will refer other cases, such as bone fracture, breast cancer, and schizophrenia to certified practitioners.

FLOWER POWER
Familiar flowers are used medicinally. The bark of the frangipani tree, ground with refined slaked lime, is applied as a *boreh* for backache.

HIBISCUS LOLOH
The hibiscus is said to aid fecundity and an easy birth. Knead the leaves, mix with a fresh raw egg, and drink.

RECIPE FOR ASTHMA
Chew thoroughly a wad of (A) laos root (*Alpina galanga*), (B) blimbing (*Averrhoa bilimbi*) leaves, and (C) turmeric with a bit of raw rice and blow it hard onto the patient's chest and shoulders. Brush your teeth.

MEDICINAL LIME
For a dry cough, dip a wedge of lime in salt and suck on it. For urinary cystitis, put some slaked lime in the navel.

PUSAT KESEHATAN MASYARAKAT
PUSKESMAS UBUD (22050301)
KECAMATAN UBUD
KABUPATEN CIANYAR

HEALTH CLINICS

The Indonesian government has set up health clinics in virtually every village throughout the archipelago.

VERSATILE DADAP TREE
The dadap tree (*Erythrina subumbrans*) has many uses. Its leaves are cooling and can be applied directly to the abdomen for intestinal troubles. Or they can be mashed and mixed with salt and coriander seeds to make a cooling drink that is safe even for pregnant women. Dadap bark is used to hasten the ripening of jackfruit. The sap is good for mouth ulcers. A pole of dadap thrust into the ground will sprout quickly into a tree.

YOUTHFUL BEAUTY POTION
Take one piece of ginger root (above), the livers of three frogs, twenty-one sirih leaves, garlic (to taste) and jangu (*Acorus calamus*). Mix together, add water, and drink.

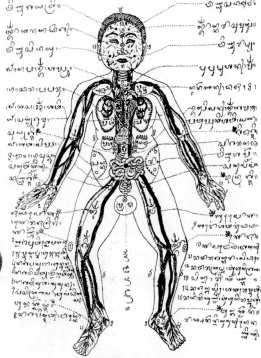

SIRIH
The leaves of the sirih plant (*Piper betle*) are used in the tonic betel nut quid, and the roots can make an abdominal *boreh* to treat diarrhea.

BODY HUMORS
Balinese medical theory is based on a complex constellation of named humors that transmute as they circulate within the body. These humors may be petitioned with offerings and mantra.

The Balinese calendar system is a mystical mathematical labyrinth based on a *saka* year of twelve lunar months and a *pawukon* year of 210 days. "Annual" temple festivals occur according to either "year".

Using these calendars, people determine the proper dates for a busy schedule of temple anniversaries, as well as the best day and time to make a fishing net, get married, and other events both large and small in the Balinese community. The system is not parallel to the Western Gregorian calendar, so major festival dates will change from month to month and year to year in this calendar.

CYCLICAL WEEKS
Simultaneously layered within the *pawukon* "year" are ten cyclical "weeks", or *wara*. The first *wara* has one day, the second has two days, and so forth up to ten. The most important of these are the three, five and seven-day "weeks". Certain conjunctions of the different *wara* are of mystical importance. The *pawukon* is also made up of thirty seven-day weeks, or *wuku*, each with a different name. For important ceremonies, the Balinese ask a priest, who consults a *tika* (below), a diagram of the *pawukon*, to determine the dates.

LUNAR MONTHS
Kasa
Karo
Katiga
Kapat
Kalima
Kanem
Kapitu
Kawulu
Kasanga
Kadasa
Jyestha
Sadha

LUNAR CALENDAR
Similar to a calendar used in India, the *saka* calendar year is based on cycles of the moon. Each month begins after a new moon, *tilem*, with the full moon, *purnama*, occurring fourteen to fifteen days later. There are twelve months of twenty-nine to thirty days each. A thirteenth month is added every thirty months to keep it synchronized with the solar year.

Balinese texts on the leaves of the lontar palm give their dates according to the *pawukon* and the *saka* year (seventy-eight years behind the conventional Western calendar).

PALELINTANGAN

The *palelintangan* (above) is a divinatory chart of Balinese character types (*lintang*) based on birth dates according to the *pawukon* calendar. The images represent mystical aspects of the five and seven-day weeks.

SABTU
Saniscara
Saturday
Doyōbi
Sing Chi Lioek

OFFICIAL CALENDAR
The official calendar published in Bali since 1950 combines Balinese calendrical systems with those of the Chinese, Muslim, and Christian communities.

GALUNGAN
The important holiday Galungan ◆ *300* fell on July 15 on this calendar from 1992. It happened to be a full moon, indicated by the small red ball. The red circle around the date indicates a Balinese holiday. The small red number refers to the phase of the moon. Inside the box are the names of the ten *wara*. There is also the name of the lunar month and the *lintang*.

Menyimpan padi di Lumbung, tgl : 15, 21.-
Mantening padi di Lumbung, tgl : 2, 13, 26.-
Mulai mengajar godel, sapi -
Kerbau membajak, tgl : 3, 19.-
Mengebiri godel, kucit, tgl : 2, 14, 20, 26.-
Mulai memelihara induk babi / bangkung, tgl : 15,
Mulai mengandangkan ternak, tgl : 13, 19.-
Menelusuk / melobangi hidung, godel, kerbau, tgl
Membakar genteng, bata, kapur, tgl : 23.-
Menebang pohon kayu untuk bangunan, tgl : 8, 20
Membuat tali pancing, tgl : 16.-
Membuat bubu / perangkap ikan, tgl : 10, 15, 24.-
Membuat bendungan / empangan, tgl : 1, 2, 4, 6, 10
28.- Menangkap Ikan, tgl : 4, 16.-

AUSPICIOUS DAYS
A column of text (above) included on the official calendar lists the auspicious days for certain activities. A glance at the list will tell someone the best day for a tooth filing, a wedding, and so on.

Lintang : Yuyu 17. Rekata Rasi Sasih Kasa		Lintang : Jongsarat 24. Rekata Rasi Sasih Kasa		Lintang : Kuda 1. Singa Rasi Sasih Kasa		Li 8. S
Muharram 7 Lak Gwee 9	Mina Pon	Muharram 14 Lak Gwee 16	Taru Kliwon	Muharram 21 Lak Gwee 23	Sato Paing	Muharram Lak Gwee
Pasah Tungleh **8**	Menga Dangu	G. tegeh Aryang **15**	Menala Pepet Tulus	Kajeng Urukung **22**	Jaya Menga rangan	Pasah Paniron
Sri Guru		Manuk Uma		Manusa Kala		Pati Brahma
Watek : Suku - Gajah Lintang : Lumbung 18. Rekata Rasi Sasih Kasa		Watek : Wong - lembu Lintang : Tiwa - tiwa 25. Rekata Rasi Sasih Kasa		Watek : Gajah - lintah Lintang : Singa Rasi 2. Singa Rasi Sasih Kasa		Watek Lin 9 S

The Balinese *warung* is a coffee-stall, convenience store, and corner pub all rolled into one. Whether a permanent structure or simply a table piled with wares, a *warung* is a place where people meet for local gossip, political debate, or private confession. Children go there for candy, older people go for company, housewives stop for coffee, farmers get betel nut, and foreigners go to immerse themselves in the language.

BETEL NUT QUID

Good for hunger, thirst, and fatigue, the betel nut quid is made up of areca nut, purified slaked lime, and *gambir*, an extract of the *Unicaria gambir* shrub. A masher (above) blends the concoction. Then it is wrapped in the peppery leaf of the sirih plant (*Piper betle*) and chewed as long as possible. Don't swallow the bright red juice; the lime will burn the stomach.

TRAVELING WARUNG

Some *warung* go where the people are: cockfights, temple festivals, or theatrical performances. Traditional wares are cigarettes, candy, betel nut, and more recently, in deference to foreign visitors, mineral water.

MODERN WARUNG

Many *warung* have televisions, and people crowd around to watch Indonesian films, dance dramas, and sports.

LOCAL CUISINE

Some of the best local cuisine one can buy is found in
warung that serve home-cooked rice meals.

NATIVE BREWS

The native brews at the *warung* include *brem,
tuak,* and *arak* (rice wine, palm toddy, and
palm gin). They are sticky, smelly, and
inflammable, respectively. All are cheap. The
best quality is homemade.

HONOR SYSTEM

Customers help themselves and pay as they
leave. The honor system is a form of courtesy;
however, the shopkeeper knows exactly how
many cakes you've had.

WARUNG WARES

The products and services found at
a *warung* vary widely, from
native brews to
photocopying
services.

Day-to-day eating for the Balinese is a private, no-fuss affair. Early in the morning, women prepare the rice and other dishes for the day. A family does not eat together; when hungry, one goes into the kitchen, takes what is there and goes to a quiet place to eat alone, quickly, and always using the right hand. Ceremonial feasts, however, are another story. A community affair, the often hours-long preparations are generally performed by the men, and the dishes feature sacrificial meats.

CEREMONIAL FEASTS
These feasts form the basis of most Balinese rituals where food is offered to the gods. People may eat the edible leftovers.

VILLAGE MARKETS
Every three days, village markets circulate around local regions. They are the best places to find seasonal produce, especially tropical fruit.

DAILY OFFERINGS
The household spirits are honored every day with little offerings after the daily rice is cooked. As in most of Asia, "rice" means "food".

NASI CAMPUR
The usual daily meal, *nasi campur,* consists of steamed rice with small amounts of spicy meats and vegetables.

FEEDING DUCKS
Ducks graze in flooded rice fields after harvest, feeding free-range on pests while fertilizing the fields. When cooked into *bebek tutu* (spiced duck), the ducks are massaged with spices, wrapped in the husk of an areca palm branch, and baked overnight in a smoldering heap of rice husks.

FEEDING PIGS
Pigs, plentiful and well-cared for in Hindu Bali, are fed soups that are prepared daily.

FESTIVE DISHES
Bali guling (spit-roasted pig) and *bebek tutu* (baked duck), two famous Balinese dishes served at feasts, owe their reputation partly to the long cooking processes required, but mostly to the care of the livestock. *Lawar*, another classic festive dish, uses the innards of sacrificial animals. These are finely minced and mixed with chopped vegetables, grated fresh coconut, chilies, spices, and sometimes fresh blood. Because *lawar* must be consumed immediately, it is not found in restaurants.

BALINESE KITCHEN
Traditional cooking fuels such as wood or kerosene make kitchens sooty and dark. In the Bali-Hindu pantheon of gods ● 46, Wisnu resides in the water jug and Brahma in the fireplace. When housewives place offerings around the house, the firewood rack in the kitchen becomes an altar to Brahma and Wisnu.

BANANA TREE
The trunk of the banana tree (right) is often used as a soup vegetable. The Balinese use complex flavorings of spices and coconut to turn almost anything edible into a delicacy.

● URAB

Urab is a rich, pungent warm salad of steamed vegetables, coconut, and spices that functions almost as a condiment to the Balinese staple food, steamed rice. The complexity of *urab* is in the seasoning; only a single green vegetable is used, normally beans, wild spinach, or Chinese cabbage. The version below comes from central Bali, where it is said to be favored by esthetes.

PREPARATION
1. Prepare ingredients for frying.

2. Gently stir fry the shallots in the oil until golden and crisp. Be careful not to burn. Set aside.

3. Pour off all but ³/₄ tbsp. oil. Stir-fry garlic for five seconds or until aroma rises. Immediately add shrimp paste/salt mixture, stirring constantly. Add tomato and stir fry until reduced to a pulp. Set aside.

4. Add oil if necessary and stir fry chilies until tender. Set aside.

7. Chop cooked vegetables finely (if using bean sprouts, leave whole).

8. Just before serving, moisten the ingredients with coconut milk. Reserve a few shallots to sprinkle on top as garnish.

9. Mix all ingredients together, adding chilies gradually to taste.

INGREDIENTS

½ cup thinly sliced shallots
½ cup frying oil
2–3 cloves crushed and chopped garlic
½ tsp. shrimp paste mixed with ½ tbsp. sea salt
2 tbsp. chopped peeled tomato
4–6 chopped hot chilies (remove seeds and ribs for milder effect)
1 lb. fresh young vegetables
1 fresh coconut
1 finely chopped fresh lemon leaf
1 lime

5. While fried ingredients cool, wash and blanch vegetables until tender. Drain and let cool.

6. Break open coconut. Discard or drink liquid. Make several deep cuts from the center to the outer edge of the meat. Remove meat with a strong blade. Grate 1½ cups coconut flesh. Set aside 1 cup. Make thick coconut milk by mixing remaining ½ cup with ½ cup hot water. Squeeze well and strain out liquid.

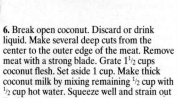

10. Mix in chopped lemon leaf and a squeeze or two of lime juice. Top with remaining shallots.

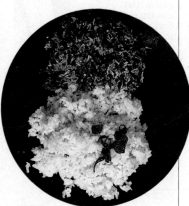

Urab tastes best served with rice on a banana leaf and eaten with the fingers, accompanied by a glass of tea or cold lager.

Etiquette and language in Bali reflect a complex order that requires constant awareness of one's social, spatial, and temporal bearings. The Balinese take pleasure in their etiquette, and a smile is as essential as correct pronunciation and vocabulary when speaking to the Balinese ● *42*.

WHERE DO YOU SIT?
Rather than "What is your name?", older Balinese still ask each other, "Where do you sit?", meaning what is your caste, so that they will know what language level to use. Caste in Bali is still observed in language and social etiquette. The four-caste system was introduced by the Hindu-Javanese of Majapahit ● *35*, and in the early 20th century it was formally encoded by the Dutch. The *Triwangsa*, or three upper castes, are the Brahmana (caste of high priests), the *Ksatriya* (caste of warrior-princes), and the *Wesiya* (merchants caste), and they comprise only about ten percent of the population, the rest being of the *Sudra* caste of farmers and artisans. The aristocratic *Pande* and *Pasek* clans were unfairly accorded commoner status by the Dutch, but they still maintain prestige in their communites.

WHAT'S IN A NAME?
In Bali, one can learn a lot about a person from his or her name. Almost everyone is called Wayan, Made, Nyoman or Ketut, but these simply mean first-born, second-born, third-born and fourth-born, at which point one starts again with Wayan. This will usually be followed by a private name which may be chosen by a trance medium. Commoner titles are "I" for males and "Ni" or "Luh" for females. Upper-caste titles are: "Ida Bagus" or "Ida Ayu" for Brahmana (male and female, respectively); "Cokorda", "Anak Agung" or "Dewa/Dewi" for *Ksatriya*; and "Gusti" for *Wesiya*.

TEMPLE ETIQUETTE

Etiquette prevents women who are menstruating from entering a temple. This is not meant to be sexist, but reflects a sanction against blood on holy ground. It is also sacrilegious to step over or stand with one's head above a sacred object or to put oneself on a higher level than that of a priest. A sash around the waist is one clothing requirement ● 92 for entering a temple.

BODY LANGUAGE

Body language still reflects old courtly manners and is strongly codified. Some tips for visitors: it is considered rude to point with one's index finger; use the thumb and always the right hand rather than the left. Use the right hand to give and receive things. The head is sacred, so don't pat children on the head. The hips and feet are considered unclean, so do not stand close to someone who is sitting on the ground. Saying "sugra" excuses you whenever you break any of these body language rules.

HOSPITALITY

Visitors are always welcomed with refreshments. Guests may acknowledge the efforts of the hostess when a tray of refreshments arrive, but they should not begin eating or drinking until the host says "*Silakan*", meaning "please begin". When leaving, a guest says goodbye by asking permission to leave, "*pamit*". It is always granted, with well-wishing for the guest's journey.

KADO

For a wedding or tooth filing ● 52, a kado (left) is in order. It is slightly smaller than a breadbox, often prewrapped, and contains something pretty and useful, such as a covered dish or drinking glasses.

PUBLIC AFFECTION

Touching between people of the same sex is unaffected and common among the Balinese, a sign of friendship not sexuality. This touching seldom occurs between people of the opposite sex, an action that would bring shame to their families. Accordingly, Westerners should avoid kissing or showing affection in public.

When people go to a temple festival, they wear their best traditional dress and make themselves as beautiful as possible to please the gods and each other. The Balinese believe the human body represents the cosmos ● *98,* heavenly at the top, demonic at the bottom, with humanity in between. Their temple wardrobe and the materials they are made of reflect this belief.

TEXTILES
Throughout Indonesia exists a mythical tradition of weaving spells into cloth. In Bali, the most magical cloth is the *geringsing* (left), said by some to be dyed with blood. The black and white *poleng* cloth symbolizes the polarity of positive and negative forces. The Javanese batik is also highly prized.

WAIST SASH
The *selendang* (waist sash) symbolically ties off the lower appetites. It is obligatory for anyone entering a temple to wear one. A white *selendang* is worn by the priest when performing holy duties. Priests are assisted by similarly sashed women, often their wives or the chief offering maker.

LATEST FASHION
Safari jackets and sports coats, along with sunglasses and gold chains, are becoming popular, and it is becoming chic to wear black for cremations.

HEADCLOTHS

The head is considered the gateway to heaven. Priests bind up their hair under white headcloths (above). Men wear headcloths, or *destar*, tied with individual flair. The hand-tied batik *destar* are preferred by fashion traditionalists over the ready-made slip-on.

MEN'S TEMPLE ATTIRE

Men wear a *kain kamben* on their lower body, tied with a flourish, the long fold falling between the legs and nearly reaching the ground. A smaller sash, or *saput*, wraps around the hips or chest, falling to the knees. A *selendang* and a buttoned shirt or jacket make up the rest of the outfit.

WOMEN'S TEMPLE ATTIRE

Women wear a close-fitting, long-sleeved jacket called a *kebaya*. A *kain kamben*, a rectangle of cloth about two yards long, is tightly wound clockwise around the waist, dropping to the ankles. A long strip of cloth or corset, a conspicuous *selendang*, lots of gold jewelry, flowers in the hair, and slip-on sandals complete the ensemble.

● GAMES OF CHANCE

Compared to Las Vegas or Monte Carlo, Bali is no gambler's paradise. In fact, the Indonesian government has forbidden any form of gambling. But Bali's wet rice agriculture permits plenty of free time for games of chance as well as other games. Apart from dance and drama spectacles, the Balinese have devised a range of entertainment, from *toplex*, a simple game played with Chinese coins, to cockfighting, with its complex rules and traditions. Taking place near the temple, in the village community pavilion, or at home, these games of chance often accompany ceremonial events such as births, marriages, cremations, or tooth filings ● *52*.

TOPLEK
In this game, a granite stone serves as the base. One to sixteen Chinese coins, called *kepeng*, are thrown and covered by the thrower's hand. The challenge is to guess exactly how many coins have been thrown.

CARD GAMES
Several games are played with Chinese cards, including *blok kiu*, a form of blackjack commonly played at cockfights. Those unsure of the rules can bet on a particular player by simply throwing their money down by him.

CRICKET-FIGHTING
The art of *mejankrikan,* or cricket-fighting, involves crickets pampered and trained for their mini-battles in bamboo tubes. Some crickets live long lives and become legendary champions.

KOCOKAN
Played on a mat decorated with snakes, turtles, demons, and other colorful creatures, *kocokan* requires players to throw money on the square or squares they choose. A toss of three large dice determines the winner. In a similar game, *bola adil*, a weighted ball wanders over a board to land eventually on the winning picture.

BULL RACES
Staged to please the god of harvest, bull races still occur in parts of Bali ▲ *247*. Teams of bulls drag their drivers, who stand on rakes hitched to the animals. Somewhat Ben Hur-esque, the Balinese and the beasts charge through the rice fields in a race for the finish.

> "...THEIR PREDOMINANT PASSIONS ARE GAMBLING AND
> COCKFIGHTING. IN THESE AMUSEMENTS...ALL THE VEHEMENCE
> AND ENERGY OF THEIR CHARACTER AND SPIRIT IS CALLED FORTH
> AND EXHAUSTED." THOMAS STAMFORD RAFFLES, 1817

COCKFIGHTING

Cockfights are still staged at religious events as blood offerings to the hungry earth spirits. In these purification rites, cockfights are sacred and occur in sacred places, so one should dress and behave accordingly. Gambling is forbidden at religious cockfights, but other cockfights where there is gambling take place secretly in village back lanes or in family compounds to exorcize malevolent spirits.

LETHAL SPURS

In preparation for the fight, lethal, polished steel daggers are bound tightly to the cock's natural spur. The blades are razor sharp, reason enough for viewers to steer clear of the fighting birds.

CARING FOR THE FIGHTING COCKS

Owners massage, bathe and train their fighting cocks each day. They feed them grains, meat, and jackfruit, selected to make the bird strong.

RULES AND ETIQUETTE

Cockfight matches are governed by a complex set of rules which determine the time and length of the rounds, etiquette, and classification of cocks by color, body shape, neck ruff, and so on. A series of hand and finger signals starts the betting. The fight itself begins with a loud gong, after which the birds are urged to fight. After first contact, the cocks are separated, and then a series of rounds determines the outcome. If a wounded cock cannot be revived, and his opponent is still standing at the end of a round, the fight is over.

Ancient, communal, egalitarian, at once civic and religious, the *banjar*, or village association, is an ingenious form of local government unique to Bali. Each Balinese village, *desa adat*, has one or more of these cooperative associations of neighbors. The *banjar* governs daily life in great detail according to local law, or *adat*. Because *adat* law is considered to be divinely ordained, it is a powerful force which few Balinese dare to disobey. The Indonesian government has astutely incorporated the *banjar* into its bureaucracy in Bali. The *banjar*, called *dusun* by the government, is effective in communicating national policies to the population, as shown by the remarkable success in Bali of the family planning program.

FINANCES

Financial matters are an important part of local administration. The treasurer keeps the books and makes loans, but is personally responsible for the funds. Cash is raised by dues, fines, and the earnings of communal enterprises such as professional dance troupes. One forward-thinking *banjar* in Sanur owns a restaurant, art market, and car wash.

TEMPLES

Temples in Bali are called *pura*, which translates literally as "place". The *desa adat* has three principal *pura* ▲ 260, which are shared by the *banjar*. The *pura puseh*, translated as the "temple of origin", is normally located in the part of the village nearest Mount Agung. It is associated with the founding ancestors of the *banjar*. The *pura desa*, associated with Brahma, is usually beside the main meeting hall, *bale banjar*, at the heart of the village. The *pura dalem*, often referred to as the "death temple", is located near the graveyard at the lower, seaward end of a village. It is associated with death rites.

BANJAR COUNCIL

Married men make up the council, which meets every thirty-five days at the community pavilion. The elected leader, or *klian*, serves more as coordinator than ruler. The *banjar* oversees such matters as property transactions, marriages, and divorces.

BANJAR BUSINESS

Banjar membership is a matter of life and death and afterlife. When a village member dies, the *kul-kul* drum ● 106 is sounded. Everyone in the *banjar* goes to the house of the bereaved to help prepare for the lengthy death rites ● 52.

ARCHITECTURE

● ORDER IN THE BALINESE UNIVERSE

The Hindu-Balinese universe permeates all aspects of life in Bali, from architecture to the making of *wayang* puppets. According to the Balinese, the universe is divided into three realms: the realm of the gods, the realm of the demons and ground spirits, and the realm of people. Just as the universe is divided into three parts, the microcosmos is split into three areas: the mountains, or home of the gods; the sea, where the powerful forces of dissolution dwell; and the intermediary region, where people live. This three-part division is repeated endlessly, in the layout of the villages, homes, shrines, and even in the human body (bottom).

KAJA AND KELOD
The most important points of reference in Bali reflect the tripartite view of the universe. Mountainward, upward, or *kaja*, is in the direction of the gods and the ancient mountain dieties. Downward, seaward, or *kelod*, is in the direction of those not yet made pure by the forces of dissolution. In ancient mountain villages, pre-Hindu structures were built down the village's spine along this imaginary line from the mountains to the sea.

HINDU SWASTIKA
The swastika, ubiquitous in the architecture of Bali, is an ancient Hindu symbol of cosmic energy and harmony.

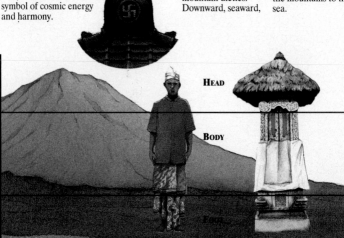

HEAD

BODY

FOOT

KAJA ▲

KELOD ▼

VILLAGE LAYOUT

Since the fundamentals of architecture are tied so directly to cosmology in Bali, it is natural that as society evolved, so too did the conventions of architecture and the village layout. In the 11th century under the Javanese sage-architect Mpu Kuturan, the three main village temples, or *pura* ▲ *260*, reflected the unification of religious sects. With the rise of the "age of kings" in the 17th to 19th centuries, village layouts became organized around the palaces (*puri*) of the

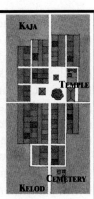

KAJA

TEMPLE

CEMETERY

KELOD

local nobility, with large central squares, usually shaded by a banyan tree. A village today comprises three areas: temples, family compounds, and a cemetery.

PRIEST-ARCHITECT

Javanese priests had a tremendous influence both on the religion of the Balinese, and on

their architecture. The Javanese introduced the concept of a priest-architect, or *undagi*. The *undagi* uses a measuring system that ensures harmony between the dwelling and the dweller, and thus harmony within the macrocosmos. To do this, he tailors the building's measurements to the owner-user. Critical measurements from the parts of the body of the head of the family provide measurements for the structure.

MANDALA

The cardinal points are associated with various Hindu deities and corresponding numbers, colors, magical syllables, and other mystical attributes. The mandala, which may be expressed in three, five, nine, or eleven points, is referred to in ritual as well as architecture.

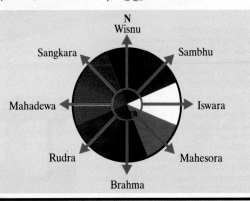

N
Wisnu

Sangkara   Sambhu

Mahadewa   Iswara

Rudra   Mahesora

Brahma

● THE FAMILY COMPOUND

The heart and hearth of Balinese cultural life is the family compound. The compound is a microcosm of the Hindu-Balinese universe ● *98* with realms for the gods, man, and the impure spirits. The house shrine is always in the *kaja*, the mountainward side of the compound. The pigsty is in the *kelod*, or seaward part of compound. In between are the pavilions for ceremonies, sleeping, and day-to-day activities. The compounds, which typically house two or three generations of families, line village lanes, grouped in units called *banjar* ● *96*.

Kaja

Kelod

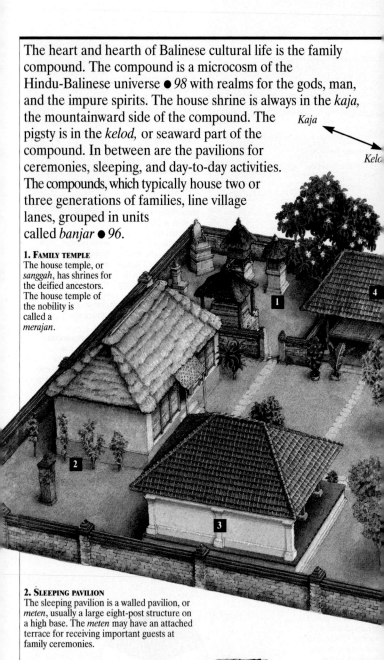

1. FAMILY TEMPLE
The house temple, or *sanggah*, has shrines for the deified ancestors. The house temple of the nobility is called a *merajan*.

2. SLEEPING PAVILION
The sleeping pavilion is a walled pavilion, or *meten*, usually a large eight-post structure on a high base. The *meten* may have an attached terrace for receiving important guests at family ceremonies.

3. WEST PAVILION
The west pavilion, or *bale dauh*, is the workhorse of the compound, serving a variety of purposes, from gathering place to sleeping quarters.

In large families, the *bale dauh* becomes a lesser *meten* for the families of the second and third sons who have yet to establish homes of their own.

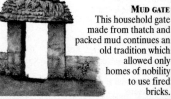

MUD GATE
This household gate made from thatch and packed mud continues an old tradition which allowed only homes of nobility to use fired bricks.

Architectural styles vary according to the construction materials available. This wall from northern Bali is made from flat black stones gathered from nearby beaches and cemented together.

4. SAKENAM

The guest pavilion for relatives and children varies in size and number according to each family's needs.

5. CEREMONIAL PAVILION

The east pavilion, or *bale dangin*, is the ceremonial pavilion. It has one or two platform beds set between six, nine, or twelve posts. The base is often tiered, providing seating for members of the extended family and visitors. The most important pavilion in the compound, this is where life rites and death rituals occur.

6. GRANARY

Called *lumbung* (six posts) or *jineng* (four posts), the granary is the house of Dewi Sri, the rice goddess. Beneath the storage area for rice is a large platform bed which serves as a kitchen extension and guest bedroom. It is often the coolest spot in the compound.

BALINESE DOORS

Often beautifully carved and painted, Balinese doors (above) may be single or double leaf. *Meten* have twin leaf doors mounted in carved frames. Kitchens have single leaf doors, hinged the ancient Chinese and Indian way, with post and socket hinges.

7. KITCHEN

The kitchen, or *paon*, is in the south because of the association with Brahma, the god of fire, whose place in the cardinal points is the south ● *99*.

Even in a simple column (right), a bricklayer shows the Balinese flair for the artistic.

9. COMPOUND GATE

The only official entry into the compound is the front gate. Its position in the right section of the perimeter wall is of spiritual importance to the welfare of the courtyard. The gate needs constant "recharging" for it to continue its job of welcoming higher spirits and discouraging evil influences. Residents place offerings in the small offering boxes located in side pillars of the gate or in freestanding shrine boxes.

8. PROTECTIVE WALL

An *aling-aling* wall, behind most temple gates and some house gates, deflects malign influences, which find turning corners difficult.

● PAVILIONS

PIASAN PAVILION
Painted religious decorations in the interior of a pavilion (left) called a *piasan* establish it as a holy place. Though not a place of worship, it often houses religious articles.

Attuned to the climate and the culture, economical but sophisticated in design, the traditional pavilions, or *bales*, of Bali are the result of centuries of experimentation and the blending of the best of Javanese, Nepalese, Chinese, and Indian styles. The *bale* is a microcosm of the Hindu-Balinese universe ● 98; the roof is the "gods" portion, the body is for the humans, and the base is for the netherworld. Considered a living organism, the *bale* is afforded consecration rites and even has its own shrine.

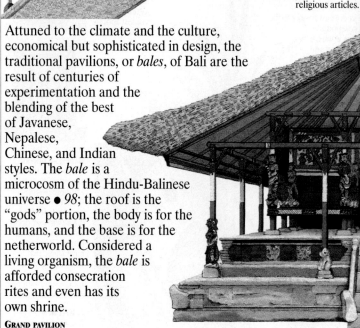

GRAND PAVILION
The *bale agung* (grand pavilion) is the most ancient building form in the archipelago. Modeled after the high mounds of stone on which the ancients held tribunals, it is the one pavilion that has been accorded the status of a temple.

GRANARY PAVILION
The *lumbung* (granary) is the only two-storied structure in Balinese pavilion architecture. Its style is often used in tourist bungalows.

METEN
The *bale meten* is an eight-posted pavilion often used as sleeping quarters. This mountain *meten* (right) is small and warm. At lower elevations the *meten* is often large and ornate.

KITCHEN PAVILION
The *paon* (kitchen) is a separate building. Smoke from open fireplaces escapes through small windows or loosely woven bamboo.

> "A WELL-BUILT *BALE*, THE ARCHETYPE OF BALINESE
> CONSTRUCTION, IS A MASTERPIECE OF
> SIMPLICITY, INGENUITY AND GOOD TASTE."
> MIGUEL COVARRUBIAS, *ISLAND OF BALI*, 1937

BALE BALI
The most classic of all Balinese pavilions is
the stately, square twelve-poster, or *bale Bali*.
It is most often found in the houses of
noblemen, where it serves as a ceremonial
pavilion, or in village temples, where it is an
elaborate grandstand for the gods. This *bale
Bali*, found in the famously polychromatic
Pura Desa Sebatu, has a three-tiered base;
column bases depict the main gods of
the Hindu-Balinese pantheon
● 46.

ROOFS
Black *ijuk*
thatch is
used in
temples;
alang-alang
thatch in lesser shrines,
ceremonial buildings,
and important buildings
such as the *meten* and
kitchen; and bamboo
shingles in mountain
pavilions as the bamboo
● 78 lasts longer. Since
colonial times,
terracotta roof tiles
have been used
increasingly in
Balinese
architecture.

Alang-alang thatch

Screen
wall

Taban

Sendi

Stereobate

COLUMNS
Jackfruit timber or
teak are used in
many columns. The
sendi (supporting
block) on which a
post sits is made of
paras (volcanic tuff)
or coral blocks.

FLOORS AND WALLS
The floors of a
community hall and
bale Bali are usually
tiled, but packed dirt
serves as the flooring
in the kitchen and
granary pavilions.
Walls in Balinese
architecture are
rarely load-bearing.
They are screens for
privacy.

COMMUNITY HALL PAVILION
The two- or three-tiered pavilion
often found adjacent to the village
temple is the town's *wantilan*
(community hall). It usually has solid
coconut wood columns and chunky
proportions for the base, plinth,
and roof trussing. The *wantilan*
is used for meetings,
cockfights, political
rallies, and dance
performances held as
part of village temple
festivals.

Bali has more temples than houses, as every house shrine is a fully fledged temple. Add to these the myriad temples to village-founding deities, to Lord Siwa, to Lake Batur and to many, many others ● *46* and it becomes clear why Bali is called "island of the gods". Typically, every major temple is divided into courtyards separated by beautifully carved gates.

COURTYARDS
Temples generally have three courtyards, such as those shown in this diagram of Pura Gunung Lebah at Campuhan ▲ *158*. The *jeroan* courtyard (top) contains shrines ● *106* for the gods. The *jaba tengah* courtyard (center) often includes a *gamelan* pavilion and the priests' meeting pavilions. Ceremonies to appease the ground spirits occur in the *jaba pura* courtyard (bottom).

Kaja

Kel

KORI AGUNG
This type of gate is said to show the reunion of the halves of the *candi bentar*. Shrines for offerings often flank such gates, as they do at Pura Penataran Dasar (right) in Gelgel.

CORAL GATE
Builders of the Pura Desa near Tanjung Benoa used white coral from nearby in the construction of this *kori agung*. It features a *boma* with a large mouth and big hands over the door, a common architectural decoration on *kori agung*.

SIDE GATES
Two doorless gateways flank the main gate at the Pura Dalem in Sudaji (above), which looks out over a dramatic sloping hill to the ocean. It is through such side gates, or *betelan*, that most people enter a temple, reserving the main gate for use during temple ceremonies.

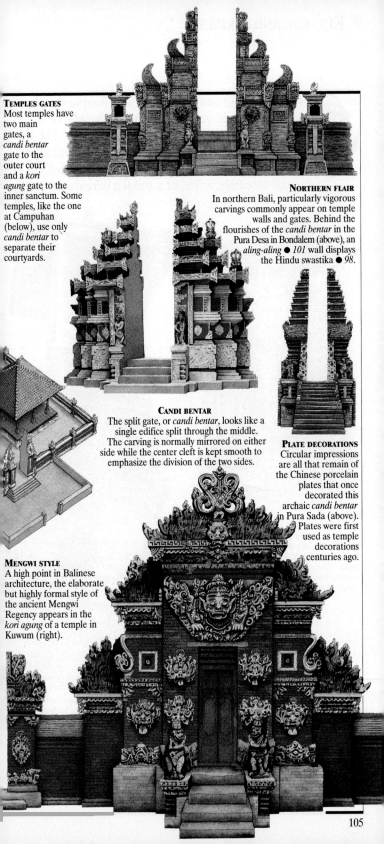

TEMPLES GATES
Most temples have two main gates, a *candi bentar* gate to the outer court and a *kori agung* gate to the inner sanctum. Some temples, like the one at Campuhan (below), use only *candi bentar* to separate their courtyards.

NORTHERN FLAIR
In northern Bali, particularly vigorous carvings commonly appear on temple walls and gates. Behind the flourishes of the *candi bentar* in the Pura Desa in Bondalem (above), an *aling-aling* ● 101 wall displays the Hindu swastika ● 98.

CANDI BENTAR
The split gate, or *candi bentar*, looks like a single edifice split through the middle. The carving is normally mirrored on either side while the center cleft is kept smooth to emphasize the division of the two sides.

PLATE DECORATIONS
Circular impressions are all that remain of the Chinese porcelain plates that once decorated this archaic *candi bentar* in Pura Sada (above). Plates were first used as temple decorations centuries ago.

MENGWI STYLE
A high point in Balinese architecture, the elaborate but highly formal style of the ancient Mengwi Regency appears in the *kori agung* of a temple in Kuwum (right).

● KUL-KUL AND SHRINES

Towers and shrines abound in Bali. Temple shrines may be simple or ornate, a small cabinet-like structure, or a towering pagoda-like *meru*. The *kul-kul*, or drum tower, is not a shrine; it is used to call villagers for any number of reasons, including a regular assembly, a fire, or a sudden bereavement.

KUL-KUL
A *kul-kul,* most commonly a four-poster pavilion, has one or more slit wooden drums hanging within it. The rhythm of the drum beats varies according to the reason for the summons. The pavilion, a tall, masoned stereobate, often straddles a wall corner.

SIMPLE KUL-KUL
The architectural style for *kul-kul* varies widely from the simple, as seen in this drum tower in northeastern Denpasar (right), to the ornate.

KUL-KUL MAOSPAHIT
This *kul-kul* is part of the Pura Maospahit, in the Grenceng neighborhood of Denpasar ▲ 267. Some of the shrines within the temple are said to date from the Majapahit era, when the eastern Javanese of Majapahit conquered Bali in the 14th century.

TAKSU SHRINE
Found in the corners of temples and family compounds, this shrine (right) honors *taksu,* the life force that acts as interpreter for the deities and speaks through mediums.

DEITY'S HOME
The simple *palinggih,* or "seat" shrine, is the most common shrine in Bali. Found in house temples and in larger versions in village temples, it is the spirit "box" or home for a deity's effigy. The shrine's doors are open only on ritual occasions, when the deity is invoked to descend into the effigy. The "head" of the *palinggih* is especially sacred. The favored roofing material for shrines is *ijuk,* the black fiber of the sugar palm (above, left). A shrine may be crowned with a terracotta pot (above, middle), a twisted tassel (above, right), or other ornaments, even a light bulb.

PADMASANA
The *padmasana* (lotus throne) (above) is an open seat-type shrine. It was introduced by the 16th-century Javanese priest Danghyang Nirartha ▲ *156.* The more elaborate ones include the Hindu-Buddhist symbol of the cosmic turtle caught in the embrace of a pair of serpents. The shrine honors the god Sang Hyang Widhi Wasa ● *46* in his manifestation as the sun god.

ULUWATU MERU
This three-tiered *meru* in the temple of Uluwatu ▲ *277* was recently rebuilt to replace one destroyed by lightning. It is dedicated to Danghyang Nirartha.

MERU
The towering *meru* (left and above) with its tiered sugar palm fiber roofs and elegant silhouette is the prima ballerina of many temple courtyards. This Balinese pagoda, a shrine to the higher deities, always has an odd number of roofs, with a maximum of 11. The number depends on the status of the divinity in the local hierarchy.

The Gianyar Palace (Puri Agung Gianyar) is a particularly fine example of a Balinese palace ▲ *199*. The palace has pavilion and royal courtyard features – Dutch fountains, Indian water gardens, Portuguese gates – used much as they were in the golden era of Hindu-Bali, the 16th to 19th centuries. Then, grand palaces were the physical manifestation of the popularity of the royal dynasties of Bali. The grand palace era ended abruptly with the arrival of the Dutch, and in the 1920's and 1930's only a few summer palaces and water gardens were built. Unfortunately, the Gianyar palace is not open to visitors.

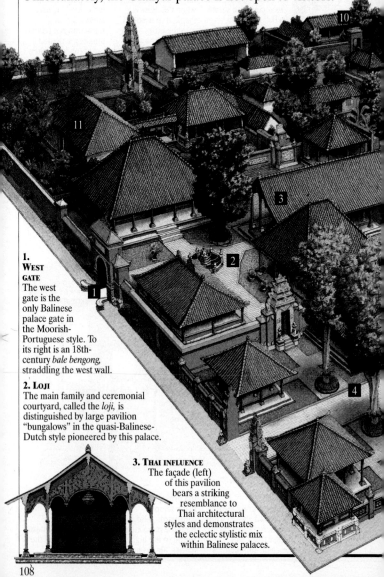

1. WEST GATE
The west gate is the only Balinese palace gate in the Moorish-Portuguese style. To its right is an 18th-century *bale bengong*, straddling the west wall.

2. LOJI
The main family and ceremonial courtyard, called the *loji*, is distinguished by large pavilion "bungalows" in the quasi-Balinese-Dutch style pioneered by this palace.

3. THAI INFLUENCE
The façade (left) of this pavilion bears a striking resemblance to Thai architectural styles and demonstrates the eclectic stylistic mix within Balinese palaces.

"THE SOUTHERN STYLE OF ARCHITECTURE (BADUNG, GIANYAR, TABANAN, BANGLI, KLUNGKUNG) IS CHARACTERIZED BY MASSES OF RED BRICK RELIEVED BY INTRICATELY CARVED ORNAMENTS..."

MIGUEL COVARRUBIAS, *ISLAND OF BALI*, 1937

4. ANCAK SAJI COURTYARD
Various viewing pavilions and reception pavilions, which come to life during palace ceremonies, are set in the magnificent *ancak saji* courtyard, resplendent with giant shade trees and flanked on all sides with exquisite gates.

5. KORI AGUNG GATE
This main palace gate, or *kori agung*, viewed from above (below), is seen to consist of many forms flowing out from one central point, a fundamental element of Hindu architecture.

10. PENYUCIAN COURTYARD
This courtyard contains the offering-making pavilions and temple kitchens.

8. ABIAN COURTYARDS
These field-like courtyards are the setting for dances related to the palace ceremonies.

11. WATER PAVILION
Guardian statues provide a refined sense of security to the raja's personal water pavilion.

6. SEMANGGEN AND
7. RANGKI-RANGKI
The holy quarters of the palace, the *semanggen* and *rangki-rangki* courtyards, are used for the poetic readings of ancient manuscripts, for tooth filings, and for the laying in state of corpses.

9. PALACE TEMPLE
The palace temple, *merajan agung*, is where the deified ancestors of the royals are honored.

● WATER PALACES

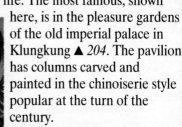

The water gardens and water palaces of the Balinese rajas were most probably inspired by the formal palaces and the temple water gardens of Sri Lanka, Cambodia, and Thailand. The Balinese added a floating pavilion, or *bale kambang*, in the center of a large walled pond or lake. Many water palace complexes are thought to represent the holy Mount Meru of Hindu cosmology, floating on a sea of *amerta*, the elixir of life. The most famous, shown here, is in the pleasure gardens of the old imperial palace in Klungkung ▲ *204*. The pavilion has columns carved and painted in the chinoiserie style popular at the turn of the century.

Panels (above) painted in the traditional Klungkung style of *wayang* paintings cover the ceiling of the *bale kambang*.

Whimsical column bases and guardian statues make this water palace one of the most beautiful and most visited in Bali.

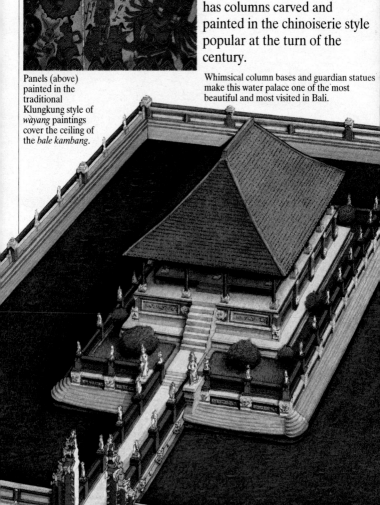

BALI AS SEEN BY PAINTERS

"THE BALINESE PAINTERS WHOM HE HELPED AND INSPIRED
TREATED HIS WORK WITH THE KIND OF AWE WHICH THEY
RESERVED FOR THE MIRACULOUS…"

MARGARET MEAD

The true impact of German artist and musicologist Walter Spies (1895–1942) on Balinese art and culture is hard to assess. After internment during World War One, he plunged into the artistically expansive world of postwar Germany, where his paintings, influenced by Rousseau, Chagall, and Klee, began to make their mark. He settled in Bali in 1927, and over the next thirteen years became the nucleus around which spun an enlightened group of expatriate scholars and artists.

A co-founder of Pita Maha, the first Balinese association of artists, and curator of Bali's first museum ▲ 268, he encouraged Balinese artists to seek new directions, gave them painting materials, and helped them sell their works. His paintings, with distorted figures, multiple horizons, and disturbing light patterns, as shown here in *View from Above* (1934), tread dangerously close to the realm of kitsch, but the universal symbolism in them usually comes to their rescue. In 1940 his life came full circle as another world war invaded his paradise. Interned by the Dutch, he was lost at sea in 1942 when a prison ship carrying German internees was sunk by Japanese bombers.

A meticulous academician from Amsterdam, Willem Gerard Hofker (1902–81), arrived in Indonesia in 1938 to deliver in person a portrait of Queen Wilhelmina to customers in Batavia (now Jakarta). He and his wife, also a painter, soon found their way to Bali, where they lived for several years. In 1940, with a world war poised to engulf even remote Bali, his oil painting *Offerings to Jero Gede* (1) strikes a threatening note. Jero Gede Mecaling ▲ 155 is the demonic bringer of pestilence who must be appeased at times of disharmony. He is sometimes associated with the *barong landung* effigy. In 1942 the Japanese interned the Hofkers in Java, but so impressed were their gaolers by Hofker's portraits that in return for paintings they allowed the Hofkers to live out the rest of the war in their house in Ubud,

so long as they did not discuss politics. While under house confinement in 1943, Hofker painted in pencil and pastels on paper the portraits of his neighbors, *Gusti Made Tuwi* (2) and *Gusti Nyoman Kelopon* (3). Gusti Nyoman Kelopon was a renowned proponent of the classical *arja* dance. In his female portraits Hofker lavished special care on the features for which the "Island of Bare Breasts" was famed. But it is the personality glowing from Gusti Made's face and her languid pose, particularly noticeable in her hands, that linger longest in the mind, conjuring a Balinese world of mellow grace even during the hardships of war.

1		2
		3
4		

A rie Smit was born in Holland in 1916 and arrived in Indonesia the same year as Hofker (1938) to work as a lithographer. Unlike Hofker, he felt his future was with the new republic and he was accepted as a naturalized citizen in Indonesia in 1950. He taught art in west Java until 1956 when he went to pursue his own muse in Bali. He is credited as the "father" of the colorfully naive "Young Artists Movement" of Penestanan village, close to his home in Campuhan. But he discounts this as pure myth, insisting that he only gave the village children materials and encouraged them to follow their own direction. His painting *Banyan Tree* (4) (1990), is dominated by the sacred tree found in the grounds of every Balinese temple, but this canvas also echoes the structure of the Balinese shadow puppet plays, as seen from the puppeteer's side of the screen, with the cosmic tree of life at the center, while female, inward turning elements associated with age are ranged to the left, and youthful, masculine and external ones are to the right of it. Arie still works in Ubud.

Indonesia's most internationally respected artist, Affandi (1907–90), was born and died in Java. The vibrant dynamism of the Balinese culture and landscape was a constant source of delight to his own bold and eccentric soul. The apparent absence of all restraint in his brushstrokes and colors is illusory; the master's mind and hand strove to keep them always in his control. Affandi's first step into professional art was painting cinema billboards, which provided grounding for his revolutionary posters during the war of independence.

He produced many self-portraits (top), saying that when a painting frustrated him he would paint his face all over it. In *Dead After Fighting* (1975), the cockfight leaps from the canvas (1). Affandi worked fast on such paintings, sometimes applying swirls of pure color directly from the tube. The outrigger canoes in *Balinese Fishing Boats* (1975) (2) are monsters with dripping fangs beneath a swirling sun (3). Art historian Claire Holt compared his boats to prehistoric cave paintings of New Guinea: "It is somehow moving to find that the well-known contemporary artist Affandi, with his characteristically stormily sweeping strokes, unknowingly renders the same spirit of boats bound to the elements – the sea, the sky, and the land – as do the Sosorra cave paintings."

● DONALD FRIEND

Enfant terrible of the Australian art world, Donald Friend (né Donald Stuart Leslie Moses, 1915–89) was trained

in Sydney and London before flitting off to the wider spaces of Africa and Asia. In 1966 he settled in a beachside house in Sanur, where he lived in exuberant style – usually with a glass and cigarette in hand – until several years before his death in 1989. His vivid sense of color, composition, and draftsmanship was complemented by a puckish sense of humor, which he also brought to bear on his wittily written and illustrated books (1). Although not reclusive by nature, the swelling stream of visitors obliged him to post a sign at his gate reading: "If You Are a Friend of a Friend, Go Away!" There is mischievous irony in Friend's work *Batu Jimbar Village* (1976) (2) because the two boys in the foreground are probably from the old village, invisible behind the palms, while all the buildings we see are the beachfront houses of Sanur's "international set", Friend's own home being the two-story building at the extreme right.

The advancing fishing boats in *Black Sand Beach* (1975) (3) are far friendlier creatures than Affandi's ● *116*, and the human figures, who cast no shadows on the black sand, seem at peace with a gentle sea. Painted in east Bali, where the beaches are mostly of volcanic ash from the eruptions of Mount Agung, there is a sense of midday heat although only a hint of red sun is rising into a sky of gold-leaf. *Careening* (c. 1975) (4) shows one of the many colorful boats from every corner of the Indonesian archipelago which would be beached to have their hulls cleaned in front of Friend's house in Sanur.

Batudjimbar

● ABDUL AZIZ AND SUHADI

L ike numerous Javanese artists who have been lured by the charms of Bali, Abdul Aziz has lived in Ubud since 1966. His controlled academic touch, honed at the Accademia di Belle Arti in Rome, is tempered with restrained playfulness. He takes pleasure in painting his subjects at doorways or windows, giving us a sense of looking into their world from outside. Sometimes his painted frame replaces the window or door, and his subjects appear to lean out of the picture, casting their shadow onto the frame. His twin panels of a young couple, entitled *Mutual Attraction* (1975), present the flirtatious glances and body language of Balinese courtship, while the eternal war of the sexes simmers just beneath the surface.

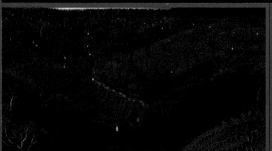

S uhadi (1937–88) painted *Fertile Earth* in the Bali highlands during the drought of 1980. Rice has been replaced by maize in the dried-out terraces, but there is an optimistic brightness to the scene which indicates the artist's confidence in the volcanic fecundity of the soil.

Bali as seen by writers

WESTERN WRITERS

FIRST SIGHTINGS

The first European views of Bali were presented by the Dutch travelers on the "First Fleet" led by Cornelis de Houtman in 1597. Although he claimed to have discovered Bali, various Portuguese and probably Sir Francis Drake had been there before, and of course hundreds of thousands of Balinese and other Indonesians were well aware of Bali's existence. These first reports, unlike those which followed, were positive ones. Portuguese or mestizos had earlier stayed to live on Bali as translators, and similarly some of the crew of the Dutch visit stayed on. Their residence was seen by later writers as proof of Bali's continued attractions, although recent historical research has shown that they actually stayed because the King of Bali paid them well to serve as mercenaries and advise on military technology. This report of the first visit is a synthesis of a number of different Dutch accounts, produced for an English audience who were interested in the competition to expand trading empires, and in the allure of strange and distant lands. Commentaries such as this often tell more about the commentators than the object of commentary.

❝They sent to the King, who accompanied the Messenger to the shoare in a Chariot drawne with Buffals, holding the Whip in his owne hands, having three hundred followers, some with flame-formed Crises and long Speares, Bowes of Canes with poysoned Arrowes. Hee was feasted in Dishes of solid Gold. The Land is an equall and fertile plaine to the West, watered with many little Rivers (some made by hand) and so peopled that the King is able to bring into the field three hundred thousand foot, and one hundred thousand horsemen. Their horses are little like Islanders, their men blacke and using little Merchandize, but with Cotton Cloth in Prawes. The Iland is in compasse about twelve Germane miles. Their Religion is Ethnike, ordered by the Brachmanes or Bramenes, in whose Disciplines the King is trayned up.❞

SAMUEL PURCHAS, *HAKLUYTUS POSTHUMOUS OR PURCHAS HIS PILGRIMES*, 1625

A PREACHER'S VIEW OF BALINESE RELIGION

From the time of their first voyage to the East Indies the Dutch continued to send emissaries to Bali. Their interests in politics and trade also meant an interest in Balinese religion, which they referred to as "heathen", the term they used for Hinduism. As non-Muslims the Balinese were potential allies against Java's greatest power, the kingdom of Mataram. One of those who traveled to Bali was the preacher Justus Heurnius. Originally based in the Dutch East India Company's first headquarters at Ambon, Heurnius traveled from there to Batavia (now Jakarta) via Ende (Flores) and Bali, in 1638. The following is from a letter to Antonio van Diemen, one of the most aggressive of the Governors General of the Company. Heurnius came to Bali in the last decades of the kingdom of Gelgel, when the ruler was a teenager.

❝The nature of their false religion... 1. Their clerics are few in number and no different in habit or dress from the other people. There is a general head over them, and he resides with the king and is held in great respect by him, so that he sits with him in judgement over criminal cases. This position (as is appropriate) is hereditary, and when he dies the son succeeds to his father's place. These give the common idolatrous priests, called Songoho, coming only from the people, who foolishly desire it, their idolatrous knowledge. The condition of these priests or Songoho is not passed on to their children, instead others come in their place. They receive no payment from the king. Their decadent state comes from the fact that they only teach those whose wish is to know how properly to serve their idols so they may achieve a blessed state after this life, and from such teachings the Songoho receive an honorarium.

2. The nature of teachings that they recite to the people:

That they maintain that there is an almighty and universal God, whom they call *Sangian toengal*, and under this they place their Saints, whom they call Betâra, which (so they maintain) are judged to be men who have, in their time, been virtuous and famous, whether on Bali or in other lands. They make no images of the *Sangian toengal* and offer nothing to him, whereas all their idolatrous images are of the Betâra or Saints, and to these they make their offerings. 99

JUSTUS HEURNIUS, *SCHRIFTELIJCK RAPPORT OVER ENDE EN BALI*, 1638

SLAVES AND SOCIETY IN BALI

Between the early 17th and the early 19th centuries, Europeans had little contact with Bali. One of the only points of interest was slaves, for Bali supplied many of the slaves for the Dutch city of Batavia (Jakarta). Although relying on secondhand accounts, the Dutch prelate and encyclopedist of the Indies, François Valentijn (1666–1721), provided a summary of outside knowledge of Bali in the early 18th century, particularly of slaves and the slave trade.

66 In their country they are generally lazy, and great little lords, who, when they have bathed, have their wenches *ramass* and *oeroet*, or pummel and rub, all their members, and even smear them with coconut oil and *bobori*. Then they dress and adorn themselves very elegantly, after which with their krisses at their sides they go out like bannerets to saunter the length of the village. They leer here and there, with a view to stealing something or other, or if strikes their fancy, to kill someone or other; or, yes, to sell one or the other of their friends, unbeknownst to them, to this or that slavetrader, who happens to be there with his sloop. They'll oh so slyly know how to deliver them. So they make the one whom they will sell go with them to one of these sloops, and then lure him below and shut him in irons for the sum which they have so treacherously extracted for it beforehand, dumping them. I have had several amongst my own Balinese slaves who have been sold by their own brothers and close relatives. 99

FRANÇOIS VALENTIJN, *OUD EN NIEUW OOST INDIEN*, 1726

A 19TH-CENTURY CREMATION

Balinese cremations have fascinated Western observers since the time of the first European visit to the island. Today's accounts are concerned with the beauty of the cremation tower (badé) and the ritual processions. From the 16th to the 19th centuries the chief preoccupation of Western descriptions was with the acts of suicide known as béla or satia (suttee) by which a king's wives, concubines, or servants joined him in death. Descriptions of such things produced suitably horrified reactions among European audiences, and in the 19th century the "barbarism" of such practices was used as a prime justification for colonial conquests. This description by the German student of Hinduism, R. Friederich, is one of the most concise.

❝On 20 December 1847 the prince of Gianyar, Dewa Manggis, was burnt… The three women (concubines) who were to become *Belas* came behind the body of the prince. They were taken to the place of cremation in procession, seated in the highest stories of their *bades*. These *bades*, which had only three stories, were carried by a large group of men. After the body of the prince had arrived at the place of the cremation, the three *Belas*, sitting in their *bades*, were conducted in procession to the three fires.

Their *bades* were turned around three times before being carried round the whole place of cremation. The women were then lifted from their *bades* and carried up the steps of the places constructed for their sacrifices. These places consisted of squares of masonry three feet high, filled with combustibles which had been burning since the morning and which threw out a scorching heat. Behind these furnaces stood bamboo structures shaped like bridges. These structures were of the same width as the squares of masonry; they were about forty feet long and between sixteen and eighteen feet high. Bamboo steps led up to them in the rear. In the centre of these bridges stood small houses which afforded final resting-places to the victims…

The victim sat in the little house on the bridge, accompanied by a female priest and by her relatives. They all spoke to her of the happiness which she would soon enjoy. She groomed herself; combed her hair, looking into her mirror, rearranged her garment, in short she arrayed herself as if she was going to a party. Her dress was white, her

Great cows serve as sarcophagi. Hewn out of tree trunks, they are covered with felt, velvet, and silks.

breasts were covered with a white *slendang*, and her hair had been made up in such a way that it would continue to hang down during the jump into the fire. When fire had almost consumed the body of the prince, the three *Belas* readied themselves; they glanced at each other to convince themselves that they were all prepared. This was not a glance of fear, but of impatience and it seemed to express the wish that they might leap at the same moment. When the doors on the bridges had been opened and when the oiled planks had

been pushed out, each victim took her place on the plank; each made three *nyembahs* by joining the hands above the head and each received a small dove (*titiran*) upon the head from one of the bystanders. As soon as the doves flew away, symbolizing their escaping souls, they leaped down. At the moment the women leaped down the attendants

appointed to watch the fire poured upon it a quantity of oil and *arak* so that if flared up to a height of eight feet. There was no cry during the fall, no cry from the fire; they must have suffocated at once...

During the whole time, from the burning of the prince till the jump of the victims, the air resounded with clamour and noise of the numerous bands of music. The soldiers had drawn up outside the square and contributed to noise by firing their muskets. In addition, some small cannon were discharged. There was no one among the fifty thousand Balinese present who did not show a merry face; no one seemed filled with repugnance or disgust except a few Europeans, whose only desire was to see an end of such barbarities. **99**

R. T. FRIEDERICH, "VOORLOPIG VERSLAG VAN HET EILAND BALI", *VERHANDELINGEN BATAVIAASCH GENOOTSCHAP* 23, 1849–50

LIFE IN BULELENG

At the beginning of the 19th century, sailors from all over the world passed through Bali. As the 19th century progressed, trade between the island and the British colony of Singapore increased, and commensurate with that more reports in English appeared. The following was originally published by Dr W. H. Medhurst, a missionary to China, in the "Singapore Chronicle" of June 1830, and was later reprinted in J. H. Moor's "Notices of the Indian Archipelago". Medhurst's report is of the north Balinese port of Buleleng and mainly based on sailors' accounts and his own visit with his assistant, Tomlin.

66 The king's palace at Baliling... with the exception of a new and rather elegant doorway differs little from the dwellings of the common people; indeed I have seen some, that for compactness and durability exceeded the residence of the rajah. The whole enclosure occupied by the king's palace did not seem above 200 yards square, surrounded by a wall about 12 feet high, over which none of the buildings are seen to top, so that they cannot be either extensive or lofty. The interior was undergoing some repair, when we entered it, and what with the workmen carrying mud backwards and forwards, and the late rain which made the ground sloppy, it was difficult for us to pick our way without being over our shoes in the soil. The Chinese say, that the rajah abstains from beautifying his palace out of compassion to his people, who would have to work much and without hire, in order to bring it into a state of complete repair: but I rather suspect the real cause is sheer idleness, which prevents him from superintending the work, and making himself as comfortable as he might be. **99**

J. H. MOOR, *NOTICES OF THE INDIAN ARCHIPELAGO*, 1837

ARRIVING IN GIANYAR

Medical doctor Julius Jacobs arrived in Bali in 1881 in the service of the Netherlands East Indies colonial government. Jacobs made a lifetime career in the Indies, and observed all that he saw with the eye of a fascinated ethnographer. He visited all the courts of Bali and was entertained in style. The interior of Bali was still then a strange wilderness to the Dutch, although only three years after Jacobs' visit a series of wars began which saw Gianyar defeated, broken up, and then reestablished under Dutch sovereignty.

❝We stood on the *Boekit Djongdjang*, a hill on the border between *Bangli* and *Gjanjar*. Some state officials, attired in festive ornateness, came up to us with due reverence, to call on us to welcome us to their land in the name of their king. There was spirit in their respectful stances, a becoming confidence in their faces and a generous cordiality in the manner in which the oldest of them, a man already aged, with grey hair hanging loose and a fiery gaze, invited us to come down from the hill and make use of a fine, daintily decked out piebald horse which stood ready. This did the heart good in a strange valley, especially after what we had been through. What a magnificent view of the valley stretched out before us. The number of men in uniform, gay colored clothing; the multiplicity of banners, among them two Dutch flags, stirred into gay undulating motion by the wind; the fantastically dressed up horses which, as it were, welcomed us with their neighing; the assembled state lances which shimmered in the sun; the uniformly dressed coolies, who lifted out goods as one and lined up in front at the nod of the headman who had been charged with the care of our baggage; and most of all the magnificent forest scene which framed this colorful panorama, lo and behold, that must have reconciled us to *Bali* to some degree.❞

J. JACOBS, *EENIGEN TIJD ONDER DER BALIËRS, EEN REISBESCHRIJVING*, 1883

FROM BULELENG TO DENPASAR

Once the Dutch had established their rule in Bali and opened the island up for tourism, Western travelers came in ever increasing numbers. Two of these were Hickman Powell and André Roosevelt, American adventurers, beachcombers, entrepreneurs, and film makers.

❝Everywhere was humanity. Roads streaming with girls. Heads proudly bearing burdens. Ankles, elbows, balanced curve of breast and armpit. Soft eyes, hair negligently hanging. Deep-shadowed backs of laden coolies. Breasts of aged, brittle women, and of fragile, unsexed children. Everywhere life, swarming, seething. Life, surging in the market place beneath a massive banyan. Youths lolling by the roadside, fighting cocks brilliantly preening... The road ran on and on, a wide avenue between stone walls. Everywhere temples lifted their stone gates, carved as feathery as the banyan trees above them. The villages were miles of walls, thatched against the rain, with hundreds of prim pillared porticos, and groups of damsels sitting by them. Beyond those parapets were homes. What sort of people lived there? What manner of life did they lead behind their sheltering barriers?

If, with Roosevelt and me, you had travelled this route one morning in April, 1928, you would have gone from Buleleng 129 kilometres to Den Pasar, the capital of the South, then on a mile to the town of Sumerta, which is a group of nine *banjars*, villages. You would have stopped before a gate in the *banjar* of Bengkel, and there, amidst a gay welcoming group, you would have beheld the smiling visage of our friend Kumis.❞

HICKMAN POWELL, *THE LAST PARADISE*, 1930

EATING IN BALI

The classic description of Bali is still Miguel Covarrubias's book "Island of Bali". Covarrubias (1904–57) was a Mexican cartoonist who became famous as much for his lifestyle with the fashionable set of the 1930's as for his art, but in his homeland he became something of a national hero. This masterpiece of the travel writer's art manages in 417 pages to capture everything that Covarrubias saw and read about Bali when he was there with his wife, Rose, in the 1930's. That meant that as well as containing what Covarrubias observed firsthand, it also reproduced earlier travelers' tales, and in this sense the book is as much an encyclopedia of the images and stereotypes of the island as it is an encyclopedia of Bali. He was at his best writing about the everyday aspects of Bali, as with his descriptions of Balinese cooking.

❝Although the daily meal was frugal, the Balinese seemed exceptionally well fed, and people were always nibbling at something. They were continually eating at odd hours, buying strange-looking foods at public eating-booths, in the market, at the crossroads, and particularly at festivals when the food vendors did a rushing business in chopped mixtures, peanuts, and bright pink drinks. Every day a young vendor came into the compound and invariably found many customers. For five cents she served a large piece of delicious roast chicken with a strong sauce, accompanied by a package of rice that sold for an extra five cents. Even small children, accustomed to looking after themselves, bought their snacks from the street vendors, waiting silently for their orders to be mashed and wrapped in neat little packages of banana leaf…

Balinese food is difficult for the palate of a Westerner. Besides being served cold always, food is considered uneatable unless it is violently flavoured with a crushed variety of pungent spices, aromatic roots and leaves, nuts, onions, garlic, fermented fish paste, lemon juice, grated coconut, and burning red peppers. It is so hot that it made even me, a Mexican raised on chili-peppers, cry and break out in beads of perspiration. But after the first shocks, and when we had become accustomed to Balinese flavours, we developed into Balinese gourmets and soon started trying out strange new combinations.❞

MIGUEL COVARRUBIAS, *ISLAND OF BALI*, 1937

LUNCH AT LAKE BATUR

Frank Clune (1893–1971) was Australia's most colorful travel writer. He traveled throughout Asia and the Pacific in the period between the World Wars, cultivating the image of the hobo or vagabond, although his books, stylishly written, thoroughly researched and well-illustrated, were usually produced from the exclusive Sydney suburb of Vaucluse. Unlike other Australian travel writers of his time he did not try to be more English than the English, but attempted to find a distinctively Australian voice with which to comment on Asia.

66 We drove across the isle to Singaradja, climbing over the volcanic mountain for lunch at the pasanggrahan of Kintamani, 5100 feet high, perched on the lip of the Batoer crater — which erupted in August, 1926, and is still wispily smoking.

Lo, from the pasanggrahan we beheld the valley with its blue lake alongside the lava-blackened slopes of the death-dealing volcano, which belched brimstone from three craters. We ordered a lunch *de luxe* of chicken followed by strawberries. While waiting for the chook to be cooked, we had some entertainment from live chooks. Here, as elsewhere, the lads of the village have thought up ways of earning money. Two urchins arrived with cocks beneath their arm to stage a fight. I paid five cents to each, and the affray was on. Then one of the midgets mulcted me an extra five cents because his warrior had drawn blood from his opponent's comb.

We drove through coffee and banana plantations, lined with hedges of hibiscus, and passed through many villages where pigs with roach backs and underslung bellies rooted for grubs and stubs. 99

FRANK CLUNE, *TO THE ISLES OF SPICE*, 1940

A PIECE OF SAYAN

In the 1980's the little village of Sayan, just above Ubud, became the place that the longer-term tourists and expatriates moved to to get away from the overcrowding that was encroaching on the larger village, which by the end of that decade was more of a town. The first Western resident of the village, Colin McPhee (1900–64), described the qualities that have drawn so many to this tiny backwater.

66 The village of Sayan stretched along the top of a narrow ridge that ran up into the mountains. Every three days a crowded bus rattled down from the Chinese coffee plantations to Den Pasar, choking and stalling as it climbed back again at night. The land I wanted lay at the end of the village, next to the graveyard, on the edge of a deep ravine. Far below ran the river; across the valley ricefields rose in terraces and disappeared in the coconut groves. Behind these ran the mountains of Tabanan, and far off to the south a triangle of sea shone between the hills. The land had once been terraced to grow rice, but now was covered with grass and shaded with coconuts. It descended in several steps to the edge of the cliff, where it dropped four hundred feet. From below came the faint roar of the river as it rushed along the rocks and stones…

Sayan was a peasant village, not very old, but running according to old Balinese law. There was not even a village school, and very few men spoke Malay, which meant I would have to learn Balinese… There were half a dozen small temples, and a crumbling palace which belonged to the Chokorda Rahi, a poverty-stricken prince from the ancient and highborn family which once ruled in Pliatan, across the valley to the east. The rest of the village were simple farmers; when they heard a white man was coming to live among them the signal drums beat loudly, and there was meeting after meeting of the village elders. **99**

COLIN McPHEE, *A HOUSE IN BALI*, 1946

KUTA IN THE 1950's

John Coast's introduction to Southeast Asia was harsher than that of most other travelers. He was in the British forces captured at the fall of Singapore, and from there was sent to the infamous Burma railway, where he first met Indonesians and studied Malay. He became involved in postwar Thai politics, but is best remembered as an enthusiastic supporter of the Indonesian struggle for independence. After the Revolution he settled in Bali, inspired by Colin McPhee's account of the island, and organized a dance troupe which toured the world.

66 We sat in two bamboo chairs, looking towards the beach, where we could hear the breakers gently pounding the white sweep of Kuta Bay. Between our grass-thatched hut and the sea lay only a shallow strip of coconut palms, beneath which the grey, sandy soil baked in the afternoon sun. The breezes blowing in steadily off the Indian Ocean made us want to sleep twelve hours a day. We had only been living in Bali for two weeks, but already we wanted to stay there indefinitely.

Kuta was a fishing village. Along the beach there stood a series of long, ragged huts, placed under trees just above the high-water mark. In these huts were the narrow boats with prows carved like fanciful masks to scare the monsters of the ocean, with their outriggers leaning drunkenly in the sand. But in these huts no Balinese lived; for according to the beliefs of the people, the low-lying sea is the habitat of demons, while always from the sea Bali's invading enemies have come. The sea, therefore, is not to be trusted, but to be placated. It is in the Great Mountain, whose vast peak dominates the whole of the island, that the gods of Bali prefer to live. The real village of Kuta, therefore, lay behind us, slightly inland. **99**

JOHN COAST, *DANCING OUT OF BALI*, 1954

ERUPTION OF MOUNT AGUNG

The English traveler Anna Mathews came to Bali in the early 1960's, when few tourists visited the island, let alone stayed. She and her husband had heard about a house to rent in east Bali, in the village of Iseh. The house had belonged to artist Walter Spies, who left it in the 1940's, and was chosen by the Mathews because of the spectacular scenery and the quietness of this village nestled on the slopes of Bali's highest mountain, Mount Agung. Little were they to know that in February 1963 Mount Agung would erupt, devastating the whole of east Bali. Here are excerpts from her vivid account of the eruption.

66 The noise was pandemonium: the vast powerhouse was out of countrol. How could it stand it? How could that bulk of rock and stone contain such monstrous force without flying into splinters?... It was as if, under that shroud, rivers of flame were flowing towards us.... Immediately below was the river-bed, already filled with yesterday's mud. In this now shallow track ramped something treacly, black, horrible. It pushed before it a flaming lip of burning trunks of trees and bits of houses. It squeaked, plopped, bubbled. The river shrivelled up before it. There was no water. There was no river. Trees at its touch burst into flames, and it passed on, leaving bonfires flaring.... The sight was fantastic. The noise was fantastic. The whole thing was infernal.... The stench was upon me, the smoke curling down, heavy with destruction. I began to run...

It was at this point that I Gusti Lanang Putuh, head of our village, achieved the stroke which calmed everyone. Down towards the lava flowing in the river-bed he walked at a firm pace. Behind him came the village priest, and I Gusti Lanang Kebon, our carpenter, carrying the ceremonial kris in his right hand. Various other elders accompanied them, one of them carrying a small black chicken. The gong, drum and cymbals brought up the rear, with a group of women who brought hastily made but fairly elaborate offerings. Twenty yards from the lava, in spite of strong opposition from those who thought it should have been beheaded nearer, Kebon made the blood-sacrifice of the black chicken. The priest prayed. The elders seized the body and bore it right down to the flaming lip of the lava and cast it in. One by one, showing no signs of nervousness, the women walked down and laid their offerings before the lava. And the lava stopped. It stopped just there, beside the offerings. ... Early in the morning of the 19th, for the first time there was enough clear sky to see the mountain. The sight was incredible. Agung had changed its shape. The rim of the crater had collapsed and lost in height as much as five hundred feet. 99

ANNA MATHEWS, *THE NIGHT OF PURNAMA*, 1965

UBUD IN THE 1980'S

Most recent visitors to Bali, especially those who have visited before, are shocked by the rapid pace of tourism development. Recent travel writing on Bali records and comments on the pace of change, as with the writings of the Italian-born Australian novelist and travel writer of Hungarian extraction, Inez Baranay. She observed sardonically the changes Bali was going through in the 1980's in her collection of travel writings, "The Saddest Pleasure", continued later in her novel "The Edge of Bali".

66 After some weeks I moved to the mountains.
In Ubud (heart of Bali heart of the world) the arts have thrived forever and the roots of a foreign community have been feeling their way into this outlandish soil.
There are subcultures abundant besides the ones anthropologists study and apart from the first-time short-stay tourists. There are, for instance, the White Balinese, the White

Rajahs and the White Natives.

Ubud is the home of the White Balinese.

'Where do you come from?'

'I come from Bali.'

'But where were you born?'

'I was reborn in Bali.'

It's the home of the White Rajahs, who live in solar-powered palaces in the hills. They're the business people who have workshops and factories turning out up-market clothes and jewels for the big cities and jet set resorts of the world; or they spend half the year in the high-powered rat races of the West and keep a Balinese alternative for the balance. Ubud is also the base for White Natives and Serious Visitors. They return over and over, often on scholarships, grants and endowments. They have a house in the rice fields, or plan to. They study dance, gamelan, singing, batik, carving; some go back to universities and present their Findings. They try to speak Indonesian, with a range of skill. They all attend, with foreign religiosity, ceremonies and celebrations, scorning the buy-your-ticket commercial dances. They visit famous artists, masseurs, dukuns, priests and balians — healers and magicians of all kinds. (I have lots of massages and they're all good and then there's the one that's something else again; he kneads and pulls and cracks, restructures your whole body, melting every block; the energy flows and you float home through the rice fields.)**

INEZ BARANAY, *THE SADDEST PLEASURE*, 1989

BALINESE VIEW OF THE WORLD

A resident of Bali since 1981, Diana Darling is an American sculptor trained in Paris and Carrara, Italy. In this excerpt from her first novel, "The Painted Alphabet", she explains the Balinese view of the world.

**One day, Mudita asked his grandmother, "Nini, is Bali the whole world?"

Ni Sabuk clacked her loom. "In a way. Why do you ask?"

"I saw some strange-looking people coming out of the palace today. I thought they must be sick people asking for help, but somebody said they were tourists – they come from beyond Bali. Is that true, Nini?"

"That could be true."

"But how? You said Bali was the whole world. Are the tourists from outside the world?"

"It's like this, 'Dita," she said, drawing with her finger on the palm of her hand. "The world is like a circle. Here in the center is Bali. Then around Bali is Java. People from Java look like normal human beings. Then all around outside is Holland. The people from there are called Dutch and they are very big and pale, it's true."

"Are they human beings?"

"So they say."

"What were Dutch people doing at the palace?"

"They're all aristrocrats," said Ni Sabuk. "They like to travel around staying in palaces.**

DIANA DARLING, *THE PAINTED ALPHABET*, 1992

131

INDONESIAN WRITERS

DRINKING OF THE COR

A. A. Panji Tisna (1908–78), scion of the royal house of Buleleng, was one of the first generation of writers in the Indonesian language. His novels on Balinese themes include "Ni Rawit, Seller of Souls"; "Sukreni, a Girl of Bali"; and "I Suasta, One Year in the Kingdom of Bedahulu". A central concern in all of these works is the notion of karma, an inexorable force binding together one's deeds and their consequences. Panji Tisna's great strength as a writer was his ability to combine plot and character development with themes of a particularly Balinese character. This comes out in the novel "Ni Rawit" in a description of a ritual oath-taking aimed at identifying the perpetrators of a crime.

66 The two men set out from the temple, at the same time looking to the left and right to see if the man they were looking for was among the passers-by. When they arrived at the temple they chose a seat in a spot sheltered from open view. As the day advanced more and more people arrived. Soon Anak Agung Made Pemecutan, the ruler of the western part of Badung district, arrived. After greeting the other local dignitaries he assembled those present in the temple and began to question them.

But not a soul would admit to having burned a house, let alone to having stolen the harbor master's goods or a treasure box belonging to a Chinese merchant. Furious the raja ordered everyone over the age of ten to drink a cor, the water of an oath, to prove that they were blameless. The High Priest, his expression revealing his extreme displeasure, added that the town of Kuta had become unclean, polluted. The gods, he said, had abandoned Kuta, driven away by the constant noise and confusion, by crimes ranging from petty larceny to grand theft and the frequent stabbings and murders. Though its terms brought terror to the heart, only the drinking of the cor could purify Kuta, cleansing it of the devils and evil spirits that had come to dwell there.

As each of the assembly came forward to drink their share of the cor from a banyan leaf, I Kerta and his friend inspected their faces. But I Lempod was nowhere in evidence. Finally they too took their share, then sat down close together next to the village signal gong, not far from the Anak Agung and Tuan Dubois.

One by one the villagers drank their share of the cor and returned home. When the ritual was complete, Nang Rame gave a sign to I Kerta that they too should return home, for the man they sought was clearly not among those who had come to the temple that day. 99

A. A. PANJI TISNA, *NI RAWIT, SELLER OF SOULS*, 1935

PANDAWA BROTHERS AT SANUR BAY

Ida Pedanda Ketut Sideman was born into a Brahman family from the priestly household of Geriya Taman in Sanur, south Bali. As a young man he showed a keen interest in the religious lore recorded on the lontar palm leaf texts ● 42. His strong speaking and singing voice were noticed by his neighbor and mentor, Ida Pedanda Made Sidemen, a priest and literary figure of legendary renown, who encouraged him to master the entire range of Balinese traditional poetic forms. This excerpt from "Satua Panca-Satya" is part of his retelling of the Wana Parwa from the Hindu epic "Mahabharata". The scene describes the arrival of the Pandawa brothers at Sanur Bay after being driven from

> "LITERATURE WILL NOT DIE BECAUSE OF THE CENSOR'S HAND OR THE BUREAUCRATIC MUZZLE; LITERATURE WILL DIE WHEN IT IS NO LONGER ABLE TO MAKE US DANCE WITH MEANING."
>
> GOENAWAN MOHAMMED, POET AND ESSAYIST

their kingdom by their evil cousins. The bay (center), a favorite of the author's, is protected by a reef and at low tide, the receding waters reveal the riches of the marine life.

❝Now we tell of the time when the Pandawa brothers arrived at the seacoast. Happily they gazed at all the sights there, for at the time the water was shallow and clear, revealing everything, right down to the sand of the sea floor. Many creatures of the reef had been left stranded as the waters receded, so as they hung limply on the surface of the water they looked like invalids or the bed-ridden. Many shrimp and shellfish had piled up on the reef too. It seemed that they had been too late to catch the receding waters. Perhaps they too were sick at heart seeing the sad fate of the Pandawa brothers.

At the same time great waves were pounding the reef, sending up a white foam that looked like the white flowers offered up by worshippers in a temple, so the sea itself appeared to showing its devotion to the Pandawas.

One could see crabs peeking out from the mouths of their burrows, afraid to come out for fear of an octopus lurking nearby, while the fish in the deeper water that darted this way and that in the current made one think of a young bachelor who is trying to get a peek at his sweetheart when her parents are keeping a close watch over her.

And there were a multitude of tiny fish leaping into the air, flashing silver-white, so the ocean seemed to be glowing brightly with a luster of its own.

On the reef a multitude of sing-sing crabs were piling up, jostling and pushing each other, almost like visitors to the court, as if they were seeking audience with the Pandawas.

Only the rocks sat motionless, showing no inclination to move even as they were pounded by the waves. Yes, if one thought carefully it appeared that they were carrying out holy vows of austerity and meditation, not to be moved by any temptation.❞

IDA PEDANDA KETUT SIDEMAN, *SATUA PANCA-SATYA*, 1984

AT BESAKIH TEMPLE

K. Landras, born into a Bali farming family in 1961, is a writer of poems and short stories that have appeared in many local newspapers and journals. In this poem, he describes his rediscovery of the special connection between man and God, represented by the Besakih temple ▲ 208.

❝I climb the high steps
following the edge
of the road to heaven
the road to the house of my love.
When I descend
I carry with me your love.

The echoing ring of the priest's bell,
the smoke of incense and smouldering sandlewood,
strike my feet and make them tremble.

The whistle of the cold wind of evening
makes me wary
while scattering rays of sunlight
remind me of evening's close. ❞

K. LANDRAS, "AT BESAKIH TEMPLE", 1989

GRANDMOTHER

I Gusti Putu Arya Tirtawirya, living in the Balinese community on Lombok, has composed short stories, poetry, essays, children's books, and reworkings of traditional stories. A writer with a keen sensitivity toward social issues and their effect on human relationships, he frequently develops these themes against a Balinese cultural background. This excerpt from "Grandmother", one of the short stories in his collection "Sands of White, Sands of the Sea", offers an insight into life in the family compound.

❝Grandmother's section of the compound straddled the boundary marking the "status quo" between the two halves of the family that had separated into two sections since the formalization of her own marriage many years ago. The shape of the compound could thus be compared to that of a great winged bird: Grandmother's sections represented the body, from head to tail, while the quarters of her two daughter's families made up the two wings, Rai's on the west, Raka's on the east.

Grandmother's age had brought with it all-too-frequent illness. Now the tense atmosphere that pervaded the house-yard seemed to press in on her soul as well. The current tension had arisen when word went round the large household that one of Rai's sons was going to go all out for his child's six-month ceremonies, complete with hired entertainment and a feast prepared from freshly slaughtered pork.

The connections that for so long had held together the two descent groups had begun to come undone the moment the gossip from Raka's quarters about the planned festivities reached the ears of the eastern wing.

They say that a single spilled drop of indigo will ruin a whole pail of milk, and just so was the effect of the news that made its way to Gusti Ayu Rai. It made her eyes – nay her heart – begin to burn, for the question of the planned-for rituals was a subject that touched upon her honor as a mother.

For Gusti Ayu Rai knew that several months ago, even before the birth of the child whose six-month ceremony was to be celebrated, the child's father had been beaten half to death by a crowd in a neighboring village. It seemed that Rai's son had lost big in gambling on the cockfights. He'd then borrowed a motorbike from a friend and pawned it hoping to use the money to recoup his losses. But it seems that he lost everything a second time, and had made himself scarce for a few days, afraid of what might happen. The owner of the bike had looked for him for days, his anger rising by the minute as he grew tired of chasing around from this place to that looking for Rai's son. Finally he'd caught up with him in the neighboring village and collared him on the spot. The crowd that gathered round was itching for a fight anyway and had gladly taken the occasion to gang up on Rai's son and beat him within an inch of his life.

Grandmother knew what Raka's side wanted from her. They hoped that she would use her position as mother of them all to expel Rai's son. It seemed to them he'd brought the misfortune on himself, and it seemed clear from this that it was his karma that had brought him to this sorry pass. How else could one explain such events?❞

PUTA ARYA TIRTAWIRYA, *SANDS OF WHITE, SANDS OF THE SEA*, 1973

CAK DANCE AT MIDNIGHT

Nyoman Tusthi Edy, raised in an east Bali village, is a high school principal as well as writer of poetry, short stories, and essays on Indonesian language and literature. The cak dance ● 63, also called the kecak dance or monkey dance, tells the classic story of Rama's exile and is seen by Edy as a symbol of the eternal struggle between greed and honesty in the world.

"A thousand hands, a thousand feet
Thrust forward their shadows
Grasping for the obscurity of the sky
Stamping out the torporous sleep of ancient powerful things
Victorious king,
Monkey warriors a million strong.

A thousand hands, a thousand feet
Impale the shaking earth and make it firm
In the pale light of neon lamps
The darkness too is swallowed up
By the dance of torchlight
Shadows of a thousand fingers
And the thunder of the sound CAK.

A thousand hands, a thousand feet
Plant firm the swaying earth
The night grows old at the peak of the temple gate
The sky too opens out
In the eyes of every monkey
An ancient enmity burns
Alengka, your fire will be extinguished
And darkness will swallow
The flames of the traitor Rahwana
A thousand hands, a thousand feet
Rama, his sorrow half submerged
Stumbles along in painful longing
Haunted by remembered images of Sita
Who knows now where she is
Faithful Laksmana
Sounds out a hero's lament
For Rama, elder brother
For Sita, sister-in-law.

A thousand hands, a thousand feet
Thunderous stamping of the monkey host
Embers of passion flare up, burning for revenge
Rahwana has set foot at the gateway of darkness
And the curse of the gods can no longer be washed away
He will live eternally now among the damned."
NYOMAN TUSTHI EDY, "CAK DANCE AT MIDNIGHT", 1989

FOR NI RENENG, THE DANCER

In this tribute to dancer and teacher the late Ni Reneng, Hartanto expresses his sadness at the near extinction of gambuh, one of the most basic of Balinese dances ● 66. Hartanto, a native of Java, has written poetry since high school. He is a reporter for MATRA magazine and contributor to many Indonesian publications.

66 The sky that you net
with your hands
seems to flash in my blood
while the unspoken moments of your magic
begin to find a place of burial
at the tip of a promontory.

Silent leaves
count the measure of my speechlessness
transfixed by the wild profusion of the trees
and a voice that touches my silence. As if
the waves of the sea had come
to carry off the flower offerings
within my heart.

Fresh water springs out from
among cracks of the parched earth
as if demanding repayment for the promise of tears.
But no gongs are sounded now
to accompany the dance of your ancient sinews. Only
the snap of your bones grows louder,
becoming an unearthly song:

"I have stored you deeply below
so you become one with my heartbeat" 99

HARTANTO, "IN MAESTOSO: THE YLANG-YLANG FLOWERS", 1993

CRAZY NYOMAN

Painter and poet Frans Nadjira was born in Makassar, the capital of Sulawesi province. He began writing in 1960, his short stories appearing first in newspapers of the Makassar area and later in the Indonesian literary magazine "Horison". His love of travel has led him to the docks of Indonesia and the Philippines, and he now resides in Bali. This poem expresses his concern over the effect of the westernization of Bali.

66 That Nyoman is really crazy
Probing the marketplaces
With his lantern in the early morning light

The gods are dead chak chak chak
Come on then Sita, let's dance to the wasteland
And place offerings on the TV set

(Hanoman leaps from branch to branch
Sobbing, from shore to shore
Searching for Rama, who in fact is long gone
Shot dead by Mannix)

A tourist gulps down palm wine
From a section of bamboo
This must be the enchantment of the fabled East
He says, while searching carefully for the meaning
Of the carnelians he holds in his hand. 99

FRANS NADJIRA, "SPRINGS OF FIRE, SPRINGS OF RAGE", 1976

A JOURNEY THROUGH BALI

▲ Mount Agung.

▼ Mount Batur.

▼ Batur Caldera.

▲ Pura Besakih.

▲ Sideman Mosque.

▼ Pura Luhur Uluwatu.

▲ Pura Mengening, Tampaksiring.

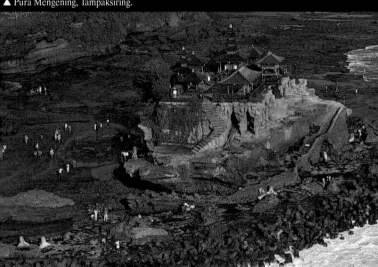

▲ Pura Tanah Lot, Kediri. ▼ Subak temple.

▲ Balinese rice terraces.　　　　　　▼ Plowing in the rice fields.

▼ Seaweed farms, Nusa Penida.

▲ Kusamba Beach.

▼ Benoa Harbor.

▼ Kuta Beach.

On the road to Ubud

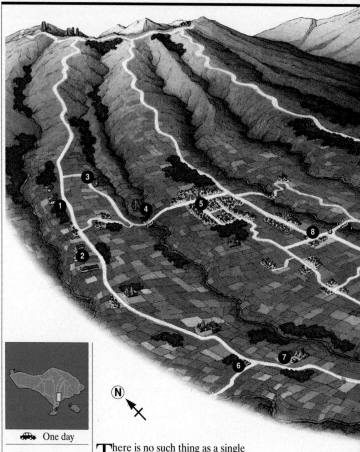

1 KEDEWATAN 2 SAYAN 3 NEKA MUSEUM 4 PURA GUNUNG LEBAH 5 UBUD 6 KENGETAN 7 PURA PUSEH SILAKARANG 8 PELIATAN

N

One day

"Now *this* is the real Bali": Western visitor overheard at the daily trance dance in Batubulan.

There is no such thing as a single "real Bali". Each one of the island's thousand faces is an aspect of the real Bali of today, but the first time you leave the beaches of Sanur and Kuta behind ▲ 274 and turn off the bypass at Tohpati onto the busy road toward Gianyar, it is easy to feel that you are entering a different and more entrancing Bali. Despite the vigorous commercialism emanating from the shops which line the road, you can sense that only a few feet behind those imposing emporiums, hundreds of thousands of Balinese are still living attuned to their old beliefs and long-held priorities. The road to Ubud is the island's major tourist route, a sort of shopper's and collector's circuit that can leave even the most acquisitive among us sated. But there are good reasons why this area has become Bali's "heart of art". Just after leaving the bypass and shortly before the Batubulan bus terminal, the hub of all public transport heading east, you cross the border into the old kingdom (now the regency ● 41) of Gianyar. Around the turn of the century, the royal house of Gianyar ▲ 199 allied itself with the Dutch against its traditional foes in the rival palaces, thus avoiding

TO DENPASAR

the fate of the other kingdoms whose royal lines were almost completely decimated in ritual *puputans,* or "fights to the end" ● *38.* The palaces here, as elsewhere, were the traditional patrons of the arts, so in the early 20th century Gianyar was the one kingdom left with all the elements required for a new flowering of the arts. With the birth of tourism in the 1930's, the artists of Gianyar found a new market and while fine art continues to flourish, its offspring, handicrafts, has become a more dynamic contributor to the rural economy. Although the regency of Gianyar is agriculturally rich and diverse, the majority of its population of 330,000 is either directly or indirectly involved in the tourism and handicrafts export industries. The distinctions are starting to blur, but each village still retains its own specialization in materials, subjects, and styles, many of which have their roots in the era of royal patronage.

WARNING
As you leave the bypass, this "crash art" reminds you that driving in Bali, where the rules of the road are almost as esoteric as the religion, requires total concentration, an enjoyment of gamesmanship, and a sense of humor. In this island of gods and demons, most of the demons can be met on the roads.

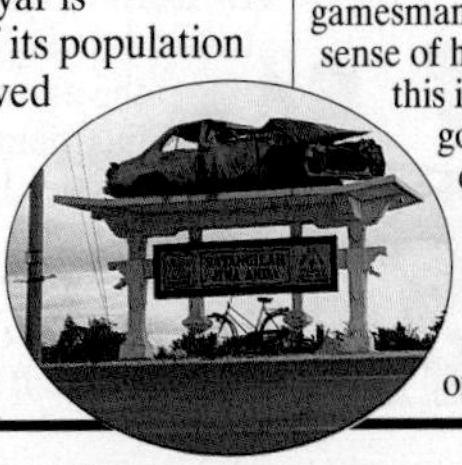

147

BATUBULAN

The numerous *banjar* (wards) ● *96* of this large village line the road for almost 2 miles starting just beyond the bus terminal. Batubulan has always been famed for the fine stone sculptures that used to grace only the entrance gates and pavilions of temples and palaces. They are carved from soft volcanic tuff called *paras*, compacted volcanic ash quarried from the nearby river gorges. The main road of Batubulan is lined with workshops where statuary ranging from the old Hindu deities and mythological heroes to modern fantasies is carved to order or sold from stock to passersby.

ANTIQUES GALORE. In recent years a new breed of shops has sprouted along the road through Batubulan and beyond. In these you can find a bewildering array of "antiques" of all ages, not just Balinese but bounty from the farthest-flung corners of Indonesia. Tenth-century Javanese bronzes vie for shelf space with Chinese porcelains, Balinese lontar leaf books ● *42*, intricate Sumatran jewelry, and penis sheaths, and the like from the cannibal tribes of New Guinea. The eye is assailed by an infinite variety of rich textiles ranging from the meticulous batiks and gold embroideries of Java and Sumatra to the haunting *ikats* of the eastern isles. Primitive tribal house ornaments from Sumba, Flores, and Timor stand alongside massive Dayak totems from inner Borneo, and Toraja death effigies from the highlands of Celebes. Although many are fakes, a discerning eye can excavate a veritable treasure trove of rich pickings from the mysterious past of the world's largest and most culturally diverse archipelago.

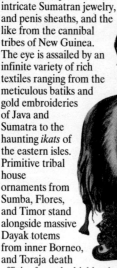

THE BARONG DANCE. Batubulan's other great claim to fame is trance – every morning at 9.30 sharp. Here you can witness the eternal conflict between Ratu Barong, the faithful guardian of the community, who looks like an overdressed cross between a lion and a Pekinese dog, and the pendulous-breasted Rangda, demonic mistress of the graveyard (above). At the height of the drama, Barong's entranced acolytes (left) turn their serpentine-bladed krises upon

themselves, usually with no ill effect. Even the Balinese, who find a trance state easy to slip into, draw the line at trancing every day, so they have invented more mundane tricks to avoid being wounded by their sharp blades. The *barong* dance, as the performance has recently been renamed for accuracy, is nonetheless an impressive spectacle, and it is not unusual for one or two of the players to unexpectedly drop into a genuine trance. Three very professional groups perform the *barong* dance each morning, with an additional night repertoire of the *kecak* (monkey chant) and the *sanghyang jaran* (fire trance), either in the Pura Puseh Bendul, on the east side of the main road, or a hundred yards farther along and down a short road east, behind the Pura Desa Batubulan.

PURA DESA BATUBULAN ★. The great gate of Pura Desa Batubulan is a fine example of monumental architecture, displaying the styles of numerous different rebuildings over the last century and incorporating Buddhist as well as Hindu elements. Massive recumbent elephants form the bannisters of the central steps while life-sized Buddhas meditate in niches in the walls either side. As in most Balinese temples, above the central door glowers the massive face of Boma, a protective earth spirit whose elemental essence Ratu Barong so energetically expresses in dance. Four *paras* sculptures of the god Wisnu (above), giver of water and preserver of life, sit before the steps atop hexagonal pedestals into which have been carved several tales from the *Tantri* myths, Bali's equivalent of Aesop's fables, in which animals act out, and reap the rewards of, the virtues and vices of humankind. These pedestals have been completely hollowed out, leaving only enough *paras* for the yarns to be spun in almost impossibly delicate fretwork, remarkable proof of the stone-carving skills of the masters of Batubulan.

CELUK, VILLAGE OF ALCHEMISTS

Just beyond the turnoff to the Pura Desa, at a statue of Ratu Barong, the main road makes a sharp turn east toward Celuk, while a smaller one continues straight ahead along a more leisurely rural route to Ubud. In the two short miles between Batubulan and Celuk there are perhaps as many as fifty shops, most of which specialize in the gold and silver jewelry for which Celuk is the island's undisputed center. Turning left off the main road in the center of the village you can enter a maze of back alleys where from almost every household emanates the sounds of hammering, chiseling, and filing as people work to supply these shops with small masterpieces, and to fulfill large export orders. In the homes of the gold and silversmiths business transactions in the form of the buying or commissioning of their workmanship take place. Traditionally, the working of metals could be performed only by members of the *Pande* caste, but expanding business opportunities have drawn almost every family of Celuk into the industry.

"The blacksmiths, makers of krises, belong to a special caste, the *Pande,* aristocrats among the lower classes who worship the fiery volcano Batur and are regarded as powerful magicians who understand the handling of iron and fire, two elements held in reverence since earliest times."
Miguel Covarrubias, *Island of Bali,* 1937

THE PANDES
These alchemists, who fell outside the normal caste hierarchy when their ancestors "stole" from the gods the secret of forging fire and base metals into power, are still considered to be the only people who can be entrusted with the creation of sacred paraphernalia for the high priests (above). *Tumpek Landep,* the day of the Balinese calender when all Balinese make special offerings to their sacred krises and other metal tools and weapons (including cars), is of particular importance to the *Pandes,* whose family temples become the scene of lavish rites.

149

Celuk, a center for the manufacture of jewelry in Bali, is a close-knit community that has organized its phenomenal jewelry production around family-based cottage industries. Most of the families are of the *Pande*, or blacksmith's, caste ● *90*.

KRIS

The beautifully wrought sword, or kris, that completes a Balinese man's ritual attire exemplifies the finest of the *Pande*'s craft. The hilt (left) is sometimes made of silver or gold and set with precious and semi-precious stones.

RELIGIOUS LINKS

Like all aspects of Balinese life, the smith's craft is linked to the religious and superstitious beliefs that abound on the island. Traditionally, when a *Pande* was asked to make a piece, he was required to make the appropriate offerings, to say the correct mantra, and to make sure the elements used were appropriate to the piece's function.

COMPASS POINTS

Each cardinal point of the compass is associated with one of the major gods of the Hindu pantheon and corresponds with a color ● *99* and day of the week. The learned *Pande* knows what color stone should be worn by an individual depending on the day of the week he or she was born.

REPOUSSE AND CHASING METHOD

Smiths traditionally used this method to decorate kris handles, ritual cups, and jewelry (right). The beaten metal is alternatively hammered and heated into the desired shape. Chasing gives fine detail to the basic shape.

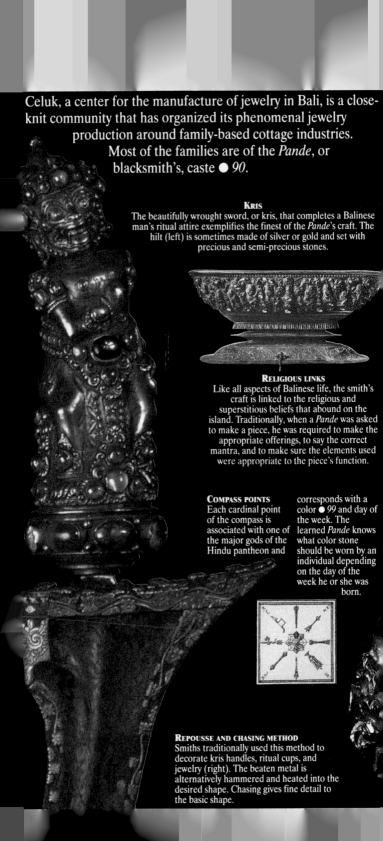

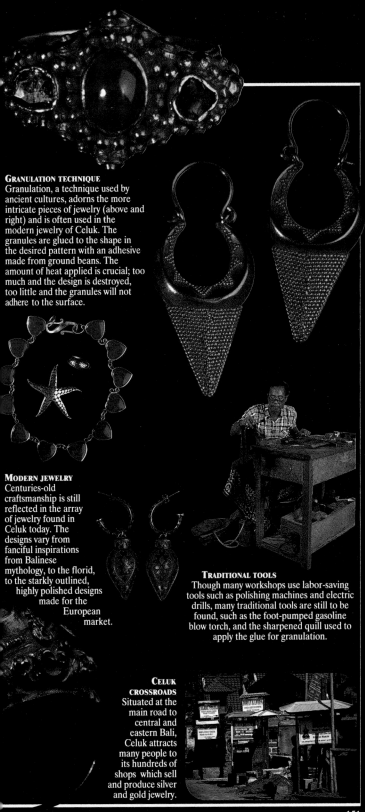

GRANULATION TECHNIQUE

Granulation, a technique used by ancient cultures, adorns the more intricate pieces of jewelry (above and right) and is often used in the modern jewelry of Celuk. The granules are glued to the shape in the desired pattern with an adhesive made from ground beans. The amount of heat applied is crucial; too much and the design is destroyed, too little and the granules will not adhere to the surface.

MODERN JEWELRY

Centuries-old craftsmanship is still reflected in the array of jewelry found in Celuk today. The designs vary from fanciful inspirations from Balinese mythology, to the florid, to the starkly outlined, highly polished designs made for the European market.

TRADITIONAL TOOLS

Though many workshops use labor-saving tools such as polishing machines and electric drills, many traditional tools are still to be found, such as the foot-pumped gasoline blow torch, and the sharpened quill used to apply the glue for granulation.

CELUK CROSSROADS

Situated at the main road to central and eastern Bali, Celuk attracts many people to its hundreds of shops which sell and produce silver and gold jewelry.

SUKAWATI SUCCESSION
Dalem Sukawati's sons were made of more dissolute stuff than the popular ruler, so he willed his entire kingdom to whichever descendant was prepared to take the tongue of his dead body into his mouth. When his sons rushed to his deathbed they discovered such a grotesquely festering corpse that they fled back to their harems. But when a more distant relative from Gianyar braved the stench to perform the unsavory deed, the corpse instantly reverted to sweet-smelling perfection. Since that day the links between the royalty of Sukawati and Gianyar have, despite occasional conflicts over the centuries, been close.

SUKAWATI

A short distance east of Celuk the road crosses a deep gorge carved by the Wos River. Alongside the new bridge trembles the old iron one dating from Dutch days. Around a sharp bend to the north stretches Sukawati, merging into its almost inseparable companion Batuan. Sukawati is an important market town for the farmers of the region, but most visitors race through at high speed with a possible pause at the new art market where all the standard handicrafts can be bought. By so doing, they are missing fascinating glimpses into Bali's history and art. A plaque in a village temple records the separation of Batuan from Sukawati early in the 11th century, and fragments of historical accounts tell us that for two glorious generations in the 18th century, Sukawati, then known as Timbul, became the seat of Bali's second most powerful kingdom. Sukawati's Camelot was presided over by I Dewa Agung Anom, also called Dalem Sukawati. With the help of a sacred kris borrowed from his father's palace at Klungkung far to the east, he overthrew the incumbent raja of Timbul, reputedly a powerful black magician, and established a glittering court based on his

visions of the long-defunct Hindu Javanese palaces of his Majapahit ancestors. It is said that Bali's most famous dance (above), the *legong kraton* ● *70*, a courtly dance by little girls, was first performed in the perfumed courtyards of his palace, and semi-mythical anecdotes from his long life are still recounted in dance dramas throughout the island.

PURI AGUNG. The palace of Sukawati remains today, as it was then, a strong supporter of the performing arts, with several forms of traditional music and dance long since lost to other parts of the island remaining vigorous in Sukawati and Batuan. Even more notable is the high percentage of Bali's most respected *dalang*, or shadow puppet masters, living in the streets just to the east of the palace. The palace, the Puri Agung, now architecturally fairly modest, stands at the central crossroads diagonally across from the new art market, while the more traditional market (left) spreads down the side streets. Here, goods of necessity to the Balinese can be bargained for, including intricate basketry and some of the island's finest ceremonial parasols, fans, and dance costumes made from the gold-painted cloth known as *prada*. In several homes behind the market, leatherworkers can be found making shadow puppets (top) of buffalo hide for the *dalang*.

PURA DESA SUKAWATI. With its regal past, Sukawati is well endowed with fine temples, each expressing its unique personality. Most have been completely rebuilt this century since the collapse of their predecessors in a devastating earthquake in 1917. Turning east off the main road a short distance north of the palace leads one away from the racing buses to a peaceful corner of the village where several small temples are dominated by the towering gates of the Pura Desa (right). Although the carvings on the Pura Desa are, by Balinese standards, almost minimalist in their paucity of detail, the temple's pure proportions are emotively powerful. There is no such thing as a typical Balinese temple, but in the simplicity of the two-courtyard Pura Desa Sukawati it is easy to come to grips with the basic principles which dominate all temple design ● *104*. Donning sarong and waist sash, obligatory wear for entering any temple in Bali, the visitor passes through the split gate into the outer courtyard.

To the right is a long raised pavilion which would be crowded with brightly colored worshipers during festivals but is normally the place where the wooden palanquins in which the effigies of the deities are carried during festival processions are parked. Directly ahead looms the massive gate, the *kori agung*, which protects the inner courtyard. The central door, up a steep flight of stone steps flanked by demonic giants, is open only for the occasional passage of the deities in procession. The carving of Boma above the door is minimally hewn to give only a stylized hint of its features, but there is no mistaking its protective power. Taking one of the side doors, one enters the inner courtyard which is towered over by three *meru*, layered pagodas which house the temple's most sacred effigies. The *meru*, along with other shrines, are spread around the northeast corner, the closest point to Mount Agung, the great mountain and abode of the gods who descend to take their seats on the shrines during festivals. In the extreme northeast corner is the only elaborately carved element in the temple. This is the *padmasana*, a shrine representing the entire universe, from the cosmic turtle upon whom the universe rests at its base to the shallow relief of Atintya, or Sang Hyang Widhi Wasa, the all-powerful deity in the Balinese religion ● *46*, behind the raised seat at the peak.

UNFINISHED SCULPTURES?
Many Balinese claim that "unfinished" sculptures, such as the *boma* in the *kori agung* at the Pura Desa Sukawati, are awaiting the time and money for the community to carve them in detail. It is more probable that they are exactly as the master architect intended because to whittle them further would destroy the classical proportions of the gate. The shape is what is essential, functional, and magical.

AN ESSENTIAL ALTAR
In the house temples of Sukawati's renowned shadow puppeteers, *dalang*, the *taksu* shrine is the seat for the interpreter of the deities. The *dalang* makes offerings to ensure that during the performance he is possessed by the intermediary between men and gods.

153

BATUAN PAINTINGS
The "Batuan Style" of painting, with its meticulous attention to detail and tendency to pack every square inch of space, is more closely related to the classical style than that of Ubud.

GAMBUH
Every full moon at the Pura Puseh Batuan, the ancient classical dance of *gambuh* is performed in its proper temple setting. Oversized flutes (right) with hauntingly resonant sounds are unique to *gamelan gambuh*. The performance begins at 8 pm. Proceeds from the Rp 15,000 ticket go to the Gambuh Preservation Foundation.

SPELLING CONFUSION
Balinese writing is similar to Old Javanese. It was first latinized by the Dutch, and that in turn was recently simplified, which accounts for the variety of spellings found in the Latin form of many Balinese words.

BATUAN

Continuing north along the main road, Sukawati merges imperceptibly into the village of Batuan. The village attained fame in the 1930's for the individualistic style of its young painters who, while responding to a newly encountered international audience, were less influenced by Western techniques than were the artists of Ubud, among whom several European painters settled ● 74. Some of the more successful artists have established large shops on the main road beyond the first sweeping curve to the left, but most sell their work from their family compounds in the back lanes. Their subject matter covers the full range of Balinese experience, from the most subtle religious concepts to the strange carryings-on of foreign visitors, with occasional plunges into the murky world of sorcery, which even today is seldom far from the minds of the villagers. By the 17th century Batuan had become a center for high caste Brahman families both of the Siwa (Shivite Hindu) and the far less prevalent Buddhist sects. It was also home of Gusti Ngurah Batulepang and his powerful family of prime ministers to the rajas of south Bali, until a priestly curse scattered his descendants far and wide. The courtly attitudes of those days have been preserved in Batuan in the form of the elegant *gambuh* dance dramas ● 66, which are generally accepted to be the ancestors of all Balinese palace dances. The two groups still performing it, one led by Ketut Kantor and the other by Made Jimat, are in constant demand for temple festivals and palace ceremonies throughout the island.

PURA PUSEH BATUAN ★. Because there is a healthy population here of every religious sect and caste, each requiring its own complete set of temples, Batuan boasts more interesting temples than many far larger villages. Probably the most impressive among these is the Pura Puseh Batuan (the Temple of Origin, literally the "Navel Temple"), a short distance down a secondary road heading west from the crossroads, where the main road takes a sharp right-angle turn to the north. Directly opposite a large meeting hall, the temple is difficult to miss as a pair of six-foot stone *raksasa* (guardian giants), standing either side of the road, guard the approach from both directions. Almost all the sculpture in this temple, whether dating from past centuries or made for the 1992 restoration, combine superb technical craftsmanship with imaginative personality. The newly rebuilt *gedong rum*, a three-tiered rectangular shrine (above) on the east side of the inner courtyard, and the *meru alit*, the shrine next to it, both with traditional murals of the gods beneath their eaves, are fine examples of what is still possible in sacred Balinese architecture. The lively stone faces growing out of a floral

scroll at the base of the *meru alit* are particularly striking (right). The earnest scholar can profit from the small signs which name each of the temple's shrines in both Balinese and modern Indonesian text for the benefit of worshipers who do not wish to misplace their offerings.

A doorway through the west wall, flanked by two reclining rams, leads to an unusual water garden whose massive gate, reminiscent of Javanese Hindu temples, and pond have been freshly restored for the first time since their collapse in the earthquake of 1917. At the center of the pond is Bedawang, the cosmic turtle (right) upon whom the universe rests. In a peaceful corner, an orderly array of broken statues and architectural details, casualties of the earthquake, await their turn to be incorporated in future restorations of the pavilions.

PURA GEDE MECALING. From the crossroads there is another small road heading due south. A few hundred yards down it on the left-hand side, just beyond a village school (Sekolah Dasar VI), was a temple upon which such loving care has not been lavished. It is extremely rare in Bali for a temple to be completely abandoned to the elements, but that has been the fate of Pura Gede Mecaling. It is told that at some hazy point in history the arch-demon Jero Gede Mecaling ● *114*, a grotesque giant whose very name most Balinese are hesitant to speak after dark, lived in a palace in Batuan before being driven across the straits to his present home on the arid island of Nusa Penida. For centuries, nobody has dared to build on the site except for one small temple to remember him by. Now even that has been allowed to crumble and all that

remains, half-strangled by the luxuriant undergrowth, is one dilapidated gate and a small statue of a long-tongued witch (left). The unclean grounds of Jero Gede Mecaling's evil palace are no longer completely unused. Close by the ruined gate, a primary school has now been built where the children of Batuan take their first educational steps into the modern world.

HISTORIC BATUAN
The earliest surviving written mention of Batuan is a stone inscription locked away in Pura Desa Batuan. Recording the separation of Batuan from Sukawati in AD 1022, it is proof of Batuan's long unbroken history. Some scholars suggest that the old name "Baturan" implies that it may have been a ritual megalithic place of worship many millennia earlier.

DANGHYANG NIRARTHA
This Javanese Hindu priest traveled throughout Bali in the 16th century, consolidating and revitalizing the religion which he found to have fallen into an even more anarchical state than it is today. He settled in Mas and married a daughter of the local prince. Royal counselor and high priest to Bali's "King of Kings", the Maharaja of Gelgel, he was able to consolidate the power of the high priests, or *pedanda*, most of whom claim descent from his loins.

GOLDEN NAME
Mysterious purple flowers can sometimes be seen budding from a small tree in the middle courtyard of Pura Taman Pule. Some say that Danghyang Nirartha himself planted the tree in the 16th century, and some time later it sprouted a flower of pure gold, giving the village its present name, "Mas", or "gold".

MAS

About 2 miles beyond Batuan, at a thirty-three-foot stone statue of an exceptionally well-fed baby Buddha (right), the main road takes a sharp turn to the right, while a smaller one continues straight up the hill toward Ubud, passing first through the prosperous village of Mas. While Ubud and Batuan were attaining fame in the 1930's as centers of painting, Mas was firmly staking its claim to become Bali's preeminent center of modern woodcarving. Long before reaching the village itself, the first shops begin to appear, offering anything from crude mass-produced carvings in local soft woods which can be bought for less than a dollar, to the works of recognized masters in fine-grained ebony, jackfruit, or sandalwood that can set one back many thousands of dollars, particularly if accompanied by a guide whose very healthy commission must be passed on to the customer. The skills of Mas did not descend out of the blue but evolved over many generations. Woodcarving (left) was traditionally the exclusive domain of the powerful clan of Brahmana, the high-priest caste which, as in Batuan, is exceptionally well represented in Mas. Until this century, these craftsmen confined their activities to producing ritual objects, musical instruments, dance masks, and sacred statues, but then a few of the younger members discovered that producing carvings for export could be a profitable business. Several of the Brahmana artists still find time between fulfilling export orders to carve sacred art objects for the temples.

PURA TAMAN PULE. Most Brahmana in Bali trace their ancestry to the wandering Hindu sage, Danghyang Nirartha (also called Danghyang Dwijendra and Pedanda Sakti Wau Rauh). To the right of the main road, behind a playing field in the center of Mas, on the site of Danghyang Nirartha's original home, stands the village's most important temple, Pura Taman Pule (left), in whose shrines some of his personal relics are said to be hidden. The five-day temple festival held every six months around Kuningan, a high-point in the ritual calendar ● *82*, is one of the most glittering events in the

Fine woodcarvings have long been associated with the prosperous village of Mas.

Balinese year, with commoners as well as high-caste descendants of the sage bringing offerings from every corner of the island. The delicate leaf-shaped inner gate is reminiscent of a *kayonan*, the shadow puppet representing the tree of life or sacred mountain, universal nature, and

the gateway to the world beyond ● *59*. Carved into its wings is the disembodied head of the demon Kala Rau who, in an unusual reversal of fortune, lost his body in an argument with the god Wisnu and obsessively pursues his revenge by trying to gobble both the sun and the moon. At the extreme northeast corner of the inner courtyard, closer to the great mountain than even the tall *padmasana* shrine, is a small well, supplying holy water. It is carved with imaginatively dramatic *nagas*, the mythological serpent-dragons who live in the dark waters of the underworld, and in front of it is a simple stone *lingam* shrouded in cloth. A touch of sly humor is provided by the distinctly clownish ladies (above) who serve as legs for two of the main offering altars. Uniformed schoolgirls flutter into the temple every day to place fresh hibiscus flowers behind the ears of all the statues.

ON TO UBUD

Turning left at a T-junction shortly beyond Mas brings one into Peliatan and then to the "painters' village" of Ubud. With its relatively cool climate, many small but comfortable hotels, and excellent restaurants, Ubud makes a sensible base from which to explore the backroads of inner Bali ▲ *162*. One can return to the south coast by the same route to call in at those shops missed on the way up, or continue through town, crossing the bridge at Campuhan. In the gorge below, on a rocky outcrop at the confluence of the Wos and a lesser tributary perches Pura Gunung Lebah ▲ *158*.

EVIL AT ECLIPSE
Even today in some remote villages the Balinese beat all their gongs and drums during an eclipse, fearful that celestial beings might not slip out safely through the demon Kala Rau's severed throat. They say that on the night following a lunar eclipse, the moon is unusually bright because of the bath she has been obliged to take after passing through the demon's unsavory gullet ▲ *169*.

Doorways to homes of Brahmana.

157

▲ PURA GUNUNG LEBAH

Pura Gunung Lebah, which is also referred to as the Campuhan Temple, is one of the most dramatically situated of the many interesting and unusual temples near Ubud. Located in the deep gorge west of Ubud, it perches on the rocks where two branches of the Wos River meet. The confluence of rivers, or *campuhan,* is believed to concentrate powerful earth energies as well as unusual psychic dangers. At night only witches would venture here to cast spells, or seekers of wisdom to meditate. In the daytime, however, colorful processions from far-flung villages can be seen crossing the arched stone bridge to collect holy water for use in temple festivals.

The temple was probably founded in the 8th century by Rsi Markandya ▲ *186* or his Buddhist followers and was considerably expanded in the 16th century by the great Hindu priest Danghyang Nirartha ▲ *156.* The cliffs of the gorge are honeycombed with sacred springs, hermits' meditation niches, and caves, one of which is said to have been the abode of a notorious *raksasa,* a demonic giant, who enjoyed snatching virgins when they came to pray at the temple.

BALI'S BEL-AIR
At some of the finest vantage points on Sayan Ridge, the passing visitor is no longer made welcome, as the ridge has become Bali's Bel-Air. Numerous

foreigners and wealthy weekenders from Jakarta have built luxury villas on the edge, and small but exclusive hotels have also been established, notable among them the Amandari (above) which was recently rated one of the world's ten best.

MASK BY LEMPAD
Pura Dalem Tengaling Pejeng in Singapadu is the sanctuary of one of Bali's most famous *barong* masks (below). Carved late last century by the illustrious Gusti Nyoman Lempad, it was brought here as booty in the 19th-century wars of the rajas, but returns twice a year to be reunited with its twin in Pejeng.

SAYAN RIDGE

Beyond the bridge at Campuhan the road climbs steeply north, passing the Neka Museum ▲ *166*, then turns sharply west and reaches a T-junction in Kedewatan, about 2 miles from Ubud. A right turn

here leads all the way up through Payangan to the Batur crater ▲ *182*, while the left goes through the village of Sayan to Batubulan and the coast. Between Kedewatan and Sayan, the road follows the contours of the Sayan Ridge, skirting close to, but usually just beyond sight of, one of Bali's most dramatic gorges (above), carved by the churning coils of the Ayung River. Travel companies offer half-day white water rafting adventures down it ◆ *308*.

SILAKARANG

South of Sayan, the Ayung River bears away from the road to be replaced on the other side by the gorge of the Wos River. Excellent volcanic tuff, called *paras,* is quarried from its walls and some of it ends up as fine sculpture in the numerous temples along the roadside. Not far beyond Kengetan, one reaches the Pura Puseh Silakarang (right), one of the most delightful of these temples. All the carving in this temple, whether old or recent, is to a very high standard.

SINGAPADU

The last village before rejoining the main road at Batubulan, Singapadu has a long history of involvement in the arts and close links with the palace of Sukawati, with which it was always allied. The late prince Cokorda Oka was famous for the inner power of the sacred masks he carved, and his creative contribution is evident in the large Pura Puseh Singapadu, which stands at the corner where a sideroad heads east into the heart of the village and beyond to Celuk and Batuan. Some people credit the artistic abundance of Singapadu to the royal family's ownership of the sacred kris, Sekar Sandat, which is said to possess supernatural energy. Dancers and musicians from here were once legendary throughout the island, and they still perform *legong* and *barong* dances in the Pura Dalem Tengaling Pejeng.

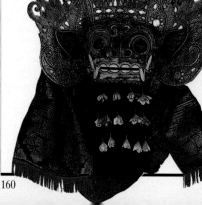

GREATER UBUD

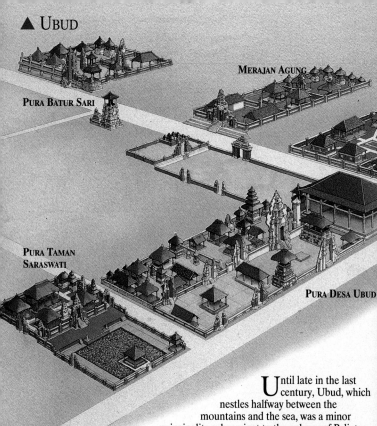

MERAJAN AGUNG

PURA BATUR SARI

PURA TAMAN SARASWATI

PURA DESA UBUD

U ntil late in the last century, Ubud, which nestles halfway between the mountains and the sea, was a minor principality subservient to the palaces of Peliatan and Gianyar, but some well-chosen alliances during the 19th-century wars of the rajas ● *37* dramatically expanded the power, lands, and influence of the prince, or *cokorda.* His prospering little kingdom attracted refugee artists, sculptors,

and architects who had fallen foul of the rulers in other kingdoms, and his descendants' hospitality toward Western artists and scholars such as Miguel and Rose Covarrubias, Margaret Mead, Walter Spies ● *112*, and Rudolph Bonnet ▲ *166* helped secure Ubud's position as the heartland of the Balinese art scene. Under their impetus and that of the then prince, Cokorda Agung Gede Sukawati, the local painters founded an association called Pita Maha to maintain high artistic standards in the face of the first whiffs of commercialism. Although Pita Maha encouraged island-wide membership, Ubud remained its nucleus. The Ubud of today, with its plethora of small hotels, fine restaurants, eager hawkers, and fancy boutiques, is no longer the sleepy artists' refuge that it was even a decade ago. But a few steps back

DANCE PERFORMANCES
Every night in Ubud, in some palace, temple, or community hall, there are regularly scheduled performances of traditional music and dance. In some ways tourism has even enhanced the performing arts, allowing groups to purchase costumes and instruments they could never have afforded in the past.

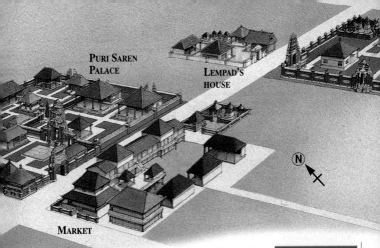

PURI SAREN PALACE

LEMPAD'S HOUSE

MARKET

Four hours

from the main streets one can still immerse oneself in the timeless flow of Balinese life; and venturing farther on foot in almost any direction, through wild tropical gorges and dramatic rice terraces, one stumbles upon hamlets where the gods, spirits, and celestial bodies still reign supreme.

PURI SAREN PALACE. One of the most respected dance groups in Bali performs several nights a week in the outer courtyard of the principal palace (center), at the northeast corner of the central crossroads. Their backdrop is a grand gate, *kori agung*, built by Ubud's most famous artist, I Gusti Nyoman Lempad. It separates the outer courtyard from the inner sanctums of the palace where the current ruling *cokorda* lives. The Puri Saren was demolished by the great earthquake of 1917, so the maze of courtyards, pavilions, and elaborate gates extending far behind the *kori agung* were mostly built soon thereafter.

MERAJAN AGUNG. The towering gate above a steep flight of steps immediately north of the main palace is one of the finest of its kind, with a striking pyramid of *boma* faces rising above its door. This is the main entrance to the Merajan Agung, the private palace temple of the royal family within which are housed the palace's most revered heirlooms.

PURA BATUR SARI. About 300 feet farther north, past the palaces of the *cokorda*'s close relatives, stands the small but elaborate Pura Batur Sari, which is also a royal temple but of a more unusual sort. Easily recognizable by the small army of statues of demon guardians and clowns which line the roadside in front, and the fierce lions (below) guarding the *kul-kul* tower, it is a *penyawang* temple, recalling days when travel on the island was more difficult than it is today. Specific gods from remote temples can be invited to visit such temples, in this case the goddess of Lake Batur, so that she can be worshiped without having to make a long and hazardous journey to her mountain home. For three full days, during Batur Sari's annual festival, a dance stage is set up in the middle of the street, closing off the road north toward many mountain villages. This is a refreshing example of the Balinese keeping their priorities straight by regarding the entertainment of the gods as more important than the convenience of impatient travelers.

RANGDA
In the inner courtyard of Pura Batur Sari, a shrine with very fine doors carved with golden images of Rangda, the legendary queen of the witches, houses the sacred masks of Rangda and one of Ubud's most powerful *barong* masks ▲ 148.

163

NIGHT MARKET

NIGHT MARKET
A large parking lot immediately east of the day market is transformed at sunset into a brightly lit

arena of food stalls offering dishes from Java and Madura as well as Balinese and Chinese cuisine. This night market is one of the cheapest places in Ubud to dine, and it is hoped renovation plans will not close it for long. It provides a splendid opportunity to rub shoulders (literally) with interesting characters from every corner of Indonesia and, indeed, the world.

LEMPAD'S DEATH
The Balinese love to tell the well authenticated circumstances of artist Lempad's death. After waiting many months for the most appropriate day in the Balinese year, Lempad called his numerous scattered descendants together and asked them to bathe him and dress him in white, the

color of purity. He told them that their inheritance was the duty to complete those tasks he had left unfulfilled during his short lifetime, bade them farewell, and then died.

UBUD MARKET. From the southeast corner of the main palace crossroads sprawls Ubud's ever-growing market. Although active every day of the year, each third day (*Paseh* in the Balinese calendar) it is almost overwhelmingly frenetic. The building right at the crossroads is devoted to souvenirs, crafts, and textiles, although these also overflow into the recently built two-story block running east along the main street. In a temple just east of the main buildings, the stall-holders make daily offerings to a well-fed Ganesha, the elephant god, who is believed to be supportive of traders.

THE LEMPAD HOUSE. Continuing east from the market, on the north side of the main street, is the family compound which, for almost a century, was home to Bali's most venerated artist of this century. I Gusti Nyoman Lempad ▲ *167* arrived as a young refugee from Bedulu late in the 1870's and died here in 1978 at the remarkable age of 116.

PURA TAMAN SARASWATI ★. West of the palace crossroads, on the north side of the main street beyond the austerely monumental grey gates of Ubud's Pura Desa (right), is a large pond, almost a lake, overflowing with lotus blossoms (below). A small pavilion overhangs this pond, whose waters flow from a gracious temple behind. A small door set into the western corner of the temple wall grants access to the inner courtyard of the Pura Taman Saraswati. This water temple honoring Dewi Saraswati ● *46*, goddess of wisdom, learning, and the arts, was commissioned in the 1950's by the *cokorda* of Ubud to celebrate his release from political imprisonment. Craftsmen came from far and wide to work under the direction of Gusti Lempad, who personally sculpted the striking ten-foot statue of the demonic spirit Jero Gede Mecaling, lord of epidemics and pestilence. In the northeast corner is an impeccable *padmasana*, a delicate pyramid rising from the back of the cosmic turtle through the many

layers of the universe to the seat of the high god.

MUSEUM PURI LUKISAN. Continuing west from the lotus pond one reaches the entrance to a bridge across a deep, shaded gully and up again into a landscaped garden of ponds, statues, and fountains. This is a calm retreat from the heat and clamor of downtown Ubud at mid-day, and its three buildings house the island's finest collection of Balinese art, ranging from the turn of the century to contemporary ▲ 168.

Stonecarving at Museum Puri Lukisan ▲ 168.

CAMPUHAN

The main street of Ubud runs west for about a half mile past numerous shops and restaurants before dipping down a steep hill toward a bridge across the deep cleft of the Wos River at Campuhan. Alongside the new bridge hangs its venerable predecessor, built in the days of Dutch rule and now only strong enough to support pedestrians. In the gorge below perches Pura Gunung Lebah ▲ 158. For those who enjoy long walks far from the main roads, the path behind the school on the Ubud side of the new bridge leads far up along the crest of the elephant grass ridge toward Keliki and the road to Taro. Passing through several isolated hamlets and with several side paths down to bathing pools in the river, it offers a cornucopia of wildlife and grand views of Mount Agung and the sea.

EAST MEETS WEST. Since the 1930's, Campuhan has been a meeting point of East and West, with all the associated dangers and stimulating energies entailed. Many of Bali's best known expatriate artists built their homes and studios here, Walter Spies ● 112, Rudolph Bonnet, and Arie Smit ● 114 among them. And just beyond the bridge, a grand drive sweeps uphill to an eccentric house and studio (right), open to the public, where the Spanish artist Antonio Blanco still lives.

NEKA MUSEUM ★. About half a mile on up the road from Campuhan, hanging on the edge of a ravine over the Wos, is the Neka Museum, with its exceptional collection of work by foreign and Balinese artists ▲ 166.

ANTONIO BLANCO
An unabashed admirer of his own work, who describes himself as "Bali's Dali", Antonio Blanco settled in Campuhan in the early 1950's after abandoning his career as a stage magician to pursue his love of art and gracious living. His timber and thatched house and its gardens contain some fine traditional

Balinese sculptures collected during his forty-year residency. The centerpiece of his studio is a large unfinished nude on an easel (above) and a carefully scattered array of paint tubes and brushes with a dance mask tossed casually among them, in exactly the same position as it has been for three years. None can deny that he is a true artist of life and has established himself as a rare phenomenon, without which Ubud would be a poorer place.

Indonesia's largest privately owned art museum was officially opened in 1982 by art dealer Suteja Neka, who had been accumulating a private collection of works by his favorite Balinese painters since the 1960's. The collection comprises a century of Balinese art, ranging from the traditional *Meeting of the Gods* (detail top right) by an anonymous 19th-century artist, to modern oils such as *Distractions* (detail above), painted in 1988 by Wayan Atjin Tisna (1942–). Western artists who have worked in Bali over the last seventy years are also well represented, as well as Indonesian painters from other islands.

GARUDA AND THE BATTLING BEASTS This work is an example of the balancing act between traditional and modern styles that has long been exercised by I Gusti Ketut Kobot (1917–) of Pengosekan. The painting (above) depicts how the mythological Garuda bird, on his way to heaven to steal the elixir of life from the gods, attacks and eats the greedy brothers, Wibhawasu and Supratika, who in their endless fight over their inheritance have cast spells to turn each other into an elephant and a turtle.

RUDOLPH BONNET *Arjuna's Wedding* (above) by Dutch artist Rudolph Bonnet (1895–1978) is one of Neka's many paintings by foreign artists who, over the decades, have been seduced by the island's charms. Arriving in Bali in 1929, Bonnet spent most of the rest of his life in Ubud and was one of the two most influential Westerners on the Balinese art scene. Unlike his friend, Walter Spies ● *112*, Bonnet did not hesitate to give formal classes in western academic style and anatomy drawing, so his strong influence is still to be seen in the work of local artists, particularly those from Padang Tegal and Taman.

TWO WOMEN IN THE GARDEN

This painting (left) is typical of the lush and sensuous canvases that Dewa Putu Bedil (1921–) began producing in the 1970's. An attentive student of Rudolph Bonnet in the 1930's, he became a fine exponent of the "half-dressed figure in a landscape" school. Over the years, as he became freer with his colors and his symbolic jests, the landscapes became more erotic than the figures. If all his naked women look remarkably similar, he explains, it is because they are all portraits of his wife as a young girl.

BATTLE OF LANGKAPURA

At right is one of the many works in the Neka collection by the great master, Gusti Nyoman Lempad (1862–1978); indeed, a whole hall is devoted to his drawings and paintings. This drawing in ink on paper depicts a battle in the *Ramayana* epic between Rama's allies, the monkeys, and the demonic army of Rawana, abductor of the lovely Sita. Drawn during the 1960's, at a time of violent political upheaval, Lempad's wicked sense of humor comes through, while he conveys the dangerously chaotic mood of the period.

RAJAPALA STEALS SULASIH'S CLOTHES

This is a popular theme in Balinese art because the descent of the celestial nymphs to bathe in an earthly pool offers great erotic potential. The detail at left is from a large canvas by Ida Bagus Rai (1933–) in which the peeking Rajapala steals the sarong, effectively the wings, of Sulasih so she cannot fly back to the heavens until she has given him a child. Electric in its execution, it is rich in symbolism and subtly hints at aspects of the story that cannot be shown in a single canvas.

MUSEUM PURI LUKISAN

Museum Puri Lukisan ("Palace of Paintings") houses what may be the world's finest permanent display of works from Bali's pre-war artistic flowering. Opened in 1956 as a showcase for the best of modern Balinese art, it was the dreamchild of Prince Agung Sukawati of Ubud, Dutch artist Rudolph Bonnet, and survivors of the Pita Maha artists' association of the 1930's ▲ *162*. All the works have been donated by the artists and their descendants or are bequests from early European buyers who wanted their paintings returned to Bali after their deaths.

Four

FOUR AGES OF THE WORLD
Dewa Nyoman Batuan (1939–), leading painter of the 1970's, is famous for his rich cosmological and tantric mandalas which radiate out from the highest gods through the many layers of the Balinese universe. He was the driving force behind the Community of Farmers and Artists of Pengosekan village, Bali's first and most genuine "community of artists".

SLENDER WOMAN
Carved in 1955 by Anak Agung Gede Raka of Peliatan (1910–81), this piece (left) shows the exaggerated elongation typical of one school of modern Balinese sculpture.

A DEER ABOUT TO LEAP
Carved from amber jackfruit wood in 1956 by I Leceng (1919–), this work possesses all the tactile sensuality that is a trademark of sculptures from his village of Nyuhkuning. The fact that the artist is familiar with cows but has never seen a live deer only adds to the work's charm.

THE ARROGANT MONKEY
The work above presents a detail of a popular yarn from the *Tantri* cycle. Painted in 1932 by Anak Agung Gede Sobrat (1917–92), it is one of the earliest known works by this artist whose influence stretched from prewar days through the 1980's.

LUNAR ECLIPSE
According to myth, a lunar eclipse occurs when the disembodied head of the demon Kala Rau (left) swallows the moon goddess, only to have her escape through his severed throat ▲ *157*. This painting is by Ketut Budiana (1950–), whose paintings draw on Balinese archetypes to delve into the darker corners of his own personal subconscious.

MEN FISHING
Sanur is the subject of this painting by Ketut Regig (1919–), donated to the museum in 1956. Its style falls between the busyness of inland artists and the more open treatment found in paintings from Sanur, the artist's chosen home.

A TRANSITIONAL MASTER
Ida Bagus Kembang (1897–1952) was one of a handful of adventurous artists who, during the late 1920's and early 1930's, first began to liberate themselves from Bali's rigid conventions. In this early painting of the priest Basubaya giving religious instruction to forest beasts (right), the figures have the traditional profile similar to the *wayang* puppets but they are softer and less formal, a dramatic new approach to composition.

Agung Rai, a young prince from Peliatan and successful art dealer who started his career selling his family's and friends' paintings on the beach in Kuta, has accumulated a remarkable private collection of works by Balinese, Javanese, and foreign artists, including the only original Walter Spies paintings in Bali. For years the collection had been on display in a back corner of his art shop in Peliatan, but in 1994 he moved the collection to its permanent home in an imposing new group of buildings a few hundred yards west of the southern end of Peliatan, on the road to Pengosekan.

A MAGICAL TALISMAN OF SEDUCTION

was the inspiration for this work in tempera and ink on paper by Ida Bagus Made (1915 –), one of the stars of the 1930's who is still going strong. He is best known for the sophisticated religious content of his paintings, which stems from his priestly background. Painted in 1974 and entitled *Tumbal* (left), this work shows the male and female principles emanating in the form of *naga* dragons from Semara, the god of love, as he performs the dance of desire. Simpler versions of this *tumbal* are still used by suitors to bewitch the reluctant targets of their affections.

DANCE OF THE WITCHES

Painted by Ketut Budiana (1950 –) of Padang Tegal, the work below displays a more sinister dance performed in the graveyard by *leyaks*, witches who can transform themselves into animals and objects to go out and bedevil their enemies during the dark phase of the moon. One of Bali's most acclaimed living artists, Budiana is also a respected *sangging*, a creator of sacred art both for the temple and for cremation rituals.

The Undersea World

The rich imagination of Anak Agung Gede Raka Turas (1917 –), who has never been under water, conjured this aquatic scene (details above and below). Although many of his marine denizens are familiar and realistic, their reef conveys the mood of the forest groves near the old artist's home in Padang Tegal, just south of Ubud.

Garuda Challenges the Gods

The detail above is from an anonymous 19th-century ceremonial painting. It depicts the flight of the mythical bird, Garuda, to the heavens to steal the elixir of life from the high gods in order to release himself and his mother from slavery. In the process he ironically agrees to become the beast of burden for Wisnu, the god of life.

Greeting Dance

The *pendet*, or traditional greeting dance, is performed by little girls to welcome both worldly visitors and the gods when they descend to the village temple at the time of its annual festival. The delightful rendition below by Nyoman Meja (1952–) of Ubud displays his special approach to daily and ritual life in Bali.

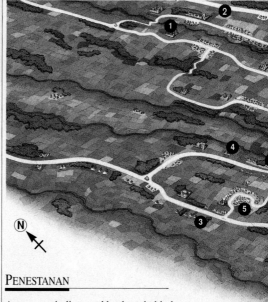

🚗 One day

TOURISTS BEWARE
The Monkey Forest would be a most peaceful sanctuary had the resident monkeys not become so fearless of strangers in recent years. Some say these monkeys are vehicles for the capricious spirits of the yet unsettled dead, and wise visitors leave it to others to bring gifts of peanuts and bananas, for this mischievous troop are the first Balinese to have been corrupted by tourism. Although they rarely bite, their opening ploy is often a head-on, fang-gnashing assault which causes all but the most stubborn visitor to drop the goodies and retreat in disorder, saving the monkey a lot of inefficient time wasted in pickpocketing, arm wrestling, or, as the last undignified resort, being reduced to the use of charm.

PENESTANAN

A narrow winding road leads up behind Blanco's house in Campuhan and across the fields to the village of Penestanan, where a new style of painting called the "Young Artists" style exploded onto the Bali art scene in the late 1950's. It was the result of an experiment by Dutch-born but Indonesian-naturalized artist Arie Smit ● *115*, who gave the village children canvases, brushes, and primary acrylic colors. The result was a rainbow of images of daily life which broke all the traditional color rules of Balinese art, with the sky perhaps being violent red above rice paddies of eye-straining orange. The hair of many of the original "young artists" is now grey, but they and their grandchildren continue to explore their hallucinogenic world of vibrant dreams. On foot, one can return to Ubud from the north end of Penestanan, following a path through an overgrown ravine and open rice fields, arriving at the top of a steep flight of steps which descends to the main road a few hundred yards beyond the Campuhan bridge. Drivers can take a longer route, heading west out of Penestanan to the road through Sayan ▲ *160*, turning right and right again to loop back down, past the well-signposted Neka Museum to Campuhan and central Ubud. The more adventurous might like to strike out on foot south from Penestanan through the rice paddies, eventually crossing the Wos lower downstream by a rickety bamboo bridge and coming out at or close to the Monkey Forest.

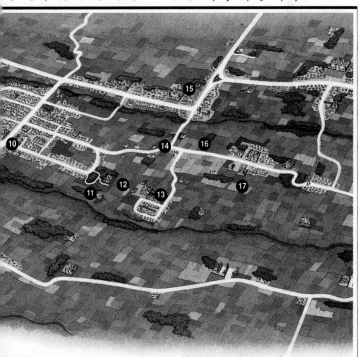

MONKEY FOREST

Scattered throughout Bali are numerous temple groves and woods which have been set aside as sanctuaries for monkeys, to thank them for the assistance they gave Rama in the rescue of his bride Sita from the clutches of King Rawana, in the *Ramayana* epic. The most extensive of these, at Sangeh near Mengwi ▲ *262,* is the only one that can truly be called a forest, but a half-mile walk due south from the central crossroads of Ubud along Monkey Forest Road, Bali's most famous shopping and eating street, brings one to a small grove of ancient trees and winding paths around a death temple and graveyard which is sanctuary to a fearless troop of long-tailed macaques (above). Passing the entrance gate, one soon reaches a triangular area shaded by a large banyan tree where the path splits in two. The left fork curves around a hillock, at the top of which the people of Banjar Padang Tegal bury and cremate their dead, while the fork bearing slightly right leads to the death temple, the Pura Dalem Padang Tegal, at the southern edge of the grove. Just before the fork, steep steps descend to the right into a far larger banyan tree which straddles a deep cleft. A bridge of great stone slabs, miraculously suspended from the tree's aerial roots, spans the cleft 30 feet above the rushing water. Beyond is a small water temple and more steps, carved from the rock, lead down to a bathing place beside the stream.

MONKEY BUSINESS
Few places have faced a more dramatic transformation than Monkey Forest Road. Only a decade or so ago it was a rural lane through rice paddies and boasted not a single building all the way to the Monkey Forest. Today it is hard to glimpse a field through the barrier of restaurants, hotels, shops, money-changers, and travel agents. Old-timers, as is their wont, moan about the changes, but the anarchical nature of its evolution gives it a unique charm.

FROG SPECIALISTS
Carvers in Nyuhkuning have come to be regarded as Bali's "frog specialists", turning out many thousands of them each month for the export market. Because of the wealth these have brought them they agreed that every household should place a statue of a frog at the entrance to their compounds. An eccentric honor guard of dancing frogs, warrior frogs, and business-suited frogs lines the walk down the village's two long parallel lanes.

A SACRED PYTHON
The villagers of Pengosekan tell numerous stories about the seldom-seen python which resides in their Pura Dalem. In 1992, when the temple's *barong* ▲ *148* was danced for the first time in many years, the snake made a rare appearance and sat on the high gate to watch the show. During another temple ceremony, when the priest had forgotten to place special offerings on the ground for the spirits of the underworld, the python slithered through the praying crowd and up into a pavilion to eat the overlooked offerings.

NYUHKUNING

Continuing on foot a half mile south from the death temple of the Monkey Forest, one reaches the wood-carving village of Nyuhkuning. As the elders of Padang Tegal have steadfastly refused to permit a road through their monkey sanctuary, this route is only possible by foot. A vehicle must take a longer, circular route via Pengosekan to Nyuhkuning. There are no painters in Nyuhkuning, but the villagers have developed a distinctive style of woodcarving founded by such masters as I Leceng and Mangku Tama, who participated in the artistic flowering of the 1930's. They sculpt softly rounded humans and animals, familiar inhabitants of daily village life, and prefer to work with the fine-grained, yellowish wood of the jackfruit tree.

THE NYUHKUNING MUSEUM ★. At the north end of the village the villagers have built a modest unofficial museum to which all the more important carvers and their descendants have donated wood sculptures. This is an excellent starting point for anyone looking for the homes of the most creative carvers.

Those with a strong head for heights can cross the "circus bridge" (left), an iron girder spanning the Wos at the southwest corner of the village, and head north to Penestanan and Campuhan. A less hazardous route towards Ubud is a paved road east from the south end of Nyuhkuning and then north at a T-junction in the famous artists' village of Pengosekan.

PENGOSEKAN

In 1969, the villagers of Pengosekan established the "Pengosekan Community of Farmers and Artists", Bali's first, and much imitated, village-level artistic co-operative. This experiment, based on ancient traditions, in sharing knowledge, techniques, materials, and outlets for their paintings, forged a prominent place in the Balinese art scene for little Pengosekan and its idiosyncratic painters.

No important collection of Balinese art is considered complete without the inclusion of works by such luminaries as Gusti Ketut Kobot, Dewa Putu Mokoh and his brother, Dewa Nyoman Batuan, and Dewa Putu Sena (in photo, left to right). Dewa Nyoman Batuan's imaginative ambition was the driving force behind the original co-operative as well as many other artistic experiments. On a more commercial level, it was in his workshops that Bali's first floral wooden mirror frames (left) were created, a departure which led to a vast array of products. A right turn (south) at the T-junction leads past the homes and studios of many of Pengosekan's artists to the

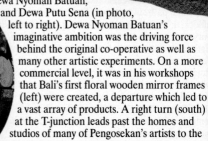

heart of the village. Tucked away to the west is the architecturally and sculpturally intriguing Pura Dalem ★ (above) . Returning north past the T-junction toward Ubud, one almost immediately reaches a turn to the east (right) which leads down a hill, past the Agung Rai Museum ▲ *170* and the studios of Dewa Nyoman Batuan, before reaching the main Denpasar road at the southern end of Peliatan, a village best known for its remarkable dancers and musicians.

PELIATAN

The royal families of Peliatan boast longer pedigrees than the more recently established ones in neighboring Ubud, with whom they are now closely linked by marriage. All the arts, too, have a long tradition here, but most notably the performing arts. It was the musicians and dancers of Peliatan, with their now famous Gong Gunung Sari *gamelan* orchestra, who stunned European audiences at the Paris Colonial Exhibition of 1931. **PURA DESA GEDE PELIATAN ★.** This complex of adjoining temples is on the right, a short way up the main street of Peliatan. Some of its very fine sculpture can be enjoyed without even going beyond the guardian statues of the *punakawan* clowns. The more elaborate of two *kori agung* gates, adorned with nymphs, monkeys, and monsters, belongs to the Pura Puseh, while the simpler, more recent gate leads to the Pura Desa (above). To the left, next to a classical *kulkul* tower, a modest iron gate (usually left unlocked) grants access to the Pura Agung with its long and recently rebuilt *bale agung* pavilion. Built of the finest timbers and decorated with many pounds of gold leaf, it houses an excellent traditional painting of deities riding on the back of the white *naga*, Basuki. The tall *gedong* shrine, housing the community's most precious religious relics, marks the border with the Pura Puseh. Just beyond it, in the two *arca* shrines, are some very old stones and statues, and the back of the *kori agung* displays some newer sculpture, humanistic in style.

PELIATAN PERFORMERS
In 1937 Peliatan's Gong Gunung Sari *gamelan* orchestra won an island-wide *gamelan* competition, a memorable victory because the main prize was a year's exemption from the dreaded *kerdja rodi*, a corvée slave labor service building roads for the Dutch. Since then the orchestra has toured on every continent except Antarctica. Today there are at least fifteen performing troupes in Peliatan, including one all-female orchestra, Mekar Sari. One of Bali's most adventurous and respected performing groups, the Seka Gunung Jati troupe of Banjar Teges Kanginan, performs on an open-air dance stage in the southeast corner of Peliatan. By special request they will perform their dramatically unusual *kecak*, as well as an excellent *legong*.

SAFE SANCTUARY
In the early 1960's, with communism and anti-traditionalism on the increase throughout Indonesia, the magical powers of Bali's temples, and fear of karmic punishment, were no longer sufficient to protect their sacred relics from politically inspired desecration and theft, so high, protective towers were installed in temples throughout the island. The *gedong* (left), taller than the tallest *meru* in the Pura Desa Gede Peliatan, was recently built to guard against a new wave of more materialistic sacrilege.

At the north end of Peliatan, the main road to Ubud turns off to the left, but there is a longer and more rural route which leads back to the central crossroads of Ubud via quiet country quaint temples and Petulu, the village of herons.

PETULU

A mile north of the turnoff to Ubud, a road leads left into the little village of Petulu. In the late afternoon, the trees of Petulu come alive with a squabbling mass of white herons and egrets, while stragglers glide in from all directions, the bold white strokes of their V-formations etched across the evening sky, for Petulu is the nesting place of almost all the herons and egrets of southern Bali. The presence of so many of these graceful birds in one place is, in itself, a remarkable phenomenon but the story of their arrival (left), less than forty years ago, is one of those typically Balinese events that, however well documented, most Westerners find hard to believe. From the Pura Desa, which is at the northern end of the village and one of the best spots from which to view the birds, a bumpy back road winds back toward central Ubud via the village of Junjungan.

JUNJUNGAN

Despite its proximity to busy Ubud, Junjungan is a welcoming backwater and the home of many skilled woodcarvers, whose homes are always open to those who have time to pause. Immediately upon arrival from the Petulu direction, one passes the well-worn Pura Desa, which sits in a grove guarded by two towering pule trees (*Alstonia scholaris*). Passing through the outer split gate which is adorned with four medallion masks of guardian spirits (left), one approaches a *kori agung* gate that, although not particularly old, seems to draw its power from the age of megaliths. The *boma* above the door and the naga bannisters leading up to it are so stylized as to be almost unrecognizable, and the gate is flanked by two large stone cylinders, altars for offerings. At the foot of the severe steps are delightful statues of Twalen ● *61*, the divine clown and teacher of heroes. An unusual but not unique feature of this temple is that the wall in which the *kori agung* is set ends abruptly a few feet to the left of the gate, allowing direct access from the outer courtyard to the inner sanctum, an example of how gates and walls in Bali are purely symbolic. A right turn at the center of the village leads through open rice fields and past the charming temples of Bentuyung and Sakti to come out eventually at the palace crossroads in the center of Ubud.

BACKROADS TO BATUR

▲ BACKROADS TO BATUR

VILLAGE SPECIALTIES
Every little retail stop along the road toward Pujung seems to offer the same wares, but there are local variations from village to village. Gentong, the first village past the Petulu turnoff, specializes in

small, amusing woodcarvings such as chains of monkeys. Tegallalang is known for its flowers and fruit trees, while Ceking, with its world-famous view of steep rice terraces, has some of the best carvers of Garuda, the mythical bird who carries the god Wisnu on his back. Some of these Garuda are of a monumental scale.

The shrines (below) in the house temples become progressively more colorful as one drives up the mountain.

"Batur" is the generic name for a profoundly sacred part of Bali. It encompasses the volcanic Mount Batur at the center; Lake Batur, Bali's largest lake, alongside; and a lava-scarred terrain sprinkled with a constellation of temples, the gods who animate them, and the villagers who serve them. The usual way from Ubud to the Batur caldera is via Tampaksiring to the east, but there are other less-traveled options: rugged secondary roads which demand a motorbike, a tough little jeep, or, for the very fit, a mountain bicycle.

TEGALLALANG

Heading due north from the T-junction east of Ubud, the road toward Tegallalang soon quits the realm of restaurants and lodgings and enters the region of wood-carvers. Like other Balinese handicrafts, this is a wholesale cottage industry, with craftsmen producing to order. Often the designs are those of foreign entrepreneurs, but there are some artists to be found among the artisans.

PUJUNG

The land rises sharply after Ceking into fresher country, some of it not yet obscured by art shops, to Pujung, where serious exporters may be seen loading container transport with carved doors, hobbyhorses, and large carved animals that have evolved from a fantastical gene pool. At heart rustic, Pujung is a market village with a number of shops which sell more practical items than wood carvings. Household goods on offer include such essentials as faux-gilt foil and colorfully beaded lids for offerings. From a T-junction at the center of Pujung, a sadistically surfaced road continues north to Batur or you can turn east (right) toward Tampaksiring, through which runs the main road to Batur. At a crossroads about half a mile along this route, there is a left turn to Pura Gunung Kawi and the village of Sebatu.

PURA GUNUNG KAWI ★

The water temple of Pura Gunung Kawi (not to be confused with the royal tombs of the same name in Tampaksiring ▲ 196) is only a few hundred yards along this sideroad. Although tourist buses are often parked there, that's no

JASAN
14 TARO
15 PURA PAMWOS, APUH
16 SEKAHAN
17 BAYUNG GEDE
18 PURA PENULISAN
19 KINTAMANI
20 PURA ULUN DANU BATUR
21 PENELOKAN
22 MOUNT BATUR
23 KEDISAN
24 PURA JATI
25 TOYABUNGKAH
26 SONGAN
27 PURA ULUN DANU
28 TRUNYAN
29 MOUNT ABANG

(N) ↑
🚗 One day

TO TAMPAKSIRING

reason to avoid this otherwise delightful complex. A natural spring flows from the heart of the temple (right) into a pool so clear that you can count the scales on the huge goldfish ghosting around the opulent island shrine at its center. Holy water is requested at an adjacent small shrine while nearby, and still within the temple walls, are the open-air public baths. Visitors are welcome to explore the other courtyards where the shrines and pavilions are lovingly maintained by the people of nearby Sebatu.

RAWANA AND HANUMAN

There are carvings everywhere at Pura Gunung Kawi, many of them old, but there are two new ones in the left-hand pavilion of the inner courtyard that are particularly striking. One is of Rawana, demonic king of Lanka in the *Ramayana* epic, and the other is of Hanuman, the white warrior monkey who challenges him.

179

SEBATU DANCERS
Sebatu's exceptional dance troupe travels internationally every year. It has revived several traditional dances that had been all but forgotten on the island. One of the more unusual of these is the *telek* (above), a refined version of the classical masked dance *jauk*.

TELAGA WAJA
Not recommended for the nervous, the footpath to Telaga Waja (above) leads down toward the river ravine until it reaches a set of very steep concrete steps which descends to the peaceful complex of Telaga Waja. Still sacred and an important source of water for Ubud, Telaga Waja has been partially restored in an unobtrusive way and you can see the old meditation niches hewn from the cliff behind the two pools.

SEBATU

Just behind Pura Gunung Kawi is the booming woodcarving village of Sebatu, also famous among the Balinese for the superiority of its *gamelan* orchestras.

Sebatu's snug layout makes it a pleasure to explore by foot; along its two main parallel lanes, nouveau riche domestic architecture is sandwiched between crumbling old mud walls and traditional kitchen huts. From the village entrance, a road to the left leads one to a broad space where it is easy to park near the Pura Desa and the village meeting hall. The temples can be visited with permission from any local official. The Pura Desa is, in fact, two large temples, densely populated with painted sculpture. The surrounding Pura Panti are clan temples. At the northern end of the village, overlooking the other temples, is the simple Pura Jaba Kuta, signifying the "head" of the village. From these temples, a little road leads northwest out of Sebatu and soon rejoins the backroad to Batur at the north end of Pujung. Those not wishing to continue to the caldera might choose to return to Ubud by a little-traveled route through Kenderan. Several miles along the road from Pujung to Tampaksiring (just before a bridge over a deep ravine) there is a turning south to Kenderan through quiet rice-growing villages.

MANUABA

Almost 3 miles down this road, in the hamlet of Manuaba, is the splendid Pura Griya Sakti, a temple of great importance to the highly respected Manuaba clan of Brahmana for whose venerable dynasty the village is named. Artefacts from the Bronze Age have been found here, most importantly a stone mold for imprinting wax in the casting of enormous bronze Pejeng-style drums ▲ *194*. Behind the temple, three huge trees have grown around each other in a provocatively symbolic way. The *wantilan* (large public pavilion) (below) in front of the temple is a particularly handsome example of this traditional building ● *102*. Farther down the road in Banjar

Kapitu, where the road makes a right-angle turn and a dirt track continues straight on, a small sign indicates the footpath to Telaga Waja, an ancient ritual bathing place at the meeting of two important rivers. The Kenderan road

Ijuk, fiber from the sugar palm, is a mountain cash crop, used exclusively for the roofs of temple shrines.

continues south for a few more miles and rejoins the Tegallalang-Ubud road in Gentong.

MOUNTAIN HAMLETS

The highlands between Pujung and Batur are considered by the Balinese to be *gunungan* ("of the mountains"). Although the agriculture changes as the land rises, the demarcation is more cultural than physical, a subtle shift of attention away from the courtly glamor of the Javanized south toward the elemental realities of mountain farming. The road north rises into the cool air of the mountain villages of Jasan, Tegalsuci, Apuh, and Sekahan before reaching the rim of the Batur caldera.

JASAN. Jasan is yet another famous woodcarving village, specializing in massive *boma* carved from the roots of lychee trees. The late Cokot of Jati (west Jasan) was the first to carve figures of phantasmagoria into the natural forms of tree roots ● 73. The rice fields between Jasan and Tegalsuci are the northernmost wet-rice fields on this road, and the landscape has an unusually gentle quality. Then the landscape takes on a new look. Here, "dry" rice (a particularly tasty but labor-intensive strain planted in dry, hilly ground instead of rice paddies), cabbage, maize, ginger, coffee, and oranges are the main mountain crops.

SEKAHAN. From the bleak town of Sekahan, the rim of the Batur caldera can be seen on the horizon. One can only try to imagine what this area was like before it was deforested to make way for farming. The aesthetics of architectural ornamentation here is painfully bizarre. Although it doesn't look "Balinese", the shameless pursuit of decorative uses of new materials such as cement, ceramic tiles, and lurid hues of paint is true to the experimental Balinese spirit. The road from Sekahan leads to the rim of the caldera, where a road skirting the ridge goes left to Kintamani or right to Penelokan. A pause at the junction is advisable as the view of the great Batur caldera can be dangerously distracting.

PURA PAMWOS
Just beyond the village of Apuh, a village noted for its rustic mud walls (above) and colorfully painted little house shrines, is an irrigation temple honoring the god of the Wos River. The relative grandeur of this temple reflects its importance to those who live downstream and are thus able to grow "wet" rice. Many houses along the road appear poor, especially where the shrines are flimsy constructions of bamboo and tin, but most are field huts, secondary houses for farmers who live in larger villages to the south.

SEKAHAN MARKET
Sekahan holds its major market on *Hari Kajeng,* every third day in the Balinese calendar, in the new marketplace at the end of a dirt lane to the southeast of the village. Like most rural markets, it begins at about four in the morning, has peaked by 7am and is all over by 9pm. In the early morning there is an almost frightening view of Mount Agung from the marketplace, but it is difficult to see anything else because the sun strikes at eye-level during the shopping hours, compelling one to go to the far end of the market and work back with the sun on one's shoulders, most welcome in these chilly highland dawns.

The Batur caldera, 8½ miles across, was once a far larger volcano than little Mount Batur, at its center, will ever be. At the rim, one is gazing into the inner organs of what was once a mountain ■ *19*. Mount Batur is still active, as is evident from the steam drifting around its crown. The lava flows on the southwestern flank were as recent as 1975, but this does not deter people from farming in the caldera. Lake Batur (right) stretches about 4 miles north to south, but no one has yet been able or willing to measure its depth.

PENELOKAN PEDDLERS
A demonic offspring of tourism, Penelokan (above) is for many Westerners a waking nightmare of being trapped between gargantuan tour buses on one side and peddlers on the other. It helps to realize that the local people are still living under hard conditions; many have to climb far for such necessities as water and firewood. By steering clear of the mega-restaurants, a delicious lunch of fried lake fish can be sampled here.

PENELOKAN

Meaning "the view" or "look-out" in Balinese, Penelokan is not a village but a cluster of restaurants, vendors' stalls, and overnight lodgings on the ridge close to the only road down into the caldera. This is where the tour buses arrive from Bangli and Tampaksiring, and the hustling is ferocious. A steep and twisty road descends to a T-junction in Kedisan where a right turn can be taken to the lake ferries for Trunyan or a left toward the hot springs at Toyabungkah.

TRUNYAN

Just visible on the eastern shore, the sinister village of Trunyan squats beneath Mount Abang. Getting across the lake to Trunyan can be expensive. Although the ferries are basically market boats, the big scam on Lake Batur is pressuring visitors into a private charter, with the agreed price sometimes being renegotiated halfway across. This is no ordinary place, for Trunyan is regarded as the ultimate "Bali Aga" village ▲ *218*. Some say "Bali Aga" means "original Balinese people" or "pre-Javanese invasion". Some scholars say that it refers to an ancient migration from the east Javanese village of Aga to Taro. The people of Trunyan insist, however, on the aboriginal interpretation and archeological evidence appears to support their claim to having been here first. Stone tools found in Trunyan attest to habitation by *Pithecanthropus erectus*, hunting and gathering here before the last Ice Age.

PURA GEDE PANCERING JAGAT. This temple harbors evidence of pre-Hindu megalithic traditions. Upright stones are venerated in a small shrine, and inside the *meru* is a 13-foot statue of the Bhatara Da Tonta ("the god who is the center of

TAX EXEMPT
One of Bali's earliest written records, a royal edict in AD 911, exempted Trunyan from certain taxes, a concession these tough mountain people probably did not attain without a struggle. They are so defiantly idiosyncratic, so convinced that their village is the true center of Bali, that they believe Trunyan to be immune to earthquakes.

TRUNYAN GRAVEYARD
A tree in the Trunyan graveyard (right) has the strange property of keeping corpses from smelling as they putrefy, obviating the need to bury the dead.

the world"). This statue appears more akin to the primitive ancestor effigies of the outer islands than to other Bali deities. What intrigues most visitors about Trunyan, however, is the fact that the villagers neither cremate nor bury their dead, so its principal attraction is its graveyard.

PURA JATI

Back on the "safe" side of the lake, along the road toward Toyabungkah, is the lakeside temple of Pura Jati (left), an important source of holy water for ceremonies throughout Bali. Said to have been built by Mpu Jayamaireng, of the ancient Pasek Kayuselem clan, it is associated with the god of the sacred river of life.

TOYABUNGKAH

Also called Air Panas, Toyabungkah is the site of another important spring temple, but it is more conspicuously a tourist spot. The hot springs, flowing into a cement-lined pool on the lakeshore, are small, crowded, and popular with Indonesian students and foreign backpackers. From here one can hike up Mount Batur, but those who prefer to observe the work of an active volcano without climbing into it may take a close look at the lava flow left by the 1965–74 eruptions. The road through Toyabungkah toward Songan comes to an abrupt halt at the lava flow. The reason the road goes no farther becomes dramatically clear.

PURA ULUN DANU

Ulun danu means "head of the lake" and this temple, far from the tourist circuit at the northeasternmost shore, is not to be confused with the Pura Ulun Danu Batur on the rim of the caldera. Although comparatively modest in size, it is specially revered by the Balinese, for only here can they can find holy water of a particularly sacred variety. The water is collected from the lake itself, directly in front of the temple, and since the lakewaters here, the ultimate source of most of the island's irrigation systems, are already intrinsically holy water, bathing is forbidden. Visitors are advised to wear a temple sash and not to go near the water. The temple is maintained by the villagers of nearby Songan whose entire social structure revolves around this sacred trust. Other than on foot, the only way out of the Batur caldera is back up the same twisting road to Penelokan.

BHATARA DA TONTO
Every three years at Trunyan's Pura Gede Pancering Jagat, in a rare ceremony no outsider is permitted to witness, Bhatara Da Tonta is ritually painted with a plaster of chalk, volcanic tuff, and honey and adorned with gold jewelry. This ceremony was already being performed at the time of the royal edict of AD 911, but it is not clear whether the statue is the original one or has been replaced over the centuries.

In this drawing by W. O. J. Nieuwenkamp, he offers a bird's -eye view of the lava flow from the 1917 Batur eruption.

TREKKING
A three-hour trek from Toyabungkah leads up to Mount Batur. By setting out around 2.30am, one can see the sunrise from inside the active volcano. The ground within the crater is springy and steaming, a potent reminder of the instability of our earth. A slightly shorter route to the top, taking about two hours, starts from Pura Jati.

MEAD AND BATESON
In the more rustic 1930's, Margaret Mead and Gregory Bateson pursued research in Bayung Gede in their quest for psychoanalytic clues to patterns of cultural behavior. They also documented the propitiatory ritual *sanghyang deling* in which two little girls in a trance animate puppets suspended on a string held between them. Sometimes the girls themselves become dolls of the gods, climbing with their eyes closed onto the shoulders of village men and dancing there, blind and blithely, as if they were trained *legong* dancers.

BAYUNG GEDE

From Penelokan, the ridge road heads northwest along the caldera rim to Kintamani and on toward Bali's north coast. Between Penelokan and Kintamani there is a signposted turnoff to the left that descends about half a mile to the village of Bayung Gede. With its dense layout of tiny, steep-roofed huts (above) and neat narrow lanes, this is a fine example of an ancient mountain village. It is also visibly prosperous and well integrated into the Republic of Indonesia, as can be seen by the post office and the medical clinic. The Pura Puseh of Bayung Gede, in the northeast of the village, is unusual for its shrines maintained in their original archaic forms: low structures in simple materials. Sacred stones, echoes of a megalithic era, are surrounded by bamboo fences. This is a place in which to tread gently and to resist the temptation to enter the temple unless specifically invited.

PURA ULUN DANU BATUR ★

Back on the ridge road and just before entering Kintamani is the dramatic temple complex Pura Ulun Danu Batur.

Regarded as Bali's second most important temple after Besakih ▲ 208, it is the ceremonial throne for Ida Bhatari Dewi Danu, the goddess of the lake. In clear weather, the temple's many-tiered *meru* are visible from miles away, but it is perhaps most beautiful in the tumbling fogs that swirl around the caldera. The goddess is honored with a tall *meru* of eleven tiers, sign of the highest divinity. The *meru* of her consort, the god of Mount Agung, has only nine, while two other nine-tiered *meru* are dedicated to the god of Mount Batur and to the deified King Waturenggong ● 35. One of the most interesting shrines in the inner courtyard is a distinctly Chinese-looking pavilion to the far left, dedicated to a Chinese princess whose image is recalled in the *barong landung* dance play. No one knows how old this temple is, although there are references to it in 11th-century texts. We do know that in the early 20th century it was still situated in the village of Batur, on the southern slopes of Mount Batur, and that it was damaged in the eruption of 1917, although the lava flow halted at its very walls (above). Neither temple nor village, however, survived the eruption of 1926, for both are now buried beneath many feet of lava rock. As many of its dismantled shrines as could be rescued were hauled up the cliff to the safety of the ridge, and the new temple built around them. In its present form, Pura Ulun Danu Batur is a reconstitution of nine earlier temples, all rescued from the eruption. Pura Tulukbiyu, the adjoining temple to the right, was similarly relocated from the inconvenient peak of Mount Abang, the mountain behind Trunyan.

SUBAK SUPPORT
Pura Ulun Danu Batur is maintained by the irrigation societies (*subak* ■ 24) of surrounding regions. Besides paying homage to the goddess of the lake and seeking rulings about water distribution from her high priest, people come here to appease the forces of crop pestilence, to pray for skill in domestic crafts and to honor a pantheon of ancient mountain gods and deified ancestors.

> ## "So now, my wishes are, remember the goddess!"
> ### Jero Gede, High Priest of Pura Ulun Danu Batur, 1986

KINTAMANI

Despite its administrative importance as the seat of district government, Kintamani looks more like an outpost than a town. In Dutch colonial times, visitors to Bali arrived at the port in Buleleng, on the north coast, and traveled to the glamorous south via Kintamani, where the second-ever tourist hotel in Bali was built. The market here is a lively site of mountain agricultural commerce, and takes place once every three days, on *Hari Paseh* in the Balinese calendar.

PURA PENULISAN ★

Pura Penulisan, as it is familiarly called although its proper name is Pura Tegeh Koripan, is several miles beyond Kintamani. This temple is actually a complex of five small temples on ascending terraces, and its pyramid-like design (below) suggests very early, possibly even megalithic, origins. The summit temple, Pura Panarajon, houses a number of stone figures, several dating from the 11th century. One of them is inscribed as being Bhatari Mandul, the barren queen of Raja Anak Wungsu, who was the younger brother of Airlangga, often associated with the *Calonarang* story (of which the *barong* and kris trance dance of Batubulan is a brief segment). Anak Wungsu is said to have forsaken his wife to meditate in the high forests of Penulisan. This is still considered a magically charged place, and modern Balinese students of meditation assemble here on auspicious nights to seek inner power.

LAKE GODDESS
Because Lake Batur is literally the spring of life for much of Bali, its waters filtering through the volcanic rock in all directions to feed the sophisticated irrigation systems of the rice-growing regions of Bangli, Buleleng, Gianyar, Klungkung, and Badung, the lake goddess is a paramount deity. Jero Gede, her earthly representative, is the island's most powerful priest because he is the final arbiter of all matters concerning the distribution of water. Upon the death of the Jero Gede, a virgin priestess goes into a trance to select his successor. The current Jero Gede was picked at the auspicious age of eleven. Like all his predecessors, he is of the Pasek Kayuselem clan, a mountain dynasty whose original ancestor was turned from a black tree standing on the summit of Mount Batur into a human at the time of the birth of the gods. Although not part of the *Triwangsa* castes ● *90*, the Jero Gede is entitled to eleven roofs on his cremation tower, an indication of his special relationship with the goddess.

185

▲ INNER KINGDOMS

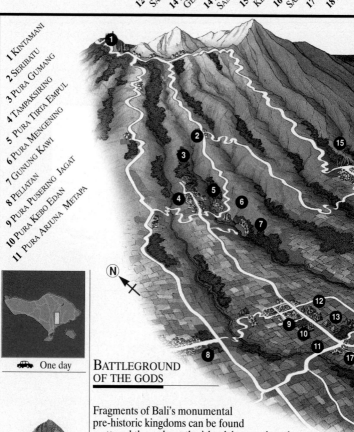

N

One day

A statue of Arjuna in Pura Arjuna Metapa is just one of the many antiquities found in this region.

BATTLEGROUND OF THE GODS

Fragments of Bali's monumental pre-historic kingdoms can be found scattered throughout the island, but nowhere have archeologists reaped richer spoils than in the valleys, cliffs, and gorges between two parallel rivers a short distance east of Ubud. The Pakerisan ("River of the Kris") and the Petanu ("River of the Curse") flow from the mountains to the sea through valleys which nurtured Bali's earliest Hindu and Buddhist kingdoms. Epic poems over the centuries agree that this narrow strip of land was the battlefield of a great war between the forces of the god Indra and the powerful ruler Maya Danawa, a semi-divine son of the goddess of Lake Batur. Furious at the Bali-Hindu gods for allowing his beloved Buddhist wife to die, the ruler ordered his people to turn their backs on the gods and direct their worship only toward him. In the war which ensued, his chief minister created and cursed a magical river which poisoned Indra's army. Indra retaliated by tapping a holy spring at Tirta Empul in Tampaksiring to revive his army and give them the supernatural strength to kill Maya Danawa. A poisonous blood gushed from his dying mouth to become the psychically contaminated waters of the Petanu. For 1700 years a curse forbade the use of its water for drinking, bathing, or even irrigation. In the 1920's, it was agreed that the 1700 years had elapsed, and with all due ceremony the prohibition was lifted. Behind this epic of magic and mysticism, we can perhaps read the historical account of a successful Hindu rebellion against

19 YEH PULU 20 CANDI TEBING 21 PURA BUKIT DHARMA 22 PURA GADUH BLAHBATU 23 PAKERISAN RIVER 24 PETANU RIVER 25 PURI AGUNG GIANYAR 26 PURA DALEM SIDAN 27 BESAKIH 28 KLUNGKUNG

a powerful Buddhist king, whose still-undiscovered capital was located somewhere near the short road between Peliatan and Bedulu. The mystical powers of later kings reached their apex in Beda-Hulu ("He of the Severed Head"), a ruler so adept at meditation that he could completely separate his head from his body. One day, however, while meditating beside the river, his head slipped into the stream. An attendant sliced off the head of a pig and stuck it on his master's shoulders. From that day on the king became progressively more greedy and pig-headed. He had a high tower built for himself, before which his subjects were forced to kneel so as never to see his curious face. He is said to have been conquered by the Javanese Majapahit general Gajah Mada, which would place his reign late in the 13th century. According to one version, his original head came to rest a short way downstream where it still stands – a face carved into the rock at Goa Gajah (right), one of Bali's most striking ancient sites.

PAKERISAN
No antiquities are found along the accursed Petanu, but all the way along the deep gorge of the Pakerisan, fed in part by Indra's sacred spring, are some of Bali's most important prehistoric monuments. Myth claims that many of these sites were the work of Kebo Iwa ● *51*, a giant who etched them from the living rock with his fingernail.

189

ELEPHANT CAVE
In the 1920's, the first Westerner seeing the head carved at Goa Gajah thought it was the face of an elephant. From this the site earned its name "Elephant Cave", although the name Lwa Gajah meaning "Elephant Waters" is far more ancient. Many Balinese insist the carving is a self-portrait of the giant, Kebo Iwa ● 51.

GOA GAJAH ★

About a mile due east from southern Peliatan, the road crosses a stone bridge over the long-accursed Petanu River and reaches the vast bus-park and gauntlet of souvenir stalls which must be negotiated before climbing down to the great head hewn from living rock at Goa Gajah ● 34. No one is sure what the figure represents, but the monstrous face, whose fanged mouth is the entrance to a man-made cave, appears to represent an earth spirit clawing its way out of the cosmic mountain, which is populated by a curious and often comical array of animals and phantoms. According to 14th-century Javanese scribes, this was one of Bali's principal Buddhist sanctuaries. Yet in the dark tunnels of its cave we find Hindu *linggas* and a statue of Siwa's son Ganesha, the elephant god of Hinduism. At every turn one is confronted with elements of both religions, ranging from the 8th to 14th centuries, suggesting that Bali's religious syncretism goes back a very long way. To the left of the cave is a small shrine housing a 1000-year-old statue of the Buddhist goddess Hariti, protector of children, surrounded by a brood of her young charges. Hariti had been a notorious baby-eating ogress until Buddhism changed her wicked ways. At the bottom of the ravine some unusual broken fragments of collapsed cliff have been found with very old and rare relief carvings of delicate stupas in the style of 8th-century Java. Farther on are two small Buddhas in the lotus position, also tentatively dated to the time of the great Javanese monument, Borobodur. Beyond the Buddhas lies the entrance to what may have been a hermit's cave. So far, it has been excavated to a depth of only 30 feet; whatever lies beyond that remains a mystery.

BATHING POOL
The top halves of several life-sized nymphs, clearly water spouts, once guarded the mouth of the Goa Gajah cave, but a 1954 excavation revealed the rest of their bodies some distance away in a large sunken bathing place (above) that had been buried for centuries.

BEDULU ★

A few hundred yards east of Goa Gajah, before reaching the main road north to Tampaksiring, there is a sign indicating the road south to Yeh Pulu. This road becomes a village street through the oldest and most charming part of Bedulu village, which was once the capital of the semi-mythical pig-headed king, Beda-Hulu ▲ 189. Once the center of all Balinese power, Bedulu is a gracious backwater in whose shady lanes tourists are still a rare enough phenomenon to be welcomed into family compounds. Gusti Nyoman Lempad, Ubud's most famous artist ▲ 164, was born and lived here until he and his father were forced to flee to Ubud late in the last century. Relatives of his still live in the old family compound and

> "THE REVERED BUDDHIST MASTERS WHO HAVE THEIR HOLY PLACES IN BADAHULU AND LWA GAJAH ARE DILIGENT IN OVERSEEING THE EXTENSIVE DOMAINS OF THE MONKS, BEING SENT THERE AS GUARDIANS BY THE ILLUSTRIOUS PRINCE."
>
> 14TH-CENTURY JAVANESE TEXT

YEH PULU RELIEFS

More than 80 feet in length and executed with exceptional boldness and vigor, the reliefs at Yeh Pulu appear to recount the adventures of Krisna, the goatherd, whose seductive music and dance made him irresistible to women, particularly as he was a divine incarnation of the god Wisnu. The first human figure seen as one descends the steps appears to be greeting the visitor, but this is a classic posture symbolic of the young Krisna's ability to playfully uproot the holy mountain and hold it up as an umbrella, much to the irritation of the senior gods. A large section of the relief probably shows a bear hunt and its aftermath (by someone who had seen more pigs than bears).

throughout his long lifetime Lempad often returned to build many of Bedulu's temple gates and shrines.

YEH PULU. A short walk into the rice paddies from the southeast corner of Bedulu brings one to Bali's most curious rock-carved reliefs (above). The experts have great difficulty agreeing on the age of Yeh Pulu because it appears to be the eccentric creation of one ascetic hermit who must have lived for many years in a hut-shaped niche he had hewn into the rock face. Aspects of its style and theme lead some to suggest a date around the 14th century, while other estimates range between the 10th and 19th centuries.

PURA SAMUAN TIGA. East of the main crossroads of Bedulu, this large and splendidly located temple (below) is of great importance to the whole island. Its annual festival is a lengthy and glittering event featuring a unique "war of the offerings" in which young men, some on the brink of trance, pelt each other with colorful offerings in Bali's version of a violent pie fight. None of Samuan Tiga's architecture pre-dates the earthquakes of 1917. It is nonetheless majestic, particularly striking features being the *kori agung*, or great gate, built by Gusti Lempad, and the cock-fighting pit beneath a mighty tree to the east. Across the street are new pavilions and guest houses.

KECAK

The modern *kecak*, combining the traditional trance-inducing "monkey" chant with a libretto from the *Ramayana*, was choreographed in Bedulu in the 1930's by the great *baris* dancer, Limbak, with encouragement from German artist Walter Spies ● *112*.

PEJENG

TANTRIC CULT
There has been much argument about the possible existence of a secretive and extremist cult of "left-handed" Tantrism practiced in 14th-century Java and Bali, and Kebo Edan may have been a center where its dark rituals were performed. Combining Tantric Buddhist and Sivaite elements, it has been called the "Bima Cult", not after the culture-hero of the *Mahabharata* epic but to honor Bima, one of the terrifying aspects of Siwa. In fact, the hero Bima from the shadow puppet plays does possess many of the characteristics of that fearful being, and it is his image that appears in the Javanese temples where the cult is believed to have been practiced. It is possible, however, that the giant of Kebo Edan was simply a temple guardian working on the universal principle that it takes one demon to see off another.

Pejeng, just north of Bedulu on the road to Tampaksiring, was once the center of a great kingdom, which either evolved from or overlapped with the Bedulu dynasty. Pejeng boasts at least forty sites housing relics of great antiquity, making it one of Indonesia's richest archeological zones. While some of the relics are housed in major temples and some in private family shrines or backyards, others crop up unexpectedly in the rice paddies. All are still venerated by the Balinese.

MUSEUM PURBAKALA GEDONG ARCA. This museum devoted to Balinese antiquities is on the right hand side of the main road about a mile north of Bedulu. Well-housed but poorly displayed are many fragments from Bali's last 400,000 years of human endeavor. The collection ranges from simple paleolithic stone tools and blades, through the pre-Hindu Bronze Age to the golden era of Balinese Hindu-Buddhism and beyond. Of special interest are the large Bronze Age sarcophagi that have been excavated from many locations on the island. Each of these would usually

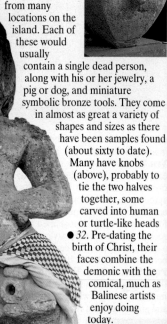

contain a single dead person, along with his or her jewelry, a pig or dog, and miniature symbolic bronze tools. They come in almost as great a variety of shapes and sizes as there have been samples found (about sixty to date). Many have knobs (above), probably to tie the two halves together, some carved into human or turtle-like heads
● *32.* Pre-dating the birth of Christ, their faces combine the demonic with the comical, much as Balinese artists enjoy doing today.

PURA KEBO EDAN
★. The "Temple of the Mad Bull", just north of the museum and across the road, houses one of the island's most imposing statues (left).

Stone carving at Pura Kebo Edan.

About 13 feet tall and dated to the 13th or 14th centuries, it is sometimes called the "Pejeng Giant". Prancing in an aggressive dance, the giant crushes a human figure beneath his great, snake-encoiled feet. A substantial (to put it mildly) penis bursts from his sarong revealing large plugs which bisect it just behind the glans. Traditional symbols of mystical and physical prowess, more modest versions of these were once sported by men throughout Southeast Asia to increase the pleasure of their ladies, and they are still in use among some Dayak tribes of Borneo. The statue never had a face. An abstract, eyeless mask reveals badly worn and highly stylized fangs and two unequal-sized horns. This could be the reason that the temple, and often the giant, is called Kebo Edan ("The Mad Bull"). Nearby is a smaller demonic figure with a belt of human skulls who holds up a cup also made from a skull.

Pura Arjuna Metapa. This is not a temple as we usually think of them, but a single small pavilion in the rice paddies clearly visible from the entrance to Kebo Edan. It houses standing statues of Arjuna, Bima's more gracious brother, as well as his clownish attendants, Twalen and Merdah (left). All three are wearing the turbans, chains, and loincloths of ascetics, a clear reference to the popular story of Arjuna, who was quite a ladies' man, meditating while celestial nymphs unsuccessfully try to tempt him away from his pure purpose.

Pura Pusering Jagat. This temple, whose name means "The Navel of The Universe", is just north of Kebo Edan, down a lane to the west. Inside is a large stone urn (right), completely covered with rich reliefs which are believed to recount how gods churned the primordial ocean to extract the elixir of life, even though many key elements of that story are only implied. The urn is not the only interesting antiquity here; most striking among the others are a four-sided sculpture of four-armed divinities and another of four intensely dancing demons. All these sculptures belong to the same period as those of Kebo Edan and Arjuna Metapa, and it is quite possible that six hundred years ago all three temples were part of a single vast Tantric complex.

BARONG MASK
In a closed shrine at Pura Kebo Edan and viewable only during temple festivals is a superb 19th-century *barong* mask carved by Gusti Nyoman Lempad when he was a young man.

URN AT PURA PUSERING JAGAT
The Balinese call this urn Naragiri ("The Mountain of Man"). It shows the cosmic mountain, alive with spirits and nymphs, beasts, birds, and humans, that floats above the ocean entwined by a rippling belt of eight *nagas* and supported by several straining gods. This dynamic work, which was clearly used as a vessel for holy water, has a pictograph date, the *saka* year 1251 (AD 1329), worked into the lotus petals of its rim.

The largest known relic from Southeast Asia's "Dongson" Bronze Age, the bronze drum known as the "Moon of Pejeng" was produced locally during Indonesia's first great cultural flowering ● *33*. Pura Penataran Sasih ("Temple of The Moon") has housed this masterpiece of art for as long as two millennia. Cast in two sections by the lost wax process, the flat tympanum and the great tubular mantle were later joined by a cuff. Modern metallurgists are amazed that ancient man could acquire such control over the temperatures and the varying ratios of the alloy (copper, tin, and lead) to produce a perfect piece of such monumental size. The fact that it is also tonally correct for drumming is even more remarkable.

This bronze drum stands a remarkable 75 inches high with a maximum diameter of 64 inches. It is modeled on the wooden, hourglass-shaped little hand drums called *tifas* still used throughout the islands of eastern Indonesia.

The Balinese believe the drum was the wheel from the chariot of the goddess of the moon (though some say her earplug) and that it fell into a tree. A thief whose nocturnal activities were curtailed by the drum's brilliance decided to dim it by urinating on it. The thief died instantly, and the "Moon of Pejeng" was cracked and lost its glow. It is now enshrined on its side in one of the temple's tallest pavilions (left and above).

Concentric circles and other decoration (right) appear on the tympanum of this huge kettle drum, which may date from 300 BC. These delicate geometric motifs are of an artistic style which still echoes through the modern art of Indonesia and Oceania.

Between the four handles are stylistic heads (left), about 8 inches high, some of the earliest representations of the human face in Indonesia.

Broken tympanums and stone molds for smaller versions have been found nearby, and miniatures of the large drum, called *mokos* (below), were being cast in east Java until the turn of the century. In the eastern island of Alor, *mokos* remain the only acceptable currency for buying a bride.

In 1875 the drum's first known Western visitor disrespectfully beat it with a stick to check its tone. The next day he fell seriously ill, but eventually recovered. Subsequent visitors were kept at a distance until, in 1906, the more sensitive wandering artist W. O. J. Nieuwenkamp was allowed to examine the drum, and made meticulous measurements and sketches (above).

ROYAL VISIT
During Gunung Kawi's annual temple festival, the royal souls still descend to take up temporary residence in the "tombs" so that their beneficial and fertilizing powers may flow down the Pakerisan and through the rice fields of the kingdom.

SUKARNO'S PALACE
Sukarno's palace squats on the hill above Pura Tirta Empul. The palace gave him a fine view of the bathing pools. In his day women bathed there, but they now use an enclosed cement block area off to one side of and beyond the temple grounds.

TAMPAKSIRING

The road north from Pejeng follows the course of the Pakerisan River, which remains just out of sight to the east. Several minor roads and lanes head toward the river, where little-known bathing places, ancient shrines, and monuments cut into the rock dot its gorge. The most important ones, however, are in Tampaksiring.

GUNUNG KAWI. In the center of Tampaksiring, a little way beyond the market corner, a clearly signposted side street leads almost to the brink of the Pakerisan gorge at Gunung Kawi, where a daunting flight of steps leads down to the river itself. You know that you are descending into Bali's "valley of the kings", for hewn into the cliffs on both sides of the river appear massive commemorative monuments to 11th-century rajas and ranis. Etched into deep, 23-foot-high niches in the cliff are five *candi* (above), temple façades with false doors leading to the "other world". The one farthest upstream is believed to have been built for King Anak Wungsu ● *34*, whose long rule over central and east Bali lasted from around AD 1050 to about 1080. The other four probably honor his senior wives who would have committed suttee ● *124* by leaping onto his funeral pyre. As kings were cremated and their ashes cast into the sea, these *candi* contain no human remains and are not, in fact, tombs but symbols of the deified rulers. Immediately south of these *candi* lies a warren of cloisters carved into the cliff. This was the inner sanctum of priestly guardians and trance oracles, who would pass on advice to the living from the long-dead and deified king. Re-crossing the bridge to the west bank and turning right, we find four more great *candi* directly facing the original five. Because all the inscriptions have worn away, it is not known whether they honor Anak Wungsu's most senior queen, his lesser wives, or a subsequent generation of his dynasty. Doubts aside, they have become known as the "Queen's Tombs". Only the very sure-footed should attempt the journey to the more isolated "Tenth Tomb", known to the Balinese as the Geriya Pedanda ("Home of the High Priest"). Just north of Gunung Kawi, the road reaches a major crossroads. The left branch leads west toward Sebatu; straight ahead the road goes to a palace built by President Sukarno in the 1950's, while the right branch curves down a hill to the most famous of the Pakerisan's many sources, Pura Tirta Empul.

PURA TIRTA EMPUL. Most of the pavilions and sculptures in this temple are neither old nor exceptional; the spring-fed bathing pools (left) are its most important feature. The ritual and historical importance to the people of Gianyar of this complex

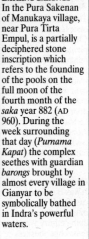

BATHING BARONGS
In the Pura Sakenan of Manukaya village, near Pura Tirta Empul, is a partially deciphered stone inscription which refers to the founding of the pools on the full moon of the fourth month of the *saka* year 882 (AD 960). During the week surrounding that day (*Purnama Kapat*) the complex seethes with guardian *barongs* brought by almost every village in Gianyar to be symbolically bathed in Indra's powerful waters.

lies in these pools in which Indra's celestial army was revived before defeating King Maya Danawa ▲ *188*.

PURA MENGENING. Just downstream from Tirta Empul, across the road and down a long flight of steps, is a far more peaceful temple complex which is also built around a sacred spring. Here, where a great tree shades the pool, a strong sense of the Balinese veneration of nature can be felt. Another flight of steps leads up to the temple itself and its large freestanding *prasada* (above). *Prasada,* now extremely rare in Bali but clearly more prevalent a thousand years ago, are square-based, multi-roofed temple buildings similar to the *candi* of ancient Java. They were the models for such rock-cut reliefs as are found just downstream at Gunung Kawi.

PURA GUMANG. About a mile north of the crossroads, beyond Sukarno's palace and Pura Sakenan, are fascinating fragments from another *prasada*. Set far back among the giant trees of a primordial forest, Pura Gumang (left) is a treasure trove of unusual antiquities: a decapitated sculpture of Nandi, the white bull ridden by Siwa; a massive *lingga*; and the remains of at least one large *prasada*. No archeological excavation has yet been undertaken in this idyllic forest grove which must, about a thousand years ago, have housed a Sivaite temple complex of great size and importance.

SACRED KRISES
Many Balinese wash their sacred krises in the waters of Mengening, where they feed into the Pakerisan ("River of the Kris") to imbue them with the magical power of Indra's celestial army.

197

The last raja of Bangli once lent money to a Chinese coffee planter who had fallen foul of fluctuations in the market. He repaid his debt with an elaborate Chinese door (above), which he had ordered from Hong Kong. A new pavilion had to be built around it.

GREGOR KRAUSE
It was Bangli which cast Bali's initial spell of enchantment over 20th-century Western mass consciousness and lured the first generation of casual tourists and escapist expatriates to the "last paradise". From 1912 to 1914, just four years after the final Dutch conquest, Doctor Gregor Krause, a German in the Dutch medical service, was posted to Bangli. His photographs (below) were published in Germany in 1926, and the book *Bali: Volk, Land, Tänze, Feste, Temple* swept through the drawing rooms of Europe and America. Bali's first known motion picture images were also shot in Bangli in 1926, eerie scenes of a royal cremation and a trance dance by little girls possessed by celestial nymphs.

BANGLI

Bangli was the second smallest of Bali's nine kingdoms and with the exception of the Batur caldera ▲ *182,* which falls within its territory, it remains the Cinderella of Balinese tourism.
Leaving the sacred spring of Tirta Empul, the road to Kintamani climbs steadily up a long ridge where rice fields soon give way to plantations of coffee, tobacco, cloves, vanilla, and other highland crops. Turning right at Seribatu toward Bangli, the road eventually curves into Bangli Town. The eight palaces of Bangli are bunched close together, most of them still home to the various branches of the royal family, and most in a state of poor repair as the aristocracy of Bangli have fallen on hard times. In order to help defray the costs of maintaining Bangli's Puri Denpasar, the grandson of the last raja of Bangli was obliged to convert a section of it into a guesthouse called Arta Sastra.

PURA KEHEN ★. Heading due north from the palaces to the second road east brings one to the imposing flight of steps up to the Pura Kehen (above). Similar both in

form and purpose to Besakih ("Mother Temple"), its ascending courtyards up a hillside are reminiscent of the stepped pyramids of the Megalithic Age. Just as Besakih became the residence of the deified spirits of the kings of Klungkung, Pura Kehen served that function for the kingdom of Bangli, whose rajas were all crowned within its hallowed courtyards. Climbing the forty-eight steps, flanked by fourteen carved demons, and passing through the great gate into the first courtyard, it feels as if the veil of centuries is being lifted. A flattened natural stone seems to emanate the same power of the similar stone altars at which Indonesian tribes in more remote islands still

In this picture, published in 1926, the chief of a small district on Bali makes a formal call on the raja in Gianyar. His servants accompany him on the visit, one of many made for consultation or to take part in ritual ceremonies.

worship. From its courtyard one ascends through split gates to the second courtyard, which houses shrines to the ancestors of the last royal dynasty of Bangli. The highest courtyard contains an eleven-tiered *meru* to the god of fire and at the northeast corner is an unusual and superbly carved "three-seater" *padmasana trisakti*. The three seats are for Brahma, Wisnu, and Siwa, the supreme Hindu trinity, but to Balinese eyes the shrine is to the sun god, Surya, of whom they are but manifestations. Traces of paint on many of the older statues indicate that Pura Kehen was once far more garishly colorful than it is today.

GIANYAR

The road from Bangli winds down toward the main east-west road between Gianyar and Klungkung. It curves around the Pura Dalem Sidan, which has a particularly graceful *kori agung* gate. Leaflike in its delicacy, it is a representation in stone of the *kayonan,* the central motif in the shadow puppet plays ● *59.* From the graveyard across the road there is a fine view over the coastal zone of the kingdom of Gianyar.

GIANYAR TOWN. Capital of the rich old kingdom, Gianyar is now the administrative center of the area and not over-endowed with touristic interest. The whole town revolves around the Puri Agung ● *108,* the palace of Ida Anak Agung Gede Agung, the tenth raja of Gianyar (although strictly speaking, his father was the last official raja). The Puri Agung ★ is the most complete traditional palace surviving in Bali. Although it is not open to the public, some of its splendid inner gates and pavilions and its first courtyard are clearly visible from the street. Particularly striking is the grand *kori agung* gate guarding a large courtyard (invisible from the street) which comes to life only during royal cremation rituals.

The *bale bengong,* a substantial raised pavilion overlooking the side street, is one of the oldest sections of the palace, having survived the burning and looting of the palace by forces of the neighboring raja of Klungkung during a setback in the 19th-century wars of the rajas. At the turn of the century, Gianyar was once again beset by enemies on all sides and sought an alliance with the Dutch. As a result, the kingdom avoided the devastation and *puputan* suffered by most of the other kingdoms of south Bali during the Dutch invasion. Under Dutch rule, during which the rajas of Gianyar retained almost unfettered autonomy, the kingdom revived its lost wealth and went from strength to strength.

A series of carvings on the outer tower of the Pura Dalem Sidan (above) feature the semi-divine hero Bima fighting with the god of death.

BABI GULING ★
The *warung* (food stalls) in Gianyar's thriving night market serve some of the island's most sumptuous *babi guling* for those who like their spitted roast pork crisp-skinned and fatty.

199

From Tegallingga, which is 3 miles along the main road from Gianyar toward Denpasar, a right turn takes you home to Ubud via Bedulu, but first there are three ancient sites nearby that are well worth exploring.

PURA BUKIT DHARMA

GODDESS DURGA
This statue in Pura Bukit Dharma shows the goddess in an energetic fighting pose, killing a demon that has taken the body of a bull. Her six arms wield a bow, an arrow, a shield, a short spear, a flaming disk, and a winged and flaming conch shell. Scholars believe this 11th-century work is a posthumous deified portrait of a powerful 10th-century Javanese queen, wife of Bali's King Udayana and mother of Airlangga ● *34*. Some Balinese suggest that she was the original Rangda ● *47*, witch of the *Calonarang* legend and *barong*/kris trance.

A few hundred yards southwest from the turnoff, right beside the main road, is a tree-covered rocky outcrop that projects the intangible aura of having been a place of worship since earliest times. At its feet, in the open shrines of Pura Bukit Dharma, numerous superb statues and sculptures can be seen that span eight centuries of Balinese art. A hundred stone steps ascend from the back of the temple, through the roots of a banyan tree to an open platform and Pura Kedarman, which consists of a single pavilion dominated by a six-foot statue of the goddess Durga. Despite being badly damaged and poorly restored, the statue retains all the grace and power of a masterpiece.

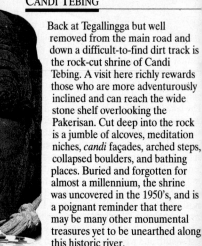

PURA GADUH

A couple of miles toward Denpasar, at the crossroads in the center of Blahbatu, is a left turn that soon brings one to this strikingly unusual temple (right) housing many old carvings. Notable among them, on a raised shrine in the eastern courtyard, is a large stone head (left) which is said to be a portrait of the giant Kebo Iwa ● *51*, who is credited with creating most of the unexplained antiquities and monuments of Gianyar.

CANDI TEBING

Back at Tegallingga but well removed from the main road and down a difficult-to-find dirt track is the rock-cut shrine of Candi Tebing. A visit here richly rewards those who are more adventurously inclined and can reach the wide stone shelf overlooking the Pakerisan. Cut deep into the rock is a jumble of alcoves, meditation niches, *candi* façades, arched steps, collapsed boulders, and bathing places. Buried and forgotten for almost a millennium, the shrine was uncovered in the 1950's, and is a poignant reminder that there may be many other monumental treasures yet to be unearthed along this historic river.

CENTERS OF POWER

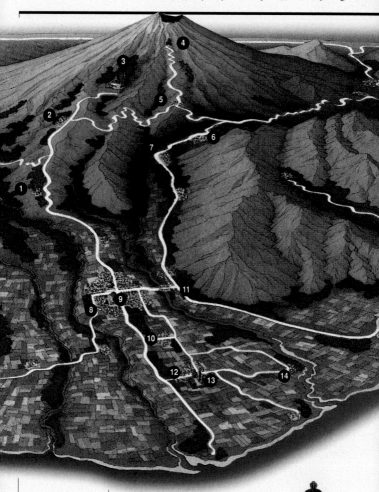

In most maps, the bustling capital of the Klungkung Regency ● *41,* 6 miles east of Gianyar, still bears the name "Klungkung"; it was only in 1992 that the town was formally renamed Semarapura in tribute to the Puri Semarapura ("Palace of the God of Love"), which once sprawled just to the southwest of the central crossroads. From its erection at the start of the 17th century until the fall of southern Bali to the Dutch in 1908, the palace (right) remained the island's political and cultural nucleus. The smallest of Bali's kingdoms, Klungkung was also the greatest. The rajas of all the other kingdoms deferred in

One day

N

word, if not action, to the raja of Klungkung, whose hereditary title, Dewa Agung, means "Great Deity". The Dewa Agungs, who were titled Dalem until the move to Klungkung in 1710, were probably directly descended from the royal family of the powerful 13th-century Majapahit civilization of east Java (although one Balinese legend holds that they were the progeny of an amorous tryst between a celestial nymph and a stone sculpture of the god Brahma). It is through their marital unions with the Dewa Agungs that the other royal houses of Bali claim varying degrees of direct descent from the emperors of Majapahit. When, in the early 16th century, Hindu Majapahit fell to newly Islamicized kingdoms in Java, many artisans, scholars, and priests sought refuge in Bali and most gravitated toward the court of the Dalem, which in those days was located at Gelgel, nearly 3 miles south of Klungkung. In the ensuing two and a half centuries, their descendants fell under the creative spell of Bali. While retaining many techniques, motifs, and themes of their Javanese ancestors, they developed a distinctive Balinese style, and the palace in Klungkung grew out of this new style. It all came to an end on April 18, 1908. While Dutch artillery pounded the palace, the last Dewa Agung sounded the call to *puputan*, or "fight to the death". At the crossroads, a towering monument, a stupa of black volcanic stone, commemorates the *puputan*, while the town's center of gravity has shifted to the bustling market east of the crossroads. Semarapura, or Klungkung as most people still call it, is neither tranquil nor at first sight particularly lovely. The multistory cement blocks of prosperous Chinese merchants that line the main shopping street and surround the market are topped with a spiky punk hairdo of television antennas and satellite dishes. Exploration of the backstreets, however, reveals glimpses of "Old Klungkung". Any day of the week the market is one of the liveliest in Bali, but every third day (*Paseh*) in the Balinese calendar, villagers flock down from the hills to make it the social event that all Indonesian markets were originally conceived as.

1908 PUPUTAN
Dressed in white, Klungkung's last Dewa Agung led a procession toward the Dutch guns in 1908. Pausing at the center of the crossroads, close to where visitors' cars and buses now park, he raised his sacred kris, the most revered and magical of all his heirlooms, and stabbed it fiercely into the ground. According to prophesy, this dramatic act should have gouged a chasm deep enough to swallow all the kingdom's enemies. Unfortunately, a new era had overtaken Bali and the power of

the kris of the Dewa Agungs had waned. A Dutch bullet caught him in the knee and as he fell, another entered his heart. Amidst the roar of field guns, his six senior wives knelt beside him and plunged their own krises into their breasts. It was the signal for the rest of his family and retainers, children included, to follow suit. The already burning palace was then systematically razed to the ground, and only a fragment has remained. Eventually, a new Dewa Agung would be selected by the Dutch from among the survivors, but he would never be more than a private citizen.

Only a minuscule fraction of Bali's premier palace survived the Dutch assault of 1908, but it includes the Taman Gili water garden in which stand two of the island's most famous and extraordinary artistic experiments: the Bale Kambang, or "floating pavilion", and the Kerta Gosa, also known as the "Hall of Justice".

KORI AGUNG ★
Nobody knows how the great gate, or *kori agung,* of the Palace of Semarapura survived the destructiveness of the invaders. Perhaps even they could appreciate the bitter joke it conveys. On either side of its superbly carved ironwood doors, where grotesque demons would normally stand guard, sit two bearded and bulbous-nosed gentlemen in top hats and frock coats (below). One of them is counting banknotes and *kepeng* coins, the archetypal early Communist caricature of a capitalist swine. Whoever built this remarkable gate appears to have foreseen what lay ahead.

BALE KAMBANG. This imposing rectangular pavilion appears to float above its lily-filled moat ● *110*. Beneath its ironwood shingled roof, every square inch of ceiling is richly painted with traditional "Kamasan style" motifs ▲ *206*, and it is only natural to assume that this must be Klungkung's renowned Hall of Justice. It is not. Kerta Gosa is the little square pavilion in the corner of the garden. The Bale Kambang (above), in the days of the rajas, was headquarters for the royal guards. Later, in Dutch times, anxious relatives of plaintiffs and transgressors waited there for judgments emanating from the Kerta Gosa. They usually had plenty of time to study the myths and legends pictured on the painted panels overhead.

The first of these eight layers of panels shows phases of the astrological calendar, while the second tells the story of Pan Brayut and Men Brayut, an impoverished couple who were blessed with eighteen children and didn't know what to do ● *50*. All the other layers to the apex relate the adventures of Sutasoma, a semi-divine hero whose wisdom and subtle powers cause arrows and spears, even those hurled at him by the gods, to turn to flowers. He is a Balinese role model of non-aggressive strength. Although the Bale Kambang survived the razing of the palace in 1908, the building seen today is not old. It was completely rebuilt and enlarged in 1942 and, due to the ravages of the climate, some of its ceiling panels were probably replaced even more recently.

BALE KERTA GOSA, THE HALL OF JUSTICE. The more famous painted ceiling of the Kerta Gosa has also gone through numerous changes this century. It had to be restored after the devastating earthquake of 1917 and was again repainted during the 1930's by Pan Sekan, a master artist from the nearby village of Kamasan. Thirty years later, Pan Sekan's son, Pan Semaris, directed the total replacement of his father's weather-eaten ceiling. With the exception of a few panels added in the last decade, which stand out because of their crudity and the fact that acrylics instead of natural pigments were used, the ceiling is as Pan Semaris created it in 1960. In the small pavilion, you find yourself on the brink of three worlds. Below you to one side is the noisy bustle of modern Bali while to the other lies the old-worldly calm of the

Several panels of the ceiling at Kerta Gosa relate tales from the *Tantri* series.

water garden, and rising overhead in a pulsating pyramid of richly painted panels (left) is the realm of gods and demons. During the thirty years of Dutch rule, suspected criminals would be tried beneath these salutary paintings. The panels are arranged in nine layers, the lowest being a series of small panels telling five tales of the *Tantri* series. (This is a Javano-Balinese version of India's *Pancatantra*, following the same concept as *A Thousand and One Nights*.) Most of the 267 panels relate episodes in the story of *Bima Swarga* in which Bima, the most unruly of the five semi-divine Pandawa brothers of the *Mahabharata*, ventures into the underworld to rescue the lost souls of his earthly parents. The karmic fate of those who have transgressed is illustrated, while Bima battles with demons and overturns cauldrons in his quest (below). We follow Bima's journey through the various stages of the heavens in quest of the elixir of immortality that will revive his parents. The entire epic is, in fact, an heroic journey of self-discovery. The astrological calendar appears on some panels, with particular emphasis on earthquakes and volcanic eruptions, which must have been on everyone's mind at the time.

"The accused, kneeling before the mighty tribunal, could not avoid the sight of the dreadful punishments depicted on the ceiling. But if he raised his eyes beyond, just a little above the horrors of Hell to the panels of Heaven, he could perhaps find some solace."

Idanna Pucci, *The Epic of Life*, 1985

SUBTLE MESSAGES
Before the arrival of the Dutch, the raja would go to the Kerta Gosa to consult with his priestly advisers. He would not have dreamed of allowing a criminal close enough to sully the purity of the Taman Gili. Perhaps then the ceiling paintings were intended as a subtle warning from lowly artisans to the raja himself. He, whose earthly power was such that a mere flick of the finger could have any pretty girl on her way to market thrust into his harem, would become as vulnerable as any other soul once he had crossed the bridge of death.

KAMASAN ★

About 2 miles due south from the central crossroads of Klungkung you reach the western fringes of Kamasan, the last stronghold of traditional Balinese painting.

BANJAR SANGGING. Close to every palace of Bali there is a *banjar sangging*, a ward for painters who work "by appointment" to the royal household, producing paintings, banners, flags, and wall hangings for ritual occasions. Only in the *banjar sangging* of Kamasan, probably the original such ward, has the traditional painting style of the "Golden Age", as seen on the ceiling of the Kerta Gosa, survived, so all traditional Balinese painting has come to be termed the "Kamasan style". Many styles of painting today are derived from the Kamasan style, in which figures resemble the two-dimensional puppets of the *wayang* shadow plays.

BANJAR PANDE MAS. The neighboring blacksmith's ward, or *banjar pande mas*, was the home of gold- and silversmiths to the court of Klungkung, and the finest examples of that semi-mystical craft are still commissioned here by the high priests of Bali. The two *banjars* are closely linked, sharing a common temple of origin (Pura Bale Batur), and households in both wards now practice goldsmithing as well as painting. Secret processes and techniques are jealously kept within the extended family.

KAMASAN PAINTING
In a Kamasan painting, the initial line-drawing in black Chinese ink, the most important phase in Balinese eyes, is performed by the master artist. He then passes it over to his children and close relatives for coloring, preferably with natural pigments. Once the coloring is completed, the painting is technically classified as *kasar*, meaning "coarse", and it is this type of Kamasan painting that is most often seen in shops today. To elevate the work to *halus*, the "refined" category, it must be returned to the hands of the master artist. Only he can be entrusted to trace with black ink over all of his original line-drawings, hiding slight smudges and runs in the coloring, but he may go far beyond that and add extra flourishes and new details.

GELGEL

For almost three centuries, before the move to Klungkung in 1710, Gelgel, immediately south of Kamasan, was the seat of power of the Dalems (later called Dewa Agungs). Most high-caste Balinese trace their ancestral roots to this out-of-the-way little village. It was here, in 1597, that Dalem Seganing entertained the first Dutch tourists who marveled at the size and magnificence of his walled palace. They wrote about the splendor of the royal processions and rituals, about his harem, and attendant dwarfs. He offered to send one of the dwarfs to the king of Holland as a token of his friendship. At the center of Gelgel, where the palace once stood, is the small but important temple Pura Jero Agung, meaning "Temple of the Great Palace". Far more impressive, however, and just as important to the kingdom, is the Pura Penataran Dasar (right), which stands just to the east on the same main street.

Here, as at Besakih, high on Mount Agung, the deified ancestors of the royal family are worshiped. During festivals the ancestors descend from the peak of the great mountain to take their seats on a raised platform. Upon it lie several natural stones, echoes of the megalithic origin of ancestral worship in Bali. Across the road from the Pura Jero Agung, shaded by a towering banyan tree, is a row of stone slabs arranged like a comfortable bench (above). Some scholars claim that these were originally megalithic altars, the predecessors of all temple shrines in Bali, while others insist that they are exactly what they appear to be, comfortable benches.

TANGKAS

About a half mile east of Gelgel is the village of Tangkas, most of which was destroyed, with considerable loss of life among its inhabitants, by the lava flow of Mount Agung's 1963 eruption ● *130*. The surviving part of the village perches on the edge of a scarred landscape where volcanic rocks and sand are quarried (right) to supply the island's burgeoning construction industry. But it was here, on the site of the Pura Dalem Gandamayu, to the north side of the road just before the quarry, that the ancestor of all Siwa high priests in Bali, Danghyang Nirartha ▲ *156*, lived and set the tenets of Balinese morality. In the temple, an altar dedicated to him is tended by his descendants.

DALEM SEGANING OF GELGEL
"His wealth and magnificence astounded them. He lived in a palace in the walled town of Gelgel, surrounded by a harem of five hundred wives, fifty dwarfs as servants (their bodies deliberately deformed to resemble the grotesque gargoyles of kris hilts), and many noblemen."
Aernoudt Lintgensz, shoreman on the Cornelis de Houtman voyage, 1597.

207

There are several chilling stories about the 1963 eruption of Mount Agung ● *130*. One, told by the few who chose to flee, recounts how almost the entire community of Badeg Dukuh, rather than abandon their place of origin, set out in procession toward the onflowing lava with the effigies from their shrines in palanquins, banners flying, gongs playing, children skipping, and priests chanting, to meet their gods. In nearby Badeg Tengah, they gathered in the temple to await their fate. A survivor, watching from a distant knoll, could still hear the priest's bell and the *gamelan* playing as the first wave of lava burst over the temple wall.

ROAD TO BESAKIH

A place of power since people first organized society in Bali, Pura Besakih is indisputably the most important temple complex on the island. Located high on the slopes of Mount Agung, the axis of the Balinese cosmos ● *98*, it was, until earlier this century, a uniquely hazardous place to visit. It was more than just the physical hardships and dangers of treacherous ravines and dense forests that made travelers hesitate to venture there alone. Far more alarming were the psychic risks of abandoning the world where humans belong to approach the supernatural realm of the spirits. Today, a well-maintained road from Klungkung makes it only too easy to overlook such subtle dangers. Driving north from the central crossroads of Klungkung, you soon find yourself climbing steeply to Bukit Jambul (above), a narrow saddle surrounded by precariously terraced rice paddies and overlooking the entire little kingdom of Klungkung. From there the road appears to level out, but this is an illusion because you are still climbing steadily up the finger of a long ridge. You pass through several villages with splendid roadside temples, many of which are worth a pause, stations on the pilgrimage to Besakih ("Mother Temple"). Continuing through the market town of Menaga, you dip into a deep valley and cross a bridge over the headwaters of the Unda River, down whose course a destructive wall of lava flowed in 1963 ● *130* all the way to Klungkung and the coast. Climbing up the other side, you begin your final approach to Besakih.

BESAKIH ★

Pura Besakih (left) is not one temple but a vast complex of temples sprawling across the mountainside. For most visitors, the first impression (apart from the hot climb from the parking lot) is of the literally hundreds of delicately towering *meru*, their many-tiered roofs of black palm-fiber thatching pointing skyward like a fleet of rockets awaiting the signal for lift-off (right). Their purpose is, in fact, the opposite. Their

"BESAKIH IS BALI'S MOST IMPRESSIVE TEMPLE IN ITS AUSTERE SIMPLICITY AND ITS GRANDIOSITY, WITH HUNDREDS OF BLACK *MERUS* RISING FROM EVERYWHERE TO THE MISTY SKY…"

MIGUEL COVARRUBIAS, *ISLAND OF BALI*, 1937

structural core ● *107* is an unobstructed square tunnel down which deities, ancestors, and spirits can descend on festive occasions to take their places in the shrines at their base. Pura Besakih is not a launch pad but a landing field for the gods. The central temple in the complex, Pura Penataran Agung, is dedicated to the god Siwa. Pura Batu Madeg ("Temple of the Standing Stone"), approached from behind the Pura Agung and to the left (northwest), is dedicated to Wisnu. Pura Kiduling Kreteg ("Temple of the South Bridge"), over a bridge and across a gully to the right (southeast), is dedicated to Brahma. There are nineteen more temples spreading up the mountain slopes, each with its own purpose and ceremonial season, but the three dedicated to the Hindu trinity ● *46* are the most important. Their orientation in relation to each other and the mountain is reflected in the three raised lotus-thrones, or *padmasana trisakti*, in the second courtyard of the Pura Penataran Agung, with Wisnu, Siwa, and Brahma sitting from left to right, though some say seats are not assigned. The *padmasana trisakti* dates back only to the 17th or 18th centuries, though Besakih was a place of worship centuries before that. Strip away all the adornments and additions to the Pura Penataran Agung, which is almost definitely the original temple of the complex, and you are confronted with a site remarkably similar to the stepped pyramids of the megalithic era, Indonesia's earliest civilization. In several of the shrines are stones that appear to date back to those pre-historic times. During the 13th century, the kingdom of Gelgel made Besakih a state temple, residence of the deified royal ancestors, and it serves as such for most of Bali's other kingdoms, but it is just as important to ordinary Balinese. Almost every day village groups can be seen coming to pray and collect holy water to take home for their local temple rituals, or to pay their respects upon completion of the complicated cycle rituals for the dead. Each temple in the complex has its own annual ceremony and approximately every tenth year the impressive Panca Wali Krama, a purification ceremony for the whole of Bali, draws almost everyone on the island. The last one was held in 1989. Not even the Panca Wali Krama can hold a joss stick to the Eka Dasa Rudra (right), the rite of universal exorcism. Rudra is the wrathful aspect of the god Siwa, and his ceremony should be performed only when the *saka* year of the Balinese calendar ● *82* ends with two zeros, which is every hundred years.

EKA DASA RUDRA

During this century, the Eka Dasa Rudra has already been held twice, in 1963 and 1979. The first one of those was a calamitous error in timing, as the god immediately made clear. As the final preparations were being completed, the volcanic Mount Agung, which was believed to be not only dormant but also dead, erupted. Beneath the ash clouds and flying boulders of the deadliest eruption in Bali's recorded history, the priests valiantly pressed on with the month-long ceremonies, regarding the event as a message of change out of which some good would come. The lava flows, although passing perilously close to the complex, left Pura Besakih intact. In 1979 an Eka Dasa Rudra was performed again without mishap.

TEXTILES
In Sideman, there is a workshop where some of Bali's finest *endek* textiles are woven (below). At the workshop and in several other households, women weave excellent, and expensive, *kain songkets* of silk, with gold and silver thread.

ISEH TRANCE RITUALS
While living in Iseh, Walter Spies discovered a veritable three-ring circus of unique trance rituals, quite distinct from those performed elsewhere in Bali. Participants would take on the attributes of snakes, pigs, puppies, monkeys, evil spirits, and even brooms and potlids. It is said that some of these can still be witnessed at the Pura Dalem Iseh on the full moon after a harvest.

SIDEMAN FOOTHILLS

There is an alternative approach to Pura Besakih which allows you to explore backroads, whose surface condition can never be guaranteed, but the journey is worth a little discomfort. Just east of Klungkung you enter the village of Paksabali, famed for a wild trance ritual, the Dewa Mapalu or "War of the Gods" (above), held every Kuningan ◆ *300* in the Balinese calendar.

At the center of Paksabali, where the main road east takes a sharp turn to the right, there is what appears to be a village street going to the left. Follow this and it will eventually take you far up the slopes of Mount Agung. You pass through numerous small villages, built high enough above the river to have escaped the lava-flow of 1963, where boulders strewn by the eruption have been put to good use as doorsteps and seats.
SIDEMAN. This is the home of the hereditary rulers of several very traditional inland villages, some of which can only be reached by foot. Up some steep steps to the right is a pleasant homestay (guesthouse) with a view all the way to the sea. It is run by one of the current *cokorda's* wives and makes a good base for the many interesting and often rugged walks through the area. At the top of the ridge behind is the Pura Puncak Leluhur, the peaceful little temple of origin of the local princes.
ISEH ★. Just up the road from Sideman, the little hamlet of Iseh boasts one of south Bali's most dramatic views of the mountain. In the 1930's, Walter Spies ● *112* built a small house here (left), a refuge from Ubud's hurly-burly pace, and on its broad verandah he produced some of his most romantic Balinese landscapes.
SELAT. About 2 miles above Iseh, where paddies give way to dry mountain rice cultivation, the road ends in a T-junction. If you turn right here, you can follow the foothills skirting the mountain all the way to Amlapura and the eastern tip of the island, while a left turn takes you west through Selat, Muncan, and an idyllic valley to Rendang on the main Besakih road. Selat was less fortunate than Iseh in 1963. Once a large and prosperous market town, it has yet to recover fully from its near total destruction, and almost every building here is relatively new.

SOGRA

A tiny road, a low-gear grind, climbs from Selat toward the few surviving or rebuilt mountain villages above. Beyond Sebudi (the new Sebudi because the original rich agricultural village lies beneath 130 feet of lava and ash) you reach a temperate zone of what appears to be tundra but is in fact lava covered with a soft veneer of grasses and a few trees (right). Here the locals hack blocks of black volcanic stone for the building industry. Rounding a sharp bend where half a temple remains, you reach Sogra (which sounds ironically like *sorga*, the Indonesian word for "heaven"). Mostly hidden from the road behind stubby shrubbery and bamboo, Sogra is not very impressive but is probably the highest village on the mountain. A small temple where many people gathered during the eruption was left unscathed by the lava, but its inhabitants must have perished suddenly from the gases. The road now extends just beyond Sogra almost to Pura Pasar Agung. Twice as far up the mountain as Besakih, this temple is seldom visited though it is of great importance to all the people of Karangasem Regency, most of whom have never seen it. Perching on a rocky and pine-covered outcrop, it is the gateway to the home of the gods and ancestors.

MOUNT AGUNG

The shortest walk to Mount Agung's 9900-foot peak (below) starts from Sogra, and the view from the jagged crater rim at dawn, before the cloud cover has closed in, is undeniably impressive. But the ascent to the misty realm of the gods, except for rare ritual occasions, is regarded by the Balinese as disrespectful and dangerous. Several tourists have disappeared without trace. If you insist on flouting Balinese proprieties, make sure to take a local guide because there are many false dead-end ravines. You can improve your odds by bearing the correct offerings, made with your own hands and carried all the way on your head, by dressing humbly in white, and, above all, by going barefoot. Better still, leave at least the gods in peace and admire their mountain home from the realm of man.

SCENE AT SOGRA
Two weeks after the 1963 eruption of Mount Agung, a search party found the inhabitants of Sogra perfectly preserved under a thin dusting of ash: "…a mother lay back, resting, an arm extended towards her baby. The baby crawled towards her on hands and knees. In fond, puppyish attitudes, a group of boys lolled against each other, near where she was lying. Others seemed to be sleeping. Under a long roof to the left of the gate, the gamelan had been playing. How long had it been silent? A boy has slipped from his stool, still holding his gamelan hammers. The big round gong mallets lie still where they have fallen, and an older man peers curiously over a low balustrade as if wondering what has happened to make the child fall."
Anna Mathews ● *130, The Night of Purnama*, 1965

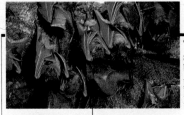

The main road east from Klungkung runs straight, wide, and fast past the black beaches of Kusamba, originally the principal port for the kingdom of Klungkung. Not far beyond Kusamba is the popular bat cave temple, Goa Lawah.

GOA LAWAH BATS
Vast clouds of Goa Lawah's harmless cave fruit bats (*Eonycteris spelaea*) flit out at night to feed on pollen and nectar. Regarded as the guardians of the temple, they are protected by the Balinese and quite easy to approach. They are not the only sacred creatures in Goa Lawah. The priests are happy to show visitors the large rock pythons, which coil luxuriously near the shrines and feed on fallen and wounded bats.

GOA LAWAH

One of Bali's state temples, Goa Lawah squats behind the beach gazing sullenly out toward the island of Nusa Penida ▲ 280. Its three chunky *meru* stand at the entrance to a deep cavern, their tiered roofs of black palm fiber stained with the droppings of the thousands of bats which dangle from the rocky overhang. Nobody knows how far the cave extends, it being taboo to venture too deep, but one story claims that it reaches all the way to Besakih, 12 miles away, while another tells that there is a submarine tunnel to the powerful temple, Pura Peed, on the facing coast of Nusa Penida.

PADANG BAI

Continuing east through spacious coconut plantations, you reach a fork to the right which brings you to Padang Bai, one of Bali's very few natural harbors. This is where the first Dutch fleet found shelter and today is the place to catch ferries and hydrofoils to Lombok and other points east. The beach-fringed village is a veritable melting-pot of Indonesia's myriad cultures and races, seafarers who came to trade and stayed.

BALINA BEACH

Back on the main road east, the sea is obscured by a ridge of small hills until you reach the village of Buwitan with its wide sweep of yellow beach, known as Balina (below). This beach is far superior to anything to be found at Candi Dasa, a few miles beyond, but there is less choice in places to stay and eat. A good argument can be made for staying on Balina Beach and zipping over to Candi Dasa for the multi-ethnic restaurants and nightlife.

East Bali

▲ East Bali

1 PURA BESAKIH
2 MOUNT AGUNG
3 TULAMBEN
4 TANAH ARON
5 SIBETAN
6 BALINA BEACH
7 CANDI DASA
8 TENGANAN
9 PURA BUKIT GUMANG
10 BUGBUG
11 BEBANDEM
12 BUDAKLING
13 BUNGAYA
14 ASAK
15 TIMBRAH

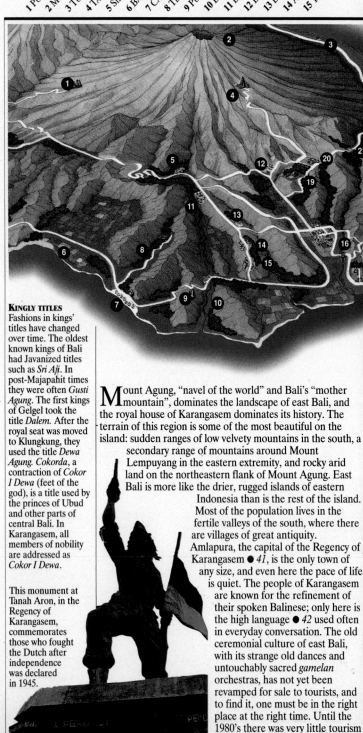

Mount Agung, "navel of the world" and Bali's "mother mountain", dominates the landscape of east Bali, and the royal house of Karangasem dominates its history. The terrain of this region is some of the most beautiful on the island: sudden ranges of low velvety mountains in the south, a secondary range of mountains around Mount Lempuyang in the eastern extremity, and rocky arid land on the northeastern flank of Mount Agung. East Bali is more like the drier, rugged islands of eastern Indonesia than is the rest of the island. Most of the population lives in the fertile valleys of the south, where there are villages of great antiquity.

Amlapura, the capital of the Regency of Karangasem ● *41*, is the only town of any size, and even here the pace of life is quiet. The people of Karangasem are known for the refinement of their spoken Balinese; only here is the high language ● *42* used often in everyday conversation. The old ceremonial culture of east Bali, with its strange old dances and untouchably sacred *gamelan* orchestras, has not yet been revamped for sale to tourists, and to find it, one must be in the right place at the right time. Until the 1980's there was very little tourism

16 AMLAPURA
17 TAMAN UJUNG
18 PURA KEBON BUKIT
19 TIRTHA GANGGA
20 ABABI
21 ABANG
22 CULIK
23 AMED
24 PURA LUHUR LEMPUYANG
25 BUNUTAN
26 MOUNT LEMPUYANG
27 SERAYA

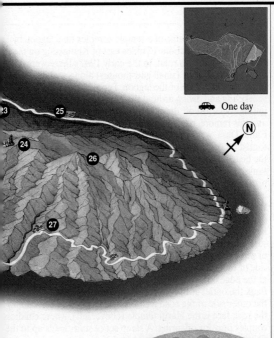

One day

N

KARANGASEM

The kingdom of Karangasem was established in the 17th century when a rebellious minister from the court of Gelgel, I Gusti Arya Batanjeruk, fled east with his wife and nephew, a small child. Batanjeruk was killed in Bungaya by his pursuers from Gelgel, and his widow sought shelter in the house of a high priest in Budakling, where she offered to help with the domestic work. It became her duty to go to market every three days in the village of Karangasem. There she met the local ruler who after a time asked to marry her. She asked permission of the high priest, who consented on the condition that her nephew I Gusti Pangeran Oka succeed his stepfather, which he eventually did. Within several generations, the kingdom stretched all over east Bali and as far as the neighboring island of Lombok. When the Dutch defeated Buleleng in 1849, it was with the help of the Raja of Lombok, A. A. Ketut Karangasem, and as a reward for this, the Dutch "granted" him the mainland kingdom of Karangasem as a vassal, although they had no legal title to do so. Less than fifty years later, the Dutch conquered Lombok, in their eyes automatically acquiring Karangasem as well. The house of Karangasem acquiesced.

in Karangasem, and what there is is still concentrated mainly in Candi Dasa, on the south coast. The usual route to east Bali is along the Denpasar-Amlapura road, which goes through Gianyar ▲ *199* and Klungkung ▲ *202*. The region can also be approached from the north along the east coast road, or across the southern slopes through Rendang, Selat, and Bebandem. All these roads lead to Amlapura, once the seat of the powerful Karangasem court.

215

SACRED GEOMETRY
In the article "Sacred Geometry on the Island of Bali" printed in the *Journal of the Royal Asiatic Society*, 1973, John James records some remarkable observations about the Candi Dasa temple complex. He discerned three principal imaginary lines aligning the temples with geographical features of southeast Bali: 1) an axis through the Shiva temple connecting it to the hilltop Bukit Glogor to the west and to Pura Bukit Gumang in the east; 2) an axis from the Shiva temple through the Hariti temple that extends precisely to the westernmost edge of the Penida group of islands; 3) an axis from the Shiva temple through the outlet of the lake in the southeast corner that extends to the easternmost edge of the Penida group.

BLOOD TYPE
A recent genetic study of the blood of Asian peoples revealed that seventeen people from Tenganan had a very rare blood configuration previously found only in a village in southern India. This, and certain rituals peculiar to both villages, suggest the Indian origin of the Tenganese.

CANDI DASA

Candi Dasa is the name of a temple complex on a lagoon by the edge of the sea about 15 miles east of Klungkung on the Denpasar-Amlapura road. In the early 1980's there were only a few simple *losmen* (small guesthouses) along a white sand beach on either side of the lagoon. People came for the snorkeling and diving around the coral reef and the islands of jutting rocks just off the coast. Then came the tourist boom, and this remote, romantic area, generically referred to as Candi Dasa, was transformed within a few years into a noisy tourist mecca, while the beach eroded at an equal pace. With the beach nearly gone, tourists no longer flock here in the same numbers, and the place is quieter now. Still, this is presently the best serviced area for visitors to stay in east Bali, and there is a great deal to explore nearby.

PURA CANDI DASA. This temple complex is found toward the eastern end of the tourist strip. Visitors will first notice the lagoon by the roadside extending to just a few yards from the surf. This spring-fed man-made lake may be considered a kind of watery forecourt to the male-female temples on the other side of the road, dedicated to Shiva and Hariti. A stone shrine at the edge of the lagoon looks out to sea. Two similar shrines flank the outlet at the southeastern corner of the lagoon. On the other side of the road a cliff rises sharply, and carved into the rock face is the Hariti temple (above, left), where childless couples pray for offspring. A steep set of stairs leads up to the Shiva temple, a small courtyard enclosing a *lingam*, the phallic-shaped symbol of Shiva. The temples, which have undergone numerous renovations, are said to have been built by King Sri Aji Jayapangus Arkajalancana in the 12th century.

TENGANAN ★

An unmarked road across from the Bali Samudra Indah Hotel at the western end of the tourist strip goes inland for about 2 miles to the village of Tenganan, the most rigorously aloof and exclusive of all the archaic cult societies referred to as Bali Aga villages ▲ *218*. The three hundred or so inhabitants of Desa Adat Tenganan Pegringsingan (as the innermost community is called) believe that their *adat*, or customary law, was granted to them by the god Indra in a special covenant, and they have protected the spiritual purity of their realm by an iron-clad obedience to their *adat* for many centuries. Despite its brittle exclusivity, Tenganan is a pleasant, tranquil place to visit, and the people are welcoming and good-natured. For decades, scholars and interested visitors have been attracted to this "living museum", many of them drawn by the magical *geringsing* cloth ▲ *222* woven by the women of Tenganan. In the recent tourism boom, the trickle of tourists has become a deluge, and the villagers' response, understandably enough, has been to put a ticket booth by the gate. Visitors are politely tolerated until dusk

In the Bali Aga village of Tenganan, traditional architectural styles are practiced with individual flair. This small window is in the back wall of a family compound.

when the village gates close and only those of the inner tribe remain within.

VILLAGE LAYOUT. The layout of Tenganan is a grid with three main streets running north to south. One enters the village

through a gate at the southern end. A broad double avenue ascends directly north toward the mountains. Single-story dwellings line both sides of the street, many of them functioning as shops or studios as well. Up the center are a series of communal pavilions for ceremonial gatherings.

Immediately to the right at the entrance to the avenue are two small temples where various female deities are worshiped. Across from these is the long *bale agung*, where the village elders sit in council making decisions about the social and ceremonial life of the village. Just north of this is the drum tower, which is beaten twenty-one times each morning to start the day. On the next level is the *bale petemu kelod,* the southernmost meeting house of the three boys' associations. The others (*petemu tengah* and *petemu kaja*) are on successive levels farther north. On the level between the *bale petemu kelod* and *tengah* is the council house of the western *banjar*, and next to that is the *bale gambang* (right) where the sacred *gamelan gambang* orchestra ▲ *221* plays during religious ceremonies. At the top of the avenue is a fine *wantilan (*community hall pavilion). Just to the east of this is a public bathing spring on a street running east and west, which leads to two more avenues farther east. At the eastern end of this street, a short lane rises to an imposing gate (below) which leads into the forest. This is the graveyard, most untypically situated on high ground in the northeast corner.

VILLAGE RULES
The calendar, social organization, and many of the Tenganese rituals are unique. Only those born within the village walls may become full members of the village and participate in its privileges and duties. And of these, only those who are without physical and moral defects can be admitted to the hierarchy of inner associations that begin with children of around the age of seven and conclude in the council of elders. Until the 1920's, for a Tenganese to marry outside the community, even into an exalted family of Brahmana, was reason for expulsion from the village. (A thriving village of exiles exists on the outskirts of formal Tenganan.) A strict protocol regarding marriages among kin groups has steered the population through the genetic dangers of intermarriage, and the people of Tenganan today are particularly handsome, looking very much the part of the spiritual elect they believe themselves to be.

▲ BALI AGA VILLAGES

Tucked away in the clefts of mountain valleys are the "Bali Aga" villages, whose way of life is distinctly archaic. The term "Bali Aga" is applied loosely to those original communities that resisted post-Majapahit kings and their Hindu-Javanese court culture and were able to maintain the ownership of their land and the authority of their local laws. Tenganan is an archetypal Bali Aga village, but there are a number of nearby villages that share many of its cultural features. These villages provide a glimpse of aboriginal Bali, traces of which still remain today in among layers of cultural influence from Java.

EARLY CHRONICLES

"Aga" means "mountain". The earliest chronicles of Bali describe migrations of gods, saints, and followers settling on the mountain tops. In one legend, the Hindu-Buddhist sage Rsi Markandya ▲ 186 came to Bali with settlers from the village Aga on Mount Raung in east Java. The unusually simple mandala-like image in the temple at right is suggestive of the particular Brahmana Buddhist cult still practiced in the village of Budakling.

LONTAR BOOKS

A village's ritual and customary laws, or *awig-awig*, are described in books of lontar leaves. The *awig-awig* of Tenganan are said to have been bestowed by the god Indra who created the village and the original ancestral parents Kaung and Keling, from whom all true inhabitants of Tenganan are descended. The villagers continue to practice traditional arts.

Lontar leaf books ● 42 of the Hindu epics are incised with fine drawings (below) and Balinese script.

HEART OF A VILLAGE

The heart of a village is the *bale agung*, the sacred council house. In a Bali Aga village, there are a number of other pavilions that serve as meeting houses with specific functions. Like the social structure, village architecture is organized around the elaborate ceremonies of the ritual cycle.

LOSING HEIRS

If a family has no heir in good standing to carry on with village duties, the land on which the house stands (above) is returned to the village and may not be occupied until another qualified village couple requires a house. It is becoming increasingly common for young people to marry outside the village.

VILLAGE GRID

In many Bali Aga villages, broad avenues run north and south on the mountain-to-sea axis ● *98*, while narrow lanes (above) run east and west. Within this grid there may be several *banjar* ● *96*, organized by clan groups.

ELDERS AT ASAK CEREMONY

One of the most distinctive features of Bali Aga villages is a social hierarchy of seniority, beginning with boys' and girls' associations, through the association of married couples, and headed by a council of elders. Priestly duties are shared by different villagers as they ascend through the ranks. For this reason, village membership is dependent on local criteria of physical and spiritual purity. In many villages, membership and rank are rewarded with a grant of land.

The arts of old Bali are embedded in religious practice. The archaic music, dances, and textile arts of the Bali Aga villages are rich with meaning, both for visitors and for the modern Balinese.

REJANG DANCE
Although the *rejang* dance is still found all over Bali in various forms, in the villages of east Bali the headgear and ceremonial dress are especially elaborate. Accompanying the *rejang* dance is the iron-keyed *gamelan selonding*, still found in a number of Bali Aga villages. It is fiercely sacred, said to be the body of a god.

WEAVING IN TENGANAN
Traditional crafts serve religious functions. The famous and very rare *geringsing* cloth ▲ 222, woven only in Tenganan, is worn by the Tengananese on ritual occasions and according to an extremely complex code of ceremonial dress.

RITUAL BATTLES
Found in various forms in a number of old Bali villages in Karangasem, ritual battles take place during the course of major ceremonies. This is not dancing, but ritually sanctioned fights (right), accompanied and controlled by the pounding of ancient *gamelan*.

SACRED SOURCES
According to an island-wide ruling by the religious authorities, the *rejang* is one of a number of sacred dances (*wali*) that may not be presented for commercial purposes. But its derivative, the "welcome dance" or *penyembrahma*, is the standard opening number for temple festival programs and tourist performances, and it is the first dance that modern Balinese little girls learn.

BARIS IN BUNGAYA
There is a great variety of sacred *baris* dances that prefigure the modern *baris*, which is performed as a virtuoso solo. "*Baris*" means "line, file", and sacred *baris* is performed by a group of men in ranks, sometimes splitting into opposing armies. As in the *rejang*, the dance is simple and repetitive. The men carry sacred paraphernalia in the form of weapons and other symbols of magical strength.

GAMELAN GAMBANG
All *gamelan* are sacred to varying degrees. In conservative societies such as those of the Bali Aga, *gamelan* have a stark ritual context. The *gamelan gambang* ● 62 is composed of four wooden-keyed xylophones played with Y-shaped mallets in each hand, and completed with a pair of seven-keyed bronze xylophones to carry the melody.

Throughout the Indonesian archipelago, occult power and meaning have traditionally been woven into cloth and encoded in design patterns, generating textiles of extraordinary beauty and complexity. In Bali, the term *payasan*, meaning "ornamentation" or "dressing-up", is used loosely to refer to the adornment of effigies, actors, and ordinary people, as well as statues, holy books, temples, and sometimes even trees. To dress up is in itself an act of reverence. The occult impulse to wrap people and things in ritually significant cloth accounts for much of the splendor of Bali's ceremonies.

GERINGSING
The *geringsing* cloth of Tenganan (above) is the only type of textile in Indonesia woven with the laborious double *ikat* technique. The pattern is dyed into both the warp and the weft threads. The dyeing process takes many months. Great skill is required in the weaving to bring the pattern of warp and weft into an exact meeting. *Geringsing* is woven on a continuous warp loom, and the uncut cloth is regarded as particularly sacred.

PRADA

The Balinese have a long tradition of painting on cloth, and the richest expression of this is painting with gold. *Prada* cloth is a requisite ingredient in the copious dress of Balinese theater. It is also used to adorn temple pavilions, ceremonial parasols, and ordinary mortals during life rites, such as tooth filings and weddings ● 52.

SONGKET

Gold is the emblem of kings as representatives of the sun, and in Bali the weaving of gold thread is a skill that is still preserved among royal women. In the relatively egalitarian era of present-day Bali, anyone who can afford a *songket* sash (below) or hip cloth may wear it.

POLENG

The Hindu notion of a revolving play of opposites is expressed in the harsh elegance of the black-and-white checkered *poleng* cloth. The totemic power of certain ambivalently charged objects is held under wraps of *poleng*.

ENDEK

The most widely produced cloth in Bali is *endek* (below), a form of the "single *ikat*" process in which the pattern is made by resist-dyeing the threads of the warp or the weft; *endek* is a weft *ikat* technique.

MORE BALI AGA VILLAGES

The drive from Candi Dasa to Amlapura is only about 8 miles east along the main road, but one may also arrive by way of an interesting inland detour, through a series of Bali Aga villages, that need not take more than a couple of leisurely hours. At the eastern end of Candi Dasa, the road suddenly leaves the coast and winds sharply upward across a range of cool green hills. The road then descends quickly into a broad valley. On the right (to the south) is the sea, and to the left is a gently cultivated landscape of rice fields, much of which is owned by the village of Tenganan and worked by the people inhabiting the eastern range of hills.

BUGBUG. Crossing the floor of the valley (above), the village of Bugbug (its administrative name is Perasi) is soon reached, whose village gates lie just to the left of the main road. Although Bugbug is a lowland coastal village, it is an interesting example of a Bali Aga village. To explore Bugbug, it is best to park by the roadside and enter the village on foot. The broad main road leads past small shops and a number of public pavilions. About halfway up the main street is an imposing square occupied by the village's *bale agung* and associated pavilions. At the end of the main street is another square, with the Pura Puseh and Pura Pasek facing each other. A few miles east of Bugbug, a secondary road on the left heads uphill into a luscious ripple of hills. Along the spine of this ridge of hills is a strip of Bali Aga villages through Timbrah, Asak, and Bungaya. These are not as strictly conserved as Tenganan, but there are clear signals of Bali Aga culture in each of these villages that an observant visitor may detect.

TIMBRAH. The southernmost village along this spine, Timbrah, has a long village center with a number of pavilions arrayed around the *bale agung* on the east side of the road. The public pavilions are neatly signposted in Balinese characters.

ASAK. Several miles north of Timbrah is Asak, famous for its *gamelan gambang* ● 62. The main road leads into Asak

On the roads between the Bali Aga villages, there are a number of small brickworks where mud bricks are baked under heaps of rice husks (above).

between the Pura Segara, or sea temple, and the Pura Dalem Alit, where certain chthonian forces are honored. The *bale agung* of Asak is located inside the Pura Bale Agung in the center of the village. This temple is the true center of Asak's village life. It is here that the village council meets and the principal deities are honored. The temple includes the communal kitchen for preparing ritual feasts and the three *gamelan* orchestras ● *64: gamelan gong, gamelan selonding,* and *gamelan gambang;* each in their own pavilions. At the northern part of the village are the Pura Puseh, and Asak's oldest temple, the simple Pura Muter. Along the east side of the road the village is a series of clan temples, the two northernmost belonging to the *Pasek* and *Pulasari* clans.

BUNGAYA. Continuing north, you soon come to the village of Bungaya. A one-way system directs the traffic around the village walls and leads to a pleasant square at the north end of the village where there is a small market and some very agreeable *warung*. Bungaya is remarkable for being one of the few, perhaps the only, Bali Aga village to include *Triwangsa* (Indic-Javanese castes) among its village membership.

BEBANDEM. About 3 miles north of Bungaya the road ends in the town of Bebandem, where every three days (*Benang Tegeh* in the Balinese calendar) there is a large market, including a cattle market.

OTHER EXCURSIONS

From Bebandem one may proceed southeast toward Amlapura or make several more side trips. A short drive west on the main road to Rendang brings you into the cool hills around Sibetan, where the countryside is dark with plantations of spiky *salak*, snakeskin fruit trees (*Salacca edulis*).

BUDAKLING. Returning toward Bebandem, a small road goes north to Budakling, a pleasant village known best for its Brahmana Buda families. Budakling has a number of gold and silversmiths, and many blacksmiths.

TANAH ARON. Toward the eastern end of Budakling there is a small road that winds north past the Pura Puseh then heads through open country toward Mount Agung and the area called Tanah Aron. The road ends at a monument on the mountain's flank. Panels of bas-relief (below) recount scenes of heroism of the guerillas led by Ngurah Rai resisting the Dutch after independence was declared in 1945. From here there is an immense vista over southern Karangasem and east to Lombok. From Budakling a road south through the village of Dukuh comes eventually to Amlapura.

Blacksmiths from villages around Bebandem come to the large market to show their wares. Some provide their smithing services on the spot.

1937 DIARY ENTRY
American dancer Katharane Mershon kept a diary of her 1937 visit to the Puri Kanginan, published in her book *Seven Plus Seven: Mysterious Life-Rituals in Bali*. Her entry upon arrival at the palace records her delight in accommodation which consisted of a private sleeping room, a bath, and a kitchen. "To show to what extent [the Raja] had extended himself to please his guests, my kitchen had plates and utensils of non-Balinese origin, soda water in bottles, tinned jam, butter (not used by the Balinese), tinned milk, canned corn beef, (Libby's!) tea, sugar, European vegetables – potatoes, carrots, cabbage – as well as a great variety of Balinese ones. Bread and cookies were provided from the prince's palace. A small boy was assigned to carry water for us..."

Amlapura, formerly called Karangasem, is the regional capital from which the present-day Regency of Karangasem is administered. It is a modest little town, but there are numerous reminders here and in the surrounding countryside of the former grandeur of the Karangasem dynasty.

TIRTHA GANGGA

The water palace at Tirtha Gangga (left), about 4 miles northwest of Amlapura, was built in 1948 by the last raja of Karangasem, A. A. Ngurah Ketut Karangasem, in a series of formal pools fed by a sacred spring. The eruption of Mount Agung in 1963, which buried much of the neighboring village of Subagan, badly damaged Tirtha Gangga. It has been gradually restored, and is open to the public for a small fee. A small hamlet of tourist accommodations and eating places has grown up here, but the main attraction is the swimming, which is permitted in several designated pools: a large one open to anyone, and a smaller one closer to the spring, for which an additional admission fee is charged. The water is indescribably refreshing, a swimming pool of holy water.

AMLAPURA

The town of Amlapura has a very small "downtown" quarter along the southern end where new three-story buildings shade the alleyways of the market. The administrative complexes are in the north, and at the heart of the town are several large *puri* (below) belonging to the still extensive Karangasem royal family. Only one, Puri Kanginan, is open to the public.

PURI KANGINAN. To get to Puri Kanginan, follow the one-way street around the town until you reach on the eastern side, heading south. About halfway down this street on the left is the Puri Kanginan, the seat of the ruling branch of the dynasty since around the beginning of the 18th century. The original palace, Amlarajja, now called Puri Kelodan, is one block farther south on the right, and the walls of several other *puri* are visible

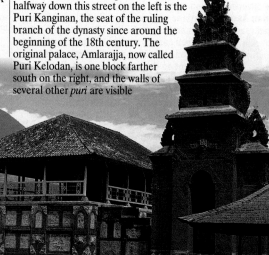

Signpost to the Ujung pleasure gardens.

nearby. Puri Kanginan is entered through a gate and a small forecourt where, according to the information sheet, "the rooms on the right and left are reserved for invited guests". It may have been here that the American dancer and student of Balinese ritual Katharane Mershon stayed in 1937 when she was a guest of the raja at the great Maligya, the splendid ceremony completing the deification of the royal deceased. The secondary courtyard, open to the public for a small fee, is an intermediary space leading to the great inner courtyard, the *pièce de résistance* of palace rejuvenation. Its main feature is a formal lake, in the middle of which is a large pavilion. This part of the inner courtyard is closed to the public, but visitors are encouraged to wander about the mansion-like Bale Maskerdam where the decoration is European.

ARCHITECTURE
The present architecture of the Puri Kanginan was completed after 1894 under the last raja, whom the Dutch appointed governor of Karangasem after their capture of Lombok. It is a revealing mix of notions of glamor at the twilight of Karangasem's royal rule. Years later, time lends a harsher light.

UJUNG

About 2½ miles southeast of Amlapura, near the village of Ujung on the road to Seraya, are the ruins of a vast royal pleasure garden (right), built in 1919 and suggestive of a kind of esthetic delirium on the part of royal Karangasem at the beginning of the 20th century.

PURA BUKIT KEBON

About ½ mile before Ujung, a secondary road heads directly north, and after about 5 miles comes to the quiet hill temple Pura Bukit Kebon. This temple, which belongs to the royal family of Karangasem, honors a child born to a princess of the fifth generation of the dynasty. The father, she said, was the god of Mount Agung. The baby was given the godly name Ida Bhatara Alit Sakti in honor of his divine parent, and his childhood was full of magical accomplishments. When he was grown to be a young man, he asked that a house be built for himself and his mother on Bukit Kebon, and when the house was ready, they all set out in a procession. The princess cut a walking staff from a kepuh tree and walked ahead with her son. Soon the two were far ahead and disappeared from sight. When the procession arrived at the Bukit, the kepuh staff was planted in the ground and mother and son were gone, absorbed directly into heaven. The sapling grew into a great tree, and the house became a temple where the deified mother and son are still venerated. The kepuh tree (below) planted by the mother stands in the middle of the single courtyard of the temple. A second kepuh, from a cutting of the original, is on the left as one enters the temple; a banyan is on the right. The handsome *bale* at the center of the northern wall is the site of the house. The flat stone nearby is said to be where mother and son achieved their miraculous death.

TAMAN UJUNG
The bas-reliefs on the surviving pavilions of the Ujung pleasure garden (above) show the same elongated style found in reliefs in the Puri Kanginan. They do not appear to have been carved (or modeled) by Balinese. This is unusual; the great architectural enterprises of princes are traditional sources of instigation and support for Balinese artisans, and there is something poetic about the collapse of this vast, effete fantasy park, another victim of Mount Agung in 1963.

227

CIRCLING MOUNT LEMPUYANG

Mount Lempuyang is the easternmost mountain of Bali, and its eastern flanks drop far into the sea. A narrow paved road goes around the mountain on a drive that is arduous and exciting, perhaps best experienced on a motorcycle with good brakes, a comfortable saddle, and a full tank. The sun beats hard on this dry country, and it is astonishing to see that the steep mountainsides are starting to be farmed, carefully terraced with volcanic rock and planted with saplings, in a heroic effort to reclaim the land. North of Mount Lempuyang the coast becomes a series of little bays where fishermen beach their boats. In the villages of Jemeluk, Bunutan, and Amed there is accommodation for tourists; there will probably be more in the next year as word gets out about the fine snorkeling and diving here. At Culik the road joins the main coastal road for the very long drive north. From Amlapura to Singaraja is 60 miles on the principal road that passes Mount Lempuyang on the west through the town of Abang and a beautiful valley which leads to Culik.

NORTH OF CULIK

North of Culik the country is dry and harsh, ravaged by the 1963 eruption of Mount Agung, which towers over all (right). Yet even here there is farming, particularly citrus trees and cashews. The lontar palm (*Borassus flabellifer*) also grows here.

TULAMBEN. About 6 miles north of Culik is the unremarkable-looking village of Tulamben, famous for its offshore wreck of the US Liberty-class warship, torpedoed by the Japanese on January 11, 1942, in the Lombok Strait. Attempts to rescue the ship were abandoned when it was found that she was taking on too much water, and she was beached at Tulamben. Shocks from the 1963 eruption broke her in half and left the wreck in the present location, about 30 yards from the shore, now an underwater city of a great variety of fish. This has become one of the most celebrated dive sites in Bali.

Along the northeast coast of Bali, many people make their living from fishing and processing salt. A water bucket made from lontar leaves (above) is used by the salt makers.

AXIAL TEMPLE
Pura Luhur Lempuyang, on the slopes of Mount Lempuyang, is one of Bail's six "axial" temples (*sadkahyangan*), points of power relating to the cardinal directions ● *99*. There is considerable variation among Balinese accounts of just which temples these are; and there are also mandalas of three, four, five, and nine axial temples, but Pura Lempuyang figures in all of them.

LONTAR PALM
The dried leaves of the lontar palm (right) are remarkably durable and can be incised to make manuscripts ● *42*. The other important use of the lontar is for *tuak* (palm juice), which is tapped from the unopened palm flower and may be either drunk directly or boiled to form a dark sugar.

NORTH BALI

▲ NORTH BALI

1 MOUNT AGUNG
2 LAKE BATUR
3 KINTAMANI
4 UBUD
5 SEMBIRAN
6 TEJAKULA
7 PURA PONJOK BATU
8 AIR SANIH
9 DENPASAR
10 LAKE BRATAN
11 PURA ULUN DANU BRATAN

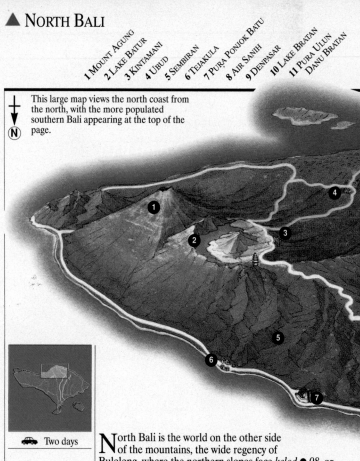

This large map views the north coast from the north, with the more populated southern Bali appearing at the top of the page.

N

🚗 Two days

This 1920's photo of Sangsit's Pura Beji shows north Bali's rococo style of temple carving.

North Bali is the world on the other side of the mountains, the wide regency of Buleleng, where the northern slopes face *kelod* ● *98,* or downstream, looking out through dusty radiance over the gentle Java Sea. This is a region of geographical superlatives. It has the wildest mountains, the richest farmers, the most waterfalls, and more dolphins to be seen than in any other regency in Bali. Buleleng also has some of the most vigorous music, oldest archeological remains, and most hair-raising temple carvings on the island, as well as a university, Bali's only Buddhist monastery, and the world's only public library

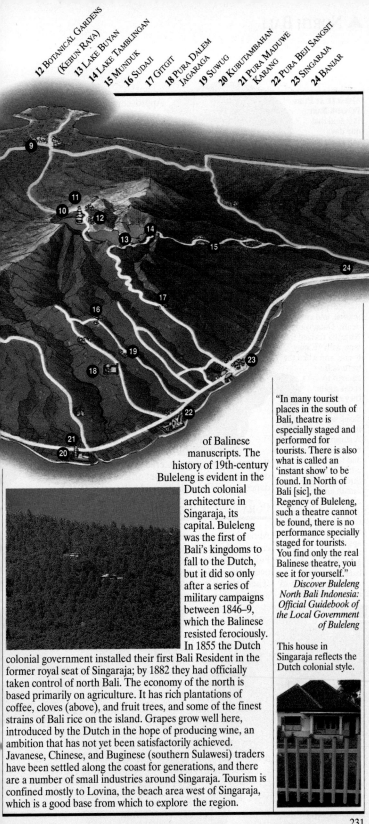

of Balinese manuscripts. The history of 19th-century Buleleng is evident in the Dutch colonial architecture in Singaraja, its capital. Buleleng was the first of Bali's kingdoms to fall to the Dutch, but it did so only after a series of military campaigns between 1846–9, which the Balinese resisted ferociously. In 1855 the Dutch colonial government installed their first Bali Resident in the former royal seat of Singaraja; by 1882 they had officially taken control of north Bali. The economy of the north is based primarily on agriculture. It has rich plantations of coffee, cloves (above), and fruit trees, and some of the finest strains of Bali rice on the island. Grapes grow well here, introduced by the Dutch in the hope of producing wine, an ambition that has not yet been satisfactorily achieved. Javanese, Chinese, and Buginese (southern Sulawesi) traders have been settled along the coast for generations, and there are a number of small industries around Singaraja. Tourism is confined mostly to Lovina, the beach area west of Singaraja, which is a good base from which to explore the region.

"In many tourist places in the south of Bali, theatre is especially staged and performed for tourists. There is also what is called an 'instant show' to be found. In North of Bali [sic], the Regency of Buleleng, such a theatre cannot be found, there is no performance specially staged for tourists. You find only the real Balinese theatre, you see it for yourself."

Discover Buleleng North Bali Indonesia: Official Guidebook of the Local Government of Buleleng

This house in Singaraja reflects the Dutch colonial style.

MIRACLE AT PURA PONJOK BATU

It is said that one day, sometime in the 16th century, the Javanese priest Danghyang Nirartha ▲ 156 stopped here to sit on the rocks, admire the sea and compose a bit of poetry when suddenly he saw a *prahu* approaching with a broken mast. The boat landed on the beach, and he saw that the seven crew members were starved, parched, seasick, and close to death. Danghyang Nirartha revived the crew with his holy magic, and when they were well enough to speak again, they explained that they were Sasak sailors from Lombok. A storm had broken their mast, and they had been adrift in the Lombok Strait for over a month and had lost all hope of survival. The priest bid them to drink from a spring that suddenly appeared in the rock, and the next day he guided them safely back to Lombok, even though they had no mast and sail.

Approaching the north by the east coast road, one skirts the desolate flanks of Mount Agung through country still ravaged from the volcano's eruption in 1963, but the beauty of the sea on the right is of some solace.

TEJAKULA ★

The first main settlement on entering north Bali from the east is the little town of Tejakula, with its sturdy houses hugging the coast. Near the center of the village is a short street to the left leading into a pleasant little square dominated by the white-washed public baths, formerly used for bathing horses. In the *banjar pande,* the neighborhood of silversmiths, a number of craftsmen make ceremonial vessels and traditional jewelry. For more than three hundred years Tejakula has been well-known among the Balinese for the brilliance of its dance troupes, especially the *wayang wong* ● 67. Both the masks and the performance are sacred and can be "awakened" only on ritual occasions; but in 1975 a secular *wayang* was created with a second set of masks for public performances, and the troupe has toured internationally. The popular dance *tari teruna jaya* (above) originated here, and its dancers from Tejakula are said to be unsurpassed.

PURA PONJOK BATU

About 3 miles west of Tejakula the road splits and circles a gentle hill crowned by the seaside temple, Pura Ponjok Batu (below). The temple, which overlooks a small projection (*ponjok*) of stones (*batu*), sits on a small, round hill, surrounded by a six-sided wall with three entrances. In the outer courtyard is an open pavilion and two very new-looking six-sided platforms, presumably bases for temporary pavilions during temple anniversary celebrations. The sacred, inner courtyard is a walled "island" within the main walls, and inside are a number of limestone shrines. On the crown of the hill is a small *padmasana* shrine shaded by tall trees. Across the road are steps leading down to a tiny beach, and next to that, hidden by a pile of black boulders and shaded by ceremonial parasols, is the holy spring. The north coastal road is lined for significant distances by stately tamarind trees planted by the Dutch, giving an almost ecclesiastical light to long stretches of the road, and one of the most seductive spots must have been Air Sanih (also known as Yeh Sanih), with its cold freshwater spring right next to the sea, before it became a tourist stop.

KUBUTAMBAHAN

In Kubutambahan, the northernmost town in Bali, one begins to see the outrageously carved temples typical of the north, and the Pura Maduwe Karang, the village temple, is a prime example. The temple is associated with crops, such as corn and coffee, grown on dry, unirrigated land. If one approaches the center of Kubutambahan from the east, the temple wall is on the right, facing a side street. Lining the front are three rows of larger-than-life statues, characters from the Indian epic *Ramayana*. There is a forecourt with a long pavilion on one side and then a grand inner courtyard with a massive complex of shrines, where the epic sculpture (above) continues in both statuary and carved reliefs. Children here will recite in unison, in English, full paragraphs of legend about the carvings. Across the street is a good *warung* that sells lots of traditional household utensils such as wisp brooms, mats, and clay water jugs. At the T-junction a few hundred yards west is the main road to Kintamani.

233

For four years the Balinese defended Buleleng from the Dutch from the hills around Sukapura. In the final assault, in 1849, it is said that Prime Minister Gusti Jelantik's wife and

her servants marched into the Dutch cannon fire, hurling their jewelry at the soldiers before stabbing themselves to death. To commemorate the martyrs, the people renamed the village "Jagaraga" (watch out for yourself), after the slogan of the resistance.

JAGARAGA

Between Kubutambahan and Sangsit, a well-marked road turns south into the foothills to the village of Jagaraga, the site of the heroic Balinese defense of Buleleng in the 1840's. The dazzling warrior-prince Gusti Ketut Jelantik, whose superior strategy kept the Dutch guns at bay until the final battle-unto-death, was declared a national hero in 1993, and has been claimed by the royal families of both Buleleng and Karangasem. Traces of the Dutch occupation can be seen in the relief carvings of the Pura Dalem Jagaraga (left), rebuilt after the Jagaraga war and renovated to commemorate the martyrs, but shriekingly vivid sculptures of Rangda form the dominant imagery of the temple. This temple, signposted "The Temple of the Dead", is on the left side of the road on the approach to the village. The articulate Ketut Suradnya of Jagaraga often gives tours of all the temple's details. If not, be sure to see the startling Singa Bersayap, a small but ferociously beautiful woodcarving of a lion under the roof of a small pavilion in the inner courtyard. Other more conspicuous aspects of this temple are the reversal of the gates; a *kori agung,* or closed gateway, leads to the outer courtyard and a split gate, *candi bentar,* to the inner courtyard ● *104.* Also unusual are the successive courtyards leading down, rather than up, to the inner courtyard. For those seeking a quiet cup of coffee, the village of Bebetin, about 3 miles up the road, has a cluster of

The Balinese portrayed the Dutch presence with humor as seen in many relief carvings (right) in the temples of north Bali.

friendly *warung* under a banyan tree at the village center. Thus refreshed, a traveler will be in good form to visit the *gamelan* smiths in the village of Sawan, about halfway back down the road to Jagaraga, and to receive knowledge about this nearly mystical craft from the energetic *pande gong*, Made Widandra, or one of his kinsmen.

THE ROAD TO SUDAJI ★

A few miles west of the Jagaraga road, and parallel to it through similarly gentle countryside, is the road to Sudaji, terminating after about 8 miles in this village famous for its rambutan and durian groves. Sudaji, with its colonial architecture, market square, and huge venerable trees, has a disconcerting and faintly European sort of charm. Halfway along the road is the similarly prosperous and seductive village of Suwug, known for its crafting of the *kendang* drums, an instrument in the *gamelan* orchestras ● *64*. An immense banyan tree (above, right) towers in front of the village's main temple, with little *warung* nestled in its roots.

SANGSIT ★

Back on the coast, in the village of Sangsit, is Pura Beji Sangsit (below), a *subak* temple; that is, it belongs to and is cared for by a rice irrigation association ■ *24*. Located about 200 yards down a small road heading toward the sea from the center of Sangsit, it was built in the 15th century on the site of a well. The temple is famous for its baroque architecture and virtuoso relief carvings. With its courtyards of clipped grass and old frangipani trees, it is a tranquil and refreshing place. The grand gate separating the forecourt from the inner courtyard spreads almost the entire length of the wall and is wonderfully carved on both the inner and outer sides. The principal shrines have staircases and turrets, and one gets the feeling here that worship has something to do with the sheer pleasure of building things.

GAMELAN-MAKING
In the casting of bronze *gamelan* instruments, the art of the *pande gong*, techniques are still used that are thousands of years old. Bronze scraps are heated in a pit crucible and then poured into molds for cymbals, keys, or small gongs. When the metal has cooled to a dull red it is hammered into its proper shape. Fine finishing is done by hand with files and abrasives. Tuning is the master's special art. The pitch of a key is raised or lowered by filing either the end or the underside, making minute changes in the thickness or length.

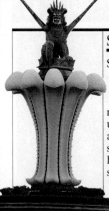

WINGED LION STATUE
Symbolism abounds in this well-known statue in Singaraja (the city's name means "Lion King"). The five-sided base stands for Pancasila, the Five Principles adopted by the Indonesian Government. The seventeen long feathers in each wing symbolize the 17 in August 17, 1945, the date of the Proclamation of the Republic of Indonesia. The lion holds a sheaf of corn with eight leaves and forty-five grains, symbolic of the eighth month, August, and 1945, respectively.

SINGARAJA

Singaraja, the capital of the Regency of Buleleng, does not bustle. It is a dusty, old-fashioned Asian town, slowed by the heat and isolated from the bombast of south Bali by the looming mountains at its back. Singaraja was once Bali's main harbor, but in recent years the harbor has become silted up. Part of Singaraja's languor is that it is no longer a port at all; the major export and import business has been recently shifted west to the more sheltered Labuan Celukbawang, halfway to Gilimanuk. Still, it has its bus terminals with their slow-motion traffic jams, exhaust fumes, and lamp-lit food stalls; and it still has its avenues, canopied by old trees and lined with dank colonial mansions, where bicycles and pony carts drift about in the aquarium light, oblivious to the motorbikes and little pick-up trucks darting past them. And it still has the full regalia of government, complete with military barracks, fervid monuments, and a number of Pertamina gas stations. There is much else to see as well. Coming into the city from the east, follow the one-way street system toward the hills, past the post office and up Jalan Gajah Mada. Nestled in the pleasantly leafy neighborhood to the right are such public institutions as the hospital, a university campus, and the art center. On the left is a large cemetery with brightly painted, particularly reptilian dragons guarding the stairway. Here there are some unusual graves (above), including that of an illustrious Chinese, guarded by lions and two life-sized black guards.

At the first traffic light, Jalan Gajah Mada intersects Jalan Veteran. To the right is a tourist information office that can provide a pamphlet on the Regency of Buleleng and a map of Singaraja. Next door is the modest-looking Gedong Kirtya.

GEDONG KIRTYA. Situated at Jalan Veteran, Gedong Kirtya has an unusual library of Balinese lontar palm-leaf manuscripts ● *42*, containing texts on Balinese ritual, healing arts, and magical formulas, poetry and chronicles. The museum was founded in 1928 by the Dutch Resident L. J. J. Caron for the collection and preservation of the manuscripts, and was named the Kirtya Liefrinck-van der Tuuk in honor of those two 19th-century Dutch philologists. In order to preserve these fragile texts , the entire collection is being gradually transcribed onto new palm leaves (left). In the 1950's a group of Dutch and Balinese scholars formed the Proyek Tik for transcribing this treasure into typewritten Latin script for greater ease of access. There are also Dutch and English books in the library, and a complete collection of calendars dating back several decades.

PURI SINAR NADI PUTRI ★. Nestled between the tourist information office and the Gedong Kirtya is a

Lontar manuscripts (below) are preserved at
the Gedong Kirtya in Singaraja.

traditional weaving workshop, Puri Sinar Nadi Putri, located
within the walls of the former residence of the king of
Singaraja. Here *endek* cloth of silk and cotton is woven on
about a dozen handlooms. Textiles can be woven to order, and
there is also a small retail shop. Returning down Jalan Gajah
Mada, one can regain the main
east-west road through the
town. The main shopping area
is in these small busy streets. In
this same neighborhood is the
Bugis quarter. Near the old
harbor, which is lined by a few
buildings from the Dutch
colonial period, is a Chinese
temple (below). The temple is
one of the few on Bali, and

evidence again of the strong impact non-Balinese have had on
Singaraja, a marketplace for seafarers for more than a
thousand years. Visitors cannot enter the Chinese temple,
which contains many antique pots and textiles, but a good
view can be found from within the compound. Jalan Achmad
Yani is the main road west out of town, heading toward
Lovina. The small Pasar Mumbul and a number of good
eating places are on the left. Or one can retrace the path
through Singaraja and head for the mountain lakes.

EARLY TOURISM
The shame aroused
by the *puputan* of
1906 and 1908 ● *38*
played a part in the
Dutch promotion of
tourism. They were
anxious to
show how
their new
"Ethical
Policy"
safeguarded
Balinese
culture.
Tourists
arrived at the
port of
Singaraja on
the government's
shipping line, KPM,
and were taken by car
to culturally
glamorous south Bali
via Munduk and
Kintamani. Early
travelers complained
about the crass urban
commercialism of
Singaraja and were
delighted by "the real
Bali" of the southern
plains.

The main road south ascends from Singaraja and crosses the range of central mountains between Lakes Bratan and Buyan. This admirably engineered road snakes upward through plantations of cloves and coffee, and there are many places along the way from which to admire the splendid vistas back to the north.

GITGIT WATERFALL

Barely 5 miles out of Singaraja is one of Buleleng's most ubiquitously touted attractions, 'the waterfall Air Terjun (below), at Gitgit. (Hard g's, by the way, or the Balinese will die laughing: *jit-jit* means "bottoms".) No amount of promotion can diminish the glory of this waterfall, but the approach with its multitude of kiosks is not what it used to be. Although Gitgit is virtually a northern suburb of Singaraja and less than an hour from Lovina, there is a hotel and restaurant just across from the ticket sellers, just in case.

MOUNTAIN LAKES AREA

The regencies of Buleleng, Badung, and Tabanan converge near the Bratan and Buyan lakes which nourish them. Lake Bratan, hooded on the east by Mount Catur, is dark and deep and only slightly ruffled by the roaring watersports industry on her southern shore that is associated with the tourist center known generically as Bedugul. The jewel of the lake is the Candi Kuning-Pura Ulun Danu Bratan temple complex.
CANDI KUNING-PURA ULUN DANU BRATAN. This is a major stop for the tourist buses, but it is too beautiful to miss. The outer grounds have been formally landscaped with clipped lawns and bold flowerbeds

CANDI KUNING
This small hexagonal stone stupa is one of the few explicitly Buddhist monuments in Bali, and the site was sacred for many centuries before the building of the present *candi*. Four Buddhas sit in niches facing the four cardinal directions, each draped in cloth corresponding with the color of the direction ● *99*, a Hindu touch which reminds one of the Hindu-Buddhist syncretism of the old Balinese religion.

Dewi Danu Bratan, like the goddess of Lake Batur ▲ *184*, is an agricultural deity whose consort is a mountain god – in this case the god of Mount Catur. She is honored by the rice farmers of Badung and Tabanan.

that reflect the elegance of the lakeside temple and its stately *meru* (below). Tourists are allowed to roam the gardens and through the outer courtyard, but entry into the inner courtyard is forbidden, though one may peer into it over the walls. The temple is said to be associated with the Bratan clan of the *Pande* caste, from which the lake takes its name. The goddess of the lake is honored at Pura Ulun Danu at the taller of the two *meru* on little islands near the shore (above).

BALI HANDARA KOSAIDO COUNTRY CLUB. The lake's other monument to splendor belongs to the kingdom of tourism. The Bali Handara Kosaido Country Club, whose split gate rivals any palace's, has an eighteen-hole championship golf course that is listed among the world's fifty greatest.

KEBUN RAYA. The road winds south around the lake past Bedugul and on to the Kebun Raya, or Botanical Gardens, with its 325 acres of tropical rain forest and hundreds of varieties of wild and cultivated orchids. The market near the Kebun Raya is famous for its fruits and vegetables. You can continue south on this road down the length of Badung to the coast, or turn back past the lakes and head northwest, taking the signposted "scenic route" at the crest of the mountain pass. This secondary road goes along the rim above Lake Buyan down to the left with Buleleng below on the right and the Java Sea far in the distance. Up here hydrangeas are grown as a cash crop. After about 3 miles, there is a T-junction. To the left, a new road (only partially paved) leads down to Lake Tamblingan; the last part, near the shore level, is a dirt track easily negotiated on a motorbike or jeep. The forest near the lake is full of staghorn ferns, mosses, hairy trees, and flowering creepers, and is now under government protection. The road to the right winds steeply down to the enchanting hill town of Munduk, through rolling valleys of coffee and clove plantations, around wealthy Banyuatis, joining the Antosari-Seririt road at Mayong. A turn toward the sea leads one toward the Lovina Beach area.

Ferns (top) flourish in Kebun Raya, and a nearby market offers flowers and fruit.

Resthouses in Dutch-style architecture are typical in Munduk.

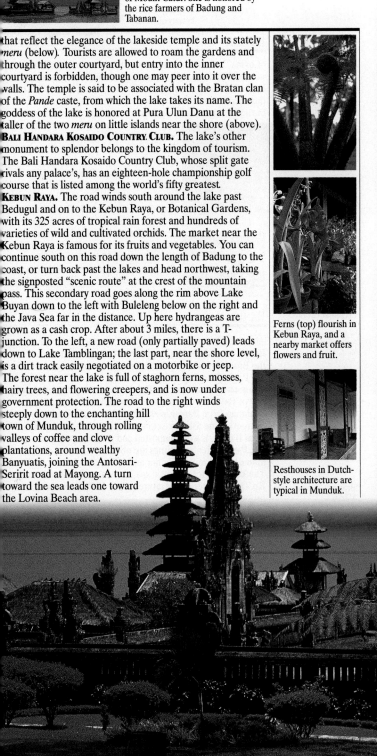

A young vendor's
bounty of shells.

LOVINA

"Lovina" refers to the outpost of tourism along the beaches west of Singaraja, actually a string of small villages and fishing hamlets. During the past decades, the bay of Lovina has been quarried for coral and intensively fished. The coral was burned to make building lime for mortar. An unexpected and

recent dividend of tourism, with its promotion of diving and snorkeling, is that now the coral is protected, and the local fishermen participate in a weekly voluntary cleanup of the beach. This is a good start, but the sea here, which is often naturally muddied by the tides and river silt, is still littered. There are some good spots, though. If you stand on the beach in front of the Nirwana Hotel, facing the sea, you need only turn right and walk about 50 to 100 yards along the shore to a pleasant cluster of little houses and *warung* with *jukung* (left) pulled up on the beach.

BANJAR

About 3 miles west of Lovina is the discreet district seat of Banjar, already on the maps for its two principal attractions: the Brahma-Asrama Vihara (Buddhist monastery), and the Air Panas ("hot" springs).

BRAHMA-ASRAMA VIHARA. The monastery is presided over by one of Bali's few Buddhist monks, Bhikku Giri Rakhita, a Brahman from Banjar, now elderly but still formidably energetic. The ashram, set into a hillside a few miles inland from Banjar, is well signposted and welcomes visitors.

AIR PANAS. The hot springs are not far to the west of the monastery; return to Banjar and follow the signs to Air Panas. The key word for this little spa is modesty: in fees (around Rp500), in water temperature (about 100° Fahrenheit), and in proper attire for bathing.

Brahma-Asrama
Vihara.

THE WILD WEST

▲ THE WILD WEST

1 BANYUWANGI 2 KETAPANG 3 GILIMANUK 4 PRAPAT AGUNG 5 MENJANGAN ISLAND 6 CEKIK 7 TELUK TERIMA 8 LABUAN LALANG 9 BANYUNWEDANG 10 PEMUTERAN 11 PALASARI 12 CANDI KUSUAMA BEACH 13 LOLOAN TIMUR 14 NEGARA 15 PUR

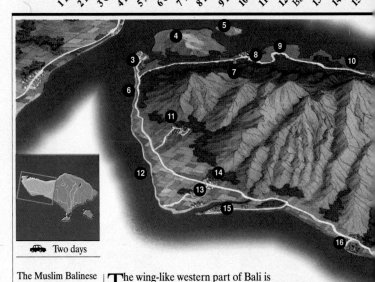

🚗 Two days

The Muslim Balinese in west Bali have retained elements of the culture of their Buginese ancestors, who began migrating here as early as 1653. A Buginese home (below), for example, has two stories with living quarters on top.

Early 20th-century Dutch map of West Bali drawn by W. O. J. Nieuwenkamp.

The wing-like western part of Bali is sparsely populated and little frequented by tourists. It is divided horizontally between the regencies of Buleleng in the north and Jembrana in the south ● 41, with most of the population centered around Jembrana's capital, Negara. The pamphlet published by Jembrana's Tourist Information Office slyly confesses that among the region's drawbacks are: no traffic jams, no noisy airport, and no discotheques. Indeed, there are hardly any roads, aside from the pan-island highway from Gilimanuk along the south coast, and few places to spend the night. The attractions are vast stretches of beaches, some very special temples, and the Bali Barat (West Bali) National Park. This 192,000-acre protected game reserve includes Menjangan Island, where there is world-class diving around its coral reefs. The park is also the habitat of Bali's one truly endemic bird, the very rare Bali starling ■ 21. Most of the people of west Bali are farmers or fishermen. An unusual percentage of them are Javanese or Balinese Muslims, or Christian Balinese. There is an important community of Balinese Catholics at Palasari before the hills north of Negara, and a village of Balinese Protestants nearby in Blimbingsari. The Buginese, a sea-faring people originally from Sulawesi, have settled around the southern deltas. The old kingdom of Jembrana, whose royal seat was in Negara, was among the first of the Balinese rajadoms to come under Dutch control at the time of the fall of Buleleng. Modern Jembrana seems to be pinning its identity to the practice of bull-racing, or *mekepung* (right), a sport introduced by the Madurese of east Java and now promoted by the local government for public entertainment and in the hope of luring tourists. Indigenous musical forms provide a different kind of excitement. For

example, *gamelan jegog* ● *63*, an ensemble of giant bamboo instruments, produces sounds so big and resonant that they are felt as much as heard. Traditional performance arts are being revived, and there are frequent scheduled performances.

JIMBAR WANA
The name of the western regency evolved from "Jimbar Wana", which means "Great Forest" of the west, understandable since more than half of the area is forested.

The huge bunut tree called Bunut Bolong stands on a slope that was probably once the foregrounds of the nearby clan temple Pura Pujangga Sakti. When the tree grew too big for people to go around it, they were obliged to go through it (*bolong* means "hole"). To cut down such a tree would have been unthinkable. The Balinese believe that all living things have a soul that must be respected. Certain trees, thought to have especially powerful souls, provide refuge for low-flying denizens of the invisible world. To unnecessarily disturb the spirits couched in nature is to risk unleashing supernatural disorder. Effigies such as the tigers at the shrine of Bunut Bolong (above) provide a local habitation for wandering spirits and a site for their homage.

ROUTES TO WEST BALI

West Bali may be approached from Java by ferry to Gilimanuk, from Singaraja along the north coastal road, or from south Bali along the main highway from Denpasar, but the most interesting way is from the north coast, through the western Tabanan hill country, the highland heart of which is the town of Pupuan.

THE NORTH-SOUTH ROUTE. A fine road runs from Seririt on the north coast to Antosari near the south coast where it joins the Denpasar-Gilimanuk road about 11 miles west of Tabanan. Ascending the hills (going south), the road twists up through plantations of clove trees tucked among wide valleys of rice fields. The luxuriant farmland (above) around Pupuan, pleasantly cool at around 2600 feet above sea level, produces much of Bali's most sought-after organically grown vegetables. Around Batungsel, just south of Pupuan, you will see many small plots planted with asparagus. Pupuan itself, the district's administrative center, is a hilly jumble of houses, shops, and little lanes. At the triangular junction near the market in the middle of town, a sign points west to Negara and south to Antosari. Both routes take you through beautiful country. The road to Antosari descends through what are perhaps the loveliest rice terraces in Bali, and then sweeps west at Soka above the surf of the Indian Ocean and follows the mostly deserted coastline for the next 34 miles to Negara. The other road from Pupuan to Negara leads you directly west over highland ridges before descending at Sepang through rain forests and plantations of coffee (above right) and cloves (right) to the coastal road at Pekutatan, 15 miles before Negara. The

highlight of the Sepang-Pekutatan road is at Bunut Bolong where the road goes straight through a banyan-like bunut tree. It is pleasant to stop at the *warung* here, take a look at the painted tigers at the shrine on the south side of the tree, and gaze into mountain jungles to the west. The prosperous villages to the south, Manggisari and Asahduren, are tidy and substantial, and the roadsides of clipped grass shaded by clove trees make for a pleasant drive. This road joins the Denpasar-Gilimanuk highway near Pekutatan. Some maps show other roads south from the hills west of Pupuan, meeting the Denpasar-Gilimanuk road at Surabratan and Pengragoan, but these are presently in bad condition. Check to see if conditions have improved before venturing along these roads. Traffic on the Denpasar-Gilimanuk road from Antosari westward thins out somewhat, mostly trucks and buses racing for the ferry. Nonetheless it takes you along some splendid coastline.

WESTERN BEACHES

For those traveling west in search of beaches, Balian Beach at Lalang Linggah, 6 miles west of Antosari, is rocky and the surf is tricky as along much of this coast, but the surrounding countryside is hilly pasture shaded by coconut groves. Nonsurfers may prefer to swim in the broad Balian River. There are a number of small beaches along this road. The next one with accommodations is at Medewi, about 28 miles farther west (10 miles east of Negara). There are long rollers here even at low tide, and the beach of grey sand stretches west as far as you can see. Candi Kusuama is another fine beach, about 8 miles west of Negara. The road is signposted, and the water here is calm enough to make it good for swimming, but there are no nearby facilities for accommodation.

MUSICAL BATTLES
West Balinese ensembles stage some frenzied competitions. *Gamelan jegog* ● *63* groups (above) often play together, or more accurately, against each other, in a sort of musical battle called *jegog mebarung*. The winner is the group that can make itself heard above the cacophony. Another competition, *kendang mebarung,* is a drumming contest between giant drums of up to 10 feet in height.

PURA RAMBUT SIWI ★

For those more interested in tourist sights than beaches, there are several stops along the road west from Pulukan. About 4 miles west of Medewi, near the village of Yehembang, a sign for Pura Rambut Siwi indicates a small road on the left near a popular truck stop. The road leads to a shady grove less than half a mile away, where the temple (above) sits on a bluff overlooking the ocean. There are a number of temples throughout Bali commemorating miraculous events in the life of the 16th-century Javanese priest, Danghyang Nirartha ▲ 156. This one contains a relic, a lock of the sage's hair (*rambut*) that is venerated (*siwi*). The story goes that when Danghyang Nirartha first arrived from Java and was traveling in the western wilderness on his way to present himself to Bali's king in Gelgel, he heard of a terrible epidemic in the village of Gading Wani. Danghyang Nirartha went there and banished the disease. The grateful villagers begged him to stay and settle there, but Danghyang Nirartha felt called to Gelgel, and left them a lock of his hair as a protective token. It was here that Danghyang Nirartha was given the honorific "Padanda Sakti Wawu Rawuh" which means "the newly arrived powerful high priest". The temple is finely built of red brick with exquisite *paras* reliefs depicting scenes from the ancient play "Arjuna Wiwaha". A particularly good sculpture of Rangda stands guard in the gateway facing the sea. Down on the beach there are several cave temples, one of the most important bearing a sacred spring. The temple art here is modern and crude. At the Pura Segara, about 50 yards down the beach, a magical tiger is said to have found a place to live in peace.

PURANCAK

Purancak is a small village just south of Negara, by the mouth of a riverlike inlet, and it takes its name from a temple there. The road to Purancak is found by turning south in the village of Tegalcangkring, about 5 miles west of Pura Rambut Siwi. There is a red brick *candi* and a sign announcing an "*obyek wisata*". You would be forgiven for thinking that the "tourist attraction" it refers to may be the deserted beach facilities at Delodbrawah, at the end of this thinly paved road, for there is little indication that you should take the paved road that goes off to the right (west) about 100 yards before the beach. After about 2 miles along this road, though, there's no mistaking the real tourist attraction. Banners and signs proclaim the Taman Rekreasi Purancak and steer you through a cow pasture toward the Kebun Satwa, which is Indonesian for "zoo".

TAMAN REKREASI PURANCAK. Jembrana has great hopes for the Taman Rekreasi

SETTLING THE WEST
Early settlers of west Bali came from the surrounding islands of Java, Madura, and Sulawesi. The sparsely settled west was, prior to the 1920's, a haven for people escaping political, economic, or legal trouble elsewhere in Indonesia. After 1920, more people settled there as a result of a transmigration program which encouraged people to come from the more densely populated areas of Bali. Others had religious reasons for moving west; Jembrana is home to the island's largest Catholic and Protestant communities ▲ 248.

OBYEK WISATA
Some travelers dislike the idea of visiting a place signposted as an *obyek wisata*, or "tourist attraction". They should bear in mind that, for many Balinese, tourism is an economic alternative preferable to stagnation and poverty or environmentally disruptive industries such as manufacturing.

Purancak. Besides the zoo and a bull-racing field (which already exist, to some extent, along with a few "facilities" pavilions), the government pamphlet mentions plans for motorized aerial sports. But for the moment, the place is one of pastoral stillness. The best way to experience the zoo is to purchase a ticket at the gate, and then go back to the *warung* in the parking lot and chat there with the charming Dayu Biang over a glass of something while you recover from the drive; then visit the animals. There is a cassowary, a pair of beautiful Bali eagles, some jungle fowl, and two little wallabies, mislabeled as kangaroo. Then there is a cage full of the monkeys you see all over Bali in the wild, a gibbon, three African lions, and some crocodiles.

Foreign visitors are likely to be more impressed with the fishing *prahu* at the harbor (top photo), a few miles farther along, at the end of the Purancak road. These are large, splendidly decorated sailing boats, some of them carrying twenty or more sailors. If you are lucky you may see them as they are heading out to sea.

PURA GEDE PURANCAK. By the river's edge just before the harbor is the temple from which the village gets its name. Pura Gede Purancak, built of limestone, is small and beautifully spare (left). It is believed that Danghyang Nirartha first arrived here in Bali and found shade under an ancak tree. This quiet and very sacred place may be visited if the priest is in attendance. There is a small forecourt and an inner court with a number of unusual looking shrines also made of limestone.

BULL RACING
Held after the rice harvest between September and November each year, these races feature Bali's handsomest and sleekest water buffalos. Two pairs run at a time around a circuitous track, hitched to a light, two-wheeled chariot. A jockey balances

precariously in the chariot, urging on his team. Decorated with bells and silks, the teams are judged for the splendor of their presentation as well as for speed. The gambling is intense ● 94.

Name spellings in Bali often vary ▲ 154. Purancak, Perancak, and Prancak are all variations of the name of one village.

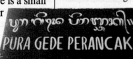

PURA GEDE PERANCAK

247

BALINESE CHRISTIANS
Northwest of Negara, in the village of Palasari, is the largest Catholic church (above) in eastern Indonesia. In the 1930's, Balinese converting to Christianity were sometimes exiled from their own villages. Many moved to Denpasar to live and work, creating an unemployment and housing problem. To

relieve the pressure, whole Christian communities, such as that of Palasari, were established in the wilds of west Bali. Nearby Belimbingsari is primarily a Protestant community, which settled in the forested west in 1939.

BALI STRAIT
The strait betwen Java and Bali is about 2 miles wide and 200 feet deep. Some tales say the strait was formed by a mythical king. In his desire to excommunicate his son, the king gouged a line with his finger through the ground. The earth parted and the waters of the Indian Ocean and Java Sea rushed in, forming the separate island of Bali.

NEGARA

As the administrative center of the Regency of Jembrana, Negara is an important town, but it looks less like a city than an airstrip. Most of the vitality of the region is found in the villages south of the town, where traces of Buginese, Javanese, and Madurese cultures are still evident. The village of Loloan Timur, about half a mile south of the market in Negara, was first settled in the 17th century by Buginese sailors from Treng Danau, in what is now Malaysia. The inhabitants have been "Balinese" for many generations, but they remain Muslim and there are still some traditional Buginese houses (above), long two-story buildings of *kayu tangi*, a kind of teak. Information about bull races and musical performances in the Negara area may be found at the Tourist Information Office in Gilimanuk.

GILIMANUK

Gilimanuk is a transit village serving the ferry between Java and Bali, a 25-minute ride across the Java Strait to Ketapang. There are a number of

budget hotels and lots of good *warung* and *rumah makan* (local restaurants).

WEST BALI NATIONAL PARK

The West Bali National Park, known as Taman Nasional Bali Barat, is a national forest reserve covering a range of geography from dry, ragged mountains in the northern and eastern parts to soft tropical rain forest on the southern slopes. The stated goal of the park is to maintain a balance between conservation and human needs, today and in the future. Portions of the park will be preserved as a wilderness resource. Other areas near settlements will continue to provide people with forest resources, including timber. The wildlife here includes the rare wild buffalo (*Bos javanicus*) and the nearly extinct Bali starling (*Leucopsar*

Detail of a carving (above) from a Buginese house.

CEKIK EXCAVATIONS
Since it was not difficult for neolithic man hunting in the primeval wilderness of east Java to cross the narrow Bali Strait, it is not surprising that stone adzes and pottery fragments have been found south of Gilimanuk at Cekik. Some one hundred burial places have been excavated, some containing funereal objects, tools ● *32*, and earthenware vessels, evidence of Bali's earliest human settlements discovered thus far.

rothschildi) ■ *21* as well as civet, leopard, monkeys, and several kinds of deer. In order to visit the park, you should buy a ticket at the park headquarters in Cekik (if you can manage to be there during the government office hours), or at the Labuan Lalang recreation center, on the road through the park toward Singaraja. It is obligatory to be accompanied by a guide.

TELUK TERIMA. Within the widespread park grounds, you can visit the tomb of Jayaprana, in Teluk Terima. Tickets can be purchased at the roadside by the steps leading to it, near Labuan Lalang. Jayaprana was a well-born orphan from Dencarik, near Seririt, raised by the lord of Kalianget. According to the songs and legends that have grown around him, Jayaprana was beautiful, brilliant, and pure of heart, and he married the lovely Layonsari, a humble girl from the village of Banjar. But the lord of Kalianget coveted the bride and he devised an evil ambush. He told Jayaprana that a band of pirates had landed in Gilimanuk, and sent him off into the western wilderness with a troop of men. At Teluk Terima, the lord's chief minister killed Jayaprana and buried him there. The lord of Kalianget then sent for Layonsari so that he could marry her himself, but she refused and committed suicide. Many Balinese women bring offerings to this shrine; it is considered a source of magical aid. It is not clear how the tomb of Jayaprana came to be a temple, but it is a busy temple indeed, with a rotating staff of priests or priestesses on hand to consecrate the offerings and guide the prayers of the petitioners. The effectiveness of the deity in granting wishes may be judged by the extraordinary number of clocks in the temple, gifts of thanks from people whose prayers have been answered.

PARK BOUNDARY
Within the West Bali National Park boundary (above) is the outcrop of land called Prapat Agung. Visitors can walk a 15-mile track along the coast of the cape, but as it is a protected area, no firewood collecting, fishing, or coral collecting are allowed.

249

As travelers continue east on the north coastal road, they will enter and leave the national park as the boundary snakes in and out to include the cape, Prapat Agung, and the nearby Menjangan Island, reachable by ferry from Labuan Lalang.

MENJANGAN ISLAND

The boundaries of the national park extend across the bay of Teluk Terima and include this small, unpopulated island and its coral reefs, said to have some of the finest diving in the archipelago. Day trips by boat and the rental of snorkeling and diving equipment can be arranged at Labuan Lalang.

BANYU WEDANG

Within the northern border of the national park is Banyu Wedang, which means "hot water". This hot spring is said to have healing properties. The place is an *obyek wisata* (tourist attraction), and an entrance fee is charged.

PEMUTERAN ★

About 6 miles farther east along the coastal road is the dusty village of Pemuteran. There is fine snorkeling and diving here, as well as accommodations, food, and a hot spring bathing place near a temple to the right of the road.

PULAKI

Several miles east are the imposing and recently restored Pura Pulaki (above, left) and Pura Dalem Melanting, both associated with Danghyang Nirartha ▲ *156*. The legends in Pulaki (formerly Mpulaki) are of a mystical nature, and the area is believed to be populated with invisible beings. A spring high in the cliff produces holy water that is highly sought after by people from all over Bali. The temples are jumping with monkeys who are very bold and naughty.

LABUAN CELUKBAWANG

About 10 miles west of Seririt, Labuan Celukbawang is now the main port for imports and exports since the harbor at Singaraja became silted up. There is a large wharf for big ships, and farther east on the beach you can sometimes see timber being unloaded from smaller boats.

MPULAKI
Soon after Nirartha arrived with his wife and children in Bali, they became lost. His daughter strayed into a village and had an experience there that so terrified and shamed her that when found, she would not speak of it, but begged her father to teach her to become invisible. He did so, and she became Bhatari Dalem Melanting. He declared that the people of the village should become invisible and honor her forever. The village became known as Mpulaki, *mpu* meaning "wise man".

Rice basket

1 ANTOSARI   2 PURA TANAH LOT   3 KERAMBITAN   4 PEJATEN   5 MELILING   6 TABANAN   7 YEH PANES

🚗 Four hours

Welcome sign at border of the Regency Tabanan.

The region east of Jembrana is as quiet and green as south Bali is noisy and commercial. The valleys streaming down from the western mountains into the regency of Tabanan ● *41* are among the most fertile in Bali. The rice terraces here, fed by Lake Bratan, are broad and serene, and in the highlands are some of the richest farmlands and natural vegetation on the island. Two of Bali's most sacred temples are found here along the north-south axis between the mountains and the sea: the Pura Luhur on Mount Batu Karu and the splendidly photogenic Pura Tanah Lot, perched on a rock in the surf. The old kingdom of Tabanan was ruled from Tabanan town, now the seat of the regional government and a model town of new-age Bali. Nearby Kerambitan was settled by a branch of the Tabanan ruling family around two hundred years ago and still maintains much of its royal ritual culture. The former kingdom of Mengwi, which lay between Tabanan and Badung and once stretched from Lake Bratan as far south as

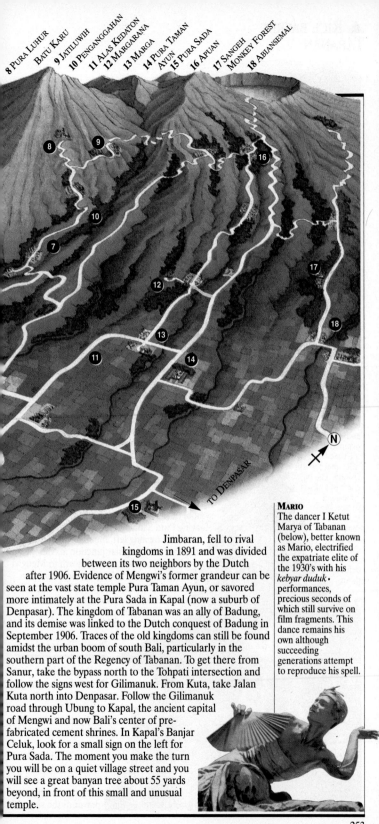

8 PURA LUHUR BATU KARU
9 JATILUWIH
10 PENGANGGAHAN
11 ALAS KEDATON
12 MARGARANA
13 MARGA
14 PURA TAMAN AYUN
15 PURA SADA
16 APUAN
17 SANGEH MONKEY FOREST
18 ABIANSEMAL

N

TO DENPASAR

MARIO
The dancer I Ketut Marya of Tabanan (below), better known as Mario, electrified the expatriate elite of the 1930's with his *kebyar duduk* • performances, precious seconds of which still survive on film fragments. This dance remains his own although succeeding generations attempt to reproduce his spell.

Jimbaran, fell to rival kingdoms in 1891 and was divided between its two neighbors by the Dutch after 1906. Evidence of Mengwi's former grandeur can be seen at the vast state temple Pura Taman Ayun, or savored more intimately at the Pura Sada in Kapal (now a suburb of Denpasar). The kingdom of Tabanan was an ally of Badung, and its demise was linked to the Dutch conquest of Badung in September 1906. Traces of the old kingdoms can still be found amidst the urban boom of south Bali, particularly in the southern part of the Regency of Tabanan. To get there from Sanur, take the bypass north to the Tohpati intersection and follow the signs west for Gilimanuk. From Kuta, take Jalan Kuta north into Denpasar. Follow the Gilimanuk road through Ubung to Kapal, the ancient capital of Mengwi and now Bali's center of pre-fabricated cement shrines. In Kapal's Banjar Celuk, look for a small sign on the left for Pura Sada. The moment you make the turn you will be on a quiet village street and you will see a great banyan tree about 55 yards beyond, in front of this small and unusual temple.

This drawing by
W. O. J.
Nieuwenkamp is very
likely Pura Tanah Lot
before the land
bridge fell into the
sea, probably during
the 1917 earthquake.
Currently, the nearby
Pura Batu Bolong
shows a similar but
less ragged bridge
caused by the sea's
erosion. Visitors are
not allowed to enter
the temples at Pura
Tanah Lot, and this is
fortunate, for they
arrive by the
hundreds everyday.
The intense
touristification of the
place is distracting,
and it's not finished
yet: a luxury hotel
and golf course are
planned nearby. For
the time being, it's
still a place worth
visiting. The big
crush of tourists
appears at
sunset; those
looking for
some peace
and quiet
should go
just
before
dawn.

PURA SADA ★

This old dynastic sanctuary of the
Mengwi kingdom dates from at least the
early 18th century. After the fall of
Mengwi in the 1890's it became
neglected, and much of it was destroyed in the 1917
earthquake. Now the temple is cared for by the villagers of
Kapal, and in 1949–50 it was restored by them with the help
of the Archeological Service of Indonesia. The beautiful split
gate leading to the first courtyard is one of the temple's few
earlier structures, badly cracked after the earthquake but
successfully restored. Visitors should enter the temple
through the small side gate next
to the house of the priest-
guardian. In the first of the
two courtyards is a large and
handsome pavilion where
visiting deities gather to
converse through trance
mediums during the temple's
anniversary. The three-tiered

roofed gate to the inner courtyard has a fine carving of Boma
● 54, crisply executed in low-relief directly in the brick. The
inner courtyard has several remarkable features, the most
surprising being the sixty-one mini-*padmasana* shrines
● 107 in tight ranks (above), captained by three larger
padma seats, and presided over by a single shrine
partially enclosed in a small pavilion. There is a tale
associated with these, of a boat bearing the ashes of
a Majapahit king from east Java in a bamboo tower,
accompanied by sixty-one retainers and three
leaders. All were lost at sea. The principal shrine
is an eleven-tiered tower of red brick (left), a
symbol of the lost bamboo cremation tower. On
leaving Pura Sada by returning to the main
road and turning left, the main road west is
rejoined. A triangular junction at Mengwitani
offers the option to head north to Mengwi
village, but if you keep to the left in the
direction of Gilimanuk to Kediri, a well-
marked left turn leads through a series of
small villages to the seaside temple of
Pura Tanah Lot.

PURA TANAH LOT

According to legend, the
temple Pura Pakendungan,
better known now as Pura
Tanah Lot ▲ 141, was
founded by the 16th-century
priest Danghyang Nirartha
▲ 156 out of sheer
adoration for the natural
beauty of the landscape
here. It's not hard to
understand why; the
power of the sea and

Carving detail from Puri Anyar,
in Kerambitan.

the abrupt drama of the coastline here are awe-inspiring. The little temple sits atop an outcrop of rock in the surf, guarded by sea snakes. Besides Pura Tanah Lot there are several other temples nearby arrayed along the coast: Pura Enjung Galuh, Pura Batu Bolong, Pura Enjung Mejaan, and Pura Beji, all of them presently in a state of disrepair, certainly due to the violence of the sea and wind which erodes the coastline constantly. The most picturesque of these is Pura Batu Bolong (meaning "the temple on the rock with a hole in it"): a wall of rock juts out into the sea with a tiny temple on the tip; a huge arch is carved out by the sea.

TABANAN

The regional seat of Tabanan is a town of prize-winning neatness. It is not yet organized for tourism, and although this in itself makes it interesting, it is a disadvantage where a place such as the *subak* museum is concerned, which was obviously conceived with visitors in mind and yet has recently declined into virtual non-existence. It is no longer the Subak Museum by the side of the road; it is buried in the "Mandala Mathika Subak", up a road that makes a switchback left-hand turn off the busy main road going into Tabanan. The complex includes several buildings for research and administration of the *subak*, the Balinese rice irrigation cooperative ■ 24. The museum in the basement of the front building is a simple room containing implements for rice irrigation and cultivation.

KERAMBITAN ★

The District of Kerambitan takes in a broad area of rice fields, but the town itself is a small village, most of which seems to be taken up with palaces. This is the seat of an old branch of the Tabanan royalty, and Kerambitan is all about palaces. The road to Kerambitan is about a mile west of Tabanan on the left. The Puri Anyar (left) on the left announces the arrival of the village rather suddenly. Across the street is the pavilion where the splendid *gamelan* is kept. Another palace worth seeing is the Puri Agung Wisata, renovated in a more modern style. Both palaces welcome visitors, and rooms are available. The main road continues south for several miles and ends at a black beach with wild surf. Returning through Kerambitan to the original T-junction,

there is a right turn which leads back to the main road, or you can take a very pretty (but badly pot-holed) road through the village of Dukuh Gede which meets the highway at Meliling, about 50 yards east of the road north to Batu Karu.

PEJATEN
A village north of Pura Tanah Lot, Pejaten is a center for the cottage-manufacture of terra cotta roof tiles and ceramic handicrafts. Great gouges in the fields attest to the natural clay structure of the soil here which is literally pressed into serviceable shapes and sun-dried in people's front yards. In recent years several potteries have been established producing ceramic ware that can be used indoors. Travelers can visit the workshops and buy things directly in the retail shops on the premises.

PURI NIGHT
Puri Anyar is the venue for "Puri Night", a festive evening that can be arranged with the family for private groups, and which includes an old-fashioned palace feast and a performance of Kerambitan's famous *Calonarang tektekan* trance drama. The *tektekan* is an exciting percussion orchestra of split bamboo and wooden bells, whose original function is exorcistic.

In the past, the crowning glory of many towering temple offerings, called *gebogan* ● *54*, would be a beautifully carved ornament. The time and attention to detail taken in creating these wood carvings were as much an offering to the gods as the *gebogan* itself. Today, rice or flour paste ornaments have taken the place of the wooden ornaments, a few of which are on display at the Bali Museum in Denpasar ▲ *268*.

The wooden stick extending from the base of the ornament would pierce the top of the layers of rice cakes, fruit, or other offering materials.

To create the ornament, the Balinese carved the face of a female deity, usually the rice goddess Dewi Sri, and then decorated it with oil paints, colored glass, or gold leaf.

YEH PANES
Yeh Panes, on the road to Batu Karu, is the well-advertised resort in Penatahan where the terrain starts to get mountainous. Here there are hot sulfurous springs and a spring temple. In the 1940's the Japanese built pools and channels, and the present resort is the third attempt to make this a recreational spa.

ATTENTION

I. THOSE WHO ARE NOT ALLOWED TO ENTER THE TEMPLE ARE:
  1. LADIES WHO ARE PREGNANT
  2. LADIES WHOSE CHILDREN HAVE NOT GOT THE FIRST TEETH
  3. CHILDREN WHOSE FIRST TEETH NOT FALLEN OUT YET
  4. LADIES DURING THEIR PERIOD
  5. DVOTEES GETTING IMPURE DUE TO DEATH
  6. MAD LADIES / GENTLEMEN
  7. THOSE NOT PROPERLY DRESSED
II. ALL DVOTEES ENTERING THE TEMPLE SHOULD MAINTAIN CLEANLINESS AND ENVIRONMENTAL CONSERVATION

MOUNT BATU KARU
According to some Balinese chronicles, Mount Batu Karu was first inhabited by the children of the god Pasupati sometime in November AD 191, about seventy years after the creation of the world. When the saint-architect Mpu Kuturan came to Bali in the 11th century, the temple at Batu Karu was already in need of renovation. He built towering *meru* and designed new shrines. In 1605, the temple was ransacked by Gusti Agung Panji Sakti of Tabanan in an excess of bravado, for which he was punished by a swarm of giant wasps. Since "Sakti" means "magically powerful", after this encounter he was obliged to change his name.

Almost as soon as you cross north of the Denpasar-Gilimanuk highway, the countryside of Tabanan starts to rise gently toward the mountains, growing steadily cooler and greener. High in the northwest is Mount Batu Karu, the geographical lord of the region.

EN ROUTE TO BATU KARU

Batu Karu can be reached from Tabanan town by way of Penebel, but there is a smaller, prettier road from Meliling on the main highway, about 50 yards west of the Dukuh Gede road out of Kerambitan. The Meliling road goes through the rice-growing villages of Ngis and Jegu. Current road maps are a bit misleading in this area. Generally, whatever road goes uphill is the correct one. In the pretty village of Penganggahan in Tengkuduk is the anomalous Catholic church St Martins de Pores (detail, above right). The congregation numbers six families. At the village of Wongaya Gede are signs directing travelers north to Pura Luhur Batu Karu.

PURA LUHUR BATU KARU ★

This temple is one of the six axial temples sacred to all Hindu Balinese ▲ 228. Standing in front of the newly restored gates, it may take a moment to appreciate that this is one of the most ancient sacred sites on the island. The temple (below) was renovated in 1991, and the grounds have been planted with the most modern civic landscaping, thus robbing it of much of its former mysterious quality. In the central temple courtyard are two large, long pavilions. The inner courtyard is small and neat, with three *meru* of three, five, and seven tiers in honor of the deified kings of Tabanan. The

lake below, to the east of the main temple, has a shrine in the center honoring the goddess of Lake Tamblingan and the god of Mount Batu Karu. On returning to Wongaya Gede, inquire about the condition of the road to Jatiluwih. This high, hilly road goes through prime vistas of rice fields, one of the island's best scenic drives. (Otherwise take the same road as far as the turnoff for Tabanan, from where one can easily get to Marga and Mengwi.)

MARGARANA

Coming from the north into Marga, you arrive at a four-way intersection. A left turn (east) leads to the main road to Bedugul ▲ *288*; a right turn leads to Margarana, the martyrs' graveyard. Margarana is a peaceful, solemn place commemorating Bali's last *puputan* against the Dutch, the fierce battle of Marga in 1946 during the fight for independence. The Balinese resistance was stomped out by the Dutch military machine, and on November 20, I Gusti Ngurah Rai, the commander of the nationalist forces, was killed with his ninety-four men.

KEDATON

From Margarana, it is a short drive to the village of Kukuh and the monkey forest Alas Kedaton and an unusual temple within it. Turn right on leaving Margarana and follow the road for about 2 miles south through the village.

PURA KEDATON. This temple is listed among the most important ones built by Mpu Kuturan, an 11th-century Javanese sage. It is remarkable for the fact that the sacred, inner courtyard is lower than the central courtyard and for two very old statues in the principal shrine.

ALAS KEDATON. The monkey forest has become a tourist site of the worst sort. The positive side is that there are lots of fruit bats that have found refuge in the trees. The temple and forest are bouncing with tame monkeys, not yet too mischievous, and there are pleasant guides to accompany visitors around the site.

WARRIOR'S MONUMENT
The tall monument in the main courtyard of Margarana is inscribed with the text of Ngurah Rai's letter refusing to surrender to the Dutch. (It was written in what was to become Bahasa Indonesia ● *42* and uses the old Dutch spelling.) The ninety-four *candi*-like stone markers, ranked with military precision, bear the name, place of origin, and date of death of each of the fallen men.

Traveling the roads of Bali, one passes through village after village which reflect many similarities in layout. The Balinese take great care to orientate their environment in accordance with their cosmology ● 98. In the layout of family compounds and villages, they observe

an imaginary axis that runs from the mountains to the sea. Enriching this is the Hindu concept *Tri Hita Karana*, which describes the three orientations of human concern for a balanced life: the relationship of humans to the gods, to other humans, and to the land. Thus the temples of origin ● *96* face toward the mountains, the houses and community buildings are in the center, and the graveyard and animals face toward the sea. The idealized village shown here is archetypal in its layout and in the civic and traditional elements listed.

1. *Pura puseh* (temple of origin), for honoring the ancestral deities who were the founders of the village.
2. *Pura desa* (village temple), for honoring the deities who guard the welfare of the village. The banyan tree is a traditional living landmark of the village center.
3. *Bale agung* (grand pavilion) ● *102*, where the village council meets. Often synonymous with the *pura desa,* or contained within it.
4. *Puri* (palace), the proper term for any *Ksatriya* ● *90* residence. There is usually one family whose traditional prestige is predominant.
5. *Sekolah* (school). Nearly every village has at least a primary school, and in every administrative unit there are secondary schools.
6. *Kul-kul* ● *106,* the drum tower used to summon villagers.
7. *Wantilan* ● *103,* a large square pavilion for cockfights and public theatrical performances.
8. *Pasar* (market).
9. *Bale banjar,* council meeting pavilion.
10. *Beji* (spring), one of many along Bali's small rivers. Water is taken from the spring to make holy water for local rituals. Bathing and laundry are done downstream.
11. *Pura dalem,* the temple for honoring the cremated dead who have not yet been fully purified into deities.
12. *Setra* (graveyard), also the cremation ground.
13. *Tanah tegal,* cultivated land that is not a rice field.
14. *Sawah,* irrigated rice fields.

BALI'S MOST EXPENSIVE BANANA
A tourist wearing expensive designer sunglasses rounds a bend in the path. A monkey pounces onto his shoulder, rips off his shades and disappears up a tree. Stunned tourist is rescued by the appearance of a sweet-faced old lady, wrinkled with smile lines, bearing on her head a basket full of succulent bananas. (It remains a mystery how all the Balinese market ladies pass with impunity through the grove with their headbaskets brimming with treasures.) She sells him Bali's most expensive banana, with which the monkey is bribed to drop the shades, and everyone continues happily on their way. Time passes. Another tourist arrives, is similarly attacked, and around the corner comes the same old lady... A sublime symbiosis.

PURA TAMAN AYUN

The most splendid remainder from Mengwi's former glory is indisputably the Pura Taman Ayun, about 2 miles east of Alas Kedaton. This is probably the largest existing Balinese house temple, built in the middle of the 18th century by Mengwi's greatest king, Cokorda Munggu. He moved the center of the kingdom from Kapal to the village of Mengwi where he founded a new palace, Puri Gede Mengwi, not far from Pura Taman Ayun. The temple (above) is surrounded by a wide moat. There is a grand *jaba pura* (outer courtyard) with a fine *wantilan* pavilion in the southeast; the lines in the floor mark out the rings and perimeters for cockfights. A split gate leads into the broad central courtyard from which you can admire the magnificent gate to the inner courtyard (*jeroan*). The low walls of the *jeroan* are shaded by flowering trees that go down to the banks of the moat. Entry to the *jeroan* is not permitted, but you can look over the walls at its fine old pavilions and the *meru* honoring the deities of the mountains Batu Karu, Agung, Batur, and Pengelengan.

SANGEH MONKEY FOREST

To get to the highly touristic Sangeh monkey forest, take the road east from Pura Taman Ayun and follow the signs. The road goes through Abiansemal and the village of Blahkiuh which has a splendid old banyan tree planted by one of the descendants of Cokorda Munggu. The Sangeh forest is a grove of nutmeg trees whose origin remains mysterious; the trees are very rare in Bali and the grove was certainly planted, perhaps hundreds of years ago. The monkeys of Sangeh, who are sacred to the Pura Bukit Sari in the nutmeg forest, are very bold and are known to attack tourists. To return to Denpasar, follow the road south through Mambal and the many small villages of suburban Denpasar, eventually meeting the Tohpati bypass.

SOUTH BALI

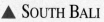

1 PURA PETITENGET 2 LEGIAN BEACH 3 KUTA BEACH 4 BEMO CORNER 5 AIRPORT 6 TUBAN 7 PURA ULUWATU 8 JIMBARAN 9 NUSA DUA 10 TANJUNG BENOA 11 BENOA HARBOR 12 SUWUNG 13 PURA SAKENAN 14 SERANGAN ISLAND 15 PURI PEMECUTAN

MAJAPAHIT
"Maospahit" is a variation of "Majapahit", the east Javanese kingdom that extended over much of the archipelago from the 13th to the 16th century and which exerted a powerful influence on Balinese art, religion, and society. In Bali the emblem of Majapahit is the deer. Shrines to Majapahit deities often have a wooden sculpture of a deer or a pair of deer antlers.

One day

COWARD TO CHAPLIN
In a poem penned to Charlie Chaplin from Bali, Noel Coward wrote:
"As I said this morning
 to Charlie
There is far too much music in Bali,
And although as a place it's entrancing,
There is also a thought
 too much dancing.
It appears that each Balinese native,
From the womb to the tomb is creative,
And although the results are quite clever,
There is too much artistic endeavour."

See **BALI**

As goes Badung, so goes Bali. By the year 2000, this might be a catchphrase for the history of Bali in the 20th century. After the Dutch conquest of Bali was completed in 1908, the colonial government opened an administrative office in Denpasar, in the Regency of Badung ● 41, and set about running things according to its own notions of Balinese culture. It also introduced tourism. The pattern has held. Today Bali is still governed through Denpasar, and Balinese culture is prepared for market in the capital's dance academies and displayed at the Werdi Budaya Art Center (center). Although Balinese art is being exported at an increasing rate, through handicrafts and international tours by its dance troupes, the biggest market

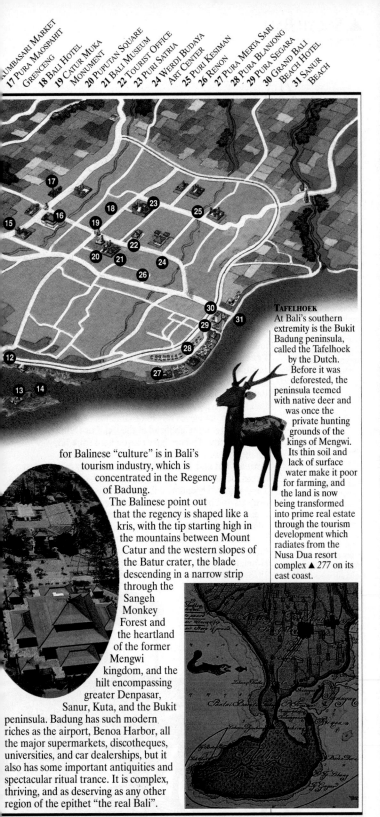

TAFELHOEK

At Bali's southern extremity is the Bukit Badung peninsula, called the Tafelhoek by the Dutch. Before it was deforested, the peninsula teemed with native deer and was once the private hunting grounds of the kings of Mengwi. Its thin soil and lack of surface water make it poor for farming, and the land is now being transformed into prime real estate through the tourism development which radiates from the Nusa Dua resort complex ▲ 277 on its east coast.

for Balinese "culture" is in Bali's tourism industry, which is concentrated in the Regency of Badung.

The Balinese point out that the regency is shaped like a kris, with the tip starting high in the mountains between Mount Catur and the western slopes of the Batur crater, the blade descending in a narrow strip through the Sangeh Monkey Forest and the heartland of the former Mengwi kingdom, and the hilt encompassing greater Denpasar, Sanur, Kuta, and the Bukit peninsula. Badung has such modern riches as the airport, Benoa Harbor, all the major supermarkets, discotheques, universities, and car dealerships, but it also has some important antiquities and spectacular ritual trance. It is complex, thriving, and as deserving as any other region of the epithet "the real Bali".

265

DENPASAR

ALUN-ALUN PUPUTAN
"In the great 'alun-alun', the playground of Den Pasar, stolid Hollanders play tennis and drink beer near young Balinese playing soccer in striped sweatshirts, shorts, and spiked shoes. All around the square are the homes of the leading white residents, neat and bourgeois, small bungalows with enormous pink embroidered lampshades on every porch and well-kept front gardens of imported roses."
Miguel Covarrubias, *Island of Bali*, 1937

PONY-CART TAXIS
Pony-cart taxis (*dokar*) provide all the disadvantages of other forms of transportation: they are subject to the same traffic rules; they cost money; and they are almost as slow as walking. Moreover, they are not allowed on the main road, Jalan Gajah Mada. For the perversely romantic, this is the ideal way to circulate in Denpasar.

Denpasar is not an easy place to visit: it's hot and noisy, and the traffic is a hurtling river of motorcycles and little trucks. For the greatest flexibility, try a combination of taxi, public transport, and walking.

PUPUTAN SQUARE. Alun-Alun Puputan, or Puputan Square, is an appropriately empty space at the very center of Denpasar. The square commemorates the mass ritual suicide of Badung's royalty in the face of Dutch cannon fire on September 20, 1906 ● *38*.

BALI MUSEUM. This well-known destination on the eastern edge of Puputan Square is a good place to be dropped off by taxi. The museum ▲ *268* was built by the Dutch after the *puputan* of 1906 and 1908 as part of their new policy to preserve Balinese culture rather than bombard it to death. The museum's architecture is itself a subject of this ethnological museum; the buildings incorporate various aspects of temple and palace architecture from different regions of Bali. The collections are very fine, but unfortunately their preservation and display are not.

PURA JAGATNATHA. Just next door to the museum, the Pura Jagatnatha is a temple founded in the 1970's whose principal deity is Sang Hyang Widhi Wasa, the godhead of the Hindu-Balinese pantheon ● *46*. Its architecture proclaims Hindu Bali's underlying monotheism in its single shrine, a towering *padmasana,* and gives way to ornamental expressionism in the gilded figure of the godhead at the top. For Denpasar's urban Hindus, many of whom have moved here from faraway villages, it takes the place of their home temples.

BADUNG TOURIST INFORMATION OFFICE. This office is just across the main road from the north flank of Pura Jagatnatha. Their yearly "Calendar of Events" is a list of major temple festivals and holy days, with a schedule of dance performances around south and central Bali. A roundabout at the northern edge of Puputan Square encircles the Catur Muka Monument, whose four faces look in the four cardinal directions. To the north, Jalan Veteran takes you past the Bali Hotel, the island's first tourist hotel, built by the Dutch in 1928 on the actual site of the *puputan*. Next door, at Jalan Veteran No. 9, is the textile factory Pertenunan AAA, where *kain ikat endek* is woven. Farther up this noisy street is the

Performances of Bali's most accomplished music, dance, and drama attract crowds of Balinese to the Werdi Budaya Art Center's open-air theater during the annual Arts Festival. Visitors can view the daily "monkey dance" performance in the small amphitheater.

bird market (left) in front of the Puri Satria and its noble red brick family temple.

JALAN GAJAH MADA. Heading west from the Catur Muka statue is Jalan Gajah Mada. This is Denpasar's "best" shopping street, where expatriates used to buy foreign products such as Scotch whisky and cheese. There are interesting shops along here and on Jalan Sulawesi, which meets Gajah Mada just east of the Kumbasari market.

KUMBASARI MARKET. The commercial crux of Denpasar, this market is southwest of the intersection of Gajah Mada and Jalan Sulawesi. This is a serious market, one that gets roaring at 2am. In daylight hours you can find mountains of things to buy, from gilt-painted parasols with a 7-foot span to sacks of cloves and baskets of blue hydreangeas.

PURI PEMECUTAN. Turning south (left) at the western end of Jalan Gajah Mada, you enter Jalan Thamrin, another important shopping street. At the south end of Jalan Thamrin where it meets the corner of Jalan Hasannudin is the Puri Pemecutan (left), one of Badung's key palaces since the 18th century. Today it contains a tourist hotel.

PURA MAOSPAHIT ★. If, at the western end of Jalan Gajah Mada you turn right and then cross the street, you will come to the quiet neighborhood of Grenceng. A short walk north brings you to Pura Maospahit, a temple of genteel antiquity secreted behind high red brick walls (below) . The entrance to this lovely old temple is through a gate about 55 yards along the southern wall. Much of the temple was damaged in the 1917 earthquake, and some parts, such as the great carved reliefs on the first gateway, were restored by the Archeological Service in 1925. The central gateway is massive and austere; its timber doors are carved with wonderful delicacy.

WERDI BUDAYA ART CENTER. On Jalan Sutomo near the corner of Jalan Gajah Mada is a rank of pony carts. The driver will know how to bring you to the Art Center, on Jalan Nusa Indah. Of all of Bali's public cultural centers this is the "mother". It is the grandest and the most successful at meeting its high-minded ambitions. The Art Center has a number of different services and events, the most famous being the Arts Festival which is held every year in June or July, but a visit is worthwhile any day.

TRANCE AT PURI KESIMAN
Once every 210 days on the anniversary of the royal house temple of Puri Kesiman, in northeastern Denpasar, a mass trance takes place.

Local people – mostly young men and boys – join the congregation for prayers, sitting on the ground of the main courtyard. A *pemangku* (priest) ● 48 moves among them sprinkling the crowd with holy water. In an instant, individuals fall into violent, sobbing trance. Those next to them who are not struck with possession half-carry the trancers (above) out through the *kori agung* in procession, circumambulating the *wantilan* next door three times before returning again to be revived with holy water. Meanwhile, inside the temple other people go into trance upon touching heirlooms such as royal garb or weapons. It is believed that during trance deified ancestors express their wishes and passions through the medium. Despite the area's booming urbanization, ritual trance is still common in South Bali.

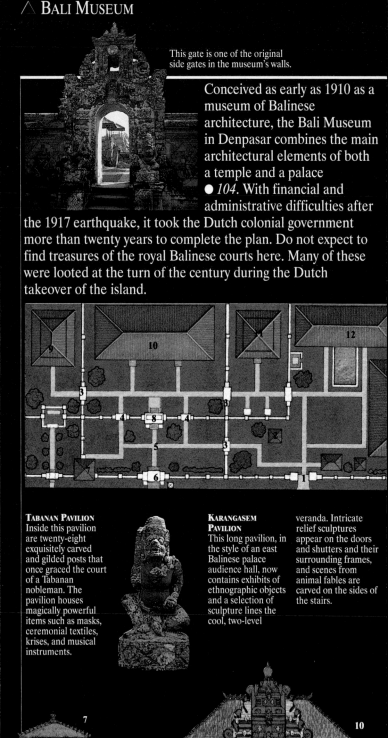

⚠ BALI MUSEUM

This gate is one of the original side gates in the museum's walls.

Conceived as early as 1910 as a museum of Balinese architecture, the Bali Museum in Denpasar combines the main architectural elements of both a temple and a palace ● *104*. With financial and administrative difficulties after the 1917 earthquake, it took the Dutch colonial government more than twenty years to complete the plan. Do not expect to find treasures of the royal Balinese courts here. Many of these were looted at the turn of the century during the Dutch takeover of the island.

TABANAN PAVILION
Inside this pavilion are twenty-eight exquisitely carved and gilded posts that once graced the court of a Tabanan nobleman. The pavilion houses magically powerful items such as masks, ceremonial textiles, krises, and musical instruments.

KARANGASEM PAVILION
This long pavilion, in the style of an east Balinese palace audience hall, now contains exhibits of ethnographic objects and a selection of sculpture lines the cool, two-level veranda. Intricate relief sculptures appear on the doors and shutters and their surrounding frames, and scenes from animal fables are carved on the sides of the stairs.

ORIGINAL MUSEUM
The four walled courtyards, five gates, and five pavilions that form the original part of the museum (right) were intended to show examples of different regional architectural styles and were paid for or contributed by several of the former kingdoms of Bali.

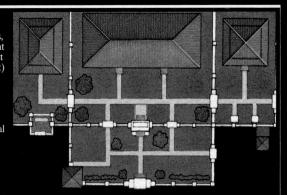

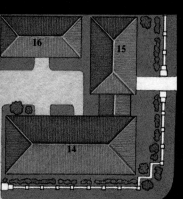

GROUND PLAN
1. Public entrance
2. Slit-gong tower
3. Original side gates
4. Side gates added after 1968
5. Center forecourt
6. Split gate (original entrance)
7. Gazebo
8. Great ceremonial gate
9. Tabanan Pavilion
10. Karangasem Pavilion
11. Buleleng Pavilion
12. Eastern exhibit building
13. Library building
14. Temporary exhibits and administration
15. Curatorial
16. Conservation, preparation, photography

BULELENG PAVILION
Representing the style of a north Bali residence pavilion, with a central post and thirty-two surrounding posts, this building was reconstructed at the museum in the early 1930's after three previous lives. It was built as the Bali-Lombok pavilion for the great Colonial Exposition of 1914 in central Java. Later it was moved to Singaraja, in northern Bali, where it became a museum and sales hall for Balinese handicrafts. Then it became the office of the Official Government Tourist Bureau. Today in Denpasar it houses traditional and modern sculptures.

The Bali Museum's collections began only in the 1930's. The Museum Association, formed in 1932, was run by a board of distinguished Balinese, colonial administrators, and representatives of the Dutch steamship company, KPM, that brought tourists to Denpasar. With the advent of the war in Europe, colonial interest faded. The museum survived the war and reopened for visitors under the guidance of a devoted Balinese, I Gusti Made Mayun. In the upheavals of the early years of independence, however, nothing was acquired until after 1966, when the museum attained its present status as a provincial museum under the Ministry of Education and Culture.

BRONZE SPEARHEAD
These two halves of a prehistoric bronze spearhead are part of the fine prehistoric and historic archeological collection at the museum. The collection of treasured bronzes, stones, and terracottas testify to Bali's technological awakening and its long established links with the Hindu and Buddhist cultures of Java and beyond.

LAKE BRATAN BRONZE
Fragments of an unidentified bronze image (right) were found near Lake Bratan. These probably date from the 13th to 14th centuries.

PRIMITIVE ART

Expatriate German artist Walter Spies ● *112* agreed to volunteer as the museum's first curator. His interest in primitive art ensured the museum's inclusion of pieces that attest to Bali's ancient Austronesian roots, reflecting deep reverence for ancestors and the forces of nature. One primitive piece is this base for a roof post, from a pavilion in the old village of Sembiran, on the northeast coast.

STUPAS

Miniature clay stupas with mantra syllables and images, probably impressed from metal stamps, are the earliest evidence of the presence of Buddhism in Bali. This piece may be from the late 8th or 9th centuries.

REVERED FIGURES

This bronze figure of a goddess or deified ancestor is of a kind still revered in a number of temples and family shrines today.

CARVED GODDESS

The goddess (below) with a tiered lotus crown and elaborate classical clothing is mounted on an animal that served as a water spout. Sturdy stone sculptures in this style are found in a number of sites in Bali, some inscribed with early 11th-century dates.

NEUHAUS COLLECTION

This monochromatic painting (right), in a style popular in the Batuan area, was acquired from Hans and Rolf Neuhaus, brothers who were interned by the Germans in 1940. The stock of their art and antique shop in Sanur was liquidated, and approximately 1500 objects, from architectural finds to modern art, came to the museum, its largest acquisition ever.

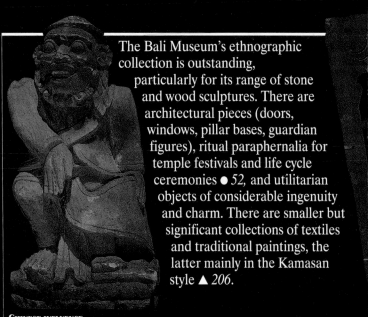

The Bali Museum's ethnographic collection is outstanding, particularly for its range of stone and wood sculptures. There are architectural pieces (doors, windows, pillar bases, guardian figures), ritual paraphernalia for temple festivals and life cycle ceremonies ● *52,* and utilitarian objects of considerable ingenuity and charm. There are smaller but significant collections of textiles and traditional paintings, the latter mainly in the Kamasan style ▲ *206.*

CHINESE INFLUENCE
Amusing sculptures of jovial, slightly demonic Chinese characters acknowledge the importance of the Chinese to Balinese trade and economy.

ELONGATED STYLE
This youthful archer is a superb example of the refined elongated style of modern sculpture that emerged from the Gianyar era in the early 1930's. During the 1930's, the museum sold selected works by artists of the day to promote contemporary art of high quality. Tourists could inspect the museum's collection of contemporary work for comparison before purchase. Neither the museum's influence on the development of modern Balinese art nor its collection of 20th-century pieces should be overlooked.

WOOD CARVING
The wooden relief panel (above), which once probably appeared above a door, features an owl in a foliate frame.

The leather image of Twalen (below), the famous clown from the shadow puppet plays ● *61*, may have been used as ornamentation on a cremation tower.

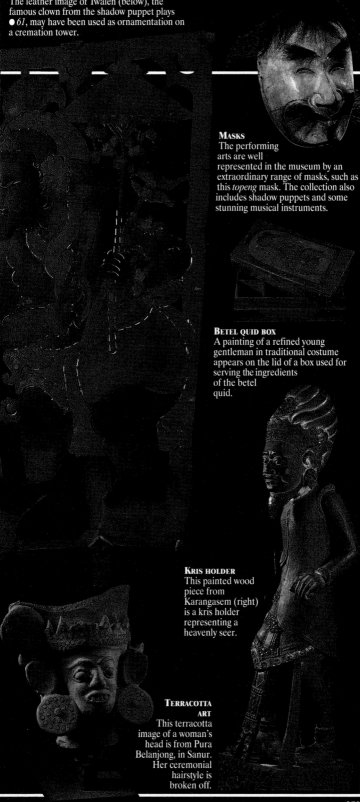

MASKS
The performing arts are well represented in the museum by an extraordinary range of masks, such as this *topeng* mask. The collection also includes shadow puppets and some stunning musical instruments.

BETEL QUID BOX
A painting of a refined young gentleman in traditional costume appears on the lid of a box used for serving the ingredients of the betel quid.

KRIS HOLDER
This painted wood piece from Karangasem (right) is a kris holder representing a heavenly seer.

TERRACOTTA ART
This terracotta image of a woman's head is from Pura Belanjong, in Sanur. Her ceremonial hairstyle is broken off.

GRAND BALI BEACH HOTEL
Sanur's venerable Bali Beach Hotel, built in 1966 and renamed the Grand Bali Beach Hotel in 1993 upon restoration after a drastic fire, is surrounded by mystical rumors. It is said that it was built on a graveyard; that room 327 is reserved for the goddess

SANUR

The tourist area on Sanur beach is just off the bypass south of Denpasar. But the Sanur that belongs to the Balinese is not easy to find. It's hidden in quiet neighborhoods behind the bypass and secretly tucked away in groves along the beach. Its traditional culture is very strong, but it wears modern dress (except of course on ritual occasions and in the hotels). Among the Balinese, Sanur has a reputation for sorcery of a high degree, both "white" and "black".

PURA SEGARA ★. Along Sanur beach are several small temples of coral with pyramid-like structures that suggest prehistoric origins. The Pura Segara is on Jalan Segara Ayu between the entrance to the Segara Village Beach Hotel and the Sanur Beach Market. *Segara* means "sea", and *pura segara* are part of a village's constellation of temples. Inland they may be just a shrine within another temple; in coastal areas they are naturally more prominent, and Sanur's Pura Segara is very curious. The gate to the outer courtyard is flanked by two black painted demons, and inside, three great piles of blackened coral fill most of the courtyard. In the inner courtyard is a stepped pyramid, topped by a small shrine (left).

PURA MERTA SARI. At the southern end of Sanur beach the coast cuts sharply around a little peninsula, forming a shallow bay. Tucked in here is the small and mysterious Pura Merta Sari, shaded by huge trees. The local people consider this place to be especially charged with supernatural force. The temple's anniversary falls two weeks after the spring equinox,

of the South Sea; and that during the fire that gutted the hotel on January 20, 1993, this was the only room unharmed. Room 327 has become a temple with offerings made daily.

the date of the highest spiritual glamor in the Balinese calendar. On this night, in the grounds outside the temple, a strange ritual dance takes place called *baris cina* (Chinese baris) and usually ends in violent trance. The dancers wear loose trousers and turn-of-the-century army helmets and carry old, bayoneted rifles. In the vicinity of Pura Merta Sari are a number of smaller temples built of coral, hidden away in the scrubby coastal vegetation.

SERANGAN ISLAND

One can only admire the candor of the Badung Government

Tourist Office, which says this about Serangan Island in its official pamphlet, "Badung the Gateway to Bali": "... It is also known as a 'turtle island'. Serangan is a scruffy low-lying slither of land, about three kms long... The attraction is a muddy pond inhabitted [sic] by greenback turtles which are now protected. (...)". There is a more to Serangan than that. There are several villages, including a Bugis community with a mosque, but the island is not an easy place to visit, nor even very pleasant except during the anniversary of its two important temples. The island lies about a third of a mile off the mangrove swamps of Suwung, and access depends on the tides. To get there at low tide you must walk across mud flats; at high tide you can charter a boat at stiff tourist prices.

PURA SAKENAN. This is another temple said to have been founded by the 16th-century Javanese priest Danghyang Nirartha ▲ 156 because of a magical force that he felt emanating from the ground there. Other records say that the original temple was built centuries earlier by architect Mpu Kuturan. The temple's main structure is a rare shrine of white coral in stepped tiers. At the nearby Pura Susunan Wadon there is a similarly *candi*-like structure, although shorter, that is reminiscent of Candi Suku in central Java in its solid proportions and ethereal relief carvings. The best time to visit these temples is during their anniversaries, around Kuningan on the Balinese calendar ● 82.

BENOA HARBOR

Benoa Harbor (below) is still under construction and looks as if it is going to be an important place. A big yacht marina was completed at the end of 1993, and a number of buildings for shops, restaurants, and maritime services are going up. At the traffic light intersection on the bypass southwest of Suwung, a signposted road leads south over a narrow, bumpy causeway to the harbor. Left of the causeway, yachts lie at anchor in the bay; on the right are replantings of mangrove. The cruise boats for the small islands east of Bali are found near the marina. Colorful old commercial fishing boats are tucked away on the other side of the harbor.

BARONG LANDUNG
No one is certain of the origin of the *landung* (tall) male-female couple of guardian effigies, found in villages throughout south and central Bali. During the temple festival at Pura Sakenan on Serangan Island, the couple (above, left) perform a dance and converse in ancient, bawdy songs.

PURA BLANJONG
In southern Sanur is the modest-looking Pura Blanjong, which contains the famous Prasasti Blanjong, an inscribed pillar ● 34. The significance of this stone pillar, dated AD 914 and "discovered" in 1932, is not only that it is the earliest Balinese inscription mentioning a royal name, but that it is written partly in Old Balinese and partly in Sanskrit using two different kinds of characters, Old Balinese and Nagari. The parts written with Old Balinese characters are in both Old Balinese and Sanskrit, thus proving that Indic Hinduism was already flourishing in south Bali by the 10th century.

MADS LANGE
Mads Lange ● 37,
one of the merchants
who prospered along
with Bali and
Lombok in the 1820's
and 1830's, is buried
in Kuta. It is possible
to go on foot to find
his tomb behind the
supermarket between
the post office and
the police station, but
it is easier to drive
there, on the
northbound bypass
and stopping just
before the first
bridge. This little
Chinese cemetery is a

sad place, squashed
in between backyards
and improvised
houses. The grave
marker is a pyramid
of black and white
painted stone and
cement. Lange
prospered in his huge
fort cum cultural
center at Kuta, then a
port. He lived in
grand style. His wives
included a daughter
of one of Kuta's
Chinese magnates,
who gave him access
to their own extensive
networks. The
Balinese know his
grave only as the
"holy Chinese place".

The beaches of Kuta, Legian, Seminyak, Jimbaran, and Nusa
Dua are the focus of Bali's world famous tourism. As in
Sanur, Balinese life still goes on behind the walls of the
temples and house courtyards much as it always has except
that the prosperity that tourism has brought allows the
Balinese to spend more on their temples and ceremonies, and
to adorn their house
compounds with
satellite dishes.

KUTA

Kuta is growing so
quickly that traffic
is continually
re-routed to
accommodate the ever-increasing number of cars. To get into
Kuta these days from anywhere but Denpasar, one has to take
the bypass nearly to the airport and approach it through
Tuban. (Locals use a back alley off the northbound side of the
bypass.) Kuta's center is Bemo Corner (above) at the
intersection of Jalan Bakung Sari and Jalan Kuta Raya. The
best way to explore the center is to alight at Bemo Corner and
walk. Along Poppies Lane I and the networks of tiny lanes
that branch off from there you can catch glimpses of
traditional house compounds behind the souvenir shops.
Jalan Pantai Kuta takes you to the famous Kuta Beach and
runs beside it for about half a mile before curving back along
Jalan Melasti, which meets the main shopping street, Jalan
Legian. At this intersection, traffic is one-way going south
(right) back to Bemo Corner, and two-ways going north (left)
into Legian and on to Seminyak.

LEGIAN BEACH

The beach from here
northward is known as Legian
Beach, heart of the sunset
scene for expatriate garment
industry moguls. Generally
speaking, the expatriate lifestyle
becomes quieter and more chic the
farther north one goes, with the present headquarters of expat
chic being in Seminyak.

PURA PETITENGET. Just north of the Oberoi Hotel is this
lovely temple where the rice fields of Krobokan meet the sea.
The *peti* (betel nut box) referred to is *tenget* (magically
powerful), because it belonged to the 16th-century Javanese
priest Danghyang Nirartha ▲ 156. This was the last place he
visited before he died at Uluwatu. The very old banyan tree
inside the temple toppled over in June 1993, destroying many
of the shrines. Restoration began immediately.

JIMBARAN

The village of Jimbaran lies on the western shore of the
narrow isthmus connecting the Bukit peninsula to the main
island. Its lovely beach-lined bay has only recently begun to be
developed for tourism. Jimbaran was once part of the

Many of the people of Jimbaran are fishermen who set out every evening in their *jukung* to fish in the quiet bay. The fish market takes place on the beach very early in the morning.

kingdom of Mengwi. The *subak* ■ *24* temple, Pura Ulun Siwi, in the middle of the village, was built by the Mengwi king Cokorda Munggu and still carries the dark glamour of the 18th century in its *meru*. Pura Muaya, very near the Four Seasons resort, has been recently restored with contributions from the hotel.

THE BUKIT

Bali's southern peninsula, called Bukit or Bukit Badung by the Balinese but increasingly referred to generically as Nusa Dua, has a geography more Australasian than tropical. There are no rivers or streams, and any surface water disappears quickly into deep fissures in the limestone rock. Topsoil is thin and precious; nonetheless farmers manage to eke out a living planting corn, tubers, legumes, peanuts, and bananas. A number of villages and temples dot the peninsula.

PURA LUHUR ULUWATU. The most famous temple is Pura Luhur Uluwatu, at the southwest extremity of the peninsula, perched on a high limestone cliff ▲ *278*. This is one of the most visited tourist destinations, especially at sunset, when for a few moments the light is unearthly. The surf just below Uluwatu is world-famous.

NUSA DUA. Life on the Bukit has been transformed in the past ten years since the building of the five-star hotel complex at Nusa Dua, on the Bukit's northeast coast (above). (The "two islands" to which the name refers are two projections of rock in the middle of this expensive stretch of beach.)

TANJUNG BENOA. Tanjung Benoa is a finger-like extension into Benoa Harbor, directly north of the Nusa Dua complex. A tiny fishing village at the tip, Desa Tanjung Benoa, has some fine Balinese temples of carved limestone. There is a large mosque presently under renovation and a Chinese Buddhist temple (right), recently restored in brilliant colors.

NUSA DUA
An experiment in five-star tourism, this self-contained complex of resort hotels was designed to minimize the negative impact of tourism on the social and natural environment. It was built by the Indonesian government and private investors under the auspices of the World Bank, under strict guidelines to ensure integrated design and maximum benefits for the local people. Nusa Dua was previously an arid stretch of coconut groves, distinguished by two peninsular islets. The wandering sage Danghyang Nirartha is said to have established several temples there, all of them still cared for by the villagers of nearby Bualu, even though some are within the grounds of international hotels.

▲ PURA LUHUR ULUWATU

Like a ship of stone afloat in the sky, Pura Luhur Uluwatu is poised 825 feet above the Indian Ocean. The temple is carved from the enormous limestone rock upon which it sits at the farthest edge. *Ulu* means "head", *watu* "rock" and *luhur* implies "heavenly", "ancestral", "original" and "transcendent" all at once. It was here that Danghyang Nirartha ▲ *156*, the Javanese high priest who brought a renewal of Hinduism to Bali in the 16th century, achieved the conscious death called *moksa*. Legend says that the temple was built by Mpu Kuturan in the 11th century, and then rebuilt several hundred years later by Danghyang Nirartha in anticipation of his ultimate release there. The architecture and temple statuary suggest that it is contemporaneous with Pura Sakenan ▲ *275*. Some of its most unusual features are the unique split gate with its inward curving wings, the arched ceremonial gate leading to the inner courtyard, and the figures of Ganesha guarding both of these gates. But the most striking aspect is the layout of the temple, long and narrow in conformity with the terrain and surprisingly intimate. Sacred monkeys roam freely over this high and airy place.

279

1. NUSA LEMBONGAN
2. NUSA CENINGAN
3. NUSA PENIDA

NUSA LEMBONGAN

The small island of Nusa Lembongan, off the southeast coast of the main island, is where the charter cruises put in for day-trips. There are a number of guest houses and eating places catering to surfers, and it is a good place to base explorations of Nusa Penida.

NUSA PENIDA

The best way to get to Nusa Penida ■ 28 is to charter a boat from Padang Bai to Sampalan and the best way to get around is with a motorbike. The crossing takes about forty-five minutes, but you cannot count on being able to find a charter much later than 11am. Nusa Penida is famous for the dread it has traditionally aroused in the hearts of the Balinese as the home of the fanged demon Jero Gede Mecaling ▲ 155. Once a place of exile, the island is surrounded by swift currents and has steep limestone cliffs (below), which make it unapproachable

except from the north. It is still so isolated that there are traces of Old Balinese ● 42 found in the language spoken there. Nusa Penida is very dry, like Bukit Badung; but there are surprisingly lush hills in the south, and its cold, clear waters ■ 28 are unusually rich in plankton. There is almost no tourism on Nusa Penida, and the people are not yet accustomed to visitors.

SEAWEED FARMS
The most important cash crop on Nusa Penida is seaweed. Looking down from the road along the east coast, seaweed beds are laid out in rectangles in crystal clear water.

KARANGSARI CAVE. This huge cave near Nusa Penida's east coast has a temple at its tiny entrance. On Kuningan night, a magically charged date in the Balinese calendar ● 82, people from all over come with offerings to an underground lake in the cave. The cave is said to be a tunnel about half a mile long.

BATUMADEG. This small inland village has few amenities, but the Pura Dalem is worth a visit. The massive *kori agung* gate is unlike anything else in Bali. Several flights of stairs lead to an impressive arched gateway into the inner courtyard. On either side of the stairway are finely carved friezes celebrating crabs, molluscs, and other sea animals.

TOYAPAKEH. Toyapakeh is a ferry and market town, where boats arrive from Kusamba. It is also the crossing point to Nusa Lembongan. The short boat trip passes through the shallow, mangrove-lined channel between Ceningan and Lembongan. The water is so clear that you can see coral clearly as if through glass. Here, at the extreme limit of Asia, you can look east from the cliffs of Nusa Penida, beyond the jagged white caps of the savage Lombok Strait, toward the volcanos of Lombok and the chain of mysterious and little visited islands of Nusa Tenggara Timur.

WIND ENERGY
The village of Tanglad feels high at 1300 feet and looks out over the south and west coasts of Nusa Penida. The wind moving over the countryside has a steady grandeur, and there is a pilot project here to harness the *tenaga alam* (earth energy).

PRACTICAL
INFORMATION

◆ PREPARATIONS

Bali is a tropical island of volcanos, rice terraces, and beaches, about half the size of Connecticut. Because it is south of the Equator, the hottest time of year is between November and March, during the rainy season. Mid December to mid January is one of the tourist high seasons because of Australian holidays. The best weather is between May and August, when it is sunny and mild to cool, so there is another tourist high season in July and August.

VISA FORMALITIES

Visitor passports must have at least six months before the expiry date and one empty page. An onward or return ticket out of Indonesia is required. Non-extendable permits for up to sixty days are granted automatically upon entry to nationals of Australia, Austria, Belgium, Brunei, Canada, Denmark, Finland, France, Germany, Greece, Iceland, Ireland, Italy, Japan, Liechtenstein, Luxembourg, Malaysia, Malta, Netherlands, New Zealand, Norway, the Philippines, Singapore, South Korea, Spain, Sweden, Switzerland, Thailand, United Kingdom, and the United States.

Nationals of Israel and Portugal must apply for a visa through Jakarta. Other nationals must apply for a visa at Indonesian consulates abroad. An airport tax of Rp20,000 is charged for international departures.

VACCINATIONS

Although not obligatory, cholera-typhoid and tetanus innoculations are recommended.

CUSTOMS

Weapons, illegal drugs, and pornographic videos are not allowed in Indonesia. You may be questioned if you are bringing in video equipment that looks professional.

EMBASSIES AND CONSULATES

AUSTRALIA
INDONESIAN CONSULATE
– 52 Albert Road,
3rd floor
South Melbourne
Victoria 3205
Tel. 03-690-7811
Fax 03-525-1588
– 133 St. George's
Terrace
Perth W.A. 6000
Tel. 09-321-9821
Fax 09-474-1261

PICCADILLY COURT
3rd floor, Pitt Street
Sydney, N.S.W.
Tel. 02-264-2976
Fax 02-349-6854

UK
INDONESIAN EMBASSY
38 Grosvenor Square
London WIX 9AD
Tel. 0171-499 7661
Fax 0171-491 4993

US
INDONESIAN CONSULATE
– 3457 Wilshire Blvd
Los Angeles,
CA 90010
Tel. (213) 383-5126
Fax (213) 487-3971
– 5 East 68th Street
New York, NY 10021
Tel. (212) 879-0600
Fax (212) 570-6206

EMBASSY OF INDONESIA
2020 Massachusetts
Avenue N.W.
Washington DC
20036
Tel. (202) 775-5200
Fax (415) 775-5365

HEALTH INSURANCE

Travelers are strongly advised to have insurance covering medical evacuation (to either Singapore or Australia). Medical emergency evacuation insurance is available in Bali through Bali International Tourist Assist (fax 62-361-231-442). The policy costs US$276/£184 for one person and is valid for a year.
Warning:
Uninsured medical evacuation begins at US$2500/£1667 and may be as much as US$24,000/£16,000 with a lot of red tape as well.

Performers at the annual Bali Arts Festival
◆ 300, held from mid June to mid July.

PRE-DEPARTURE CHECKLIST:
✓ Medical evacuation insurance
✓ Comfortable walking shoes
✓ Flashlight

AIR FARES

FROM THE US:
◆ GARUDA INDONESIA
Tel. (800) 342-7832
*Economy return fare
from LA $1,350–
1,450. First class
$4,896.*

◆ SINGAPORE AIRLINES
Tel. (800) 742-3333
*Economy from New
York, $1,360–1,510.*

◆ THAI AIRWAYS
Tel. (800) 426-5204

*Los Angeles to Bali
$1,495–1,620
economy.*

FROM THE UK:
◆ SINGAPORE AIRLINES
Tel. 0171 439 8111
*Excursion £1,195
return.*

◆ GARUDA INDONESIA
Tel. 0171 486 3011
*Return flights from
£565–700.*

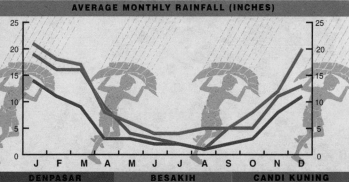

Hydrangea plantation near Tamblingan.

TOUR OPERATORS

US
◆ GARUDA ORIENT
HOLIDAYS
Tel. (212) 983-6288

◆ SITA WORLD TRAVEL
Tel. (818) 767-0039

UK:
◆ ASIA PLUS
Tel. 0171 470 0708

◆ ANGLO-FRENCH
Tel. 0171 437 4404

BUDGETING FOR ONE WEEK

Estimates in
US$/UK£.
For a couple staying
in upper-range
accommodation:
Hotel: $1050/£700
Food: $595/£397
For a couple staying
in mid-range
accommodation:
Hotel: $315/£210

Food: $210/£140
For a couple with two
children in mid-range
accommodation:
Hotel: $350/£233
Food: $245/£163
For a couple
backpacking:
Guest house:
$70/£47
Food: $90/£60

ELECTRICITY

Generally 220-240V,
50 cycles AC. Some
villages may have
110V, 50 cycles AC.
Power is in greater
demand than supply,
and shortages are
common. Some
outlying areas do not

yet have any
electricity. It's a good
idea to carry a small
flashlight with a spare
bulb and batteries.
Most large hotels
provide hairdryers.

CLIMATE

Annual rainfall is
about 70 inches in
the south central
plains with an
average of two
hundred days of rain
per year. East Bali
and the north coast
may get only 2–3
inches. Temperatures
range from 60˚F to

85˚F, depending on
season and altitude.
Bring a light jacket if
you plan to go into
the mountains.
Daylight is from
about 6am to 6pm
year-round with slight
variations between
June and December.

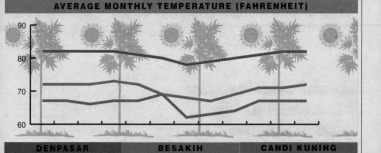

AVERAGE MONTHLY RAINFALL (INCHES)

J F M A M J J A S O N D

DENPASAR BESAKIH CANDI KUNING

AVERAGE MONTHLY TEMPERATURE (FAHRENHEIT)

DENPASAR BESAKIH CANDI KUNING

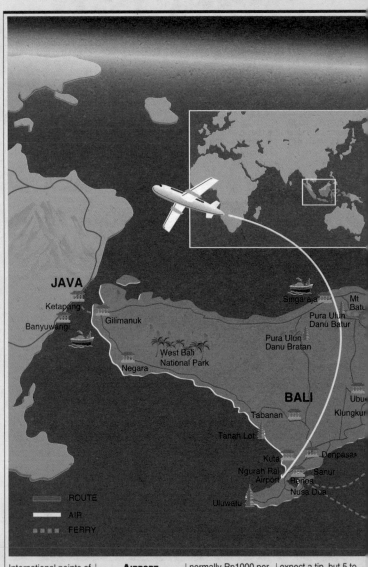

JAVA

Ketapang

Banyuwangi

Gilimanuk

Negara

West Bali
National Park

Singaraja

Mt
Batu

Pura Ulun
Danu Batur

Pura Ulun
Danu Bratan

BALI

Tabanan

Ubu

Klungkur

Tanah Lot

Kuta

Denpasar

Ngurah Rai
Airport

Sanur

Benoa

Nusa Dua

Uluwatu

ROUTE
AIR
FERRY

International points of entry into Bali, Indonesia, are Ngurah Rai Airport and the sea ports at Padang Bai and Benoa.

AIRPORT TRANSPORT

To hire an airport taxi, approach the taxi counter, state your destination, and pay directly. Tipping: normally Rp1000 per bag for porters. Airport taxis don't expect a tip, but 5 to 10 percent of the fare is gratefully received.

TRAVELING TO BALI		
Departure from	Distance (miles)	Duration (hours)
London	7800	15
Los Angeles	9000	20
Sydney-Melbourne	3000	6
Perth	1600	4

Note: Figures are approximate and will vary with carrier and number of stopovers.

TAXI FROM NGURAH RAI AIRPORT	
(DISTANCE/FARE US$1=Rp2339; UK£1=RP3175)	
Denpasar	8 miles/Rp9000
Kuta 1 (south of Jl. Bakung Sari)	2½ miles/Rp4500
Kuta 2 (Jl. Bakung Sari–Jl. Padma)	3½ miles/Rp6500
Kuta 3 (beyond Jl. Padma)	5 miles/Rp9000
Nusa Dua	7 miles/Rp12,000
Oberoi	6 miles/Rp10,000
Sanur	7 miles/Rp12,000
Ubud	20½ miles/Rp34,000

There is an advantage in using the national carrier Garuda in that it is the only airline providing city check-in services for flights to Japan, Singapore, Hong Kong, Seoul, and Taipei, as well as selected domestic flights to Jakarta, Yogyakarta, Surakarta, and Ujung Pandang.

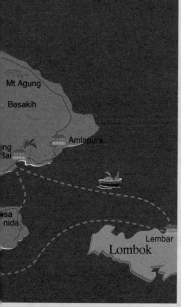

BY SEA

Bali's major ports are Gilimanuk, Padang Bai, and Benoa.

INTERNATIONAL LINES: Several major shipping lines call in at Padang Bai, often as part of a round-the-world cruise. One favorite is the *Seabourn Spirit*, from the luxury cruise company Seabourn Cruise Line, 55 Francisco St, San Francisco, CA 94133. Tel. (415) 391-7444, Fax (415) 391-8518.

DOMESTIC LINES: PELNI, the state-owned national shipping company has several ships which serve major Indonesian ports. Fares and schedules are fixed, and there are up to five classes. Main ticket office: Jl. Gajah Mada 14 Jakarta 10130 Tel. 62-21-384-4342 Fax 62-21-385-4130 Bali office: Benoa Harbor Tel. 62-361-228-962

BALI TO LOMBOK

BY AIR
Merpati and Sempati Airlines fly seven times daily from Denpasar. The twenty-minute flight costs Rp105,500 round-trip.

BY SEA
Ferries from Padang Bai depart at 8am, 11am, 2pm, and 5pm. The four-hour trip should cost Rp4000 for economy class, Rp5700 for first class, but it may be quicker and easier to pay a bit more and buy from one of the many touts.

Note: First class is a tiny, closed room with air conditioning and lots of seasick passengers. It is more fun to buy deck access and watch the flying fish.

The *Mabua Express*, a luxury high speed catamaran, departs from Benoa at 8.30am and 11am daily, returning at 5pm. Tickets for the two-hour trip are US$17.50/£12 and $25/£17, including refreshments. Book through tour agents or call 772-370/521.

GETTING TO OTHER NEARBY ISLANDS

PRIVATE CHARTERS Many boat charters ◆ *309* travel to the nearby islands, departing from Nusa Dua, Jimbaran, and Benoa.

FERRY From Padang Bai to Nusa Penida (seven daily departures, Rp5000).

JUKUNG Tiny Balinese dugout with a sail. Negotiate with boatmen along Sanur Beach, especially those just north of Hotel Bali Beach. Prices depend on season.

LONG BOAT/WATER TAXI Local sea transport operating in same places and on same principles as *jukung*. Carries about fifteen people, and will take motorbikes for extra charge.

BY ROAD/RAIL FROM JAVA

There are no trains in Bali, but you can take the *Bima II* or *Mutiara Selatan* trains from Jakarta to Surabaya, continue by bus to Ketapang, then take the ferry to Gilimanuk and a bus to Denpasar. Buses are uncomfortable. Trains from Yogyakarta to Surabaya leave around midnight.

Fares are between Rp36,000 and Rp39,000, and the journey takes about six hours. A bus/ferry trip from Surabaya to Denpasar costs Rp21,000 and takes eleven hours. An overnight air-conditioned bus/ferry trip from Yogyakarta to Denpasar costs Rp37,000 and takes sixteen hours.

◆ Getting around Bali

Hired car, motorbike, and bicycle are just a few of the ways to get around Bali. Whatever mode you choose, there are several rules of the road to keep in mind. Traffic drives on the left and is heavy both on the road and along the roadside. Beware of pedestrians, bicyclists, and animals darting suddenly into the road. It is customary to toot the horn before overtaking, at curves, and to awaken pedestrians out of reverie. Cyclists and motorbikers entering a main road from a side street do not stop or give way (or even look). Motorbikes are not supposed to pass on your left, but they do. Gas is cheap (Rp750–800/liter) and available at modern gas stations around the island.

OUT OF GAS?

In an emergency, you can also buy gas in almost any village for about the same price as in a gas station, but the quality may not be good. Look for little shacks advertising "premium".

LOST?

You can't really get lost in Bali. It is often sufficient to have the address of your origin and your destination written down.
To ask directions, stop the engine and step out of your vehicle (it's rude to ask directions from behind the wheel). Say *Permisi* (pardon me) *Ibu* or *Pak* (madam or sir), *minta tolong* (can you help me?), and then name your general destination, such as Candi Dasa (not the hotel name). Once you get to Candi Dasa, local people can give you more specific instructions. Those to ask are young people (they won't be as frightened of you), women at *warung* (food stalls), or anyone in uniform.

BEMOS

These covered pick-up trucks that service the markets were once a favorite way for travelers to get around. The term is sometimes still used for the minivans and minibuses that are replacing them as "public" transport. Routes are marked on the side of the green, yellow, or orange minivans. You may flag them down. Empty vans will take charters.

DISTANCES IN BALI (IN MILES)

	AMLAPURA	BEDUGUAL	GILIMANUK	KINTAMANI	KUTA	NUSA DUA	SANUR	SINGARAJA	UBUD
AMLAPURA		79	128	53	54	64	50	62	38
BEDUGAL	79		92	72	35	45	34	19	45
GILIMANUK	128	92		122	85	95	84	53	95
KINTAMANI	53	43	122		43	53	45	32	30
KUTA	54	35	85	43		10	5	54	21
NUSA DUA	65	49	95	58	10		15	64	31
SANUR	50	34	84	45	5	15		53	17
SINGARAJA	62	19	53	32	54	64	53		62
UBUD	38	45	95	30	21	31	17	62	

MAPS

Available in bookshops and the large hotels; rarely at tourist information kiosks. Specially recommended: the new Periplus Map (1994); *Explorers' Bali* by Silvio Santoso (Brem, Ubud); Nelles Verlag map (Germany); *Ubud Surroundings, Travel Treasure Maps,* Knaus Publications, 1994.

Street in Denpasar.

Ferry from Padang Bai to Lombok.

DAY TOURS

Prices differ between the south coast (Sanur, Kuta, Nusa Dua) and Ubud, which is more central and less luxury-oriented. Generally Ubud tours are figured by the cost of the car (or minivan) whereas the more expensive tours in the south give prices per person. Also, tour fares and itineraries differ. The rates quoted here are estimates, in US dollars and UK pounds per person.

KINTAMANI
US$8–14/£5–9 (via Batubulan, Goa Gajah, and Tampaksiring)

SINGARAJA
US$15–20/£10–13 (via Lake Bratan/ Bedugul, Gitgit waterfall, Lovina Beach, and Pupuan)

BESAKIH
US$10–15/£7–10 (via Klungkung/ Kerta Gosa, Candi Dasa/Tenganan)

DENPASAR
US$5–8/£3–5 half-day city tour (includes Bali Museum, Art Center, market, and shopping)

TRANSPORTATION

MODE/RATE	ADVANTAGES	DISADVANTAGES
Hired car w/driver $20–40/£13–27/day	Comfortable; no driving worries; drivers speak some English and act as guides.	The customer sometimes pays for gas and, on overnight trips, accommodation for the driver.
Hired car without driver $15–30/ £10–20/day with insurance; usually a Suzuki Jimney or Toyota Kijang	Flexible, private.	Traffic conditions heavy in South Bali and very difficult in Denpasar. Must have valid driver's licence from your own country and an international driver's licence.
Motorbike $5–10/£3–7/day including insurance	Economical and flexible. Excellent for touring countryside.	Dangerous in heavy traffic. Need valid driver's licence and a 30-day permit obtainable after a test at police stations with the help of a rental agent.
Bicycle/Mountain bike $5–10/£3–7/day	Great way to see countryside if you are fit.	Countryside is hilly. Dangerous in South Bali's heavy traffic.
Metered taxi $0.25/£0.17/km	Convenient, the most economical form of transport for short duration. Will go anywhere. Readily available by phone in Kuta, Sanur, and Nusa Dua.	Originate only in Kuta and Sanur. Drivers may not speak foreign languages.
Shuttle van $2.50–5.50/£1.70–3.70 depending on distance	Economical transport between common tourist destinations. Fixed prices.	Originate only in Kuta and Sanur. Drivers may not speak foreign languages.
Local mini-vans $0.05/£0.03/km	Cheap, very frequent. Recommended in Denpasar.	Routes are arcane, designed for local service, not tourists. Infrequent service after dark.

Services in Bali expand as fast as the growing sophistication of the workforce and infrastructure permit. ATMs are new and exist only in a few locations (Bank Central Asia in Kuta and Denpasar). It may take weeks to cash a foreign bank draft. Telex transfers are often routed through Jakarta. Patience and a smile are essential.

MONEY

The Indonesian currency, the rupiah, is the most common form of payment in Bali. In 1996 US$1 = Rp2339/£1=Rp3175. Coins are in denominations of Rp25, 50, 100, and 500, and bills in denominations of Rp100, 500, 1000, 5000, 10,000, 20,000, and 50,000. Keep a supply of Rp1000 and Rp500 as sellers sometimes claim not to have change for larger bills. Rp5 and Rp10 coins are going out of circulation.

HOURS

Bank and government office hours are 8am–2.30pm Mon.–Fri.; closed on Sat. and Sun. Most retail businesses are open daily with varying hours, generally 9am–5pm or 6pm, many until 9pm or 10pm. Some shops in Denpasar and Kuta close between 2pm and 5pm and are open late. Certain services like airline offices close on Sundays, but major hotels keep services open after-hours and on holidays.

CURRENCY EXCHANGE

Besides banks in the major towns, there are many authorized currency exchanges in the major tourism areas offering competitive rates. Hours vary, but they are generally open daily until 6pm (including Sun.). Currency exchanges in the major hotels charge higher than average rates.

POSTAL SERVICES

Local post offices keep government office hours. Licenced postal services abound in tourist areas for simple procedures like buying stamps and mailing letters. Look for small orange signs with white lettering: "KP&G (Kantor Pos & Giro) Postal service". Postal rates at these services may vary.

PERIODICALS

The *Jakarta Post* is the Indonesian English-language newspaper. The Indonesian-language daily newspaper, the *Bali Post*, has an English-language section. Foreign news publications available include the *International Herald Tribune, Time, Newsweek, Asiaweek, Far East Economic Review,* and *The Economist*. Large hotels also carry major European periodicals.

TELEVISION

The government-run TVRI is the major channel, broadcast from Jakarta, with local programming from Denpasar. There is an English-language news program, produced in Bali, every evening at 6.30pm on the commercial channels. CNN and Australian and French channels are available on satellite TV in large hotels and in an increasing number of private establishments.

RADIO

There are numerous local broadcasts on AM and FM. News is produced by Radio Indonesia. BBC World Service, Radio Australia, and other foreign broadcasts are accessible on shortwave.

TIME DIFFERENTIAL

Bali is GMT + 8 hours. This is the same as Singapore time, but one hour ahead of Jakarta.

The Jakarta Post
The journal of Indonesia today
SUNDAY

Local fruit strives for recognition

CREDIT CARDS

Visa and MasterCard are widely accepted in major hotels and by an increasing number of shops. A 5 percent commission is added as a surcharge.

PRICE CHART

| A CUP OF COFFEE (TOURIST RESTAURANT) RP500 | 1 PLATE *NASI CAMPUR* (TOURIST RESTAURANT) RP3500 | POSTAGE FOR POSTCARD TO ANYWHERE IN THE WORLD RP600 | 1 ROLL OF FILM (PHOTO SHOP) RP7500 |
| 1 LITER OF GAS RP750 | ADMISSION TO CULTURAL PERFORMANCE RP7500 | MUSEUM ENTRANCE FEE RP500–1000 | 1 PIECE SARONG (ORDINARY) RP5000–20,000 |

ACCOMMODATION

TYPE	RATE	DESCRIPTION
Superior (all 5-star hotels and selected fine small hotels)	US$110–$2000++ /£73–£1333++ 81 in Bali (15 5-star) Rooms: 12,360	Luxury accommodation and services of international standard. Cultural performances, complete tour and concierge services, watersports.
Moderate Great variation in quality and value for money. Inspect first.	US$15–110++ /£10–£73++ 680 in Bali Rooms: 12,247	All have private bathrooms with hot water; many with swimming pool, laundry service, restaurant, and bar.
Budget Basic accommodation, usually family run, sometimes in house courtyard. Inspect first.	US$15++ and below /£10++ 471 in Bali Rooms: 1956	Usually a *losmen* or homestay. Simple room, often with private cold water bathroom, sometimes with fan. Nearly always includes breakfast. Service is simple but gracious. Comfort greatly improved if you provide own bed and bath linen. Electricity minimal, phones rare.

Note: There are no central reservation phone numbers or local ratings. Tax and service usually additional. Because of rapid inflation, many hotels, retail shops, and services list their prices in US dollars.

TIPPING

Many hotels include a service charge of about 15 percent which is supposed to be divided among the staff. Otherwise, tipping is voluntary, and gratefully accepted: wages in Bali are very low. If someone does you a big favor (like pulling your car out of a ditch), it is correct to offer a tip (Rp10,000 in this case); a Balinese would do the same.

BARGAINING

Expected unless prices are marked as fixed. You may always ask if you can bargain (*Boleh tawar?*). Try for at least half of the first price quoted. A craftsman will expect a much smaller profit than a large shop.

MANDI

Some accommodation comes with a *mandi*, a tub of water for bathing. Don't get into it; use the dipper to throw water over yourself. A few dippersful flush the toilet. If you want to take a hot bath, ask for some thermoses of hot water. Mix the hot water in a bucket, not in the *bak mandi*.

IDD TELEPHONE CALLS
International direct dialing (IDD) and fax services are available in most hotels, in TELKOM offices, and in private shops (WARTEL, from *warung telekomunikasi*) selling telecom services. IDD calls are charged by the minute.

Telecommunications services in Bali are being greatly expanded as this book goes to print. Five-digit phone numbers are gradually being changed to six-digit; prefixes are changing. Expect inconsistency and changing information. Telecommunications are not yet island-wide. Temples, many small businesses, and most private individuals do not yet have phones – but those who do often have a fax as well. Telephone books are scarce, and there is no standard convention yet for the alphabetical listing of Balinese names.

PUBLIC TELEPHONES
Public pay phones are of two sorts: those that take Rp100 coins and those that take phone cards, available at TELKOM offices and some shops, in denominations of pulses (1 pulse = Rp75). Cards are the most economical way to phone.

Pulses	Rp
60	4950
100	8250
140	11,550
280	23,100
400	33,000
680	56,100

TARIFFS
These are high in Indonesia, and in the major hotels they are exorbitant. Use home country direct (HCD) when possible. International calls through the operator are charged a base price for the first three minutes and a secondary rate for each following minute.

FROM OVERSEAS
♦ TO TELEPHONE BALI FROM THE UK
Dial 00 62 361 and then the number, dropping the 0 before the area code.
♦ TO TELEPHONE BALI FROM THE US
Dial 011 62 361 and then the number, dropping the 0 before the area code.

SERVICE NUMBERS

Ambulance	118
Police	110
Fire	113
Rescue	751-111
Complaints	117
Foreign language assistance	(021) 489-6558
Central (national) information	(021) 385-7974
Local information	108
AIDS Information	(021) 390-3838

PREFIXES

Country code	62
International Direct Dialing	001
Inter-regional operator	100
International operator	101
International information	102
Inter-regional information (outside Bali)	106

AREA CODES WITHIN BALI

Badung, Gianyar, Tabanan	(0)361
Buleleng	(0)362
Karangasem	(0)363
Jembrana (Negara)	(0)365
Klungkung (Semarapura) and Bangli	(0)366
Pupuan	(0)369

Note: To call within Indonesia but outside Bali, use the (0). To call Bali from outside of Indonesia, dial the country code and drop the (0) before the area code.

TELKOM RATES FOR OVERSEAS CALLS (in rupiah, 1994)

COUNTRY	PHONE				FAX PER PAGE
	CPP	SS	PP	CAM	
Australia	455	13,650	22,750	4550	8085
Europe	618	18,540	30,900	6180	10,835
U.K.	520	15,600	26,000	5200	9185
U.S.	455	13,650	22,750	4550	8085

KEY:
CCP = Cost in rupiah per pulse (minimum 6 pulses)
SS = Station to station via operator (3 minutes)
PP = Person to person via operator (3 minutes)
CAM = Cost per minute after minimum 3 minutes
Rates lower on Sundays and holidays.

COUNTRY NAMES IN INDONESIAN:
England = *Inggris*; France = *Perancis*; Germany = *Jerman*; Netherlands = *Belanda*; US = *Amerika Serikat* (AS)

BUYER BEWARE

Clothes sizes are mostly "small", "medium", and "large", and sometimes "XL". Shoes follow the European system (USA 7½ = 38). None of these sizes are to an exact standard. Be sure to try things on, especially shoes (both of them). You may find cheap shirts in the supermarket that say "Made in France". They aren't.

RESTAURANT ETIQUETTE

One pays after eating. To ask for the bill, say *minta bill*. Unless a prohibition is printed on the check, tips are voluntary, at one's discretion. Waiters in tourist restaurants are often young and inexperienced and may not be able to give much advice. In *rumah makan* (local restaurants) you often write down your order. A *warung* has no menu; what you see is what is available. Pay afterward, telling the vendor what you had.

BALINESE AND INDONESIAN SPECIALTIES

BABI GULING

Spit-roasted suckling pig, a speciality of Gianyar, is available in many tourist restaurants if ordered twenty-four hours in advance. Good for groups. Try it at the *bale banjar* in Gianyar or in Ubud Tengah.

GADO-GADO

Vegetarian dish par excellence: slices of steamed rice cakes with steamed vegetables in a spicy peanut sauce. Standard fare in tourist restaurants. The same thing at a *warung* is called *tipat*, with brighter spicing and at a fraction of the price. Try it at Warung Unick, Candi Kuning, Lake Bratan.

NASI CAMPUR

The basic daily rice dish, served with a variety of spicy meat and vegetables as condiments. Try it at Made's Warung, Kuta, or the Ubud market (until noon).

SATAY

Skewers of grilled chicken, beef, pork, or goat served in a peanut sauce with rice and a meat soup. Try it at Nomad, Ubud, or the Satriya bird market, Denpasar.

BEBEK TUTU

A baked spicy duck, this must be ordered 24 hours in advance from most tourist restaurants. The duck is rubbed with spices, wrapped in banana leaf and bamboo sheath, and roasted overnight under a heap of smoldering rice husks. One duck feeds two tourists or ten Balinese. Try it at Ibu Arsa's, Peliatan.

Steamed cakes.

WARUNG

These are local stalls ● *84* offering home-cooked food at minimal prices in minimal comfort. Night markets in Denpasar offer a great variety of Balinese and Indonesian speciality. Prices are reasonable; *nasi campur* ● *86* costs Rp1000–2500 at a *warung* and Rp7000 in a hotel restaurant. Drinks include coffee, beer, soft drinks, bottled water, tea, and *arak*. Food quality varies; hygiene is very casual.

LOCAL BREW

Due to an old Dutch tax on wine that has never been repealed, the price of wine in Indonesia is several times its cost elsewhere. People make do with the very good local beers – cheap and available everywhere and especially good on tap. The common domestic beers are Bintang, Anker, and San Miguel. *Brem* (rice beer) is often called "rice wine", but should not be confused with real wine: it is heavy, sweet, and milky. *Tuak* is palm toddy. *Arak* (distilled *brem* or *tuak*) is strong, clear, cheap, and often used in local cocktails.

BRIEF FOOD GLOSSARY

aqua : bottled water
ayam : chicken
babi : pork
bir kecil : small beer
bir besar : large beer
cap cay (pronounced chap chye) : stir-fried mixed vegetables with chicken or pork
cumi-cumi : squid
goreng : fried
gula : sugar
gurami : similar to bass, a freshwater fish
ikan laut : (sea) fish
kopi : coffee
mee goreng : fried noodles
nasi goreng : fried rice with vegetables, meat, and sometimes shrimp
nasi putih : plain white rice
panggang : grilled
rebus : boiled
sapi : beef
sayur : vegetables
susu : milk (usually powdered or processed)
tampa gula : without sugar
teh : tea
telor : egg
telor mata sapi : fried egg
udang : prawns

Bali is justly famous for its unique Hindu culture, the splendor of its ritual arts, and the charm of its people. It has been romantically called the "Island of the Gods". Seen through Western eyes as an idyllic tropical paradise, it continues to attract hordes of tourists. But although tourism is intense, much of Bali's countryside is still unspoiled.

Rice terraces near Sideman.

GEOGRAPHY

Bali's 2253-square-mile surface is dominated by a range of volcanic mountains across the north, scattered with lakes which run into numerous rivers. The broad plains of the south are irrigated by an ingenious, centuries-old system of water distribution ◆ *304* that allows rice to be grown year-round and thus to support a dense population. Much of Bali is under cultivation, but there remain virgin rain forests in the western mountains which are under government protection. The ecological challenges of Bali's rapid development are tremendous and are beginning to command the attention of the government and local environmentalists.

ECONOMY

More than 80 percent of the economy is based on agriculture, the other sectors being handicrafts, tourism, small trade, and professional services. The principal agricultural products are rice, coffee, cloves, fruit, livestock such as pigs, cattle, and ducks, as well as fishing and food processing. Emerging industries are tourism, textile and garment manufacture, and the development of new produce such as seaweed, cashews, and garden vegetables for the tourism market.

POPULATION

Most of Bali's 2.9 million people live in villages in the central southern plains and in the capital towns of the eight *kabupaten* or regencies ● *41*. The Balinese have brown skin, straight or curly dark hair, and fine, expressive hands. In comparison to their Javanese compatriots, they are extroverted, playful, and proud. The most common employment for men is farming; many are also craftsmen. Most women are small merchants. Nearly all children under twelve attend public schools; many go on to secondary school and tertiary institutes, such as the Performing Arts Academy or one of Bali's three universities.

HISTORY

Bali's history ● *31* is vague until the 18th century, but there is much evidence of the influence of Hindu Java, especially that of the 14th-century court culture of Majapahit, which was absorbed and reinterpreted in the Balinese arts. Sculpture, painting, music, theater, dance, metallurgy, weaving, and poetry all thrived in the crucible of royal patronage as lords competed to express their prestige in state ceremonies and the building of palaces and temples. Although the Dutch had ruled Java since the 17th century, it was not until the mid 19th century that they became interested in Bali. After a series of military expeditions against various Balinese kingdoms the Dutch finally conquered Bali in 1908. Colonial rule froze the social order according to Dutch notions of Balinese tradition; it also improved the irrigation system, and set the example of a paternalistic bureaucracy. Dutch rule ended with the Japanese invasion in 1942. After the declaration of an independent Indonesia in 1945, Balinese guerrillas led by I Gusti Ngurah Rai gallantly resisted the Dutch. Bali became a province of the Republic of Indonesia in 1958, eight years after the founding of the nation.

INTERNATIONAL ARRIVALS IN BALI	
YEAR	NUMBER OF ARRIVALS
1973	54,000
1983	170,000
1993	739,000

Gathering salt at Kasumba.

Bedugul vegetable and fruit market.

TOURISM

To the visitor, the most visible economic activity is tourism and tourism-related industries such as handicrafts. Mass tourism in Bali is very recent, and many computer-literate Balinese grew up

before the advent of electricity and piped water. This, and the cultural chasm between Bali and the rest of the world, leads to incongruities – most often charming (such as offerings on the taxi dashboard) – and sometimes frustration. Most Balinese believe that tourism is strengthening their economy as well as promoting the prestige of their culture and thus helping to conserve their remarkable way of life.

STREET SMART

The postal address and street system in Bali can be quite confusing. It is only recently that addresses have been necessary at all. Streets may be known by several names; or the street name may be new and unfamiliar to the local people; or the name of the street may change through certain districts. Many addresses do not have numbers.
In 1994, there was still only one "bypass" in Bali. Its name is Ngurah Rai, but it is often abbreviated to

"bypass". Between Sanur and Kuta, it passes through unnamed land. Bali is divided into eight *kabupaten*. Towns, or *kota*, are divided into villages which are subdivided into districts called *banjar*. Many *banjar* and villages have the same name, and some central *banjar* have the same name as their villages. In this book, the addresses should be adequate as listed. "Kuta" alone means downtown Kuta; "Ubud" alone means central Ubud.

SOCIETY AND TRADITIONS

Balinese society is collectivist and place-oriented. Villages are organized around community temples, and collectively run by village councils called *banjar* ● 96. This social structure remains strong, even in urban areas. Family compounds ● 100 often contain three generations and three or four nuclear families, and each compound has a house temple where the ancestral deities are honored. Customary law is imbued with communal religious duties. Offerings are prepared daily and set out in the house temple and at various points around the compound, also the

shop, the car dashboard, and the market temple, if a woman sells there.

RELIGION

Most Balinese are Hindu. The roots of Balinese Hinduism (now called Agama Hindu Dharma Indonesia) are in various sects of Hindu-Buddhism, the veneration of ancestors,

and ancient Indonesian animism. The Balinese honor the supreme deity ● 46 in a variety of manifestations with offerings ● 54, some of which are spectacularly elaborate.

293

1. Pura Besakih

2. Goa Gajah

12. Pura Gunung Kawi

Singaraja
Kubutambahan

⑪

Penulisan

③ Lake Bratan
Bedugul

⑦

⑤ Ubud ⑫

Tabanan ②

④ Celuk

DENPASAR

Sanur

Kuta

⑥ Nusa Dua

11. Gitgit Waterfall

10. Bale Kambang, Taman Gili

9. Pura Ulun Danu Batur

3. Goa Lawa

4. Tanah Lot

5. Taman Ayun

6. Uluwatu

8. Pura Ulun Danu Bratan

7. Tirtha Empul

lt. Batur

ngli

Padang Bai

NUSA PENIDA

This tour is designed as a quick, intensive sampler of Bali, with a broad range of flavors and geography. It includes some famous tourist attractions and some out-of-the-way places, hedonism, and quiet. Because time is short, we suggest hiring a car and driver.

DAY 1

Check into a hotel on the beach in Sanur. Have a swim and lunch at the hotel and take advantage of Bali's famous hospitality to let yourself unwind and be spoiled for an afternoon. Make arrangements with your hotel for the next day's transportation – you want a car and driver for the day, to take you as far as Ubud – and make a booking for lunch tomorrow afternoon at the Amandari and at your Ubud hotel. Ask your hotel to arrange transport to the 6 pm *kecak* performance at the Werdi Budaya Art Center, in nearby Denpasar. After the performance, wander down the beach for dinner at the Sanur Beach Market. If you are up to it, the hottest nightspots are in Kuta at Double Six or Chez Gado Gado. The disco starts at 1 am.

DAY 2

Leave early enough to catch the *barong* dance at the Pura Puseh in Batubulan at 9.30 am ▲ *148*. This is a performance for tourists, but it is great theater and still somewhat sacred. After the dance, stop at the Sukawati Art Market and buy a temple sash for visiting temples, then follow the main road north to Batuan and visit the Pura Puseh Batuan ▲ *154*. Head west through Batuan and visit the studios of painters W. Bendi and Dewa Putu Toris in Banjar Tengah Batuan. Continue west through Batuan, then cut south and west again to Singapadu. Along this route you will find many silversmiths, several mask carvers, and very few tourists. There are good shopping opportunities here ◆ *306*. At the T-junction of Singapadu and the Sayan road, turn right (north) and have lunch at the Amandari. After lunch continue into Ubud and check into your hotel. Hire a bicycle and ride north up Jalan Suweta, following it through villages and rice fields for three or four miles until you reach the highest ground of this rice-growing plateau. Watch the sky for great V-shaped flocks of white herons returning to roost in the nearby village of Petulu ▲ *176*. Retrace your route and come back into Ubud as the lamps are coming on. Wander over to the Cafe Lotus or to Ary's Warung for a drink in the quiet chic that Ubud is getting good at, and then go to the Ubud Palace (Puri Saren) ▲ *163* a few yards away and watch the nightly dance performance. Have dinner at Griya Barbeque for great food in a quiet romantic setting. For night owls, Nomad stays open late. Beggars' Bush has old jazz music. Casa Luna has quiet live music on Thursdays and Saturdays. Ubud doesn't disco.

Stonecarver in Batubulan.

Ubud Palace.

DAY 3

Today you are heading for the mountains. If you have not engaged a car and driver, ask your hotel to help with transportation for an overnight tour to Kintamani/Batur and onward. Set out north along the Tegallalang road. If you want to buy wood carvings, today's the day. You are welcome to visit the studios that line the road, especially that of I Made Ada, near Ceking, a famous stop for viewing the rice fields. At Pujung, turn east toward Sebatu and stop at the spring temple Pura Gunung Kawi ▲ 178. Continue on to Sebatu. Stroll around the village, perhaps stopping in a *warung* for a snack, and ask to see the Pura Desa ▲ 180 with its many painted wood sculptures. From Sebatu take the road north and rejoin the road to Kintamani. As you approach the rim of the caldera, there will be stands selling seasonal fruit from the region. At the top of the road, turn left for Kintamani and Pura Ulun Danu Batur ▲ 184. Don your temple sash again and explore this temple dedicated to the lake goddess. Have lunch in north Kintamani at the very modest Rumah Makan Cahaya. After lunch continue several miles farther up the road to Pura Penulisan ▲ 185. Return back through Kintamani and on to Penelokan. There are a number of good vantage points from which to photograph the view, but be prepared to be accosted by peddlers. Take the winding road down to the lake and over the moon-like landscape to Toyabungkah and check into Under the Volcano. Enjoy an excellent dinner of lake fish here.

DEPARTURE CHECKLIST
- bed and bath linen (for day 3)
- light jacket
- flashlight
- swimwear
- personal items

Festival at Puri Penulisan.

DAY 4

If you wake up early you can see the fishermen coming in with their catch. And if you wake up very early indeed you can climb Mount Batur and watch the sunrise from the crater of the volcano itself (and even find hot coffee there). After breakfast, head for Besakih ▲ 208 via the back road through Suter. There is a good chance that one of the many temples here will be having some kind of ceremony.

Now take the road south toward Klungkung. In Klungkung there is a huge market that is not yet overrun with tourists. This is a good opportunity for shopping for things from all over the archipelago. If you can wait that long, lunch back in Sanur at the Cafe Batujimbar with the freshest of organically grown produce – an excellent way to ease back into the world of the West.

BALI IN A WEEKEND

Check into one of the following hotels and spoil yourself.

Four Seasons Resort (Jimbaran Bay) ♦ 338
Great location, architecture, food, service, and gardens. The rooms are really townhouses, made up of several pavilions and a private dip-pool.

Bali Oberoi (Legian Beach, Kuta) ♦ 336
Secluded, fine understated architecture of white coral, great beach, luxury villas.

Tandjung Sari (Sanur) ♦ 335
Simple, very personal, small luxury hotel on the beach, with beautiful old gardens.

Amandari (Ubud) ♦ 327
Superb architecture, luxury villas, some with private swimming pool. Wonderful food.

Amanusa (Nusa Dua) ♦ 338
Luxury villas on an eighteen-hole golf course. Handsome architecture, fine Italian restaurant.

Amankila (Karangasem) ♦ 328
Exciting location on a hill overlooking the sea, luxury villas, beach, and some marvelous swimming pools.

Fruitful wood carvings.

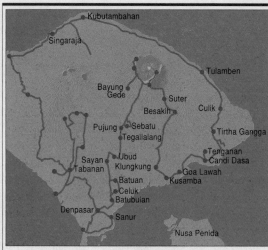

Small as Bali is, you can't see it all in ten days – and part of getting to know the island is having time to do nothing. What follows gives you a combination of exploration and leisure over a wide range of terrain. You will inevitably run into bands of tourists; this too is part of Bali's reality.

DAY 1

Check into a hotel by the sea (in Sanur or Kuta). Have lunch at the hotel and spend the afternoon slowing down at the pool, on the beach, or just indulging in Bali's famous hospitality. Walk to dinner (Sanur Beach Market, PJ's at the Four Seasons, or TJ's on Poppies' Lane). For those who enjoy a late nightlife, visit Double Six or Chez Gado Gado in Kuta.

DAY 2

Hire a car and driver for a day's tour of the Regency of Tabanan. See the splendid seaside temple Tanah Lot ▲ 254 early in the morning. Then head for Pura Luhur Batu Karu ▲ 258 on the slopes of Mount Batu Karu.

Drive through some of Bali's loveliest rice terrace country via Jatiluwih, and stop for lunch at the pleasant Soka Sari restaurant, in Soka. Turn south at Apuan. At Margarana, visit the very quiet and moving martyrs'

cemetery. From here, go back through Tabanan heading west and turn left for Kerambitan. Spend a royal evening at the palace's Puri Night which offers a banquet dinner and first-class *tektekan* trance theater.

DAY 4

Join Victor Mason's Bali Bird Walk for a morning's walk concluding with lunch. In the afternoon, visit the Museum Puri Lukisan ▲ 168 and see the morning's sights translated into Balinese painting. To buy paintings, visit the Neka Gallery, Puri Lempad, Agung Rai Gallery, or any of the many Ubud art shops. Evening: The Ganesha Bookshop offers "An Introduction to Balinese Music". Have dinner at Nomad (try the *satay*). If there is a temple festival nearby, go to it.

DAY 3

After last night's trance you can skip the *barong* dance in Batubulan but you may recognize some of the principal demons in the stone-carving studios that line the road through this village. A few miles farther is Celuk, the village of gold- and silversmiths; take Jalan Jagaraga, the small road north through the village (left off the main road) to find the little studios that furnish the big shops. Follow the back road to Batuan where you will find practitioners of most of Bali's arts, especially painting, jewelry, and weaving. Visit the Pura Puseh Batuan ▲ 154. The road west from Batuan will bring you to the Sayan road toward Kedewatan and Ubud. Head north along this road and stop for lunch at the Amandari or continue on to Ubud and have lunch at Griya or Cafe Lotus. After lunch check into your hotel (two nights). For short visits, stay in the center of Ubud. The rice fields are only a few minutes' walk away. See a dance performance at Puri Saren Agung, then walk to dinner at Ary's, Nomad, Cafe Wayan, or any of dozens of good eating places nearby.

Klungkung shop.

Warriors' monument at Margarana.

DAY 5

Rent a car or charter a mini-van and tell the driver that you want to sleep in the mountains. Take the Tegallalang road toward Kintamani and follow the plans for "Day 3" ◆ *297*, but with this important extra side-trip on your way from Kintamani to Penelokan: the mountain village of Bayung Gede ▲ *254*. At Penelokan take the road down to the lake and find a room for the night at Toyabungkah. Under the Volcano is a favorite. If still light, take a drive around the northern flank of the volcano and see the black lava flow.

DAY 6

Make an early morning visit to Pura Ulun Danu ▲ *183*, temple of the lake goddess, beyond the village of Songan. After breakfast, pack up and head for Besakih ▲ *208* via Suter, Keladian, and Kunyit. From Besakih, take the main road south to the last of Bali's former royal realms, Klungkung, whose kings were the traditional custodians of Besakih. See the Kerta Gosa, Hall of Justice ▲ *204*. In the nearby village of Kamasan, you can find painters still practicing the traditional style. On the main road east after Kusamba is Goa Lawah ▲ *212*. This is more than a bat cave. It is linked spiritually with Pura Besakih, and is also an important station in the purification of the cremated dead. This morning you have traced the path of a three-phase cycle from divine origins through human existence to the underworld. From Goa Lawah, the souls of the ancestors are escorted to Besakih and on to heaven, but you may proceed to lunch at TJ's in Candi Dasa. After lunch check into a hotel (two nights). From here it is a short trip to visit the famous Bali Aga village of Tengenan ▲ *216*.

DAY 7

Although there isn't much beach left at Candi Dasa, the snorkeling and diving are good. Or go to the northeast for diving in Tulamben ▲ *228* or in Lipah on the coast east of Culik. Or you can go to Tirtha Gangga ▲ *226* and actually swim in holy water. For lunch, try the sandwiches at the nearby Rice Terrace Coffeeshop.

DAYS 8 AND 9

(Book in advance Iskander's bike tour ◆ *310* tailored to your fitness and the countryside you'd like to see later today.) Set out early and follow the road along the coast to north Bali, via Singaraja and Lovina, and then at Seririt, head south for the mountains. You arrive at the village of Batungsel, Pupuan, by 12.30 for lunch. Spend the next few hours familiarizing yourself with your bike and the area. Enjoy your dinner and accommodation at Iskander's farm house. The next day, after breakfast, you set out on mountain bikes with guides and a picnic lunch and are met later by your car. If this is your last night in Bali, try staying on the south coast close to phones and the airport, ideally at the Four Seasons in Jimbaran where your educated eye will appreciate the references to Balinese architecture, and the sight of planes flying over the bay will help you get used to the idea of leaving Bali.

DAY 10

If you have been smitten with Baliphilia, you might want to go shopping ◆ *306*, and restore yourself afterward at Riyoshi, the Japanese restaurant in Seminyak. The Galleria Nusa Dua offers several acres of one-stop shopping. The Batik Keris Department Store in the same complex lets you do it all in air-conditioned surroundings. The mezzanine coffee shop has a comprehensive choice of Indonesian coffees. Really special things can be found at the Gallery at Amanusa,* and at the boutique at Four Seasons.

The traditional context of Balinese performing arts is religious occasions, some of which are described here. But the regularly scheduled performances for tourists are just as good, much shorter, and the viewing conditions are better than at some of the performances in temple festivals. In either case, the dancers and musicians are usually the same.

Nyepi

Nyepi, the "Day of Silence", usually falls sometime in March or April on the new moon. All the excitement is on the day before: huge ceremonies of exorcism at major crossroads, followed by parades of terrifying effigies, firecrackers, and as much noise as possible to scare the demons. The best place to see this is in Denpasar. On Nyepi itself it is forbidden to light fires or leave the house after early morning. No lamps may be lit that evening: the entire island is to remain dark and silent.

Purnama Kedasa

Purnama Kedasa is the full moon after Nyepi. There are big temple festivals lasting eleven days at Besakih and Pura Batur. If you try to go to either on the day of Purnama Kedasa itself, be prepared for immense crowds and restrictive entry policies.

Purnama Kapat

This is another important full moon holy day, usually falling sometime in October. Big temple festivals are held at Besakih and many other temples.

Galungan and Kuningan

Galungan is a holy day of obscure origin, described in tourist literature as a day celebrating the "victory of good over evil" but ritually more like an "All Souls' and Saints' Day" and

CULTURAL

	SUNDAY	MONDAY	TUESDAY
Batubulan Pura Puseh Bendul Puri Batubulan	*Barong* 9.30am *Kecak*/Fire trance 6.30pm	*Barong* 9.30am *Kecak*/Fire trance 6.30pm	*Barong* 9.30am *Kecak*/Fire trance 6.30pm
Bona Gianyar	*Kecak*/Fire trance 7pm	*Kecak*/Fire trance 7pm	
Denpasar Werdi Budaya Arts Center Jl. Nusa Indah Puri Kesiman Kesiman	*Kecak* 6.30pm *Barong* 9.30am	*Kecak* 6.30pm *Barong* 9.30am	*Kecak* 6.30pm *Barong* 9.30am
Mawang Village Center			
Padang Tegal (Ubud) Padang Tegal Stage Jl. Hanoman	*Kecak* 7pm		*Kecak* 7pm
Peliatan Puri Agung Banjar Teges Bale Banjar Central Peliatan			
Ubud Hotel Oka Kartini Jl. Raya Pura Dalem Puri Tebesaya Ubud Palace	*Wayang Kulit* 8pm *Mahabarata* 7.30pm	 Siwa Ratri Dance 7.30pm *Legong* 7.30pm	 *Ramayana* 8 pm

PRIVATE CEREMONIES

Tourists are sometimes invited to a wedding, tooth filing, cremation, or other family ceremony ● *52.* You will want to dress correctly ● *92,* and it is customary to bring a gift ● *90.* Protocol at private ceremonies is simple. Your hosts will tell you where to sit, serve you with refreshments, and point out photo opportunities. You will not have to pray or do anything at all except to appear to partake of the buffet feast, and to say goodbye to your hosts when you leave (which you may do any time after you've eaten).

socially and commercially the Balinese equivalent of Christmas. Galungan is the most disruptive of the holidays; most businesses close the day before and the day after as well as on Galungan itself. There is little for the visitor to see as this is a domestic holiday, a time for prayers, and for visiting friends and relations. On Galungan and the day after (Manis Galungan), the roads are clogged. Kuningan follows ten days later, with a fresh feast and more offerings. The ritual calendar is dense with temple festivals in the weeks following Kuningan.

HARI RAYA SARASWATI

The last day of the 210-day calendar ● *82,* this is devoted to Saraswati, the goddess of knowledge, wisdom, and the arts ● *47.* This particularly Hindu holy day, which always falls on a Saturday, has become increasingly important in Bali; it is an official holiday. Hari Raya Saraswati is most famous for being the day when books are given offerings and it is forbidden to read or write. It is also the day that people take gifts to "wise men" (sorcerers and healers and, recently, doctors) who have helped them.

ARTS FESTIVAL

The annual Bali Arts Festival is a government-sponsored, month-long jamboree, usually from mid June to mid July. It is held at the Werdha Budi Arts Center, in Denpasar. Included are exhibitions and performances of new and traditional art, dance, and music.

CULTURAL PERFORMANCES

Some of the major regularly scheduled performances are listed in the chart below (see glossary for descriptions of the performances). There are also myriad hotel and restaurant performances. Tourist performances allow dance troupes and *gamelan* groups to earn enough money to maintain costumes and instruments and to help keep these art forms alive. The schedule is subject to frequent changes, so check with your hotel or the Bina Wisata Tourist Information Center in Ubud. Admission is usually Rp5000.

ERFORMANCES

WEDNESDAY	THURSDAY	FRIDAY	SATURDAY
Barong 9.30am	*Barong* 9.30am	*Barong* 9.30am	*Barong* 9.30am
Kecak/Fire trance 6.30pm	*Kecak*/Fire trance 6.30pm	*Kecak*/Fire trance 6.30pm	*Kecak*/Fire trance 6.30pm
Kecak/Fire trance 7pm		*Kecak*/Fire trance 7pm	
Kecak 6.30pm	*Kecak* 6.30pm	*Kecak* 6.30pm	*Kecak* 6.30pm
Barong 9.30am	*Barong* 9.3am	*Barong* 9.30am	*Barong* 9.30am
	Barong 7.30pm		*Barong* 7.30pm
Ramayana 7pm	*Barong Landung* 7.30pm		
	Kecak 7.30pm		
	Mahabarata 7.30pm	*Legong* 7.30pm	
Wayang Kulit 8pm			
	Barong 7.30pm		*Barong* 7.30pm
	Gabor 7.30pm.	*Barong* 6.30pm	*Legong* 7.30pm

301

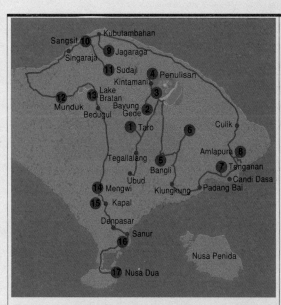

SITES OF SPECIAL ARCHITECTURAL INTEREST

Start your tour by heading north from Ubud, along the Tegallalang road. Pura Gunung Raung (1), Taro, is a large single courtyard temple at the heart of the village. Notice the very long *bale agung* pavilion, built from a single tree. The huge three-tiered *meru* is in the west, symbolic of Mount Raung, from where the village's founders originated ▲ 186.

Return to the Tegallalang road and continue north to the Kintamani road. Turn left on the Kintamani road and, several miles farther, turn left again and find the village of Bayung Gede (2), about a mile down that road. In Bayung Gede, the village layout and uniformity of the house compounds is typical of Bali Aga villages ▲ 218. The Pura Puseh, a short way to the northeast, is remarkably simple and pristine ▲ 184. The tall *meru* of Pura Ulun Danu Batur (3) are visible in the distance as you approach Kintamani. This important temple honoring the lake goddess and agricultural deities was built with the help of the Dutch in the 1920's and is periodically renovated with donations from its large congregation of rice farmers ▲ 184. One of the oldest existing royal temples is Pura Penulisan (4), on the Kintamani road toward Singaraja. The pyramidal form of the temple complex rising in terraces suggests that this site was sacred in pre-Hindu times ▲ 185.

This is a tour to take at your own pace, ideally over several days. To become familiar with the layout and elements of Balinese architecture ● *97,* we suggest beginning in Ubud with an "Ubud architectural sampler", visiting a house compound, two temples, and a palace. Then we propose a number of places around Bali that are remarkable for the beauty — or the eccentricity — of their architecture.

UBUD ARCHITECTURAL SAMPLER

Pura Gunung Lebah (a), at Campuhan, is a fine example of classic temple architecture ● *104.* Puri Saren (Ubud Palace) (b) is a small but sumptuous royal house ▲ *162.* Notice the grand gates, large first courtyard (where dance performances are held every evening), and fine ceramic *batu galang* (transparent "stones") in the walls. The *bale bengong* that looks over the palace walls was where royal women used to look out onto the world. *Bengong* means to "gaze out into space". The middle courtyard has guest pavilions. The *saren* (private quarters) are further inside. Puri Lempad (c) is a traditional nobleman's house, built by Bali's most celebrated architect and artist, I Gusti Nyoman Lempad ▲ *164* . On the outside are family businesses (art shops). The main courtyard has a handsome ceremonial *bale Bali* ● *102* on the east, *bale meten* in the north, house temple in the northeast, and kitchen in the south. Pura Taman Sari (d), in Banjar Taman Kelod, is a single courtyard temple.

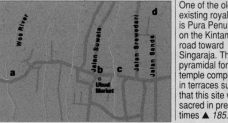

Nusa Dua Beach Hotel architecture.

Rice barn architecture, Sudaji.

Return through Kintamani and continue on to Bangli. Pura Kehen **(5)**, state temple of Bangli's kings, is a splendid example of royal temple architecture and of the virtuosity of Bangli's stonecarvers ▲ *198*. Pura Besakih's **(6)** grandeur and complexity reflect its importance to all Hindu Bali. Nearly all of the island's many clan dynasties are represented in the myriad small temples surrounding the imposing central Pura Penataran Agung ▲ *209*. To the east, the village of Tenganan **(7)**, near Candi Dasa, is remarkable for its archaic way of life, reflected in the village layout ▲ *216* and many communal ceremonial buildings . Puri Kanginan **(8)** in Amlapura shows the cosmopolitan tastes of the last ruling king of Karangasem, most evident in the Bale Maskerdam and floating pavilion in the central courtyard ▲ *226*.

Follow the east coast road toward Singaraja. Pura Dalem Jagaraga **(9)** is wildly carved in the dense manner typical of north Bali. Notice that the inner courtyard is, unusually, lower than the first ▲ *234*. Pura Beji Sangsit **(10)** has particularly fine carving in the richly ornate style of north Bali ▲ *235*. The rice barns **(11)** of north Bali are made of timber, often with

fine carving. Good examples may be seen on the road to Sudaji. Sudaji's village center is one of the most harmonious and charming in Bali, with temples and market shaded by grand old trees ▲ *235*. Head west to Seririt, then southeast to Munduk. In the rich coffee-growing valley around Banyuatis and Munduk **(12)**, domestic architecture is solid in the manner of Dutch colonial buildings ▲ *239*.

Continue toward Lake Bratan. Pura Ulun Danu Bratan **(13)** is an exquisitely sited lake temple. The nearby Candi Kuning is a Buddhist stupa ▲ *238*. Follow the Bedugul-Denpasar road to Mengwi. Pura Taman Ayun **(14)**, the ancestral temple of royal Mengwi, was built in the 18th century ▲ *262*. Despite its grand proportions, the architecture is classical and elegant. Notice the particularly fine grand gate to the inner courtyard. The nine- and eleven-tiered *meru* honor the mountains of Batur, Batu Karu, and Agung, respectively. The broad moat around the temple adds to the feeling of otherworldly serenity. Continue toward Denpasar. As you enter Kapal, look sharply for a small side road on the right to Pura Sada **(15)**. Pura Sada has very unusual shrines in the inner courtyard ▲ *254*. Follow the main road into Denpasar to Tohpati and take the bypass south (straight, toward Sanur). At the intersection by the Grand Bali Beach Hotel, turn right toward Renon. Niti Mandala **(16)**, the complex of

government buildings in Renon, shows how elements of Balinese ornamentation are applied to building façades in the "Balinization" of modern architecture. In the same area are opulent new villas. Notice the new trend to put house temples on an upper story so that in multistory dwellings one will not be higher than the gods. The Nusa Dua Beach Hotel **(17)** is one of the most flamboyant examples of the use of traditional temple architecture in hotels and other secular buildings.

Farmer smoothing the rice field.

Praying at a Balinese field shrine.

The *subak* network, Bali's traditional irrigation system ■ 24, is typically Balinese — ingeniously low-tech, highly complex, communal, and ordered by religious principles. Wet rice cultivation requires flooding and draining the fields at precise stages of growth. Bali has plenty of water, but it is seasonal and it flows in deep river gorges far below the rice fields. To solve this problem, the Balinese diverted rivers high in the mountains into tunnels, aqueducts, and channels. They built weirs, channels, and terraces, creating an "engineered landscape" of amazing complexity. The water available for irrigation is not sufficient for all the farmers to plant their rice fields at the same time; but if the cycles are staggered, there is enough water for all. On the other hand, effective pest control requires that adjacent rice fields are drained or burned off at the same time. To coordinate the sharing of water and the syncopation of planting, farmers sharing the same water source form associations called *subak*. Membership is compulsory, and the maintenance of the irrigation ditches is done collectively. A number of *subak* may

receive water from the same dam; together they work out the distribution of water. To see the *subak* system at work you need to go into the rice fields and walk "upstream". Along the way you would pass a number of temples at each important junction. The rice farmers who worship at these temples are those whose fields lie downstream and receive water from that source. Thus the farther upstream, the greater the spiritual community, culminating at a *pura ulun danu* (lake temple). The Balinese believe that water originates in the goddess of the lake, and she is honored at every stage. As Stephen Lansing points out in his book *Priests and Programmers*, the water temple network thus marks a natural system of organization based on the flow of irrigation water and unified by the lake goddess.

Important Water Temples

Pura Ulun Danu Batur, Kintamani
A source temple. Lake Batur is believed to feed the other lakes through underground springs and tunnels. *Subak* from central and northeast Bali pay homage to the lake goddess, Dewi Danu.

Pura Pamwos, Apuh, Tegallalang
Temple honoring the deity of the river Wos. This temple marks the head of an irrigation system.

Pura Gunung Lebah, Ubud
Several branches of the Wos river join here, making this a place of concentrated spiritual power.

Pura Er Jeruk, Sukawati
Temple marking the downstream end of an irrigation system. The accumulated spiritual impurities create a "negative" force here which is balanced through ritual.

Ubud Subak Walk

In Ubud there is a comfortable walk through the rice fields at the end of Jalan Kajeng. No matter what stage of the rice cycle it is, the clear geography of the terraces is constant. Each rice field has a rim of earth held together by a tight net of grassroots. Water is let into and out of the terrace with a few chops of a hoe to open and close a gap in the rim. An irrigation ditch runs alongside the path, crossed at intervals by coconut log dams. The logs have several notches that can be stopped with ditch mud to divert the water. Some hundred yards up the path is the Pura Subak Jeruk Manis, where the farmers of this *subak* meet. As

you continue north, the ditch becomes a neat channel. The building and maintenance of this channel is the work of all the farmers who receive water from it. Still following the channel, you will notice that the rice terraces on your right are now above eye level. During the flooding of the fields, the runoff pours out through openings in the banks and flows back into the channel. On your left is a narrow river gorge with the stream far below. About half a mile into the rice fields is a small dam and a footbridge. A short distance farther is a tunnel bringing the water from far upstream.

Arts, Crafts, and Sports

The Balinese handicraft industry is a cottage industry, with thousands of individual artisans working from home to produce crafts for export. Traditional arts and crafts are concentrated in specialist villages, many of them in the region of Gianyar. In this directory, the villages best known for a craft are listed first. A comprehensive arts and crafts tour from South Bali leads through Batubulan, Celuk, Sukawati, Batuan, Mas, Ubud, Tegallalang, and Tampaksiring, returning through Gianyar with a sidetrip to Klungkung and Tengenan. Or if your interest is in just one craft, you may want to limit your tour to the villages listed for it.

PAINTINGS

Ubud
The heartland of Balinese painting; several important galleries and museums and hundreds of individual studios in central Ubud, Padang Tegal, Pengosekan, Campuhan, and Penestanan. Visit AGUNG RAI GALLERY ▲ 170, ALIT'S GALLERY, NEKA GALLERY ▲ 166, PURI LEMPAD, PURI LUKISAN ▲ 168, and PURPA GALLERY.

Batuan
Numerous galleries and individual artists' studios. See especially I MADE BUDI and MOKOH. Also DEWA PUTU TORIS, Tanjar Tengah. Tel. 298-530.

Klungkung
NYOMAN GUNARSA MUSEUM Jl. Raya Klungkung (east). Tel. (0366) 22-255 Open Tues.-Sun. 9am-5pm Admission: Rp5000 *Large collection of Balinese and Indonesian paintings.*

Kamasan, Klungkung
Br SanggING for traditional *wayang* style paintings. See especially NYOMAN MANDRA, MANGKU MURA, and IBU SUCIARMI.

CAUTION
Woodcarvings are subject to splitting when moved to a drier environment, and they may carry parasites. Expect concern at Australian customs. Enquire at cargo services about fumigation.

WOODCARVINGS
Grand galleries and studios specializing in fine wood sculpture, masks, and contemporary carvings. See especially (all on the main road):
NYANA TILEM GALLERY Tel. 975-099 *Woodcarvings.*
I.B. ANOM Tel. 975-292 *Masks.*
I.B. SUTARJA Tel. 975-206 *Masks.*
WAYAN MUKA On small lane going east. *Masks.*

Nyuhkuning, Ubud
NYUHKUNING MUSEUM, ▲ 174. *Carvings in jackfruit.*

Tegallalang
Hand-carved flowers, fruit trees, *garudas,* suspended angels, and wooden trinkets ▲ 178. Garudas particularly around Ceking; carved doors and hobby horses in north Pujung; Cokot-style root carvings ▲ 181 in Jasan; and in Sebatu, dozens of studios specializing in woodcarvings of all sorts.

(Note: Name of shop first; craftsman in parentheses.)

IBU KARTINI CITRA Gentong, Tegallalang Tel. 96-428 *Exporter, retail/wholesale.*
CEKING SARI (I Ketut Suweta) Ceking, Tegallalang Tel: 96014 Fax 975-120

BUYER'S TIP
Paras, the volcanic tuff used for temple carvings, looks like cement when it is new. A hard rain will make this porous stone darker and much heavier. One rainy season will make it look like an antique, that is, mossy. Painting *paras* with a thin coat of yoghurt and keeping it damp will hasten the transformation. Ship when dry.

DEWI ANTIQUES Ceking, Tegallalang
MANGKU PICE Jasan, Tegallalang
MULYASIH ART SHOP (I Made Senor) Br Bilukan, Sebatu
PONDOK PUSPITA (Wayan Gandra) Br Bilukan, Sebatu
SUMA DANU (I Made Ranus Artawan) Jl. Bilukan, Sebatu

STONE CARVINGS

Batubulan
Main center for fine traditional *paras* sculpture. In Br Tegal Tamu, Batubulan, see especially:
I MADE KAKUL Tel. 98-208
ROTE ADHI Tel. 98-145 Fax 98-622
WAYAN MERGOG

KENGETAN
(on the Sayan road) *Specializing in carved paras architectural elements.*

Ubud
WAYAN CEMUL *Primitive-style sculpture.*

GOLD- AND SILVERSMITHS
(Note: Gold and silver jewelry is sold by the gram.)

Celuk
Center for gold and silver jewelry ▲ 150. Best places for silver are on the small road.

JUST ASK
Many village studios do not have postal addresses or phones. Once you reach the village listed, just ask for the name and someone should be able to direct you.

Jalan Jagaraga. See especially:
PUTRA KEMBAR
No. 26
Tel./Fax 298-604
EDDY SANTANA
No. 25
Tel./Fax 298-291
SUWARSA
No. 17
Tel. 298-359

For gold:
BALI SUN SR
Main road
Tel. 298-275
Fax 232-268

Kamasan, Klungkung
Br Pande Mas for gold jewelry, silver bowls, and other ceremonial objects.

Budakling, Karangasem
Br Pande Mas for traditional gold jewelry.

Denpasar
Jl. Sulawesi and Jl. Hasanudin area. Many goldsmiths and silversmiths are on these two short streets.

Kuta
Br Pande Mas for traditional gold jewelry.

TEXTILES
GERINGSING
Tenganan
Buy directly from the weavers' homes.
INDIGO SHOP
(By. I Wayan Kondri)

Candi Dasa
GRINGSING SHOP

Ubud
JANI'S IKAT SHOP
Monkey Forest Road

SONGKET
Buy directly from weavers' homes in Br Bratan, Singaraja; Jero Kanginan,

Sideman; Br. Jero Agung, Gelgel; Batuan; and Sukawati.
SUKAWATI ART MARKET
PERTENUNAN "PELANGI"
(I Dewa Ketut Alit)
Br Budamanis, Sideman, and Jl. Soka 48, Tohpati, Denpasar

ENDEK IKAT
Weaving factories:
Denpasar
PERTENUNAN AAA
Jl. Veteran 9
PERTENUNAN SETIA
CAP CILI
Jl. Ciungwanara 7

Gianyar
CAP TOGOG
Jl. Astina Utara 11

CEREMONIAL UMBRELLAS
Petulu, Ubud
PAK WUK
Jalan Raya Andong

Sukawati
KIOS MERTA SEDANA
(Ibu Made Kuki)
Main road

Paksabali, Klungkung
SATRIA AGUNG
(A.A.Gde Raka Bagus)
Pasar Satria 7

WAYANG KULIT PUPPETS
Sukawati
Famous for its *dalang* and musicians.
SUKAWATI ART MARKET
DHARMA YAS HOME INDUSTRY
(I Wayan Reka)
Puaya (one block down the small road opposite the police station)

CERAMICS
Pejaten
Traditional cottage industry production of

terracotta tiles; now getting into other wares. See especially:
THE POTTERY

Sanur
JENGGALA KERAMIK
SARI BUMI
Jl. Danu Tamblingan (opposite the *bale banjar* Batujimbar).

ANTIQUES
Legian and Kuta
Many shops; see especially:
ARTS OF ASIA
Jl. Raya Kuta
Tel. 752860
POLOS GALLERY
Jl. Legian
Tel. 751316
Fax 751218
TIMOR ARTS
Jl. Legian 423A
Traditional textiles from east Indonesia.

Denpasar
ARTS OF ASIA
Jl. Thamrin 2737, Block C5
Tel. 223350
BALI SOUVENIR
Gianyar Road
Tohpati

Batubulan
Many shops on both sides of the main road to Gianyar. See especially:
KADEK NADHI ANTIQUES
(I Made Sagetnara)
Tel. 298105
PURI SAKANA, ANTIQUES ART GALLERY
(I Wayan Dupa Suciptra)
Tel. 298205
Fax 298210
MOJOPAHIT ART
(Abu Naim)

Celuk
AMANDA ANTIQUES
(I Made Guna Wijaya)

Batuan
MARIO ANTIQUES
Tel. 978541

Sakah
DEWATA ANTIQUES
(I Made Sadia)
East of the baby "Buddha" statue.
Fine reproduction furniture.

BASKETRY
Tenganan
PAK KEDEP
Basket weaver.

Pengosekan, Ubud
MANGKU GINA
Large decorative baskets.

Ubud
MERTA JASA II
Jl. Hanoman
Baskets from Tenganan and Lombok.

Major markets (Denpasar, Ubud, Sukawati)
Common domestic baskets.

ONE-STOP SHOPPING
For those who do not have the time or inclination to tour several villages for crafts, visit the Sukawati Art Market, the Galleria Nusa Dua shopping complex, Mega Art Shop (Jalan Gajah Mada 36-38) in Denpasar, or the souvenir market at Goa Gajah near Gianyar for one-stop shopping. An assortment of fine crafts and antiques from the region may be found at Kunang-Kunang I&II in Ubud and in the boutiques at the Aman hotels.

As an island, Bali offers myriad opportunities for watersports, including white-water rafting, surfing, diving, and parasailing. There are numerous yacht charters for day trips and longer cruises from Benoa Harbor. Bali also has two world-class golf courses and a 192,000-acre nature reserve. In this directory of some of the many opportunities for sports and outdoor activities, there is something for every visitor to Bali.

DIVING

Price ranges listed below (US$/UK£) generally include two full tanks, weight belt, lunch box, soft drinks, boat, dive guide, insurance, and hotel transfer. All originate from the Kuta-Sanur-Nusa Dua area unless otherwise noted.

DIVE LOCATIONS

NUSA DUA AND SANUR: $45–50/£30–34
Surprisingly good variety of fish, but limited coral. Very gentle current.

NUSA PENIDA: $68–85/£45–57

Excellent variety of fish and hard corals ■ 28. Can be very cold with unpredictable and often fierce currents (4+ knots).

PADANG BAI: $50–60/£34–40
Good variety and number of fish and scattered outcrops of coral. Gentle current.

CANDI DASA (Gili Tepekong): $58–65/£39–44
Excellent variety of coral in underwater canyon, teeming with fish. Can be very cold, with tricky, strong currents, more than 5 knots.

JEMELUK (Amed): $58–65/£39–44
Coastal reef with excellent variety of hard coral and fish. Mild current.

TULAMBEN: $58–65/£39–44

Good variety of animals on Liberty shipwreck ▲ 228. No current.

MENJANGAN ISLAND: $68–85/£45–57
Numerous soft corals and fish. Great visibility, with slight current. Access: thirty minutes by boat from Labuan Lalang.

SURFING

APRIL TO OCTOBER:

ULUWATU: Left, hollow, long rides, consistent; sharp coral bottom, strong current. Peak at high tide; Racetrack at mid-tide.

PADANG-PADANG: Next break down from Uluwatu. Hollow left; very dangerous below mid-tide.

BINGIN: Next channel down from Padang. Left, hollow, best at low-mid tide.

KUTA REEF: At south end of Kuta Beach; fifteen-minute paddle or Rp5000 by boat. Hollow, left, medium rides; best at mid-high tide.

KUTA BEACH: Famous sandy bottom beach break called the Halfway, usually somewhere across from the Sahid Beach Hotel. All tides.

CANGGU: Right and left. North of Legian Beach, past Krobokan village.

MEDEWI BEACH: About 42 miles west of Denpasar on the Denpasar-Negara road. Long left, hollow, breaks on a rocky beach.

NUSA LEMBONGAN: Three big breaks on the north coast, two

SURF SHOPS

BLUE SURF
Jl. Melasti, Legian

THE SURF SHOP
Jl. Legian, Kuta

THE BLUE GROOVE
Jl. Legian, Kuta

of them right.

NOVEMBER TO MARCH:

NUSA DUA: Right, hollow, medium rides; consistent; strong current. Best at mid-high tide. A Rp5000 boat ride off the beach past the golf club.

SANUR REEF: In front of the Bali Beach Hotel; fifteen-minute paddle on the side of the break, or Rp20,000 by boat. Best at low or mid-tide.

OTHER WATERSPORTS

A number of companies offer activities for about the same price:

JET SKI:
$20/£13/fifteen minutes

PARASAIL:
$10/£7/one trip

WATER SKI:
$15–20 (£10–13)/ fifteen minutes

WINDSURFING:
$10–15/£7–10/one hour

Contact:
BALI MARINE SPORTS
Jl. Bypass Ngurah Rai Blanjong, Sanur
Tel. 288-829
Fax 287-872

BARUNA WATER SPORTS (see "Dive companies").

ENA DIVE CENTER & WATER SPORTS (see "Dive companies").

WATERBOM PARK
Jl. Kartika Plaza

DIVE COMPANIES

BARUNA WATER SPORTS
(PT WISATA TIRTA BARUNA)
Jl. Bypass I Gusti Ngurah Rai 300B, Kuta
Tel. 753-820, 751-223
Fax 753-809, 752-779

DIVE & DIVES
Jl. Bypass I Gusti Ngurah Rai, 23, Sanur
Tel. 288-052 Fax 289-309

ENA DIVE CENTER & WATER SPORTS
Jl. Pengembak 7, Sanur
Tel. 287-134 Tel./Fax 287-945

DIVE PARADISE TULAMBEN
Paradise Palm Beach Bungalows
Tulamben, Kubu, Karangasem
c/o The Friendship Shop
Candi Dasa
Tel. (0361) 229-052

REEF SEEN AQUATICS
Pondok Sari Beach Bungalows & Dive Village
Pemuteran, Grokgak, Singaraja
Tel. (0362) 92-339

SPICE DIVE
Arya's Cafe, Lovina Beach
P.O. Box 157, Singaraja
(0362) 23-305

Surfing at Uluwatu.

White-water rafting.

Tel. 755-676/8
Fax 753-517
9am–6pm daily.
*Adults $7.50/£5,
children five to twelve
$4/£2.60 (under
twelve must be with
an adult), children
under five free.*

CRUISES/YACHT CHARTERS

*For package details,
contact individual
operators.*

Sirius 1935
Captain David Plant
Bali International
Marina, Suite 2,
Benoa Harbor
Tel. 771-470
Fax 771-479
*Historic 62-ft
pleasure schooner.
Suitable for extended
charters of up to
eight passengers (day
charters up to
twenty-five
passengers). Charter
cruises to Komodo
and around the
archipelago.
$820/£547/day for
boat/meals*

Sri Noa Noa
Naomi Petiniaud
Jl. Raya Sesetan 46
D, Br Pesanggaran,
Denpasar
Tel./Fax 233-555
A 46.5-ft schooner,

*for two to three
passengers. Private
charter.
SS Adelaar*
ADELAAR Cruises
Bali International
Yacht Club
Benoa Harbor
Tel./Fax 772-415
*Historic 124-ft Dutch
clipper. For eighteen
passengers, five
crew. Available for
extended charter and
day cruises.*

Golden Hawk (1879)
Golden Hawk Cruises
Jl. Danu Poso, 20A,
Sanur
Tel./Fax 287-431
*Handsome tall ship,
117-ft gaff-rigged
ketch carrying eight
sails; the oldest
continuously
operated sailing ship
in the world. Day
cruises to Nusa
Lembongan $85/£57.
Diving equipment
and services
available for
+$40/£27/person.*

P&O SPICE ISLAND
CRUISES
Jl. Pelabuhan
Benoa Harbor
Tel. 234-822
Fax 231-137
*Indonesia Expedition
Cruises of six,*

*seven, eight, and
thirteen days
duration on board the
double-hulled luxury
mini-liners M/V Island
Explorer (135-ft) or
M/V Spice Islander
(122-ft). Cruises
originating in Bali to
Kupang via Komodo
and the Lesser
Sundas.
$2569–$5321/£1713
–3547/adult, not
including meals.*

RASA YACHT
CHARTERS
Benoa Harbor
Tel. 288-756
*Three steel-hulled
ketches. Day cruises
to Nusa Lembongan
or chartered cruises
of two days.
Maximum twelve
passengers. Day
cruises $79/£53
(children four to
twelve $40/£27).*

BALI CAMAR YACHT
CHARTER
Benoa Harbor
Tel. 231-591
Fax 231-592
*Ocean Lady II, 47-ft
yacht. From Benoa to
Nusa Lembongan
and return. Day trips
(maximum twelve
passengers)
$75/£50/person;
overnight (maximum
of five)
$165/£110/person.
The Wakalouka, 69-ft
catamaran, to the
Nusa Lembongan
Reef Club.
$70/£47/person;
children five to fifteen
half-price; children
under five free. The
Helsal III, maxi racing
yacht, is available for
day charter to Nusa*

Lembongan $75/£50.

ISLAND EXPLORER
YACHT CRUISES
Jl. Sekar Waru 8,
Sanur
Tel./Fax 287-473 and
287-431
*The Island Explorer
is a 60-ft luxury
cruising yacht. Day
cruises to Nusa
Lembongan
$77/£52/person.
Budget cruise
$49/£33/person.*

ODYSSEY CRUISES
MBR TOURS &
TRAVEL
Jl. Sekarwaru 17
Br Blanjong, Sanur
Tel. 262-303 and
288-612
Fax 288-612
*Eight-day cruises
around the Lesser
Sunda Islands on the
96-ft Sea Safari.
Maximum twenty-
four passengers.
$150/£100/person/
day (children under
twelve half-price).*

BALI HAI CRUISES
Bali Hai Pier
Benoa Harbor
Tel. 234-331
Fax 234-334
*The Bali Hai, 112-ft
double decker
catamaran motor
launch, to Nusa
Lembongan. Day
trips $68/£45/person;
sunset/dinner cruise
$34/£23/person.*

BIG GAME FISHING

PT Tourdevco
Benoa Harbor
Tel. 231-591
Fax 231-592
*Light and heavy
tackle supplied on
the Simone III.*

Bali Golf and Country Club, Nusa Dua.

Mountain biking.

Departs Benoa Harbor daily at 8.30 am, returning 5 pm. one to six passengers. $100/£67/person.

Yos Water Sport
Jl. Pratama, Tanjung Benoa, Nusa Dua or PT Bali Intai Tour & Travel
Jl. Bypass Ngurah Rai 1B, Tuban, Kuta
Tel. 752-005
Fax 752-985
Half-day outings. Minimum two persons. Coral fishing $59/£40/person; trolling $75/£50/person.

GOLF
Bali Golf and Country Club
P.O.Box 12
Nusa Dua
Tel. 771-791
Fax 771-797
Eighteen-hole champion-ship course designed by Nelson/Wright. Multiple tees ranging from 5208 to 6849 yards - Par 72. Course rating: Championship tees, 72.4; Men's tees, 70.4; Ladies' tees, 69.9. Greens fees: weekdays $85/57 (eighteen holes), $50/£33 (nine holes); weekends and holidays $110/$60/£73/£40. Club rental: $25/£17. Tee times available from 6.30am–4pm.

Bali Handara Kosaido Country Club
Pancasari, Lake Bratan, Buleleng

Reservations Office
P.O. Box 3324
Denpasar, Bali
Tel. 288-944
(0362) 22-646
Fax 287-358
(0362) 23-048
Eighteen-hole champion-ship golf course designed by Peter Thompson, Michael Woveridge & Associates, chosen as one of the world's greatest fifty golf courses. High mountain lake country 3769 ft above sea level, average temperature 61–68°F. Greens fees: $57.75/£38.50 (eighteen holes). 25 percent discount for guests staying at club. Club rentals: $16/£11/day.

NATURE ADVENTURES
Bali Adventure Tours
Jl. Tunjung Mekar Legian Kelod, Kuta
Tel. 751-292, 262-316
Fax 754-334
White-water rafting & inflatable kayaking on the Ayung River ($56/£37); mountain cycling ($49/£33); trekking tours ($40/£27).

Bali Barat National Park
Labuan Lalang: Park headquarters for Menjangan and Recreation Park, Bay. Boat hire Rp42,000 for four hours (maximum ten people); entrance fee Rp2000; parking Rp2000; snorkeling and equipment rental RP5000; guide for trekking or snorkeling Rp15,000.

Bali Bird Walks
with Victor Mason, author of *Bali Bird Walks* (Insight Pocket Guides). *The $28/£19 fee includes a 10 percent donation to the Conservation Fund. Sundays, Tuesdays, and Fridays at 9.15 am at the sign of the Beggar's Bush. Or call 975-009 to arrange individual outings.*

Iskander Wawo Runtu
BICYCLE TOURS
Tandjung Sari, Sanur
Tel. 288-441
Fax 287-930 or the Cafe Batujimbar, Sanur, Tel. 287-374.
Tailored mountain bike tours around Pupuan. Day tour: $60/£40 (minimum five people). Weekend: $125/£83.

Santa Bali Tours and Travel
Grand Bali Beach Hotel Arcade, Sanur
Tel. 287-628, 288-057, 263-009,
Fax 236-508
Walking tours in Karangasem and Tengenan ($40/£27), Ubud ($27.50/£18); bicycle tours around Ubud area ($37.50/£25) and Mengwi-Tanah Lot ($49/£33); waterskiing at Lake Bratan ($45/£30); archeological tour of central Gianyar

($37.50/£25); white-water rafting on the Ayung River ($57/£38); golfing at the Bali Handara Kosaido Country Club ($110/£73); bird-watching tours in the West Bali National Park ($55/£37) and the Botanical Gardens at Bedugul ($45/£30); Puri Night in Kerambitan ($65/£43).

Sobek Bina Utama
Jl. Bypass Ngurah Rai 56X, Sanur
Tel. 287-059
Fax 289-448
White-water rafting $63/£42; river kayaking $64/£43; sea kayaking $65/£43; mountain cycling $50/£33; off-road cycling $62/£41; jungle trekking $47/£31; Bali bird walks $43/£29.

PONY TREKKING
PT Jaran Jaran Kencana
Loji Gardens Hotel, Legian, Kuta
Tel. 751-672
Tel./Fax 751-746
(In Ubud: 975-298)
Pony Day and Sunset Pony Day tours $55/£37/person. Twenty percent deposit required for bookings.

Mesari Beach Inn
Jl. Dhyana Pura, Seminyak, Kuta
Tel. 753-517
Horses for hire. Rp20,000/hour.

◆ BASICS ◆

Yes: *ya*
No: *tidak*
What: *apa*
Why: *kenapa*
Where: *di mana*
When: *kapan*
Who: *siapa*
How: *bagaimana*
And: *dan*
To: *ke*
From: *dari*

◆ POLITE PHRASES ◆

Please: *tolong*
If you please: *silahkan*
Thank you (very much):
terima kasih (banyak)
You are welcome:
*terima kasih kembali/
sama-sama*
I am sorry: *ma'af*
Good morning (6 am–
11 am): *selamat pagi*
Good day (11 am–
3 pm): *selamat siang*
Good afternoon (3 pm–
6 pm): *selamat sore*
Good evening/night
(6 pm to midnight):
selamat malam
How are you?: *apa
kabar?*
I am fine: *kabar baik*
Goodbye (said by the
person leaving):
selamat tinggal
Goodbye (said by the
person staying):
selamat jalan
See you later: *sampai
jumpa nanti*

◆ TIME ◆

Now: *sekarang*
Later: *nanti*
What time is it?: *jam
berapa?*
Morning: *pagi*
Midday: *siang*
Afternoon: *sore*
Evening/night: *malam*
Today: *hari ini*
Yesterday: *kemarin*
Day: *hari*
Week: *minggu*
Next week: *Minggu
Depan*

◆ DAYS ◆

Monday: *hari senin*
Tuesday: *hari selasa*
Wednesday: *hari rabu*
Thursday: *hari kamis*
Friday: *hari jum'at*
Saturday: *hari sabtu*
Sunday: *hari minggu*

◆ THE MONTHS ◆

Month: *bulan*
January: *januari*
February: *februari*
March: *maret*
April: *april*
May: *mei*
June: *juni*
July: *juli*
August: *agustus*
September: *september*
October: *oktober*
November: *nopember*
December: *desember*

◆ NUMBERS ◆

One: *satu*
Two: *dua*
Three: *tiga*
Four: *empat*
Five: *lima*
Six: *enam*
Seven: *tuju*
Eight: *delapan*
Nine: *sembilan*
Ten: *sepuluh*
Eleven: *sebelas*
Twelve: *duabelas*
Thirteen: *tigabelas*
Twenty: *duapuluh*
Twenty-one: *duapuluh
satu*
Thirty: *tigapuluh*
Forty: *empatpuluh*
One hundred: *seratus*
Two hundred: *duaratus*
One thousand: *seribu*
Three thousand:
tigaribu
One million: *sejuta*
Five million: *lima juta*

◆ TRAVELING ◆

Walking: *jalan-jalan kaki*
Bicycle: *sepeda*
Motorcycle: *sepeda
motor*
Car: *mobil*
Local bus: *bemo*
Large bus: *bis*
Ship: *kapal laut*
Airplane: *kapal terbang*
Airport: *lapangan
terbang*
Driver's license: *Surat
Ijin Mengemudi* (SIM)
How much is the fare?:
Berapa ongkosnya?
How far is it?: *Berapa
jauhnya*
Rental: *disewakan*, i.e.
mobil disewakan
Road: *jalan*
Gasoline: *bensin*
Where is the road to…?:
di mana jalan ke…?

◆ DIRECTIONS ◆

North: *utara*
South: *selatan*
East: *timur*
West: *barat*
Beach: *pantai*
Sea: *laut*
Mountain: *gunung*
Cave: *goa*

River: *sungai*
Waterfall: *air terjun*
Close: *dekat*
Far: *jauh*
Right: *kanan*
Left: *kiri*
Middle: *tengah*

◆ MONEY AND
SHOPPING ◆

Bank: *bank*
Money: *uang*
Change money: *tukar
uang*
Do you accept credit
cards?: *kartu kredit bisa
dipakai disini?*
How much does it cost?:
berapa harganya
Expensive: *mahal*
Can you lower the
price?: *apakah harga
bisa dikurangi?*
Inexpensive: *murah*
Can we bargain ?:
boleh tawar?
Store: *toko*
Market: *pasar*

◆ SIGHTS
AND EVENTS ◆

Open: *buka*
Closed: *tutup*
Ticket: *karcis*
Temple: *pura*
Museum: *museum*
Can I take a
photograph?: *Boleh
memotret?*
Entrance: *pintu masuk*
Exit: *pintu keluar*
Cremation: *Ngaben*
Cockfight: *Tajen*

◆ FOOD ◆

Restaurant: *rumah
makan*
Food stall: *warung*
Market: *pasar*
Breakfast: *sarapan
pagi*
Lunch: *makan siang*
Dinner: *makan malam*
Menu: *daftar makanan*
Can we have a table for
… people?: *minta meja
untuk … orang*
Please bring me the bill:
saya minta rekening
I do not eat any meat :
*saya tidak makan
daging-dagingan*
Rice: *nasi*
Bread: *roti*
Noodles: *mie*
Cake: *kue/ jajan*
Vegetables: *sayur-
sayuran*
Fruit: *buah-buahan*
Fish: *ikan laut*
Prawns: *udang*
Chicken: *daging ayam*
Beef: *daging sapi*

Pork: *daging babi*
Duck: *daging bebek*
Tofu: *tahu*
Egg: *telur*
Peanuts: *kacang tanah*
Coffee: *kopi*
Milk: *susu*
Tea: *teh*
Drinking water: *air
minum/ aqua/ air putih*
Hot: *panas*
Cold: *dingin*
Spicy: *pedas*
Sweet: *manis*
Salty: *asin*
Sour: *asam*
Sugar: *gulah*

◆ ACCOMMODATION ◆

Guest house: *losmen*
Is there a room
available?: *ada kamar
kosong?*
With two beds: *dengan
dua tempat tidur*

◆ COMMUNICATION ◆

Where is the closest
post office?: *Di mana
kantor pos yang
terdekat?*
Stamp: *prangko*
Envelope: *amplop*
Letter: *surat*
Postcard: *kartu pos*
Air mail: *pos udara*
Where is a public
phone?: *Di mana ada
telpon umum?*
I want to make a long-
distance call: *Saya ingin
menelpon untuk
interlokal*

◆ EMERGENCIES ◆

Pharmacy: *apotik*
I need a doctor: *saya
perlu dokter*
I feel very sick: *saya
merasa sangat sakit*
Dentist: *dokter gigi*
Ambulance: *ambulans*
Hospital: *rumah sakit*
Police: *polisi*
Police station: *kantor
polisi*
I need a translator: *saya
perlu penterjemah*

◆ USEFUL
EXPRESSIONS ◆

I do not understand:
saya tidak mengerti
I need…: *saya perlu…*
I would like …: *saya
ingin…*
May I have…: *boleh
saya minta…*
What is this/that?: *apa
ini/itu?*
No problem!: *tidak apa-
apa!*

◆ A ◆

◆ ADAT: Local law, enforced by the *banjar* village association but considered to be divinely ordained, which governs daily life.

◆ AGAMA TIRTHA: Literally translated as "the religion of the holy waters", one of the many names for Balinese-Hinduism reflecting the vital role of water in the lives of the Balinese, not only as a tool of purification but also as the crucial element in irrigation systems.

◆ AGUNG: Refined Balinese word meaning "large" or "great", for example used to describe the sacred mountain Gunung Agung, the members of the warrior-prince "caste", Anak Agung, and the grand pavilion, *bale agung*.

◆ ALANG-ALANG: Strong wild grass used for roof thatching.

◆ ALING-ALING: Protective wall located behind most temple and house gates to deflect malign influences.

◆ AMERTA: The elixir of life, upon which the holy Mount Meru of Hindu cosmology is said to float.

◆ ARAK: Palm gin, a cheap and potent local brew dispensed at *warung*.

◆ ARJA: Classical Balinese "opera".

◆ ATINTYA: See Sang Hyang Widi Wasa.

◆ AWIG-AWIG: Specific customary rules detailing a particular village *adat*.

◆ B ◆

◆ BABAD: Literature of dynastic genealogies; historico-mythical chronicles of Balinese clans and kingdoms which provide inspiration for *topeng* performances.

◆ BABI GULING: Spit-roasted pig, a delicacy prepared for special occasions.

◆ BADE: Cremation tower; a representation of the universe, with upper tiers symbolizing the various heavens where the soul is heading.

◆ BALE: Traditional pavilion with a varying number of posts according to its function.

◆ BALI AGA: Communities, such as those found in Trunyan and Tenganan, that resisted post-Majapahit kings and their Hindu-Javanese court culture and were able to maintain the ownership of their land and the authority of their local laws.

◆ BALIAN: Generic term for traditional healer, ranging from the *balian taksu* trance medium, to the scholarly *balian usada* consultant of sacred lontar texts, to the massage therapist.

◆ BANJAR: Cooperative neighborhood association which governs daily life in great detail according to local law, or *adat*.

◆ BANJAR PANDE MAS: Village ward for goldsmiths.

◆ BANJAR SANGGING: Ward for painters who work "by appointment" to the royal household, producing paintings, banners, flags, and wall hangings for ritual occasions.

◆ BARIS: Meaning "line" or "file", this dance which often serves a ritual function may be performed by a group of men in ranks who sometimes split into opposing armies. The modern variation is most often danced as a virtuoso solo.

◆ BARONG: A splendid dragon-like creature whose protective powers are concentrated in its sacred mask. This netherworldly figure, with his consort-nemesis Rangda, is revered by the Balinese as a guardian of the village. The ritual confrontation between Barong and Rangda is the culmination of the "Calonarang" dance-drama, and depicts the complementary opposition of positive and negative forces in the universe.

◆ BARONG KEDINGKLING: Archaic form of *wayang wong* with exorcistic functions.

◆ BARONG LANDUNG: Large male and female guardian effigies (*landung* meaning "tall"). On ritual occasions they perform a dance-play in which their dialogue is an exchange of erotic songs.

◆ BEBEK TUTU: Slow-baked spiced duck, a famous Balinese dish often served at feasts.

◆ BEDAWANG NALA : Cosmic turtle upon whom the universe rests; often represented in *sarad* painted rice dough offerings.

◆ BEDEG: Slats of woven bamboo used in traditional architecture.

◆ BELEGANJUR: Processional music played with drums, big cymbals, and gongs of all sizes.

◆ BESAKIH: The most sacred of all Balinese temples, located at the great mountain Gunung Agung.

◆ BETELAN: Side gates of the temple through which most people enter, reserving the main gates for use during temple ceremonies.

◆ BETELNUT: Quid composed of areca nut, purified slaked lime and *gambir*, mashed and wrapped in *sirih* leaf, which, when chewed, combats hunger, thirst, and fatigue, and provides the brilliant crimson hue characteristic of many elderly Balinese smiles.

◆ BHATARA/BHATARI (FEMININE): Generic title used to refer to sacred Balinese powers such as Bhatara Guru, another name for the god Siwa, Bhatari Durga, the ferocious consort of Siwa, and Ida Bhatari Dewi Ulun Danu Batur, the goddess of Lake Batur.

◆ BIMA: One of the five Pandawa brothers, the heroes of the *Mahabharata*. Fiery Bima's primary attribute of ferocity is transformed into true courage through the moral contest with his cousins the Kurawas.

◆ BLOK KIU: A form of blackjack played with Chinese cards, common at most cockfights.

◆ BOMA: Son of the earth goddess, a fearsome but protective figure who represents all living things growing from the earth; often represented in *sarad* rice dough offerings and in temple sculptures as a head with a large mouth and big hands.

◆ BONDRES: Commoner clown characters in *topeng* masked dance dramas who poke fun at the faults of the lower classes and portray idiosyncrasies of local villagers, thereby providing audiences with examples of how not to behave.

◆ BOREH: Form of traditional herbal medicine. Plants are ground to a paste and applied externally to the body.

◆ BRAHMA: One of the three primary manifestations of the Supreme God. As the Creator, Brahma is associated with fire, volcanos, and the color red.

◆ BRAHMANA: The highest of the four Balinese "castes", whose members alone may become high priests. Brahman women and men are called Ida Ayu and Ida Bagus, respectively.

◆ BREM: Sweet rice wine.

◆ C ◆

◆ CAK: Vocal gamelan in which the chorus imitates the sounds of percussion instruments. Originally an accompaniment for ritual trance dances, the *cak* is now more well-known in the form of the modern *kecak* (see *Kecak*).

◆ CALONARANG: Myth incorporating historical, ritual, and exorcistic elements which relates the struggle between Rangda, a magically powerful witch, and the Javanese sage Mpu Bharadah. Many versions of this tale are enacted in dance drama performances, but all involve a battle between Rangda and the Barong (see *Barong*).

◆ CAMPUAN: The name of this site where two branches of the Wos River join comes from the Balinese word *campuh*, meaning "meeting". The confluence of rivers is believed to concentrate powerful earth energies as well as unusual psychic dangers; hence, the Gunung Lebah temple perched over these waters has particular significance.

◆ CANANG SARI: Genre of offerings, typically containing flowers, leaves, liquid fragrance, and a symbolic betel quid, said to embody the essence or *sari* of human prosperity; presented as a kind of repayment for the forces of the invisible world for their gifts to human society.

◆ CANDI: Temple façade with a false door leading to the "other world".

◆ CANDI BENTAR: Split gate used in temples which looks like a single carved edifice divided through the middle by a smooth cleft.

◆ CATUR WARNA: The "four-caste" system imposed by the colonial Dutch – Brahmana, Ksatriya, Wesiya, and Sudra. The first three, comprising about ten percent of the population, were recognized as the aristocracy; all other indigenous nobility were relegated to the residual commoner class, Sudra. (See *Triwangsa*.)

◆ CILI: Ancient symbol of both human and wet rice life cycles, often incorporated into offerings. This sign of prosperity and fertility usually takes the form of a beautiful, young girl.

◆ COKORDA: Title for a prince or his descendants.

◆ CONDONG: Archetype of the good attendant and confidant who serves the princesses of the Legong, Gambuh, and Arja dance dramas.

◆ COR: Ritual oath-taking via the sharing of a drink.

◆ D ◆

◆ DALANG: Shadow puppeteer; simultaneously a director-performer, literary arbiter, musician, comic, and priest, said to incarnate the god Siwa during performances.

◆ DALEM: Often used as a title for king, particularly in *arja* and *topeng* dance dramas, after the fashion of the first kings of Gelgel.

◆ DELEM: One of the servant-interpreters of the villains in *wayang kulit*, known for his arrogance.

◆ DESTAR: Headcloth that men wear for ritual occasions.

◆ DEWI SRI: Beloved goddess of rice, residing

over granaries and rice baskets and honored in a number of different cyclical rituals.

◆ DOKAR: Pony cart taxis still found in Denpasar.

◆ DUSUN: Indonesian governmental name for the Balinese *banjar* village association.

◆ E ◆

◆ EKA DASA RUDRA: Rite of universal exorcism performed every hundred years.

◆ ENDEK: Most widely woven cloth in Bali, produced through a "single *ikat*" process in which the pattern is created by resist-dyeing the threads of the weft.

◆ F ◆

◆ FIRE DANCE: A man in a trance dances with a hobby-horse through red-hot coals.

◆ G ◆

◆ GALUH: Generic name for princess characters in classical dance dramas such as Gambuh and Arja.

◆ GALUNGAN: Holiday celebrating the creation of the universe, during which ancestral spirits are thought to descend to the island and visit their living relatives.

◆ GAMBUH: Oldest known dance drama on Bali, considered the forebear of the classical dances and dance dramas inspired by Javanese literature.

◆ GAMELAN: Generic term for instrumental ensemble. Gamelans vary widely in size, sound, and function, from the sweet old bronze gamelan *angklung* often used for rituals, to the western Balinese bamboo gamelan *jegog*, to the virtuoso gong *kebyar* accompaniment to modern dance creations.

◆ GANESHA: Elephant god of Hinduism; Siwa's son.

◆ GARUDA: Mythical bird who carries the god Wisnu on his back, adopted as the official emblem of the Indonesian Republic.

◆ GAYAH: Meat offerings, fashioned by men, standing in contrast to the majority

of plant-based offerings constructed by women. These elaborate creations, also called *sate gede*, are said to represent the animal kingdom.

◆ GEBOGAN: Towering offerings of fruits, cakes, *canang sari*, and flowers, constructed around the base of a banana trunk.

◆ GEDONG RUM: Three-tiered rectangular temple shrine.

◆ GENDER WAYANG: Music which accompanies *wayang kulit*; these dazzlingly complicated compositions are considered the most difficult to play of all the gamelan repertoire.

◆ GERINGSING: The only textile in Indonesia woven with the laborious double *ikat* technique in which the pattern is dyed into both the warp and the weft threads. Some examples of this most magical cloth of Bali are said to be dyed with blood.

◆ GUNUNG: Mountain. (See *Kaja*.)

◆ GUWUNG: Bell-shaped baskets for fighting cocks.

◆ H ◆

◆ HALUS: Means "refined", used to describe everything from language to dance characters.

◆ HANUMAN: White monkey king of the *Ramayana* story who helps Rama defeat the evil king Rawana.

◆ I ◆

◆ IJUK: Black fiber from the sugar palm used to thatch temple shrines; a mountain cash crop.

◆ IKAT: Resist-dye technique applied to the warp or the weft threads, or both in the case of double *ikat*, to make patterns in woven cloth.

◆ J ◆

◆ JABA PURA: The outer courtyard of a temple, site of ceremonies to appease the lower spirits.

◆ JABA TENGAH: Central courtyard of a temple which is often the location of a gamelan pavilion and the priests'

meeting quarters.

◆ JEROAN: Most sacred, inner courtyard of a temple, housing shrines for the gods.

◆ JOGED BUMBUNG: Bamboo gamelan music often used to accompany the flirtatious social *joged* dance.

◆ K ◆

◆ KABUPATEN: Regency; the island is divided into eight *kabupaten* which basically follow the boundaries of the old Balinese kingdoms.

◆ KADO: Gift given at weddings or tooth filings, often a prewrapped box containing something pretty and useful, such as a covered dish or drinking glasses.

◆ KAIN KAMBEN: Rectangular piece of cloth wrapped around the lower body, worn by women and men as part of *pakaian adat*.

◆ KAJA: "Mountainward", "upstream"; associated with origins, purity, and the gods, in opposition to Kelod, the direction of the sea. The notion of Kaja/Kelod is based on the flow of water from pure mountain springs, accumulating impurities as it descends that are finally dissolved in the sea. (See *Kelod*.)

◆ KARAWAS: Cousins and enemies of the Pandawa brothers in the *Mahabharata* epic.

◆ KASAR: Coarse; used to describe language, art, character types, and behavior.

◆ KAWI: Usually called Old Javanese since it was the ancient literary language of Java, Kawi is actually a number of related languages that are forms of Javanese or Javanese Balinese and are still used in *wayang kulit* and classical dance dramas.

◆ KAWITAN: The original ancestor of a clan group.

◆ KAYONAN: Shadow puppet representing the tree of life or sacred mountain, universal nature, and the gateway to the world beyond.

◆ KEBAYA: Close-fitting long-sleeved jacket that women wear as part of *pakaian adat*.

◆ KEBO IWA: Mythical gigantic hero possessing magical

powers who is credited with creating most of the unexplained antiquities and monuments of Gianyar. He was tricked into going to Java by the Majapahit king, thereby causing the fall of Bali.

◆ KECAK: Ever-popular "monkey" dance, with a chorus of fifty to a hundred men chanting to accompany an enactment of the *Ramayana* story. *Kecak* was choreographed in the 1930's for tourist performances but draws its inspiration from the vocal gamelan *cak* of ritual trance dances.

◆ KELABANG: A quickly available building material made by plaiting the leaves of palm branches, often used for the ceilings and walls of temporary ritual structures.

◆ KELOD: "Seaward", "downstream"; associated with impurity and dissolution, and thus has a negative sacred character. The souls of the dead are cleansed in the purgatory of the sea. (See *Kaja*.)

◆ KENDANG: Drum.

◆ KEPENG: Chinese coins, used in *kwangen* offerings to represent human action, purified in the act of worship. *Kepeng* are also used to play games such as *toplek*.

◆ KERJA RODI: Corvée slave labor, imposed by the Dutch.

◆ KISA: A woven carrier used for transporting cocks to a cockfight.

◆ KLIAN: The elected leader of any group; used alone, it usually refers to the *klian banjar*. (See *Banjar*.)

◆ KOCOKAN: Game in which players throw money on squares of a mat decorated with snakes, turtles, demons, and other colorful creatures.

◆ KORI AGUNG: Type of temple gate said to show the reunion of the halves of the split *candi bentar* gate; often flanked by shrines for offerings.

◆ KOTEKAN: Interlocking counterpoint or ornamental figuration in gamelan music.

◆ KRIS: Beautifully wrought sword imbued with spiritual power.

◆ KSATRYA: Second highest "caste" in Bali,

comprising the descendants of warriors and princes. Caste members are named Cokorda or Anak Agung.

◆ KUKUSAN: Conical woven container used for steaming rice; may also be utilized to make a simple kind of holy water.

◆ KUL-KUL: Drum tower used to call villagers for any number of reasons; most often in the form of a four-poster pavilion with one or more slit wooden drums hanging in it.

◆ KUMBAKARNA: Brother of the wicked king Rawana in the *Ramayana* story; Kumbakama disagrees with the villain's actions but remains loyal to him.

◆ KWANGEN: Small conical offering containing flowers, a small betel quid, and often Chinese coins, used in prayer.

◆ L ◆

◆ LAMAK: Symbolic garment made of plaited palm leaf often used to "clothe" shrines.

◆ LASEM: Most common story used by *legong* dance performances in which King Lasem kidnaps a princess, whose brother is supposedly coming to rescue her. On the way to meet this brother in battle the King is attacked by a bird, an omen of his eventual defeat.

◆ LAWAR: A classic festive dish of finely minced innards of sacrificial animals mixed with chopped vegetables, grated fresh coconut, chilies, spices, and sometimes fresh blood.

◆ LEGONG: Classical dance of the princely courts characterized by highly disciplined body movements and an intricate pattern of synchronized steps. Two identically dressed *legong* dancers and a similarly dressed *condong*, or servant, play all the roles of the story derived from the Malat Hindu-Javanese literature.

◆ LEYAK: Witches who can transform themselves into animals and objects to go out and bedevil their

enemies during the dark phase of the moon.

◆ LOJI: Main family and ceremonial courtyard of a palace.

◆ LOLOH: Traditional herbal medicine administered as a drink.

◆ LONTAR: Palm whose dried leaves are remarkably durable and can be incised to make manuscripts which are often passed down for generations. Lontar palm juice, *tuak*, may be drunk directly or boiled to form a dark sugar.

◆ LOSMEN: A small guest house often operated as a family business.

◆ LUHUR: Simultaneously meaning "heavenly", "ancestral", "original", and "transcendent".

◆ LUMBUNG: Six-posted granary found in family compounds; not only the physical place to store rice but also the house of its goddess, Dewi Sri.

◆ M ◆

◆ MAHABHARATA: Great Indian epic depicting the battle between the five Pandawa brothers and their cousins the Kurawas which often provides the story for *wayang kulit* performances.

◆ MAHABARATA BALLET: Dance drama based on the Hindu epic of the war between the heroic Pandawa brothers and their army of cousins, the Kurawas.

◆ MAJAPAHIT: The east Javanese kingdom that extended over much of the archipelago from the 13th to 16th century and which exerted a powerful influence on Balinese art, religion, and society.

◆ MALAT: Hindu-Javanese tales about wars and rivalries between the little east Javanese kingdoms under the Majapahit empire. These stories are the basis of ancient dance dramas such as Gambuh.

◆ MEJANKRIKAN: Cricket-fighting.

◆ MEKEPUNG: Bull-racing; a sport introduced to the western part of Bali by the Madurese of east Java.

◆ MERAJAN: House temple of the nobility; in a palace also referred to

as the *merajan agung*.

◆ MERDA: One of the *punakawan* or servants of the heroes in *wayang kulit*; the son of the beloved Twalen.

◆ MERU: Balinese pagoda acting as a shrine to the higher deities which always has an odd number of roofs, with a maximum of eleven. The number depends on the status of the divinity in the local hierarchy.

◆ MOUNT MERU: Holy mountain of Hindu cosmology, said to float on a sea of amerta, the elixir of life.

◆ METEN: Walled pavilion, usually a large eight-post structure on a high base; often used as sleeping quarters.

◆ MOKSA: Liberation from the shackles of the sensory world, whereby the body becomes one with the macrocosm; also, "conscious death", practiced by sages.

◆ MPU: Title given to a wise man, such as the 11th-century Javanese sage-architect Mpu Kuturan.

◆ MUDRAS: Holy hand gestures used by priests to pray and make holy water.

◆ MUSPA: Prayer with flowers.

◆ N ◆

◆ NAGA BASUKI: Mythological serpent-dragons who live in the dark waters of the underworld; often represented in *sarad* rice dough offerings.

◆ NASI CAMPUR: Steamed rice with small amounts of spicy meats and vegetables which forms the usual daily meal.

◆ NYEMBAH: A gesture of homage formed by joining the hands above the head.

◆ NYIU: Bamboo tray, used for daily offerings and also ideal for winnowing rice.

◆ O ◆

◆ OBJEK WISATA: Tourist attraction.

◆ ODALAN: Annual commemoration of the founding of a temple; a joyful celebration during which people renew their ties to the gods and also reinforce their bonds with each other through the elaborate preparations and ceremonies.

◆ P ◆

◆ PADMASANA: Open seat-type shrine, sometimes called the lotus throne, which honors the sun god manifestation of the supreme Sang Hyang Widi Wasa.

◆ PAKAIAN ADAT: Traditional clothing worn for all ritual occasions; necessary for entrance into a temple.

◆ PALELINTANGAN: Divinatory chart of Balinese character types called *lintang*, based on birth dates according to the *pawukon* calendar.

◆ PANCA WALI KRAMA: Massive ceremony held every ten years at major temples to purify and bring blessings upon the entire world.

◆ PANDAWA: Five brothers, Arjuna, Bima, Yudhistira, Nakula, and Sahadewa, of the *Mahabharata* story who each represent some aspect of the human ideal. These heroes' attributes are transmuted into virtues through the moral contest with their cousins, the Kurawas.

◆ PANDE: Metalsmiths, traditionally belonging to the Pande clan, who are honored for their ability to manipulate fire and base metals, two revered elements.

◆ PANJI: Archetype of the refined prince, war hero, and fine dancer; the protagonist of the Malat Hindu-Javanese tales and central character of classical dance dramas.

◆ PANYEMBRAHMA: "Welcome dance"; the standard opening number for temple festival programs and tourist performances.

◆ PAON: Kitchen, associated with Brahma, the god of fire.

◆ PARAS: Volcanic tuff used for carving sculptures.

◆ PASEK: Very large kinship group who live all over the island, descended from the same Majapahit Brahman priest as the kings of Bali and appointed by them as regional leaders.

◆ PASUPATI: The awakening of magical powers; a rite that *dalang* perform for themselves and their shadow puppets before a performance.

◆ PAWUKON: Balinese year comprising of thirty seven-day weeks called *wuku*, for a total of 210 days.

◆ PEDANDA: High priest originating only from the Brahman caste and considered to be reborn at the time of consecration. *Pedanda* make potent holy water for big temple festivals and direct rituals of life and death.

◆ PELINGGIH: Simple "seat" shrine, the most common of all shrines in Bali, which serves as the home for a deity's effigy.

◆ PEMANGKU: Lay-priests who come from any caste other than Brahman; they consecrate offerings, make holy water, and preside over temple ceremonies.

◆ PENARAK: Basket of woven bamboo and rattan.

◆ PENDET: Traditional greeting dance performed by women or little girls to welcome the gods when they descend to the village temple at the time of its annual festival.

◆ PENJOR: Offering in the form of a tall, decorated bamboo pole, placed in front of each Balinese household for the Galungan holiday and also used in conjunction with important temple ceremonies and life-cycle rituals.

◆ PETI: Betel nut box.

◆ PIASAN: Holy pavilion that houses religious articles.

◆ POLENG: Black and white checked cloth symbolizing the polarity of positive and negative forces in the universe.

◆ POROSAN: Offering of red areca nut, green betel leaf, and white lime whose colors represent Brahma, Wisnu, and Siwa, the three gods of the Hindu trimurti.

◆ PRADA: Gold-painted cloth used for theatrical costumes, ceremonial parasols, and adornment for temple pavilions and humans during important ceremonies.

◆ PRAHU: Small fishing boat.

◆ PRASADA: Square-based, multi-roofed temple buildings similar to the *candi* of Java, now extremely rare in Bali.

◆ PREMBON: More recent form of drama which blends *topeng* masked characters with *arja* opera; some players are unmasked in order to be able to sing.

◆ PUNAKAWAN: Servant-interpreters of the central characters in *wayang kulit* and dance dramas. Twalen, Merdah, Delem, and Sangut provide the audience with comic relief as well as unrefined Balinese explanations of the interchanges conducted in Kawi and high Balinese.

◆ PUPUTAN: Fight to the death; a mass ritual suicide of both Badung and Klungkung's royalty in the face of Dutch artillery.

◆ PURA: Temple, of which many varieties exist. Each village contains at least three principle *pura*: the *pura puseh* "temple of origin", associated with Wisnu and the founding ancestors of the *banjar*; the *pura desa*, at the heart of the village and associated with Brahma; and the *pura dalem* "death temple" next to the graveyard and associated with Siwa.

◆ PURI: Palace; the name of a Ksatriya residence.

◆ PURNAMA: Full moon, a day observed with extra offerings.

◆ PUSKESMAS: Community health center; government-established clinic.

◆ R ◆

◆ RAKSASA: Demonic giants, sometimes considered guardian spirits.

◆ RAMA: The hero of the *Ramayana* epic, said to be an incarnation of the god Wisnu and a model of gentleness.

◆ RAMAYANA: Great Indian epic recounting Sita's abduction by the evil king Rawana and her ultimate rescue by Rama, aided by Hanuman and his army of monkeys.

◆ RAMAYANA BALLET: Dance drama based on the Hindu epic of Rama and the rescue of his beautiful wife Sita with the help of Hanuman, the monkey king. The Children's Ramayana in Padang Tegal is performed entirely by children.

◆ RANGDA: Sacred tutelary figure representing Durga, the fierce female aspect of Siwa. Often referred to in tourist literature as "Queen of witches". (See *Barong*).

◆ RANGKI-RANGKI: Holy courtyard in a palace.

◆ RAWANA: Wicked King who abducts Sita in the *Ramayana* epic.

◆ REBAB: Two-stringed, bowed instrument similar to a lute.

◆ REJANG: Sacred processional dance performed by girls or women.

◆ S ◆

◆ SADKAHYANGAN: Six "axial" temples on the island, points of power relating to the cardinal directions.

◆ SAKA YEAR: Indic solar/lunar year, seventy-eight years behind the conventional Western calendar.

◆ SAKENAM: Guest pavilion for relatives and children in a family compound.

◆ SAKTI: (Imbued with) magical power.

◆ SAMPIAN: Beautifully plaited palm leaf creations that adorn offerings and the ends of *penjor*.

◆ SANGGAH: Name for the temple in a low caste family compound.

◆ SANGGAH CUCUK: Small temporary shrine of bamboo always found beneath *penjor* pole offerings.

◆ SANGGING: Creator of sacred art both for the temple and for cremation rituals.

◆ SANGHYANG DELING: Trance dance in which two little girls animate puppets suspended on a string held between them, or, alternately, themselves become the dolls of the gods, dancing with their eyes closed on the shoulders of village men. Sanghyang is the name given to all trance dances.

◆ SANG HYANG WIDI WASA: The "One

Supreme Unknowable God", represented as Atintya, a being in meditation surrounded by flames.

◆ SANGUT: One of the servant-interpreters, *punakawan*, of the villains in *wayang kulit*; the weaselly looking sidekick to Delem.

◆ SAPUT: Cloth that men wrap over their *kain kamben* as part of their *pakaian adat* ritual clothing.

◆ SARAD: Elaborate offerings, made of dyed rice dough arranged against a framework of bamboo and cloth, which symbolize the form and content of the Balinese mythical world.

◆ SARASWATI: Goddess of knowledge, wisdom, and the arts, usually depicted as a beautiful, richly dressed woman riding a goose; she is Brahma's consort.

◆ SATIA: Acts of suicide formerly committed by a king's wives, concubines, or servants, carried out by throwing themselves on the flaming funeral pyre.

◆ SAWAH: Irrigated rice fields.

◆ SEGARA: Sea.

◆ SELENDANG: Waist sash, worn as part of *pakaian adat*, which symbolically ties off the lower appetites.

◆ SEMANGGEN: Holy courtyard in a palace; like the *rangki-rangki*, it is used for the poetic readings of ancient manuscripts, for tooth filings, and for the laying in state of corpses.

◆ SEMAT: Long wisps of bamboo used to pin together leaves to make offerings.

◆ SENDI: Supporting block, made of volcanic tuff or coral, on which a pavilion post sits.

◆ SETRA: Graveyard.

◆ SIDHA KARYA: The final character to appear in the *topeng pajegan* masked dance drama. As "the one who completes work", he blesses special offerings and hands out coins to the children in the audience.

◆ SIMBUH: Traditional herbal medicine of chewed up raw rice blown forcefully on the affected area.

◆ SIRIH: *Piper betle* plant whose leaves are used in the tonic betel nut quid.

◆ SITA: Rama's consort, abducted by the evil king Rawana in the *Ramayana* epic.

◆ SIWA: One of the three primary manifestations of the Supreme God, in the form of the destroyer.

◆ SIWA RATRI DANCE: Dance drama enacting the story of the sinner Lubdhaka who is mysteriously exalted by the god Siwa. (A new creation from an old myth.)

◆ SOK: Square basket of woven bamboo which comes in numerous sizes and acts as the Balinese alternative to cupboards and drawers. The *sok asi* stores fresh steamed rice.

◆ SONGKET: Cloth containing gold or silver thread, traditionally woven by royal women.

◆ SUBAK: Rice irrigation cooperative; these societies have provided the framework which has made Bali one of the most efficient rice growers in the archipelago.

◆ SUDRA: The so-called commoner class of farmers and artisans, comprising about ninety percent of the Balinese population after the Dutch refused to recognize the aristocratic status of non-Triwangsa clan groups such as the *Pande* and *Pasek*. (See *Catur warna*.)

◆ SUKLA: Not previously used; a quality required of implements utilized for ritual purposes.

◆ **T** ◆

◆ TAKSU: The life force that acts as interpreter for the deities and speaks through mediums. Artists also pray to obtain *taksu*, the divine inspiration for a charismatic performance.

◆ TANTRI: Bali's equivalent of Aesop's fables, in which animals act out, and reap the rewards of, the virtues and vices of humankind.

◆ TEKTEKAN: Exciting percussion orchestra of split bamboo and wooden bells, whose original function is exorcistic.

◆ TELEK: Refined version of the classical masked dance called *jauk*.

◆ TENGET: A magically powerful object, such as a mask.

◆ TIKA: Diagram of the complex *pawukon* calendar which a priest consults to determine the dates for important ceremonies.

◆ TILEM: New moon, an event which entails the giving of extra offerings.

◆ TOPENG: Ancient and still popular masked dance drama which draws its inspiration from the *babad* literature and communicates to its audience history, philosophy, moral standards, and government messages. In *topeng pajegan*, one dancer plays all the characters including Topeng Dalem, the refined king, Topeng Keras, a minister, Topeng Tua, an elder statesman and Sidha Karya, who ends the performance.

◆ TOPLEK: A guessing game involving Chinese coins.

◆ TRI HITA KARANA: Hindu concept which describes the three orientations of human concern for a balanced life: the relationship of humans to the gods, to other humans, and to the land.

◆ TRIMURTI: Hindu trinity, or three primary manifestations of the Supreme God: Brahma, the creator; Wisnu, the preserver; and Siwa, the destroyer.

◆ TRIWANGSA: The three upper "castes" or clan groups – Brahmana, Ksatriya, Wesiya – claiming descent from the Indo-Javanese Majapahit nobility, comprising ten percent of the Balinese population.

◆ TUAK: A beer of fermented palm sap.

◆ TWALEN: The beloved servant-interpreter of the heroes in *wayang kulit*, said to be a shaman and older than time. With his droll eye, gravelly voice, and love of food, Twalen is the most popular of the shadow puppet characters.

◆ **U** ◆

◆ UNDAGI: Priest-architect who uses a measuring system that ensures harmony between the dwelling

and the dweller, and thus harmony with the macrocosmos.

◆ URAB: Rich, pungent, warm salad of steamed vegetables, coconut, and spices that functions almost as a condiment to the Balinese staple food, steamed white rice.

◆ **W** ◆

◆ WALI: Ritual. Refers also to sacred dances, such as the *rejang*, that may not be presented for commercial purposes.

◆ WANTILAN: Two- or three-tiered pavilion that functions as the town community hall, used for meetings, dance performances, cockfights, and political rallies.

◆ WARA: Ten cyclical "weeks", of which the most important are those composed of three, five, and seven days; certain conjunctions of the different *wara* are of mystical importance.

◆ WAYANG KULIT: Shadow puppet theater; Bali's most complex sacred art form, not only a traditional medium of moral and spiritual instruction, but also wonderfully entertaining.

◆ WAYANG WONG: Masked drama in which human performers take on the roles played by the shadow puppets of *wayang kulit*, to the extent that the dancers' movements are inspired by the two-dimensional style of puppets.

◆ WESIYA: Third highest "caste" in Bali, traditionally comprised of merchants. Male and female caste members bear the title Gusti.

◆ WIBISANA: Brother of the wicked king Rawana in the *Ramayana* epic who disagrees with his sibling's abduction of Sita and thus rebels.

◆ WISNU: One of the three primary manifestations of the Supreme God, in the form of the preserver.

◆ WUKU: Name for the seven-day week. Thirty *wuku* make up one *pawukon*, or 210-day Balinese year.

Useful addresses

⊕	Luxury restaurant
◑	Typical restaurant
○	Budget restaurant
🏛	Luxury hotel
🏠	Typical hotel
⌂	Budget hotel
▭	Credit cards accepted
🅒	Central
☀	Exceptional view/gardens
⌂	Quiet
⤳	Secluded
⌇	Swimming pool
♫	Cultural performances
▢	Television
☎	IDD phone
🎺	Live music or disco

Price key:
♦ < US$15 / £10
♦♦ US$15 to $110 / £10 to £75
♦♦♦ > US$110 / £75

Hotel	Page	Price	Exceptional View/Gardens	Quiet	AC/Ceiling Fan	Hot Water	Exceptional Architecture	Restaurant and/or Bar	Rooms
UBUD (CENTRAL AND NORTH)									
KAJENG HOMESTAY	326	♦	●	●		●			11
KETUT'S PLACE	326	♦	●	●		●			6
PURI SAREN (UBUD PALACE)	326	♦♦		●	●	●	●		12
PURI SARASWATI BUNGALOWS	326	♦♦		●	●	●			18
SITI BUNGALOWS	326	♦♦		●		●		●	7
UBUD (MONKEY FOREST RD)									
FIBRA INN	326	♦♦			●	●		●	16
SAGITTARIUS INN	326	♦			●	●		●	12
UBUD INN	327	♦♦		●	●	●		●	26
UBUD AREA (SOUTH)									
ARTINI I HOMESTAY	327	♦	●	●	●	●			8
PURI INDAH EXCLUSIVE VILLAS	327	♦♦♦		●	●	●		●	15
UBUD AREA (WEST)									
AMANDARI***	327	♦♦♦	●	●	●	●	●	●	29
BALIUBUD COTTAGES	327	♦♦	●	●	●	●		●	14
HOTEL TJAMPUHAN	327	♦♦	●	●	●	●		●	55
MUNUT BUNGALOWS	327	♦	●	●	●	●			9
PADMA INDAH COTTAGES	327	♦♦	●	●		●		●	10
SARI BUNGALOWS	327	♦	●	●		●			6
SAYAN TERRACES	327	♦♦	●	●	●	●		●	11
ULUN UBUD COTTAGES	327	♦♦	●	●	●	●	●	●	23
VILLA BUKIT UBUD	327	♦♦♦	●	●	●	●		●	20
KINTAMANI									
LOSMEN MIRANDA	328	♦	●	●					8
LOSMEN & RESTAURANT GUNAWAN	328	♦	●	●				●	12
PURI ASTINA INN	328	♦♦	●	●				●	4
SURYA HOMESTAY	328	♦		●	●			●	22
UNDER THE VOLCANO	328	♦	●	●				●	16
EAST BALI									
AMANKILA***	328	♦♦♦	●	●	●	●	●	●	35
HIDDEN PARADISE COTTAGES	329	♦♦		●	●	●		●	16
IDA BEACH VILLAGE	329	♦♦		●	●	●	●	●	17
IDA HOMESTAY	329	♦	●	●					6
KUSUMA JAYA INN	329	♦	●	●				●	16
NIRWANA COTTAGES	329	♦♦		●	●	●		●	24
PARADISE PALM BEACH BUNGALOWS	329	♦		●				●	17
PURI BAGUS BEACH HOTEL	329	♦♦		●	●	●		●	50
SERAI HOTEL	329	♦♦♦	●	●	●	●		●	58
VIENNA BEACH BUNGALOWS	329	♦		●				●	13
THE WATERGARDEN	329	♦♦	●	●	●	●		●	12
NORTH BALI (COAST)									
ADITYA BUNGALOWS	330	♦♦			●	●		●	80
BALI LOVINA BEACH COTTAGES*	330	♦♦			●	●		●	34
BALI TAMAN BEACH HOTEL	330	♦♦			●	●		●	18
KALIBUKBUK INN	330	♦				●		●	26
NIRWANA SEASIDE COTTAGES	330	♦				●		●	46
PALMA BEACH HOTEL**	330	♦♦		●	●	●		●	45
PARMA BEACH HOTEL	330	♦		●		●		●	16
NORTH BALI (MOUNTAINS)									
ASHRAM GUEST HOUSE	330	♦	●	●				●	27
BALI HANDARA KOSAIDO	330	♦♦♦	●	●		●		●	77
PURI LUMBUNG	330	♦♦	●	●	●		●	●	5
WEST BALI									
BALIAN BEACH BUNGALOWS	331	♦	●	●				●	12
MEDEWI BEACH COTTAGES	331	♦♦	●	●	●	●		●	26
PONDOK SARI BEACH BUNGALOWS	331	♦	●	●	●			●	14
TINJAYA BUNGALOWS	331	♦	●	●				●	6

	PAGE	PRICE	EXCEPTIONAL VIEW/GARDENS	QUIET	AC/CEILING FAN	HOT WATER	EXCEPTIONAL ARCHITECTURE	RESTAURANT AND/OR BAR	ROOMS
DENPASAR									
NATOUR BALI (BALI HOTEL)	332	♦♦			●	●		●	74
PURI PEMECUTAN**	332	♦♦			●	●		●	42
SANUR									
ANANDA HOTEL	333	♦			●			●	15
BARUNA BEACH INN	333	♦♦			●	●		●	7
BUMI AYU BUNGALOWS	333	♦♦		●	●			●	58
GRAND BALI BEACH HOTEL*****	333	♦♦♦		●	●	●		●	619
HOTEL BALI HYATT*****	333	♦♦♦	●	●	●	●		●	387
HOTEL BALI WIRASANA	333	♦			●	●			20
HOTEL SANUR BEACH****	334	♦♦♦		●	●	●		●	425
HOTEL TAMAN AGUNG BEACH INN	334	♦♦			●	●		●	24
LA TAVERNA BALI HOTEL**	334	♦♦♦	●		●	●		●	34
SEGARA VILLAGE***	334	♦♦♦		●	●	●		●	125
TANDJUNG SARI***	335	♦♦♦	●		●	●		●	28
PONDOK WISATA PRIMA COTTAGES	335	♦			●	●		●	14
PURI KLAPA GARDEN COTTAGES	335	♦♦		●	●	●		●	39
WATERING HOLE HOMESTAY	335	♦			●			●	13
WERDHA PURA	335	♦♦		●	●	●		●	13
KUTA AREA									
ASANA SANTHI WILLY	336	♦♦			●	●			12
BALI IMPERIAL HOTEL*****	336	♦♦♦			●	●		●	401
BALI OBEROI****	336	♦♦♦	●	●	●	●	●	●	75
BALI PADMA HOTEL*****	336	♦♦♦			●	●		●	404
BINTANG BALI*****	336	♦♦♦			●	●		●	401
FAT YOGI	336	♦			●	●		●	18
HOLIDAY INN BALI HAI****	337	♦♦♦			●	●		●	188
KARTIKA PLAZA BEACH HOTEL*****	337	♦♦♦			●	●		●	100
KEMPU TAMAN AYU	337	♦			●				4
LEGIAN GARDEN COTTAGE	337	♦♦		●	●	●		●	25
MIMPI BUNGALOWS	337	♦♦			●				9
PERTAMINA COTTAGES*****	337	♦♦♦			●	●		●	250
POPPIES I	337	♦♦			●	●		●	20
PURI RATIH BALI**	337	♦♦		●	●	●			32
RAJA GARDENS	337	♦	●	●	●	●			6
RUM JUNGLE ROAD	337	♦			●			●	12
SAREG	337	♦			●				4
NUSA DUA AREA									
AMANUSA***	338	♦♦♦	●	●	●	●	●	●	35
BALI CLIFF RESORT*****	338	♦♦♦	●	●	●	●		●	200
BALI HILTON INTERNATIONAL*****	338	♦♦♦	●	●	●	●		●	537
BALI INTER-CONTINENTAL*****	338	♦♦♦	●	●	●	●		●	431
BALI ROYAL	338	♦♦♦	●	●	●	●		●	12
CLUB MED BALI***	338	♦♦♦	●	●	●	●		●	400
FOUR SEASONS RESORT BALI*****	338	♦♦♦	●	●	●	●	●	●	147
GRAND HYATT BALI*****	339	♦♦♦	●	●	●	●	●	●	750
KERATON COTTAGES**	339	♦♦♦		●	●	●		●	99
MELIA BALI SOL*****	339	♦♦♦	●	●	●	●		●	500
NUSA DUA BEACH HOTEL*****	339	♦♦♦	●	●	●	●		●	401
PANSEA PURI BALI*	339	♦♦♦		●	●	●		●	41
PURI JOMA	339	♦♦		●	●	●		●	10
PUTRI BALI HOTEL*****	339	♦♦♦		●	●	●		●	425
SHERATON LAGOON RESORT*****	339	♦♦♦		●	●	●		●	276
SHERATON NUSA INDAH RESORT*****	339	♦♦♦		●	●	●		●	369
NUSA LEMBONGAN									
AGUNG	339	♦						●	8
MAIN SKI INN	339	♦						●	5
NUSA LEMBONGAN BUNGALOWS	339	♦						●	8

◆ CHOOSING A RESTAURANT

Exchange rate US$1=Rp2180
£1=Rp3265
◆ < Rp12,000
◆◆ Rp12,000–Rp30,000
◆◆◆ > Rp30,000

Restaurant	PAGE	PRICE	VIEW AND/OR GARDENS	EXCEPTIONAL DECOR/AMBIENCE	INDONESIAN/ASIAN CUISINE	EXCEPTIONAL SERVICE	WESTERN CUISINE	JAPANESE CUISINE	BAR/WINE
UBUD (CENTRAL AND NORTH)									
ARY'S WARUNG	325	◆		●	●		●		●
BINTANG PARI	325	◆	●	●	●	●			
CAFE LOTUS	325	◆◆	●		●		●		●
CASA LUNA	325	◆		●	●		●		●
GRIYA BARBEQUE	325	◆	●	●	●		●		
HAN SNEL'S GARDEN RESTAURANT	325	◆◆	●		●				●
MOMOYA	325	◆◆			●	●		●	
MUMBUL TERRACE GARDEN RESTAURANT	325	◆	●		●		●		
NOMAD	325	◆		●	●	●	●		●
ROOF GARDEN RESTAURANT	325	◆◆	●		●		●		●
UBUD (MONKEY FOREST RD)									
CAFE WAYAN	325	◆◆	●		●		●		●
LOTUS LANE	326	◆◆	●		●		●		●
YOGYAKARTA TEAHOUSE	326	◆			●				
UBUD (SOUTH)									
BEBEK BENGIL	326	◆◆			●		●		●
KAGEMUSHA	326	◆	●	●		●		●	
KOKOKAN CLUB	326	◆◆	●	●	●				●
KURA KURA	326	◆◆	●		●				●
RUMAH MAKAN PADANG	326	◆			●				
SHADANA	326	◆			●				
UBUD RAYA	326	◆			●			●	
UBUD (WEST)									
AMANDARI RESTAURANT	326	◆◆◆	●	●	●	●	●		●
BEGGAR'S BUSH	326	◆◆		●	●		●		●
CAFE DEWATA	326	◆	●		●		●		
DANINO	326	◆	●		●		●		
MURNI'S	326	◆◆	●		●		●		●
SAYAN CAFE	326	◆			●		●		
WARUNG, KEDEWATAN	326	◆			●				
KINTAMANI									
LAKEVIEW	327	◆	●		●				
RUMAH MAKAN CAHAYA	327	◆			●	●			
UNDER THE VOLCANO	328	◆	●		●				
EAST BALI									
CHEZ LILLY	328	◆			●		●		●
GANGGA CAFE	328	◆			●				
RICE TERRACE COFFEESHOP	328	◆				●	●		
TJ'S	328	◆◆	●	●	●	●	●		●
THE RESTAURANT, AMANKILA	328	◆◆◆	●	●	●	●	●		●
NORTH BALI (COAST)									
KHI KHI SEAFOOD RESTAURANT	330	◆			●				
MALIBU RESTAURANT & BAR	330	◆			●		●		
RUMAH MAKAN ARINA	330	◆			●				
WINA RESTAURANT & BAR	330	◆			●		●		
NORTH BALI (MOUNTAINS)									
TALIWANG BERSAUDARA	330	◆	●		●				
WARUNG KOPI	330	◆	●	●	●	●			

	PAGE	PRICE	VIEW AND/OR GARDENS	EXCEPTIONAL DECOR/AMBIENCE	INDONESIAN/ASIAN CUISINE	EXCEPTIONAL SERVICE	WESTERN CUISINE	JAPANESE CUISINE	BAR/WINE
WARUNG UNICK	330	♦			●		●		
WEST BALI									
BALIAN BEACH CLUB	331	♦			●	●	●		●
SOKA SARI	331	♦	●		●	●			
WARUNG MUSLIM	331	♦			●	●			
WARUNG SDSB No. 205033	331	♦			●				
DENPASAR									
ATOOM BARU	331	♦♦			●				●
AYAM BAKAR TALIWANG	331	♦			●				
KAK MAN	331	♦			●				
RUMAH MAKAN BETTY	331	♦			●				
TIARA DEWATA SHOPPING CENTER	332	♦			●				
WARUNG SATE KAMBING	332	♦			●				
SANUR									
BORNEO BAR & RESTAURANT	333	♦			●	●	●		●
CAFE BATUJIMBAR	333	♦		●	●		●		●
CINTU BINDO	333	♦			●				
JAWA BARAT	333	♦			●				
LA TAVERNA	333	♦♦					●		●
NAN BAN KAN	333	♦♦♦		●		●		●	●
RUMAH MAKAH SARI LAUT	333	♦			●				
SANUR BEACH MARKET	333	♦	●						●
TANDJUNG SARI	333	♦♦♦	●	●	●	●	●		●
TELAGA NAGA	333	♦♦♦	●	●	●				●
KUTA AREA									
CAFE LUNA	336	♦		●			●		●
CHIANG MAI THAI	336	♦♦	●		●				●
THE CHINESE RESTAURANT	336	♦♦			●				●
DOUBLE SIX	336	♦♦	●				●		●
GOA 2001	336	♦		●			●		●
KRAKATOA	336	♦					●		●
LA LUCCIOLA	336	♦♦	●				●		●
MADE'S WARUNG	336	♦♦		●	●		●		●
MAMA'S GERMAN RESTAURANT	336	♦					●		
POCO LOCO	336	♦♦					●		●
RIYOSHI	336	♦♦		●				●	●
TJ'S	336	♦♦	●	●		●	●		●
WARUNG KOPI	336	♦		●					●
NUSA DUA AREA									
THE DINING ROOM, FOUR SEASONS	338	♦♦♦	●	●	●	●	●		●
EDELWEISS	338	♦♦		●			●		●
IKAN, NUSA INDAH	338	♦♦	●	●	●				●
INAGIKU, GRAND HYATT	338	♦♦♦	●	●		●		●	●
JAANSAN CAFE ET PUB	338	♦♦			●		●		●
MEI YAN CHINESE RESTAURANT	338	♦♦♦		●	●				●
PJ'S	338	♦♦♦	●	●			●		●
THE RESTAURANT, AMANUSA	338	♦♦♦		●	●		●		●
SALSA VERDE, GRAND HYATT	338	♦♦		●			●		●
THE TERRACE, AMANUSA	338	♦♦	●	●	●	●	●		●

GENERAL INFORMATION

Note : Jalan Bypass Ngurah Rai, around Denpasar, is sometimes referred to as Jl. Bypass or Jl. Ngurah Rai.

USEFUL ADDRESSES

EMERGENCIES (24 HOURS)
BALI TOURIST INTERNATIONAL ASSISTANCE
Tel. 227-271, 231-443, 228-996
AMBULANCE
Tel. 118
POLICE
Tel. 110
FIRE
Tel. 113

IMMIGRATION
KANTOR IMIGRASI
Jl. D.I. Panjaitan
Niti Mandala, Renon, Denpasar
Tel. 227-828
KANTOR IMIGRASI
Jl. I Gusti Ngurah Rai
Tuban, Kuta
Tel. 751-038

POLICE STATIONS
BADUNG
Jl. Diponegoro 10
Tel. 234-928

BANGLI
Jl. Nusantara
Tel. (0366) 91-072

BULELENG
Jl. Pramuka, Singaraja
Tel. (0362) 41-510

DENPASAR
Jl. A. Yani
Tel. 225-456

GIANYAR
Jl. Ngurah Rai
Tel. 93-110

JEMBRANA
Jl. Pahlawan, Negara
Tel. (0365) 110

KARANGASEM
Jl. Bhyangkara, Amlapura
Tel. (0363) 110
KLUNGKUNG
Jl. Untung Surapati
Tel. (0366) 21-115

KUTA
Jl. Bypass Tuban, Tuban
Tel. 751-598

NUSA DUA
Jl. Bypass, Bualu
Tel. 772-110

SANUR
Jl. Bypass
Tel. 288-597

TABANAN
Jl. Pahlawan
Tel. 91-210

UBUD
Jl. Andong, Andong
Tel. 975-316

HOSPITALS (RUMAH SAKIT)
◆ **DENPASAR**
ARMY HOSPITAL
Jl. Panglima Sudirman
Tel. 228-003
SANGLAH PUBLIC HOSPITAL
Sanglah
Tel. 227-911
MANUABA GENERAL HOSPITAL
Jl. Cokroaminoto, 28
Tel. 426-393
SURYA HUSADHA HOSPITAL
Jl. Pulau Serangan 1-3
Sanglah
Tel. 233-786/7

◆ **KUTA**
MANUABA CLINIC
Jl. Raya Kuta, Tuban
Tel. 754-748

PHARMACY (24-HOURS)
APOTIK TEUKU UMAR
Jl. Teuku Umar, Denpasar
Tel. 224-472, 224-034

FINANCIAL SERVICES

BANKS
Banking hours are 8am–2.30 pm, Monday to Friday. Closed on Saturday and Sunday.

◆ **DENPASAR**
BANK NEGARA INDONESIA 1946 (BNI)
Jl. Gajah Mada 30 80113
Tel. 227-321/4
Fax 234-799
Telex 35114 BNIDPR IA
BANK DUTA
Jl. Raya Hayam Wuruk 165, Tanjung Bungkak
Tel. 226-578, 231-481
Fax 228-465

Telex 35140, 35141
DUTA DPIA 35233 VC
DUTA IA

◆ **KARANGASEM**
BANK SERI PARTHA
Jl. Sudirman 27X, Amlapura
Tel. (0363) 232233

◆ **KUTA**
BANK CENTRAL ASIA
Jl. Raya Kuta 121
Tel. 754-113
Fax 750-4060
Telex 35643
24-hour AMT (BCA card)
PANIN BANK
Jl. Legian 80X
Tel. 751-076/7/8
Fax 752-815
Telex 352-78 PIBDPR IA

◆ **SINGARAJA**
BANK BUMI DAYA
Jl. Erlangga 14
Tel. (362) 41243/5,
Telex 35132 BDDPR IA

◆ **UBUD**
BANK DUTA
Jl. Ida Bagus Manik (Main Street)
Banjar Ambangan (Peliatan)
Tel. 975-247
Telex 35233 VCDUTA IA

CREDIT CARDS
Visa and MasterCard offices:
BANK DUTA
Jl. Raya Hayam Wuruk 165, Tanjung Bungkak, Denpasar
Tel. 226-578, 231-481
Fax 228-465
Telex 35140, 35141
DUTA DPIA, 35233 VC
DUTA IA

CURRENCY EXCHANGE
CV MASAJA MONEY CHANGER
Jl. Raya Airport 30, Kuta (at Jl. Bakung Sari)
Tel. 751-978
Good rates.
CV DIRGAHAYU
Jl. Legian 1, Kuta
Tel. 751-002, 751-821
Also provides safe deposit locker service.

POSTAL SERVICES

CENTRAL POST OFFICE
Jalan Raya Puputan
Renon, Denpasar
Tel. 223-565/8
Hours: 8am–8pm Monday to Saturday. Closed Sunday.
KUTA POST OFFICE
Jalan Raya Tuban
SANUR POST OFFICE

Jalan Danau Buyan
Taman

COMPUTER SERVICES

ADI COMPUTER
Jl. Tukad Yeh Penet 2
Renon, DenpasarBranch in Nusa Dua
Tel. 236-531
Fax 236-753

CONSULATES

AUSTRALIA
Jl. Mr. M. Yamin Kav. 51, Renon, Denpasar
Tel. 235-092
Jl. Legian, Kuta
Tel. 751-977

DENMARK & NORWAY
Jl. Jayagiri VIII/10, Denpasar
Tel. 234-834, 235-098

FRANCE (CONSULAR AGENT)
Jl. Raya Sesetan 46 D, Banjar Pesanggaran, Denpasar
Tel. 233-555

GERMANY (HONORARY)
Jl. Pantai Karang 17, Sanur
Tel. 288-827, 288-535
Fax 288-826

ITALY (HONORARY)
Jl. Cemara, Semawang, Sanur
Tel. 288-896, 288-996, 287-642

JAPAN
Jl. Mohamad Yamin 9, Renon, Denpasar
Tel. 231-808, 234-808

NETHERLANDS
Jl. Imam Bonjol 599, (in KCB Tours building) Denpasar
Tel. 754-934

SWEDEN & FINLAND
Segara Village Hotel
Jl. Segara Ayu, Sanur
Tel. 288-407, 288-408

SWITZERLAND & AUSTRIA
c/o Swiss Restaurant
Jl. Pura Bagus Taruna, Legian Kaja, Kuta
Tel./Fax 751-735

UNITED KINGDOM
128 Jl. Agus Salim, Jakarta
Tel: 3907484
No UK consulate in Bali.

USA (CONSULAR AGENT)
Jl. Segara Ayu 5,
Sanur
Tel. 288-478

TOURIST INFORMATION

BADUNG TOURIST OFFICE
Jl. Surapati 7, Denpasar
Tel. 223-399
Bali monthly calendar of events available.
BALI TOURIST GUIDE
Jl. Bypass, Kuta
Tel/fax 754-322
Free tourist publication available.
BINA WISA TOURIST INFORMATION
Jl. Raya Ubud (at the main crossroad)
Tel. 96-285
PERAMA TOURIST SERVICE
Jl. Legian 20, Kuta
Tel. 751-551, 751-875
Fax 751-170
REGIONAL TOURIST OFFICE
Komplek Niti Mandala,
Jl. Raya Puputan
Renon, Denpasar 80235
Tel. 225-649, 233-474
Tel. 222-387, 226-313

TRANSPORT

AIRPORT
Ngurah Rai Airport
Tuban, Kuta
Tel. 751-011, 753-207
Information extensions:
1313, 1127, 3114

AIRLINES
AIR NEW ZEALAND
Kartika Plaza Beach Hotel, Kuta
Tel. 751-067

ANSETT AIRLINES
Grand Bali Beach Hotel, Sanur
Tel. 289-637

BOURAQ INDONESIA
Jl. Sudirman 19A, Denpasar
Tel. 223-564

CATHAY PACIFIC AIRWAYS
Grand Bali Beach Hotel, Sanur
Tel. 288-576,
288-511 ext 1592/3

CHINA AIRLINES
Airport: Tel. 754-856
CONTINENTAL MICRONESIA
Grand Bali Beach Hotel, Sanur
Tel. 287-774
Airport: Tel. 752-106

GARUDA INDONESIA AIRWAYS
Jl. Melati 61, Denpasar
Tel. 289-135
Grand Bali Beach Hotel
Tel. 287-920,
288-511 ext 130
Sanur Beach Hotel
Tel. 287-915,
288-011 x 1789
Nusa Dua Beach Hotel
Tel. 772-231
Reconfirmation:
Tel. 751-178

KLM
ROYAL DUTCH AIRLINES
Grand Bali Beach Hotel, Sanur
Tel. 287-576, 287-577
Fax 287-460
Airport: Tel. 753-950

KOREAN AIR
Grand Bali Beach Hotel, Sanur
Tel. 289-402

LUFTHANSA GERMAN AIRLINES
Grand Bali Beach Hotel, Sanur
Tel. 287-069

MALAYSIA AIRLINES
Grand Bali Beach Hotel, Sanur
Tel. 288-716

MERPATI NUSANTARA
Jl. Melati 57, Denpasar
Tel. 228-842
Airport: Tel. 751-374

QANTAS AIRWAYS
Grand Bali Beach Hotel, Sanur
Tel. 288-332, 287-896
Airport: Tel. 751-472/3

ROYAL BRUNEI AIRLINES
Nusa Dua Beach Hotel
Tel. 772-618/20
Fax 772-621

SCANDINAVIAN AIRLINES SYSTEM
Grand Bali Beach Hotel, Sanur
Tel. 288-141

SEMPATI AIR
Grand Bali Beach Hotel, Sanur
Tel. 288-823
Fax 287-917
Airport: Tel. 754-218/9
Fax 754-218

SINGAPORE AIRLINES
Grand Bali Beach Hotel, Sanur
Tel. 287-940, 288-124, 289-340
Fax 287-176
Airport: 752-174,

751-011 ext 1309
Fax 754-190

THAI AIRWAYS INTERNATIONAL
Grand Bali Beach Hotel, Sanur
Tel. 288-141

UTA FRENCH AIRLINES
Jl. Bypass Ngurah Rai 87 X, Sanur
Tel. 289-225/6/7
Fax 289-228

HELICOPTER AND CHARTER SERVICES
GATARI
Ngurah Rai Airport:
Domestic Arrival Hall
Tel. 754-063
Helicopter and fixed wing services.

P.T. INDONESIA AIR TRANSPORT
Ngurah Rai Airport,
Domestic Arrival Hall
Tel. 753-957, 753-730
Air charter and helicopter service.

MANTRUST ASAHI AIRWAYS
Jl. Hang Tuah 4, Sanur
Tel. 288-007
Fax 287-948
Heli tour & charter service.

TRAVEL AGENTS

Here are a few of the many reputable licenced travel agents.
BALINDO STAR TOURS & TRAVEL
Jl. Gatot Subroto 778X, Denpasar
Tel. 235-060, 228-669
(After hours: 222-497)
Fax 232-545

BSA TOURS & TRAVEL
Jl. Imam Bonjol 209, Denpasar
(open 24-hours)
Tel. 231-665
Fax 223-788
Jl. Legian 75, Kuta
Tel. 754-491
Jl. Suweta 1, Ubud
Tel. 975-575/6/7

JAN'S TOURS & TRAVEL SERVICE LTD.
Jl. Nusa Indah 62, Denpasar
Tel. 234-930, 232-660
Fax 231-009
PACTO LTD.
Jl. Ngurah Rai, Denpasar
Tel. 288-247/8
Fax 288-240

UBUD AREA

Note: Jl. Raya Ubud Ubud is also called Main Street. Puri Saren Agung is also called Ubud Palace. The wantilan is the large public pavilion at the central crossroads of Ubud.

USEFUL ADDRESSES

EMERGENCIES
POLICE
Jl. Andong
Tel. 975-316

MEDICAL CLINIC (24-HOURS)
Darma Usada Clinic,
Jl. Abangan (by the aqueduct)
Tel. 975-235

PHARMACY (APOTIK)
Dwi Sandhi,
Jl. Andong
Tel. 975-465
Toko Obat (next to Dharma Usada Clinic)

TOURIST SERVICES AND INFORMATION CENTERS
ARY'S TOURIST SERVICES CENTER
Main St., across from the Pura Desa.
8am–9pm. Closed 12.30pm–1.30pm
Tel./Fax 975-162

BINA WISATA UBUD
TOURIST INFORMATION
Crossroads, Jl. Raya
Ubud
Tel. 96-285
Nyoman Baula, Mgr.
Best source of
information about
performances, local
temple festivals, tours,
and transport.

BSA (BAHTERA SUJUD
ANUGRAH) TOURS AND
TRAVEL
Jl. Suweta 1 (north of
the wantilan)
Tel. 975-575,
975-577

CAMPUAN TOURIST
INFORMATION SERVICE
Main St. (on the curve
down toward the bridge)
Tel./Fax 975-298.

NOMAD GROUP
Jl. Raya Ubud 33.
Open daily 8am–7pm
(Telecommunications
office open till 11pm).
Tel. 975-131
Fax 975-115

PERAMA TOURIST
SERVICE
Jl. Padang Tegal
Tel. 96-316

UBUD NEWSTAND
Main St. (across from
the lotus pond)
Silvio Santoso is an
authority on local
culture. His excellent
map "Explorers' Bali"
available at Rp10,000.

COMMUNICATIONS

Phone, facsimile, IDD,
telegram, phone cards
available at TELKOM and
WARTEL (warung
telekomunikasi or
telecom shops).
Telecommunication
items also available in
numerous local tourist
services at varying
rates.

TELKOM
Jl. Andong
Fax 975-120
Card phones in the
parking lot. 8am–7pm.
Closed Sunday.

WARTEL
Nomad Group (upstairs).
Tel. 975-114
Fax 975-115.
8am–11pm daily.
Rates are posted
Telkom rates + 10
percent

TRANSPORT
AIRLINE TICKET AGENCIES

BSA TOURS AND TRAVEL
Jl. Suweta 1
Tel. 975-575/7

BEMO SERVICE

Going east, north, and
south from in front of
the market; going west
from in front of the
wantilan.

SHUTTLE SERVICE

To airport, Kuta, Sanur,
Denpasar, Lovina,
Kintamani, Candi Dasa,
Padang Bai, and
Lombok. Competitive
rates and coordinated
schedules. Reservations
recommended.

GANDA SAKTI TOURIST
INFORMATION
Jl. Raya Ubud 33
Tel. 975-131

PERAMA TOURIST
SERVICE,
Jl. Padang Tegal,
Ubud
Tel. 96-316

BINA WISATA TOURIST
INFORMATION
Crossroads, Jl. Raya
Ubud
Tel. 96-285

MUTIARA
Main St. (across from
Pura Desa)

MINIVAN CHARTER

Near the central
crossroads. They'll find
you.

CAR AND MOTORBIKE HIRE

See Tourist Services
listings for:
ARY'S TOURIST SERVICES
CENTER
GANDA SAKTI TOURIST
INFORMATION

PURPA
Monkey Forest Rd
Tel. 975-068, 975-234
Fax 975-016.
CV THREE BROTHERS
WISATA CAR RENTAL
Monkey Forest Rd
Tel. 975-396

CULTURAL ACTIVITIES

MUSEUMS/GALLERIES

All open daily except on
Nyepi and Galungan
◆ 300.
AGUNG RAI FINE ART
GALLERY ▲ 170
Main Road, Peliatan
Tel. 975-444
Fax 975-332
9am–6.30pm
ALIT'S GALLERY
Jl. Raya Ubud (west of
Puri Lukisan)
Tel. 96-280
ANTONIO BLANCO ▲ 165
Campuhan (next to
Bridge Café)
7am–5pm
Admission Rp1,000
KAMARKINI GALLERY
Jl. Raya Lungsiakan
Kedewatan, Ubud
Tel. 975-296
LA LUNA ART GALLERY
Penestanan, Ubud (at
Padma Indah Cottages)
MUNUT'S GALLERY
Jl. Raya Ubud (across
from post office)
Tel. 975-171
7.30am–6pm
MUSEUM PURI LUKISAN
▲ 168
Jl. Raya Ubud
Tel. 975-136
9am–5pm.
Admission Rp1000.
NEKA GALLERY
Jl. Raya Ubud (across
from post office)
Tel. 975-034
8am–5pm
NEKA MUSEUM ▲ 166
Campuhan
(Sanggingan)
Tel. 975-074
9am–5pm
Admission Rp1000
NGURAH K.K. "YOUNG
ARTISTS" SCHOOL OF
PAINTING
Campuhan (past bridge,
left side)
PURI LEMPAD
Jl. Raya Ubud
PURPA GALLERY
Monkey Forest Rd
Tel. 975-068
Fax 975-016
9am–6pm
PURI BUKIT MAS
Jl. Raya Ubud
Tel. 96125
7am–8pm

SENIWATI: ART BY WOMEN
Jl. Sriwedari 2B
Taman, Ubud
10am–5pm (or on
request, call Mary at tel.
975-568)
WAYAN CEMUL
(stone carver)
Jl. Kajeng

DANCE/THEATER

There is a choice of
performances nightly.
Schedules and
programs change often.
Check with Bina Wisata
Ubud Tourist Information
for current information.

UBUD PALACE
Dance and gamelan
rehearsals
Dance: 4pm Sun. &
Tues. Gamelan: Sun.
9–11am; Tues. 4pm

TEMPLES ▲ 162

PURA DESA UBUD
Central Ubud, west of
Puri Saren Agung
PURA GUNUNG LEBAH
Campuhan
PURA DALEM PADANG
TEGAL
Monkey Forest
Scary carvings.
PURA TAMAN SARASWATI
Central Ubud, at the
lotus pond
PURA BATU KARU
Jl. Suweta

STUDY OPPORTUNITIES
BATIK PAINTING

NYOMAN SURADNYA
Nirwana Homestay
Jl.Gautama 10, Padang
Tegal
Tel. 975-415
CRACKPOT BATIK
WORKSHOP
Monkey Forest Rd
Open daily from 9am
Rp25,000 includes shirt,
instruction, dyes.

COOKING CLASSES

Casa Luna
Jl. Raya Ubud
Tel. 96-283
Wed. 10.30am
Balinese cooking
classes. Rp20,000.

DANCE

Agung Kompiang
Jl. Kajeng
Ask teachers at Ubud
Palace rehearsals; also
at Padang Tegal's
Stage.

MASK-CARVING

Ida Bagus Anom
Main Road, Mas
Tel. 975-292

MUSIC
GANESHA BOOKSHOP
Jl. Raya Ubud (opposite the post office)
"Introduction to Balinese Music"
Tues. 6pm
Rp15,000/person
NYOMAN TINGGAL
Pengosekan
Kendang lessons

PARAS CARVING
Wayan Cemul
Jl.Kajeng
Rp15,000 includes three days' instruction, stone, loan of tools.

WOOD CARVING
Wayan Lebah
Junjungan,
Ubud
Enquire at Bina Wisata Tourist Information.

SHOPPING ◆ 306

Shops are generally open daily from 9am–7pm unless otherwise noted.

ANTIQUES/CRAFTS
THE GALLERY
Amandari
Kedewatan, Ubud
Tel. 975-333 .
KUNANG KUNANG I & II
Campuhan and Jl. Raya Ubud West
Tel. 975-714
THE SHOP
Amandari
Kedewatan, Ubud
Tel. 975-333

BASKETS
MERTA JAYA II
Jl. Hanoman
UBUD MARKET
Central Crossroads

BOOKS AND TOYS
ADINDA
Jl. Hanoman 10
Padang Tegal
Tel. 975-393
CINTA BOOKSHOP
Jl. Dewi Sinta.
CRACKPOT COFFEE HOUSE & BOOK EXCHANGE
Monkey Forest Rd
DEWA HOUSE
Monkey Forest Rd 68
GANESHA BOOKSHOP & MUSICAL INSTRUMENTS
Main St Ubud
UBUD BOOKSTORE
Main St Ubud (across from the post office)
UBUD NEWSTAND
Main St Ubud (across from lotus pond)

CLOTHES AND ACCESSORIES
BABYLON BALI
Sangingan, Ubud
(west of Neka Museum)
Quality clothes in linen, cotton, and rayon in sizes XS to XL.
SAKTI
Monkey Forest Rd
THE WIZ BOUTIQUE
Jl. Raya Ubud
Tel. 975-811
Locally designed clothes and shoes at reasonable prices.
TOKO
Monkey Forest Rd (just southwest of the market)
Tel. 975-046
Indonesian designer fashions in original textiles, in an idiosyncratically elegant shop.

GOLD AND JEWELRY
DEWI SRI
Monkey Forest Rd
Tel. 975-056
10am–9pm.
PURPA SILVER GALLERY
Monkey Forest Rd
Tel. 975-068

HOMEWARES
CASA LINA
Jl. Raya Ubud
Tel./Fax 96-282

TEXTILES
A.A.RAI PASTI, TAILOR
Monkey Forest Rd
Tel. 96-259
7.30am–9pm
KAMAR SUTRA
Monkey Forest Rd (next to Cafe Wayan)
Tel 975-135.
LOTUS STUDIOS
Jl. Raya Ubud
Tel. 975-363
WARDANI BOUTIQUE
Monkey Forest Rd
Tel. 975-538

RESTAURANTS

Note: All restaurants open daily from 11am to 10pm unless otherwise noted. Reservations not necessary unless noted.

UBUD (CENTRAL AND NORTH)

ARY'S WARUNG
Jl. Raya Ubud
Tel. 975-053
Eclectic menu with many vegetarian dishes. Charming atmosphere, food average.
Rp7500
○ C

BINTANG PARI
Jl. Suweta, Sakti, North Ubud
Beautifully airy thatched pavilion overlooking rice fields. This Balinese-Japanese collaboration provides exquisite hospitality and nice dishes with Japanese names. Open from early lunch until very early dinner.
Rp6500
○ ☀ ⌂

CAFE LOTUS
Jl. Raya Ubud
Tel. 975-053
On splendid lotus pond. Specialties: homemade pasta and dessert. Used to be better.
Rp15,000
◐ C ☀

CASA LUNA
Jl. Raya Ubud
Tel. 96-283
Eclectic light cuisine (Mediterranean and Indonesian); salads; kids' menu; Italian breads; bakery. Spacious and pleasant. TV room for laser disk movies nightly. Open for breakfast until late at night. Popular with expats.
Rp7500
○ C

GRIYA BARBEQUE
Jl. Raya Ubud
(west of Puri Lukisan)
Tel. 975-428
Specialties: barbecued grills. Always good.
Rp9000
★ ○ C

HAN SNEL'S GARDEN RESTAURANT
Jl. Kajeng 3
Tel. 975-699
Specialties: Indonesian dishes. Full bar.
Rp10,000
◐ C ☀ ⌂

MOMOYA
Jl. Suweta 18
Tel. 96412
Balinese and Japanese delicacies by a Balinese-Japanese couple. Balinese banquets on request.
Rp12,000
○ C ⌂

MUMBUL TERRACE GARDEN RESTAURANT
Jl. Raya Ubud
Tel. 975-136
Western eclectic. Specialties: Western breakfasts; fresh fruit juices, homemade ice creams, and sherbets; cocktails. Pleasant, central.
Rp7500
○ C

NOMAD
Jl. Raya Ubud
(east of the Market)
Tel. 975-131
Hearty food at reasonable prices; good bakery; full bar. A friendly place. Open early, closes late.
Rp7500
○ C

ROOF GARDEN RESTAURANT
Jl. Raya Ubud
(across from Griya BBQ)
Tel. 975-086
Specialties: Italian and Indonesian dishes. Wine list. Fine desserts. Tranquil, intimate place on upper story.
Rp15,000
◐ C

MONKEY FOREST ROAD

CAFE WAYAN
Monkey Forest Rd
Tel. 975-447
European and Indonesian food. Selection of wines. Casual; pavilions and terraces. Balinese buffet Sundays. Popular with expats. Reservations advisable during high season.
Rp15,000
◐ C

LOTUS LANE
Monkey Forest Rd
Tel. 975-357
Italian and Indonesian food in a quiet lane. Balinese maitre d' speaks fluent Italian. Selection of wines.
Rp17,000
◐ ⦶ ⅏

YOGYAKARTA TEAHOUSE
Monkey Forest Rd
Tel. 96-482
Central Javanese cooking. Lunch and dinner in a charming two-story building. Good value.
Rp5000
○ ⦶

UBUD (SOUTH)

BEBEK BENGIL (THE DIRTY DUCK)
Jl. Hanuman (at the Y-junction to the Monkey Forest)
Tel. 975-489
Eclectic menu in an airy pavilion. Best tables on tatami mats. Great ginger chicken; good desserts.
Rp15,000
◐

KAGEMUSHA
Jl. Hanuman, Pengosekan
Tel. 96-134
Japanese country cooking in a charming, modest pavilion. Highly recommended. Lunch and dinner. Closed Sun. Reasonable prices.
Rp7500
★ ○ ⅏ ⌂

KOKOKAN CLUB
Jl. Pengosekan (at the entrance to Puri Indah)
Tel. 96-495
Opened in 1993; unprecedented grandeur for Ubud. Elegant drinks lounge downstairs, elegant dining upstairs. Thai cuisine. Lunch and dinner. Live music or performances Sat.
Rp20,000
◐ ♫ ⅏

KURA KURA
Jl. Hanuman (next to Bebek Bengil)
Tel. 975-659
Mexican food. Pleasant upstairs loft. A favorite with expats.
Rp15,000
◐ ⅏ ⌂

RUMAH MAKAN PADANG
Jl. Hanuman, Padang Tegal
Authentic Padang (Sumatran) food.
Rp7500
○ ⦶

SHADANA
Jl. Raya Ubud (opposite Jl. Hanoman)
Vegetarian. Simple place, wide choice. Very reasonable.
Rp5000
○ ⦶

UBUD RAYA
Jl. Hanuman, Pengosekan
Tel. 975-607
Japanese and Indonesian food. Good food in a clean and comfortable place.
Rp7500
○ ⅏ ⌂

UBUD (WEST)

AMANDARI RESTAURANT
Sayan, Kedewatan
Tel. 975-333
Gourmet experience in one of the world's most exquisite small hotels. International and Indonesian cuisine. Bookings required for non-guests.
Rp45,000
★ � ⅏ ⌂ ⌷⸱⸱

BEGGAR'S BUSH
Campuhan (just after the bridge)
Tel. 975-009
The publican is Victor Mason, authority on Balinese birds and Dixieland jazz. Good grills, excellent beer on tap.
Rp12,000
◐

CAFE DEWATA
Penestanan Kelod
Tel. 96-076
Balinese, Indonesian, Chinese, and Italian food.
Rp5000
○ ⅏ ⌂

DANINO
Penestanan Kelod
[No phone]
Indonesian and Western food; video movies.
Rp5000
○ ⅏ ⌂

MURNI'S
Campuhan (Just before the bridge)
Tel. 975-233
An old favorite. American and Indonesian specialties; grills downstairs. Good bakery. Closed Wed.
Rp12,000
◐ ⅏ ⌂

SAYAN CAFE
Sayan Terrace
Charming place with an uneven history of quality. Under new management; deserves yet another chance. Western and Indonesian dishes.
Rp6500
○ ⌂

WARUNG
Jl. Payangan, Kedawatan (just north of the T-junction to Ubud)
Big, clean-looking warung with white ceramic tile on the walls. Great nasi campur. Famous with locals.
Rp2000
○

ACCOMMODATION

UBUD (CENTRAL AND NORTH)

KAJENG HOMESTAY
Jl. Kajeng 29
Tel. 975-018
Rooms with private bath, four with hot water. On a hill; nice garden and pond. Breakfast included.
Rp10,000–25,000
⌂ ⦶ ⅏ ⌷⸱⸱

KETUT'S PLACE
Jl. Suweta (north of the Pura Puseh)
Tel. 96-426
Bungalows with private bathroom (one with hot shower). In an orchid garden behind a family compound. Special Balinese buffet dinner available on request. Breakfast included.
Rp15,000–35,000
⌂ ⅏

PURI SAREN (UBUD PALACE)
Across from the Ubud Market
Tel. 975-057
Fax 975-137 (Hotel Tjampuan)
Pavilion rooms in Ubud's main palace. All have private bath, fan, veranda. Quiet, clean, royally opulent surroundings. Absolutely central. Gamelan rehearsals in the forecourt every Sun. am; full performances almost every evening. Breakfast included.
US$40/£27
★ ⌂ ⦶ ♫ ⌂

PURI SARASWATI BUNGALOWS
Jl. Raya Ubud (next to the Cafe Lotus)
Tel./Fax 975-164
Rooms and bungalows, all with private bath, fan, some with hot water. Breakfast pavilion. Very central but surprisingly quiet. Adjoins the splendid temple, Pura Taman Saraswati, on the lotus lake. Good family hotel.
US$22–40/£15–27
⌂ ⦶ ⌂ ⌇

SITI BUNGALOWS
Jl. Kajeng 3
(P.O. Box 227, Denpasar 80001)
Tel. 975-699
Fax 975-643
Bungalows in secluded garden, but very central location. Siti is the Balinese wife of the Dutch painter Han Snel, whose studio and restaurant are on the same grounds. Very clean and quiet. Good value. Breakfast and afternoon tea included. Deposit required.
US$40–50/£27–34
⌂ ⦶ ⌂ ⌷⸱⸱ ⌇

MONKEY FOREST ROAD

FIBRA INN
Tel./Fax 975-451
Villa-style rooms and suites with hot water, ceiling fans, veranda; garden; airport transfer service. The proprietress is a dancer.
US$30–40/£20–27
⌂ ⦶

SAGITTARIUS INN
Tel./Fax 975-492
Twelve rooms, four with hot water; fan. Good restaurant with video films. Breakfast included.
Rp15,000–30,000
⌂ ⦶

UBUD INN
P.O. Box 171,
Ubud
Tel. 975-071/96-257
Fax 975-188
*Villa-style rooms and
suites, including four
family rooms (one double
and two single beds)
with hot-water showers,
fan or AC, veranda.
Pleasant, popular.
Breakfast included.
US$30–70/£20–47*

UBUD (SOUTH)

ARTINI I HOMESTAY
Jl. Hanoman, Padang
Tegal
Tel. 975-348
*Rooms in garden; hot
water; fan. Access to
swimming pool at Artini
II across the street
(Rp5,000). Lovely
garden. An old favorite.
Breakfast included.
Rp20,000*

PURI INDAH
EXCLUSIVE VILLAS
Jl. Pengosekan
Tel. 975-742
Fax 975-332
*Villa-style rooms and
suites with hot bath, fan,
veranda. Also two-story
family house. Impressive
architecture and
gardens, but expensive.
Breakfast included.
US$65–230/£43.40–154*

UBUD (WEST)
AMANDARI
Kedewatan
Tel. 975-333
Fax 975-335
Reservations:
Tel. 771-267
Fax 771-266
*Luxury villas
(single-story and duplex
suites, six with private
pool), each with private*

*garden, outdoor sunken
marble bath, music
system, private bar.
Superb architecture in
traditional materials, set
in rice terraces
overlooking the Ayung
River valley; first-class
cuisine; expertly
managed. The ultimate
retreat. Discreet luxury.
Considered one of the
best hotels in the world.
US$300–700/£200–467*

BALIUBUD COTTAGES
Penestanan
Tel. 975-058
Tel./Fax 287-223
*Rooms with hot-water
baths, some with AC;
bar pavilion, airport
transfer service.
Balinese buffet
available on request.
Handsome grounds on
high, airy location.
$50–75/£34–50, extra
bed $15/£10*

HOTEL TJAMPUHAN
[also spelled Campuan
and Campuhan]
Campuhan
P.O. Box 3015
Denpasar 80030
Tel. 975-368/9
Fax 975-137
*Bungalow rooms with
private bath & veranda,
fan; two tennis courts,
badminton. Situated in
steep gardens on a
river gorge where Walter
Spies built his famous
house. Romantic, very
"old Ubud". Breakfast
included.
US$52–80/£35–54,
extra bed $14/£9*

MUNUT BUNGALOWS
Campuhan
Tel. 975-039
Bungalows with veranda,

*fan, some with hot water.
In Penestanan, on a hill
in the rice fields.
Breakfast included.
Rp20,000–Rp25,000*

PADMA INDAH
COTTAGES
Penestanan, Campuhan
Tel./Fax 975-719
*Rooms in two-story, rice
barn-style cottages, all
with hot-water baths,
king-size beds, art
gallery. Two family
cottages with two
bedrooms, kitchen,
large veranda, and
second-floor studio.
US$90–180/£60–120*

SARI BUNGALOWS
Penestanan Kelod
Tel. 975-547
*Rooms with double
beds, mandi-style
bathroom, and bungalow
with two bedrooms,
kitchen, and bathroom.
Charming homestay..
Breakfast included.
Rp250,000–500,000 per
month*

SAYAN TERRACES
Sayan, Kedewatan
P.O. Box 6, Ubud
Tel./Fax 975-384
*Cottage-style rooms
overlooking the Ayung
River valley; private
bath, veranda, some
rooms have fans.
Restaurant nearby. A
little settlement of typical
accommodation in an
upmarket neighborhood.
Breakfast included.
US$20–60/£13–40*

ULUN UBUD COTTAGES
Sanggingan
P.O. Box 3, Ubud
Tel. 975-024, 975-762
Fax 975-524
*Bungalows on a river
gorge; private bath, hot
water. Charming
architecture and
furnishings; good view.
The site is quite steep.
Breakfast included.
US$55–110/£37–74*

VILLA BUKIT UBUD
Sanggingan
P.O. Box 20, Ubud
Tel. 975-371
Fax 975-787
*Bungalow rooms with
garden bath (tub and*

*shower), hot water, most
with AC, refrigerator.
Free shuttle around
Ubud area. Wonderful
view of grassy river
gorges. Spacious, clean.
US$40–200/£27–134*

CULTURAL
ATTRACTIONS

PURA JATI
*Lakeside temple
▲ 183 on the road to
Toyabungkah.*

PURA ULUN DANU
Songan
*Temple ▲ 183 at the
head of the lake
dedicated to the lake
goddess.*

PURA ULUN DANU
BATUR
Karang Anyar
*Impressive temple
complex ▲ 184 in
Kintamani dedicated to
irrigation system and
lake goddess.*

PURA PENULISAN
*Ancient mountaintop
temple ▲ 184.*

TRUNYAN
*Famous Bali Aga village
▲ 182 on far side of
Lake Batur.*

RESTAURANTS

MARKET FOOD STALLS
*On market day (once
every three days, Hari
Pasah on the Balinese
calendar), there are
dozens of food stalls
open at the market until
around 11am.*

LAKEVIEW
Penelokan
*Indonesian food; buffet.
Specialty is lake fish.
Rp6000*

RUMAH MAKAN CAHAYA
Kintamani (north)
Simple warung with

very good
Chinese-Balinese home
cooking. Lovely people.
Rp2000
○

UNDER THE VOLCANO
Toyabungkah, Lake Batur
Grilled or fried lake fish.
Simple place; great
home cooking.
Rp5000
○ ⚒

ACCOMMODATION

Note: Air conditioning
not necessary in
Kintamani. Hot water for
bathing available on
request. None of the
places listed have
phones.

LOSMEN MIRANDA
Pasar Kintamani
Rooms share cold-
water bath. Basic
accommmodation in a
clean, modest Dutch-
style house across the
street from the
Kintamani market.
Breakfast included.
Rp10,000
⌂

**LOSMEN &
RESTAURANT
GUNAWAN**
Penelokan
Perched on a bluff
overlooking the lake.
Stupendous view.
Under renovation.
US$7–9/£5–6
⌂ ⚒

PURI ASTINA INN
Kintamani (north), about
220 yards from the main
road.
Rooms with large beds,
cold-water baths. Clean,
spacious, chilly. Remote
location with wonderful
view looking out toward
Mt. Batur, Mt. Abang,
and Mt. Agung.
US$15–30/£10–20
⌂ ⌂ ⚒ ⌂⋯

SURYA HOMESTAY
Kedisan, Lake Batur
Twenty-two rooms, all
with bathrooms, some
with hot-water showers.
Breakfast included.
Rp10,000–25,000
⌂

UNDER THE VOLCANO
Toyabungkah, Lake
Batur
Rooms with cold-water
shower and mandi.

Good simple restaurant.
Clean, hospitable.
Breakfast included.
Rp10,000–20,000
⌂

EAST BALI
USEFUL ADDRESSES

DIALING CODE
0363 in Karangasem,
0366 in Manggis

The main town is
Amlapura. The main
tourism center is Candi
Dasa, about 6½ miles
west of Amlapura.
Addresses are still
simple in East Bali,
outside of Amlapura.
What is listed should be
sufficient identification.
Telephone service is still
infrequent. Some hotels
in Candi Dasa use
Denpasar numbers and
do not require the
(0363) prefix. Padang
Bai is the harbor for
ferries to Lombok and
Nusa Penida.

EMERGENCIES
RUMAH SAKIT UMUM
(GENERAL HOSPITAL)
Jl. Ngurah Rai,
Amlapura
Tel. (0363) 21-011
POLICE
Jl. Bhayangkara,
Amlapura
Tel. 110

**TOURIST INFORMATION
AND SHUTTLE
SERVICES**
PANDAWA TOURIST
SERVICE
Candi Dasa

THE FRIENDSHIP SHOP
Candi Dasa
Tel. 229-052

DEPOT SEGARA
Jl. Silayukti
Padang Bai

KARANGASEM
GOVERNMENT TOURISM
OFFICE
Jl. Diponegoro
Amlapura
Tel. (0363) 21-196

CULTURAL
ATTRACTIONS

BUDAKLING
Village of iron-, gold-
and silversmiths.
**CANDI DASA TEMPLE
COMPLEX**
Siwa temple and lagoon
▲ 216.

PURI KANGINAN
Open daily 9am–5pm.
Admission Rp500
Palace of Karangasem
royal family ▲ 226.

TENGANAN
Open daily from 8am–
6pm. Small donation
requested.
Bali Aga village ▲ 216.
Good textile market in
the parking lot.

TIRTHA GANGGA
Always open. Admission:
Rp500
Water gardens ▲ 226
and spring-fed
swimming pools.

UJUNG WATER PALACE
Ruins of former royal
water gardens ▲ 227.

WATERSPORTS

Note: Most diving trips
should be arranged with
a diving company ◆ 308,
but if you have your own
equipment you can
usually arrange
something directly on
the spot.

PARADISE PALM BEACH
BUNGALOWS,
Tulamben, Kubu,
Amlapura
Tel. 229-052
(The Friendship Shop,
Candi Dasa)

BARUNA DIVE
Puri Bagus Beach
Hotel,
Candi Dasa
Tel. 235-291

RESTAURANTS

CHEZ LILLY
Candi Dasa
Western, Indonesian,
seafood, and vegetarian
dishes. Pleasant setting.
Rp7500
○

GANGGA CAFE
Tirtha Gangga
Indian and Indonesian,
with large menu of
homemade yoghurt
dishes.
Rp5000
○

**RICE TERRACE
COFFEESHOP**
Tirtha Gangga
French bread
sandwiches

recommended.
Rp7000
○

TJ's
Candi Dasa
Tel. 235-540
Asian and Western
dishes. French and
Australian wines; full bar.
Casual chic setting in
water gardens.
Rp15,000
★ ◐

**THE RESTAURANT,
AMANKILA**
Manggis, Karangasem
Tel. (0366) 21-993
Indonesian Straits
(Nonya) cuisine in
elegant pavilion.
Reservations required.
Rp45,000
◍ ⌂ ⌂⋯ ⚒

ACCOMMODATION

AMANKILA
Manggis, Bali
Tel. (366) 21993
Fax (366) 21995
Reservations:
Tel. (363) 41333
Luxury suites, seven

with private pool. On a steep forested hill overlooking a secluded beach cove; dramatic architecture; gloriously private and spacious. Aman-class hospitality and luxury in all details.
US$300–1100/£200–734
★ 🏠 🏠 ⛗ ⚓ 🛌 ☎

HIDDEN PARADISE COTTAGES
Lipah, Amed, Karangasem
Fax (0361) 431-273, (0363) 21-044
Bungalows on the beach with fan or AC, hot-water baths. Very comfortable and well-run. American breakfast included.
US$30–60/£20–40
🏠 🛌

IDA BEACH VILLAGE
Desa Samuh, Candi Dasa
P.O. Box 270, Denpasar
Tel. 229-041
Fax 751-934
Balinese-style houses each with garden and courtyard; hot-water bath, AC, or fan. Large, handsomely built bungalows of timber and brick; gracious staff.
US$45–50/£30–34
🏠 ⛗ 🛌 🎵

IDA HOMESTAY
Candi Dasa
Rice barn-style bungalows with cold-water bath, fan. Simple accommodation in a large coconut grove. One of the original Candi Dasa hideaways, and has refused to change. Romantic. Long-time favorite.
Rp25,000–50,000
🏠 ⚊ 🏠 ⚓

SERAI HOTEL
Buitan, Manggis, Karangasem 80871, Bali
Tel. (363) 41011
Fax. (363) 41015
A new concept on Bali:

high quality, medium-priced accommodation. Built and run by the Aman people. Stylishly simple, on the beach. Good restaurant, very reasonably priced.
US$90–175/£60–117
★ 🏠 🏠 ⛗ 🛌 ⚊ ⚊ 🔲 ☎

KUSUMA JAYA INN
Tirtha Gangga
Bungalows with private bath, a few with hot water. Up a steep flight of stairs and girdling a hillside with wonderful views of rice fields, sea, and eastern mountains. Breakfast included.
Rp20,000–40,000
🏠 ⚊ 🏠

NIRWANA COTTAGES
Sengkidu, Candi Dasa Beach
Amlapura, Bali 80871
Tel. (361) 236-136
Fax (361) 235-543
Cottages with AC, hot showers, and baths, terrace; refrigerators. Airport transport on request; good beach front. Very clean and well-run. Restaurant has home-style cooking. Highly recommended.
$40–50/£27–34, extra bed $10/£7, baby cot $5/£3.
🏠 ⛗ 🏠 ⚓ 🔲

PARADISE PALM BEACH BUNGALOWS
Tulamben, Kubu, Karangasem
Tel. 229-052 (Friendship Shop, Candi Dasa)
Rooms by the sea, fan, cold-water bath. Near the Liberty wreck dive site. Narrow rocky beach.
Rp22,000–30,000
🏠

PURI BAGUS BEACH HOTEL
Candi Dasa
Tel. 235-291
Fax 235-666

Rooms in pleasant bungalows on beach; AC, hot-water baths. Comfortable and quiet.
US$60–175 /£40–117 (children under twelve free if sharing room with parents)
🏠 ⛗ 🛌 🎵

VIENNA BEACH BUNGALOWS
Lipah, Amed, Karangasem
Double bungalows on the beach; cold-water baths. Modest and pleasant. Breakfast included.
Rp25,000
🏠

THE WATERGARDEN
Candi Dasa, Bali
Tel./Fax (361) 235-540
Fan-cooled thatched cottages, each with its own goldfish pond and garden; hot showers; adjacent restaurant and bar with poolside dining; saltwater swimming pool; airport pick-up on request. Two-minute walk to the beach. Wonderfully soothing Zen-like place. You can hear the carp jumping and the sound of the surf. Marvelous hospitality.
$65/£43, extra bed $10/£7
★ 🏠 🇨 ⚊ 🛌 ☎

NORTH BALI
USEFUL ADDRESSES

DIALING CODE
0362 in Singaraja and Lovina Beach

EMERGENCIES
HOSPITAL (RUMAH SAKIT)

Rumah Sakit Umum Kertha Usada
Jl. Jend. A. Yani 108, Singaraja
Tel. (0362) 22-396, (0362) 23-067

TRANSPORT
GANDA SARI TRANSPORT
Arya's Cafe, Lovina Beach
Tel. (0362) 63-797

PERAMA TOURIST SERVICE
Tel. (0361) 751-551

CULTURAL ATTRACTIONS

TEMPLES
PURA BEJI, SANGSIT
Kubutambahan
Subak temple with virtuoso stone carving ▲ 235.
PURA DALEM JAGARAGA
Jagaraga
Famous temple of the dead ▲ 233.
PURA MADUWE KARANG
Kubutambahan
Grand village temple with fine statuary and bas reliefs ▲ 233.
PURA ULUN DANU
BRATAN AND CANDI
KUNING
Bedugul
Elegant lakeside temple and Buddhist stupa ▲ 238.

BUDDHIST ASHRAM
BRAHMAN WIHARA
ASRAMA
Desa Banjar, Singaraja

TRADITIONAL WEAVING
Puri Sinar Nadi Putri
(Mme.A.A. Ayu Agettis)
Jl. Veteran 22, Singaraja
Tel. (0362) 21-585

GAMELAN SMITH
Sida Karya (I Made Widandra)
Desa Sawan, Singaraja

SPORTS

SNORKELING AND DIVING
BARUNA WATER SPORTS
Palma Beach Hotel, Kalibukbuk, Lovina Beach
Tel. (0362) 23-775
Fax (0362) 23-659

SPICE DIVE
Arya's Cafe
Lovina Beach
Tel. (0362) 23-305
REEF SEEN AQUATICS
c/o Pondok Sari Beach
Bungalows & Dive Village
Pemuteran, Grokgak,
Singaraja
Tel. (0362) 92-339

GOLF
BALI HANDARA KOSAIDO
COUNTRY CLUB
Pancasari, Buleleng
Tel. (0362) 22-646
Fax (0362) 23-048

RESTAURANTS

NORTH BALI (COAST)

*Note: Restaurants are
generally open daily, all
day, as long as there
are customers.*

KHI KHI SEAFOOD
RESTAURANT
Kalibukbuk, Lovina Beach
*Grilled seafood;
Chinese. Two big
kitchens where you can
watch them cook. Very
casual service and
setting; great food; huge
portions.*
Rp6500
★ ○

MALIBU RESTAURANT
& BAR
Lovina Beach
*Indonesian and
Western food; full bar;
video movies; live band.*
Rp6500
○ ⬆

RUMAH MAKAN
ARINA
Jl. Ahmad Yani 53,
Singaraja
*Javanese-Chinese
cooking. Specialty is
ayam bakar Taliwang
(grilled local chicken).
Grilled seafood
depending on supply.*
Rp3500
○

WINA RESTAURANT &
BAR
Lovina Beach
*Huge pavilion with full
bar, Indonesian and
Chinese menu, video
movies every evening.*
Rp6500
○ ☐

NORTH BALI
(MOUNTAINS)
TALIWANG
BERSAUDARA
Candi Kuning, Bedugal
(across from the
mosque).
*Grilled local chicken is
the specialty, but also
some vegetarian dishes.
Right on the lake.*
Rp2000–4000
○ ⬆ ⌂

WARUNG KOPI
Puri Lumbung, Munduk,
Banjar, Singaraja
*Open daily from
breakfast until 10 pm.
Balinese-style cooking
served in a pleasant
setting.*
Rp7000
○ ⬆ ⌂ ⬜··

WARUNG UNICK
Candi Kuning, Bedugal
(about 200 yards north of
Candi Kuning)
*Old Dutch house; buffet
(Rp11,000) caters for
tour groups, but a la
carte is very
reasonable. Excellent
gado-gado for Rp3000*
○

ACCOMMODATION

NORTH BALI (COAST)
*Note: All hotels listed are
beachfront properties.*

ADITYA BUNGALOWS,
RESTAURANT & PUB
Lovina Beach, P.O. Box
134, Singaraja 81101
Tel. (0362) 23-342
Fax (0362) 22-059
*Eighty rooms
(seventeen w/fan; sixty-
three w/AC, hot water).
The non-AC cottages
on the beach are a
good deal. Continental
breakfast included.*
US$20–60/£13–40
⬆ ⬇ ⬜

BALI LOVINA BEACH
COTTAGES
Lovina Beach
P.O. Box 186, Singaraja
Tel.(0362) 22-385
Fax (0362) 23-478
⬆ ☐ ☐ ⬇

BALI TAMAN
BEACH HOTEL
Tukadmungga, Lovina
Beach
P.O. Box 198, Singaraja
Tel. (0362) 22-126
Fax (0362) 22-840
*Rooms with AC or fan,
hot water w/ bathtub.
Very pleasant.
Continental or
Indonesian breakfast
included.*
US$23–55/£16–37
⬆ ☐ ⬇ ⬜

KALIBUKBUK INN
Kalibukbuk, Lovina
Beach
*Twenty-six rooms (nine
w/AC). Close to the sea.
The AC rooms are a
good deal.*
Rp15,000–35,000
⌂

NIRWANA SEASIDE
COTTAGES
Kalibukbuk, Lovina
Beach
Tel. (0362) 22-288
Fax (0362) 21-090
*Rooms in bamboo
cottages; some with AC.
Long beach front;
popular. Breakfast
included.*
Rp25,000–50,000
⌂

PALMA BEACH HOTEL
Jl. Raya Lovina,
Kalibukbuk, Singaraja
Tel. (0362) 23-775
Fax (0362) 23-659
*Rooms in AC cottages,
hot-water baths, tennis
court. Baruna Water
Sports diving facilities.
The fanciest hotel so far
in north Bali.*
US$60–160/£40–107
⬆ ⬇ ♫ ⬜

PARMA BEACH HOTEL
West Lovina Beach (next
to Aditya Hotel)
Tel. (0362) 23-955
*Close to the sea; good
hospitality; very good
value. Breakfast
included.*
Rp15,000–25,000
⌂

NORTH BALI
(MOUNTAINS)

ASHRAM GUEST HOUSE
Candi Kuning, Bedugal
Tel. (0362) 22-439,
(0368) 21-101
*Some rooms with hot
water, most with private
bath. Quiet location on
Lake Bratan. Breakfast
included.*
Rp15,000–70,000
⌂ ⬆ ⌂ ⬜··

BALI HANDARA
KOSAIDO COUNTRY
CLUB
Pancasari, Buleleng
Reservations:
P.O. Box 3324, Denpasar
Tel. (0361) 288-944
Fax (0361) 287-358
*Luxury suites and
bungalows with optional
adjustable heater.
Japanese bath, spa,
fitness center, tennis
courts, full golf facilities
◆ 310. Can be
chilly July–Aug.*
US$65–350/£44–234
⬆ ⌂ ⬜·· ⬜

PURI LUMBUNG
Munduk, Banjar,
Singaraja
Reservations: P.O.2,
Nusa Dua, Denpasar
Tel. (0361) 772-078
Fax (0361) 771-532
*Two-story cottages in the
style of north Bali
wooden rice barns, with*

garden baths. Balinese breakfast included. Low-key, high quality, ecologically sensitive tourism. (An off-the-beaten track absolute must.) US$30–40/£20–27
★ ⌂ ⚡ ⌂ ⤳

WEST BALI
USEFUL ADDRESSES

DIALING CODE
0365 in Negara
0361 in Tabanan

POLICE STATION
J. Pahlawan, Negara
Tel. (0365) 110
Jl. Pahlawan
Tel. 91-210, Tabanan

TRANSPORT
Ferry to Java, every half-hour Gilimanuk

CULTURAL ATTRACTIONS

BULL-RACING
Purancak
Check locally for details.

GAMELAN JEGOG PERFORMANCES
Negara
Check at tourist information centers for details.

PURA PULAKI
Pulaki
Impressive seaside temple in northwest Bali ▲ 250.

PURA RAMBUT SIWI
East of Negara
Seaside temple with lovely carved reliefs ▲ 246.

SPORTS/NATURE

SNORKELING, DIVING
MENJANGAN ISLAND
Bali Barat National Park
Information, permits, boat transport at Labuan Lalang.

NATURE EXPLORATION
BALI BARAT NATIONAL PARK
Information ◆ 310, permits, guides (obligatory) at Labuan Lalang and Cekik.

RESTAURANTS

BALIAN BEACH CLUB
Lalang Linggah, Tabanan
Good food and hospitality in a very casual setting; gorgeous countryside by the sea. Accommodation also available.
Rp15,000
○ ⚡ ⤳

SOKA SARI
Soka, Jatiluwih, Tabanan
Reservations: Jl. Muding 43, Denpasar
Tel. (0361) 435-909
Pleasant restaurant with terrace overlooking the gorgeous Jatiluwih rice fields.
Rp9000
○ ⚡ ⤳

WARUNG MUSLIM
Gilimanuk Ferry Terminal
Good, clean, Javanese home-cooking.
Rp2000
○

WARUNG SDSB No. 205033
Pupuan (near the three-way intersection)
Clean warung with excellent nasi campur.
Rp1500
○ ★

ACCOMMODATION

BALIAN BEACH BUNGALOWS
Lalang Linggih, Selemadeg, Tabanan
Bungalows w/ fan and cold-water baths. Short walk to beach; bathing in Balian river. Great hospitality; rooms a bit funky. Beautiful country. Breakfast included.
Rp10,000–50,000
⌂ ⊟ ⌂ ⤳

MEDEWI BEACH COTTAGES
Pekutatan, Jembrana
Reservations:
P.O. Box 126, Negara
Tel. (0365) 40-029, 40-030
Fax (0365) 41-555
Rooms w/ AC, hot-water baths w/ tub. On a rocky beach.
US$20–60/£14–40
⌂ ⊟ ⤳ ⊿ ▢

PONDOK SARI BEACH BUNGALOWS & RESTAURANT
Pemuteran, Grokgak, Buleleng
Reservations: (0361) 289-031, 288-096
Fax (0362) 289-031
Rooms with fan; cold-water garden bath. Diving center. Very clean and comfortable; very quiet. Snorkeling off the beach.
Rp20,000–45,000
⌂ ⌂ ⤳

TINJAYA BUNGALOWS (MEDEWI SURFING POINT)
Pekutatan, Jembrana (next to Medewi Beach Hotel)
Six rooms in three two-story lumbung-style bungalows; private cold-water baths. Sandy beach nearby. Good value. Breakfast included.
Rp20,000–25,000
⌂

DENPASAR
USEFUL ADDRESSES

DIALING CODE
0361 in Denpasar

POLICE STATION
Jl. A. Yani
Tel. 225-456

CULTURAL ATTRACTIONS

BALI MUSEUM
Puputan Square
Open 8am–5pm, weekends and Tues.–Thurs; 8am–3.30pm Friday; Closed Mon ▲ 268.

PURA JAGATNATHA
Next to Bali Museum
State temple dedicated to Sang Hyang Widi Wasa ▲ 266.

PURA MAOSPAHIT
Jl. Sutomo, Grenceng
Very old, handsome, red brick temple ▲ 267.

PURA SADA
Kapal (West Denpasar)
Unusual old temple ▲ 254.

WERDI BUDAYA ART CENTER
Jl. Nusa Indah
Open daily 8am–4pm. Closed on holidays. Annual Arts Festival held in June–July ▲ 267.

SHOPPING

TRADITIONAL MARKETS
PASAR BADUNG
Jl. Sulawesi
PASAR KRENENG
Jl. Kamboja
PASAR KUMBASARI
Jl. Gajah Mada
PASAR SATRIYA
Jl. Nakula

DEPARTMENT STORES/ SHOPPING MALLS
KERTA WIJAYA PLAZA
Jl. Diponegoro 98
LIBI DEPARTMENT STORE
Jl. Teuku Umar 104-110
M'A DEPARTMENT STORE
Jl. Diponegoro 50
MATAHARI DEPARTMENT STORE
Jl. Dewi Sartika
TIARA DEWATA
Jl. Sutoyo

RESTAURANTS

ATOOM BARU
Jl. Gajah Bada 85
Tel. 222-623
Cantonese and Szechuan food.
Rp9000
◐ ⊟

AYAM BAKAR TALIWANG
Jl.Teuku Umar
Tel. 228-789
Open daily 9am–9pm.
Specialty: grilled local chicken.
Rp5000
★ ○

KAK MAN
Jl. Teuku Umar
Tel. 227-188
Open daily 11am–10pm.
Unusual: Balinese food with tablecloths. Authentic.
Rp6500
○

RUMAH MAKAN BETTY
Jl. Sumatra
Tel. 224-502
Daily 8am–8pm.
Good Indonesian food;

SANUR

menu in Indonesian and English.
Rp4000
○ **C**

TIARA DEWATA SHOPPING CENTER
Jl. Sutoyo
Open daily from
11am–10pm.
Food bazaar has dozens of specialty food stalls with Balinese, Javanese, Sumatran, Chinese, and Western food.
○

WARUNG SATE KAMBING
Pasar Burung Satriya, Jl. Veteran
Specializes in goat satay and soup.
Rp2500
★ ○

ACCOMMODATION

NATOUR BALI (BALI HOTEL)
Jl. Veteran 3
Tel. 225-681
Fax 235-347
All rooms with AC, private hot-water baths. Art deco colonial Dutch tourist hotel now surrounded by roaring Denpasar and bisected by a busy street. The better rooms (built by the Dutch in 1927 and recently restored) are on the other side from the circa 1942 standard rooms (which are overpriced).
US$60–100/£40–67
⌂ ⌷ **C** ⟲ □ ☎

PURI PEMECUTAN
Jl. Thamrin 2
Tel. 223-491
On the grounds of the royal palace of Pemecutan.
Rp50,000
⌂ **C** ♫

Note: The main road in Sanur is Jl. Danau Tamblingan, also known as Jl. Tandjung Sari and Jl. Bali Hyatt. Jl. Sri Kesari is also called Jl. Danau Poso. Sanur Beach has white sand from the Bali Beach Hotel south, black sand north of the hotel.

USEFUL ADDRESSES

EMERGENCIES
POLICE
Tel. 110
AMBULANCE
Tel. 118 or 227-911
DOCTOR (24-HOUR CALL)
Tel. 287-314
MEDICAL CLINIC
Hotel Bali Beach

PHARMACY (APOTIK)
Jl. Segara Ayu at the Bypass
Jl. Danau Tamblingan, Batujimbar
Jl. Danau Poso, Br Blanjong

TRANSPORT
METERED TAXI
Tel. 289-090, 289-191
BEMOS
Bemo service is cheap and convenient for local transport. Station is near the entrance to the Sanur Beach hotel; or just flag one down.

CAR AND MOTORBIKE RENTAL
CV BALI SETIA MOTOR
Jl. Danau Tamblingan 44
Tel. 288-698, 287-819
Fax 288-979
Although the sign says "Rent a car/self-drive", drivers are available for an extra $10/£7/day (maximum ten hours). Reasonable rates, nice people, good sevice. Mechanic permanently on call.
BALI CAR RENTAL
Jl. Bypass Ngurah Rai (northbound)
Tel. 288-550
Fax 288-778
Self-drive or with driver.
CV. WIRASANA
Jl. Danau Tamblingan 126
Tel. 288-706

CULTURAL ATTRACTIONS

TEMPLES
Sanur ▲ 274 is famous for its white coral temples. There are many small ones hidden away along the south beach. In December and January, watch for huge processions to the sea with purification ceremonies on the beach, especially at Sindhu (Sanur Beach Market). There are often gamelan rehearsals in the evenings at the various bale banjar. Visitors are welcome to watch. Ask for information at a nearby warung.
PURA BLANJONG
Banjar Blanjong
An inscribed pillar in this temple is from AD 914, Bali's earliest dated writing ▲ 275.

DANCES
Dance performances are scheduled regularly in all the major hotels. The performances organized by the Tanjung Sari hotel on Saturday evenings are particularly good, but they are expensive (Rp27,500 just to watch; Rp67,500 with buffet dinner). Check the Calendar of Events (Badung Tourist Office) for other dance performances ◆ 300.

DIVING COMPANIES

DIVE & DIVES
Jl. Bypass I Gusti Ngurah Rai, 23
Tel. 288-052
Fax 289309
ENA DIVE CENTER & WATER SPORTS
Jl. Pengembak 7
Tel. 287-134
Tel./Fax 287-945

SHOPPING

GENERAL/SUNDRIES
BAGUS DRUGSTORE
Jl. Danau Tamblingan at Jl. Duyung
TOKO TELAGA TUNJUNG
Jl. Danau Tamblingan 204

ARTS / CRAFTS
ANCESTORS
Jl. Danau Tamblingan 97
Primitive sculpture and tribal arts of Indonesia.
ASMAT ARTS
Jl. Danau Tamblingan 200X
BATIK GANDY
Jl. Bypass 146X
Tel. 289-541
Batik items from all over Indonesia.
SARI BUMI
Jl. Danau Tamblingan (next to Cafe Batujimbar)
Ceramics made in the workshop in Batujimbar.

BOOKS/NEWS STANDS
For foreign newspapers and periodicals, general reading, and books on Bali and Indonesia:
BATUJIMBAR BOOKSHOP
(next to Cafe Batujimbar)
DRUGSTORE
Sanur Beach Hotel
DADY BOOKSTORE
Jl. Danau Tamblingan (across from Laghawa Beach Inn)
KLICK GALLERY
(Next to Cafe Batu Jimbar)
Jl. Danu Tamblingan
Photo gallery, books, periodicals, gifts, art T-shirts.

For second-hand books in English, French, German, and Dutch:
DONALD'S NEWS AGENCY & DRUGSTORE
(next to the entrance of the Sanur Beach Hotel)

CLOTHES
NOGO BALI IKAT CENTER
Jl. Danau Tamblingan 98
(across from the

Tandjung Sari)
Specializing in ikat and handwoven fabrics. Ready-made clothes and quick service made-to-order. Multilingual staff on hand.

PISCES
Jl. Danau Tamblingan 105
Smart-looking clothes in black and white batiks. Very reasonable prices.

RASCALS
Jl. Danau Tamblingan (southern end)
Children's wear; very attractive clothes in batik cotton.

PHOTOGRAPHIC SERVICES

BAGUS DRUGSTORE
Jl. Danu Tamblingan & Jl. Duyung
SANUR FOTO CENTER
Jl. Tamblingan 68 (across from the Gazebo hotel)

RESTAURANTS

BORNEO BAR & RESTAURANT
Sindhu Beach Rd
Sindhu
(No phone)
Seafood, meaty Western dishes like chilli con carne, steaks; Indonesian dishes. Good value. Breakfast, lunch and dinner.
Rp7500
○ C

CAFE BATUJIMBAR
Jl. Danau Tamblingan 152
Tel. 287-374
Specializing in freshest quality salads and seafood. Daily specials; bakery, and homemade desserts. Shady terrace. A favorite for lunch; open till around 9pm.
Rp10,000
★ ○ C

CINTU BINDO
Jl. Danau Tamblingan 178
Open 24 hours.
Padang food.
Rp5000
○ C

JAWA BARAT
Jl. Kesuma Sari 2
Br. Semawang, Sanur
11am–10pm.
West Javanese cooking, specializing in live sweetwater fish, but there's a lot for vegetarians to choose from: the tempeh bacam is especially good. Big, airy place with good food at very reasonable prices. Popular with locals and expats.
Rp3500
○ C

LA TAVERNA
Jl. Danua Tamblingan
Tel. 288-387
Italian. Good pizzas. The marinated kokak is exquisite. Wine list. Open daily for breakfast, lunch, and dinner.
Rp20,000
◑ C

NAN BAN KAN
Jl. Danau Tamblingan 67
Tel. 288-388
Evenings only.
Japanese restaurant and bar: sushi, sashimi, robata yaki; live seafood. Beautifully simple decor (entirely indoors), serious menu; generous portions. Set menu Rp25,000 and 35,000. A la carte 3500–15,000
◑ ▭ C ★

RUMAH MAKAN SARI LAUT
Blanjong Market (near the entrance to the Sanur Beach Hotel).
Upmarket Sanur warung serving good Indonesian food, specializing in seafood, gurami fish; generous nasi campur.
Rp3000
○

SANUR BEACH MARKET
On the beach at the end of Jl. Segara
11am–10pm
Indonesian, Chinese, and Balinese dishes, specializing in seafood and live gurami fish. Great location. This community-run place has decent food at reasonable prices. Full bar.
Rp7500
○ C ⤢

TANDJUNG SARI
Jl. Danau Tamblingan
Tel. 288-441
Indonesian and Western food, seafood, good salads. Elegant pavilion on the beach, fine service. The menu and quality here have run the gamut of change over the years; currently one of the nicest places in Sanur. Wine, full bar.
Rp30,000
◑ C ⤢

TELAGA NAGA
Opposite the Bali Hyatt
Tel. (Bali Hyatt: 288-271)
Chinese food (lunch and dinner) in a private park with lotus pavilions.
Rp30,000
◑ C ⤢

ACCOMMODATION

ANANDA HOTEL
Jl. Hang Tuah 43
Tel. 288-327, 288-713
Budget hotel on the black sand beach. Rooms with private bath, cold water only. Fan. Clean and simple. Funky part of the beach where the little jukung sail boats park and wait for customers.
Rp30,000
⌂

BARUNA BEACH INN
Jl. Pantai Sindhu
Tel. 288-546
Fax 289-629
Bungalows on good beach. AC, hot water with tub or shower. Former beach retreat of Sukarno. Charming gardens; whimsical antiques everywhere. A special place in a central, rather noisy beach location. Continental breakfast and afternoon tea included. No credit cards.
US$35–65/£24–44
⌂ C

BUMI AYU BUNGALOWS
Jl. Bumi Ayu
Tel. 289-101
Fax 287-517
Bungalow-style hotel a ten-minute walk from the beach. Large rooms in lush gardens, all with AC, full bath. Attractive, well-run hotel. Good value.
US$45–150/£30–100, extra bed $15/£10.
⌂ ⌂ ⤢ ☎

GRAND BALI BEACH HOTEL
Sanur
Tel. 288-511
Fax 288-917
Luxury hotel, 125 acres, good beach front, two restaurants, three bars, nine-hole golf course, two tennis courts. Excellent staff. Recently restored after being gutted by fire.
US$110–375/£74–250. No charge for children under twelve sharing room with parents.
⌂ ▭ C ⌂ ⤢ ♫
▢ ☎ ⊨

HOTEL BALI HYATT
Jn. Danau Tamblingan
Tel. 288-271
Fax 287-693
Luxury hotel in 36 acres with good beach front, six restaurants, five bars, tennis courts, three-hole golf course. Gorgeous gardens, great swimming pool, glamorous lobby, and piano bar; but the rooms are rather small and stacked in four-story blocks. Recently renovated.
Rates:
$150–660/£100–440, extra bed $20/£13, but free of charge for children under eighteen. No charge for children under eighteen sharing room with parents.
⌂ ▭ C ⌂ ⤢ ⏦
♫ ▢ ☎ ⊨

HOTEL BALI WIRASANA
Jl. Danau Tamblingan 126
Tel. 288-632
Budget hotel 600 feet

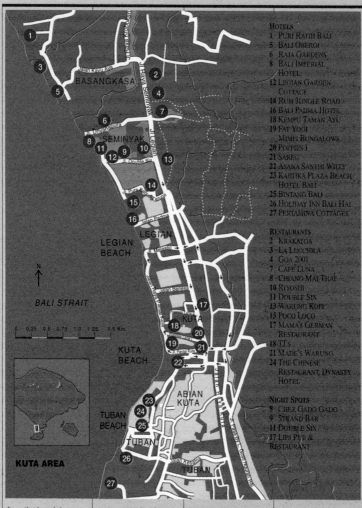

BASANGKASA

SEMINYAK

N

BALI STRAIT

LEGIAN
BEACH

LEGIAN

KUTA

KUTA
BEACH

ABIAN
KUTA

TUBAN
BEACH

TUBAN

TUBAN

0 0.25 0.5 0.75 1.0 1.25 1.5 Km.

KUTA AREA

HOTELS
1 PURI RATIH BALI
5 BALI OBEROI
6 RAJA GARDENS
8 BALI IMPERIAL
   HOTEL
12 LEGIAN GARDEN
   COTTAGE
14 RUM JUNGLE ROAD
16 BALI PADMA HOTEL
18 KEMPU TAMAN AYU
19 FAT YOGI
   MIMPI BUNGALOWS
20 POPPIES I
21 SARI
22 ASANA SANTHI WILLY
23 KARTIKA PLAZA BEACH
   HOTEL BALI
25 BINTANG BALI
26 HOLIDAY INN BALI HAI
27 PERTAMINA COTTAGES

RESTAURANTS
2 KRAKATOA
3 LA LUCCIOLA
4 GOA 2001
7 CAFÉ LUNA
8 CHIANG MAI THAI
10 RIYOSHI
11 DOUBLE SIX
13 WARUNG KOPI
15 POCO LOCO
17 MAMA'S GERMAN
   RESTAURANT
18 TJ'S
21 MADE'S WARUNG
24 THE CHINESE
   RESTAURANT, DYNASTY
   HOTEL

NIGHT SPOTS
8 CHEZ GADO GADO
9 STRAND BAR
11 DOUBLE SIX
17 LIPS PUB &
   RESTAURANT

from the beach in central Sanur. Rooms w/ verandas in old single-story and new two-story buildings, all with private bath and fan, some with AC and hot water. Access to swimming pool at the Swastika Hotel next door. Quiet gardens; nice people; pleasantly modest. Popular with European backpackers. Rp25,000–40,000

HOTEL SANUR BEACH
Tel. 288-011, 288-980, 287-740
Fax 287-566, 287-749
Luxury resort on good beach; three

restaurants; two bars. Recently well renovated. Excellent staff.
US$120–900/£80–600, extra bed $20/£13. No charge for children under twelve sharing room with parents.

HOTEL TAMAN AGUNG BEACH INN
Jl. Danau Tamblingan 146
Tel. 288-549, 289-161
600 feet from the beach in central Sanur. Twenty rooms in all, of which two are suites complete with kitchen, twelve with AC, eight with fan and

hot water, four with fan and cold water only. Reasonably priced restaurant and bar. Very clean, recently refurbished in surprisingly good taste. Charming staff, pleasant garden. Good value.
US$18–40/£12–27, extra bed $7/£5.

LA TAVERNA BALI HOTEL
Jl. Danau Tamblingan
Tel. 288-387, 288-497
Fax 287-126
Luxury-class rooms and bungalows in old gardens on good beach. Restaurant specializing

in Indonesian and Italian food; big wood-burning pizza oven. Cozy. Decor is slightly eccentric.
US$80–195/£54–130, extra bed $30/£20. No charge for children under twelve sharing room with parents.

SEGARA VILLAGE
Jl. Segara Ayu, Sanur
Tel. 288-407, 288-408, 288-021, 287-150
Fax 287-242, 288-022
Luxury-class rooms and bungalows in big gardens on good beach; two restaurants; three bars. Culture

Club with classes in Balinese dancing, flower arranging, Balinese decoration, woodcarving, painting, batik. Childrens' Club with play group, babysitting, children's activities. Well laid out in "village"-like clusters of low thatch-roofed buildings. Highly recommended for families.
US$55–200/£37–134, extra bed $20/£13; baby cot $15/£10.
🏠 🖾 C 🛏 🍴 ♫ ☎

TANDJUNG SARI
Jl. Danau Tamblingan
Tel. 288-441
Fax 287-930
Unusual luxury hotel on good beach; individually furnished bungalows of various designs, built in traditional materials by Balinese craftsmen, each with private gardens. A sophisticated family-run hotel created in 1962 with love and great attention to detail. Quiet, lovely, expensive.
US$200–380/£134–254, extra bed in certain bungalows $25/£17.
🏠 🖾 C ⛵ 🛏 🏊 ♫ ☎

PONDOK WISATA PRIMA COTTAGES
Jl. Bumi Ayu 15
Tel. 289-153
Fax 289-153, 288-548
Rooms and bungalows ten-minute walk from the beach. Salt-water swimming pool, solar heated water, fans, or AC. Very clean and pleasant; nice family. Very good value, especially the two-bedroom house with kitchen and huge veranda.
Rp25,000–50,000
🛏 🏊 ☕

PURI KLAPA GARDEN COTTAGES
Jl. Segara Ayu
Tel. 288-999, 287-416
Fax 287-417
Four-minute walk from Sanur beach. Rooms in two-story buildings or individual bungalows. Swimming pool with sunken bar. All rooms with AC, hot water. Very

clean, quiet, and pleasantly furnished.
US$60/£40, extra bed $14/£9.
🏠 ☕ 🛏 ☎

WATERING HOLE BAR-RESTAURANT & HOMESTAY
Jl. Hangtuah 35
Tel. 288-289
Budget hotel in northern Sanur 160 feet from the black sand beach. Rooms with veranda in two-story building; private bath; AC or fan.
Rooms face a small common garden; atmosphere is very friendly and casual. Jovial management.
Rp25,000–35,000
☕

WERDHA PURA
Jl. Danau Tamblingan
Tel. 288-171
Cottages on the beach. AC and hot-water baths. Small, austere rooms in a government-owned "tourism prototype" complex built in the 1960's. First-class address at discount prices. Breakfast included.
Rp50,000
🏠 C ☕

KUTA AREA

The "Kuta" area includes, from south to north along the coast and with no demarcation: Tuban, Kuta, Legian Kelod, Legian Tengah, Legian Kaja, Seminyak, and Krobokan. "Raya" means "main". Jl. Raya Legian, others use Jl. Legian. As Jl. Legian goes north, it's sometimes called Jl. Raya Seminyak. It is never called Jl. Raya Kuta: that refers to the road that goes to Denpasar.

USEFUL ADDRESSES

EMERGENCIES
KUTA CLINIC
Jl. Raya Kuta 100X
Tel. 753-268
Doctors and ambulance on 24-hour call.

SURYA HUSADA CLINIC
Jl. Kartika Plaza 9X
(near Kartika Plaza Beach Hotel)
Tel. 752-947

POLICE
Jl. Raya Tuban (near the corner of Jl. Bakung Sari and the airport road).
Tel. 751-598

BUSINESS CENTER
CV KRAKATOA
Jl. Raya Seminyak 56
Seminyak
Tel. 752-849
Fax 752-842, 752-011
Open Mon.–Sat.
8am–10pm and Sun.
9am–3pm.
Telecommunications, travel, cargo.
CV RUDY'S INDOTAMA
Jl. Dhyana Pura 5A
Seminyak
Tel. 754-355
Fax 754-354
Open daily
Telecommunications, travel, computer services.

TOURIST INFORMATION
KUTA TOURIST
INFORMATION
Mastapa Building (2nd floor)
Jl. Legian
Tel. 751-660 ext 145

TRANSPORT
BALI BERINGIN CAR
RENTAL CV
(At the airport)
Tel. 753-744
BALIVAN
Jl. Raya Tuban 108
Tuban
Tel. 752-486
Rental and limousine service
GANDA SARI
Jl. Raya Legian, Kuta
Tel. 754-383
MEGA JAYA RENT CARS
Jl. Raya Kuta 78 X
Tel. 753-760
PERAMA TOURIST
SERVICE
Jl. Legian 20, Kuta
Tel. 751-551, 751-875
Fax 751-170
SURYA AGUNG DEWATA
RENT CAR/SELF DRIVE
Jl. Raya Kuta 39
(opposite Supernova)
Tel. 752-866
Fax 754-433
TAXI
Tel. 751-919, 752-299
TOYOTA RENT-A-CAR
Jl. Raya Tuban, Kuta
Tel. 751-282, 751-356, 753-744

SPORTS AND LEISURE ACTIVITIES

DIVING
BARUNA WATER SPORTS
(PT WISATA TIRTA BARUNA)
Jl. Bypass I Gusti
Ngurah Rai 300B,
Kuta
Tel. 753-820, 751-223
Fax: 753-809, 752-779
Numerous sales desks in Bali and Lombok.

HORSEBACK RIDING
MESARI BEACH INN
Jl. Dhyana Pura,
Seminyak
Tel. 751-401
Rp20,000/hour

SURFING
Ask for information at Tubes, Poppies Lane II, Kuta, or at any of the many surf shops
◆ 308.

WATER PARK
WATERBOM PARK
Jl. Kartika Plaza
Tel. 755-676/8
Fax 753-517
9am–6pm daily
About 900 feet of waterslides set in 8 acres of gardens. Fun for children and adults. Good casual restaurant. Adults US$7.50/£5, children five to twelve US$4/£3 (under twelve must be accompanied by an adult), children under five free.

SHOPPING

CLOTHES
ASSE BY ASIH
Jl. Pantai Kuta 24 A
Tel. 751-514
High chic for women. Asih designs and Italian imports.
BAIK-BAIK
Jl. Legian 370, Legian
Kelod
Tel. 751-622
Clothes for men by the designer Asih, especially exclusive batik shirts on silk and cotton.
HARROD'S LEATHER
BOUTIQUE
Jl. Pantai Kuta 44, and
Jl. Melasti
Tel. 754-225
Suede clothes, ready-made and made-to-order. Good prices.
HEY
Jl. Melasti
Casual clothes for men & women in black & white.

HOP ON POP
Jl. Pantai Kuta, 45C
Children's clothes.
KAYAGAYA STUDIO
Jl. Raya Seminyak
Clothes, accessories, and objects from the Indonesian archipelago.
MUTI SHOP
Jl. Legian 402
Cloth shoes in pretty colors. Embroidered shoes next door.
RASCALS
Jl. Legian at Jl. Melasti
Smart swimwear for women.

OTHERS
GUNATAMA TEXTILE
Jl. Legian 504, Legian Kaja
Tel. 752-855
Wholesale and retail textiles.
HOUSE OF BIRDNEST
Jl. Kartika Plaza 90X/12 (across from Bali Bintang Hotel)
Tel. 752-212
Birds' nests and other hard-to-find Indonesian groceries.
KERTA I BOOK SHOP
Jl. Pantai Kuta
Standard books on Bali and many second-hand paperbacks in English and European languages.
MAHOGANY
Jl. Raya Seminyak
Tel. 752-478
The best selection of tapes and CDs in Bali.

RESTAURANTS

CAFE LUNA
Jl. Legian 499, Legian Kaja
Tel. 751-514
Italian. Smart, spare; good pasta and desserts. Evenings only.
Rp8000
❍

CHIANG MAI THAI
Jl. Dhyana Pura, Seminyak
Tel. 752-255
Authentic Thai cuisine. Beachside terrace garden.
Rp15,000
◐

THE CHINESE RESTAURANT
Bali Dynasty Hotel
Jl. Kartika Plaza, Tuban
Tel. 752-403
From 4 pm.
Yum Cha at lunch.

Rp25,000
◐

DOUBLE SIX
Jl. "66", Legian
Tel. 753-366, 753-666
Italian. Short, serious menu with homemade pasta and seafood. Grilled squid salad is famous. Special chocolate menu of desserts. Lunch and dinner. Big pavilion by the beach becomes a raging disco after midnight.
Rp20,000
★ ◐ ↯ ➤

GOA 2001
Jl. Raya Seminyak
Tel. 753-922
Eclectic, specializing in sushi, with Western and Indonesian dishes. Big, casual; sexy lighting. Favorite dinner place with expats. Evenings only.
Rp8,000
★ ◐

KRAKATOA
Jl. Raya Seminyak 56
Tel. 752-849
Café with good breakfasts, sandwiches, salads, and two big TVs tuned to CNN. Laser disk movies daily; kids' matinee Sat. 3.30
Rp5,000
❍

LA LUCCIOLA
Krobokan, Kuta
Tel. 261-047
Smart Italian cuisine; seafood. Deep fried mozzarella is especially good.
Rp15,000
★ ◐ ↯ ➤⋅

MADE'S WARUNG
Jl. Pantai Kuta, Kuta
Tel. 751-923
Eclectic menu includes sushi, prosciutto di Parma, bagels, and smoked salmon, and such New Zealand imports as steaks and green-lipped mussels. First-rate nasi campur. Imported beers and wines. Cozy, crowded; a favorite with expats for breakfast, lunch, dinner, and onward.
Rp15,000
★ ◐ 🄲

MAMA'S GERMAN RESTAURANT
Jl. Legian, Kuta
Tel. 751-805
Open 24 hours
Bavarian food and delicatessen.
Rp10,000
❍

POCO LOCO
Jl. Rum Jungle Rd, Legian
Mexican. Big, noisy, fun. Evenings only.
Rp12,000
◐

RIYOSHI
Jl. Raya Seminyak, Seminyak
Japanese. Small, simple, air-conditioned. This is an unusually restoring place. Age mono, yaki mono, robata yaki, gohan mono, menrui, sashimi, sushi. Menu of the day.
Rp17,000
★ ◐

TJ's
Poppies Gang I, Kuta
Tel. 751-093
California-Mexican. Spacious, comfortably chic place for lunch and dinner. Great salads, excellent margaritas.
Rp15,000
★ ◐ 🄲

WARUNG KOPI
Jl. Legian 427, Legian Tengah
Tel. 753-602
Lunch and dinner. Closed Sun.
Middle Eastern and vegetarian dishes, fresh seafood, satays, and traditional Indonesian food. Fabulous desserts. Charming small café with garden restaurant.
Rp15,000
❍

ACCOMMODATION

ASANA SANTHI WILLY
Jl. Tegalwangi 18, Kuta
Tel. 751-281, 752-273
Fax 752-641
Small hotel, three-minute walk from the beach; rooms with AC, hot water, full bath, veranda. Very clean; charmingly furnished. Breakfast included.
US$35/£24 +10 percent
🏠

BALI IMPERIAL HOTEL
Jl. Dyana Pura
Legian, Kuta
Tel. 754-545
Fax 751-545
$140–2000/£94–1334
🏠 ▭ ⌕ ♫ ▢ ☎
➤

BALI OBEROI
Seminyak, Kuta
Tel. 751-061
Fax 752-791
Fifteen luxury villas, eight of which have their own pools, and sixty lanai bungalow rooms; in secluded park on Legian beach. Tennis court, health club w/sauna and massage. Superbly discreet architecture, beautiful gardens. Isolated; truly luxurious, very romantic.
US$200–850/£134–567 + 17.5 percent. 10 percent surcharge in peak season.
★ 🏠 ⌕ ↯ 🄐 ➤⋅
⌕ ▢ ☎

BALI PADMA HOTEL
Jl. Padma 1
Legian, Kuta
Tel. 752-111
Fax 752-140
Luxury resort on Legian Beach; four restaurants, three bars, tennis courts, squash, fitness center. Well-designed. Relaxed atmosphere. Good Japanese restaurant.
US$110–1500/£74–1000 + 17½ percent. Extra bed $20/£14
🏠▭ 🄲 ⌕ ♫ ▢
☎ ➤

BINTANG BALI
Jl. Kartika Plaza, Kuta
Tel. 753-292/3
Fax 753-288
US$95–888/£64–592
🏠 ▭ ⌕ ♫ ▢ ☎
➤

FAT YOGI
Poppies Lane I, Kuta
Tel. 751-665
1000 feet from the beach; private baths, some with hot water; fans. Clean; central location. An old favorite.
US$12–20/£8–14 + 15½ percent. Extra bed $8–10/£6–7
🏠 🄲 ⌕

**HOLIDAY INN
BALI HAI**
Jl. Wana Segara, 33
P.O. Box 2054
Tuban, Kuta 80361
Tel. 753-035
Fax 752-527/8/9
*Beach front. Very close
to the airport.*
US$120–550/£80–367
+ 17½ percent
🏨 ⌷ 🍴 ♫ ▢ ☎
🍽

**KARTIKA PLAZA
BEACH HOTEL**
Jl. Kartika Plaza,
Kuta
Tel. 751-067/9
Fax 752-475
US$110–1100/£74–734
🏨 ⌷ 🎿 ⌣ ♫ ▢
☎ 🍽

KEMPU TAMAN AYU
Off Poppies Lane I
(near TJ's), Kuta
[No phone]
*Rooms with private
bath, cold-water
showers, fan. Modest
losmen in a simple and
pleasant family
compound.*
Rp9,000–12,000
⌂

**LEGIAN GARDEN
COTTAGE**
Jl. Legian Cottage,
Seminyak
Tel. 751-876/7
Fax 753-405
*Bungalows a minute's
walk from Legian
Beach, all with AC, hot
water; pleasant
gardens. Well-designed,
low-key, attractive
place. Good value.*
US$45–65/£30–44,
extra bed $10/£7. No
charge for two children
under twelve occupying
room with parents.
🏨 ⌷ ⌣ ☎

MIMPI BUNGALOWS
Off Poppies Lane I, Kuta
Tel./Fax 751-848
*Short walk from the
beach; rooms with
ceiling fans, some with
hot water.
Very clean and well
maintained.*
US$17–35/£12–24
🏨 ⌷ ⌣

PERTAMINA COTTAGES
Tuban Beach, Kuta
Tel. 751-161
Fax 752-030
*Beachfront, three
restaurants, two bars.
Very, very close to the*

airport. Popular with
Indonesian VIPs.
US$128–800/£86–534
🏨 ⌷ ⌣ ♫ ▢ ☎
🍽

POPPIES I
Poppies Lane I, Kuta
P.O. Box 3378
Denpasar 80033
Tel. 751-509
Fax 752-364
*Two-minute walk to the
beach; twenty
bungalows with hot
water, baths and
showers with garden,
AC and/or ceiling fans,
optional cooking
facilities.
Lush gardens;
comfortable,
well-designed cottages
with traditional
architectural features;
good service. Highly
recommended,
especially for families.*
US$63/£42, extra bed
$12/£8; baby cot free of
charge.
🏨 ⌷ ⌣

PURI RATIH BALI
Jl. Puri Ratih Bali,
Petitenget, Krobokan
Tel. 751-546/8
Fax 751-549
*Small resort on quiet
beach; bungalows, villas
and residences, some
with two double
bedrooms, all with
pantries and kitchens
with stocked
refrigerators; AC
bedrooms. Fitness
center, sauna, tennis
court. Pleasant,
somewhat remote; good
for families or small
groups.*
US$80–320/£54–214,
extra bed $15/£10.
🏨 ⌷ ⌣ ⌣ ⌣ ▢

RAJA GARDENS
Jl. Dhyana Pura,
Seminyak
Tel./Fax 751-494
*Bungalows in lush
garden, one-minute
walk from Legian
Beach. Double beds,
private bath, cold water,
fan. Simple but
luxurious homestay.*
US$25/£17
★ ⌂ 🎿 ⌣ ⌣

RUM JUNGLE ROAD
Jl. Pura Bagus Taruna,
Legian
Tel./Fax 751-992
*Most rooms with cold-
water bath and fan, one*

with AC and hot water.
Attractive, popular place.
Rp15,000–40,000
⌂ ⌣

SAREG
Jl. Pantai Kuta 32, Kuta
[No phone]
*Rooms with or w/o fan;
private cold-water
bath. Vintage losmen in the
heart of Kuta.
Well-maintained.*
Rp15,000–20,000
⌂ ⌣

NIGHTLIFE

CHEZ GADO GADO
Jl. Dhyana Pura on the
beach
Tel. 752-255
*Disco from midnight to
5am Tue, Wed, Fri, Sun.*

DOUBLE SIX
Jl. "66", on the beach
Tel. 753-366, 753-666
*Disco from midnight to
5am Mon., Thur., Sat.*

**LIPS PUB &
RESTAURANT**
Jl. Legian, Kuta
Tel. 754-630

STRAND BAR
Jl. "66", Legian

NUSA DUA AREA

*Nusa Dua has become
the general name for
the peninsula area.
Jimbaran Bay is on the
west side of the isthmus
leading to the peninsula,
and Tanjung Benoa is a
finger of land extending
from Nusa Dua proper
into Benoa Harbor on
the east side of the
isthmus.*

USEFUL ADDRESSES

EMERGENCIES
*Medical services
available in all the major
hotels*

NUSA DUA CLINIC
Jl. Pratama 81 A-B
Tanjung Benoa
Tel. 771-324
24-hour medical service,

ambulance, and on-call
doctors.

POLICE
Jl. Ngurah Rai Bypass,
near Tragia
supermarket.
Tel. 772-110

TRANSPORT
METERED TAXI
Tel 751-919, 752-299
NUSA DUA RENT CAR
23 Pantai Megiat Street
Tel. 771-905

CULTURAL
ATTRACTION

PURU LUHUR ULUWATU
*Small, dramatically
situated temple
overlooking the sea*
▲ 278.

SHOPPING

GALLERIA NUSA DUA
Nusa Dua Hotel
Complex
*Keris Galley
department store and
numerous boutiques,
restaurants, travel
services.*
THE GALLERY
Amanusa, Nusa Dua
*Fine art objects, crafts,
antiques from the
archipelago.*
PASAR SENGGOL
Grand Hyat Bali, Nusa
Dua
Shopping mall.
TRAGIA SHOPPING
COMPLEX
Jl. Ngurah Rai Bypass
(northbound)
*Supermarket, specialty
shops, eating places.*

SPORTS

SURFING
*The surf off the south
coast of the peninsula is
among the most
challenging in the world*
◆ 308.

GOLF
BALI GOLF AND COUNTRY
CLUB
P.O.Box 12, Nusa Dua
Tel. 771-791
Fax 771-797
*Eighteen-hole
championship course
designed by
Nelson/Wright* ◆ 310.

RESTAURANTS

*The road to Tanjung
Benoa is lined with local
restaurants, rumah*

makan, *on the non-beach side of the road. Reservations recommended for all the following restaurants.*
All restaurants in major hotels are subject to 21 percent surcharges.

THE DINING ROOM
Four Seasons Resort
Jimbaran Bay
Tel. 771-288
6–11am and 6–10pm.
Contemporary Western and Indonesian cuisine. Open-sided pavilion with custom-designed cooling system. Lovely.
Rp50,000
⑪ ⤼

EDELWEISS
Nusa Dua Bypass
(eastbound) Nusa Dua
(No telephone)
6–10pm
Austrian cuisine in an Austrian cottage.
Rp30,000
◑

IKAN RESTAURANT
Shearton Nusa Indah Resort, Nusa Dua
Tel. 771-906
Authentic Balinese cooking and seafood specialties in a casual beachside pavilion. Charming tableware.
Rp25,000
◑ ▭ ⤼ ⌂ ⊶

INAGIKU
Grand Hyatt, Nusa Dua
Tel. 771-234
Built in the style of a Japanese country house; tatami rooms, sushi and teppanyaki bars. Famous for its tempura.
Rp40,000
⑪ ▭ ⌂ ⤼

JAANSAN CAFE ET PUB
Nusa Dua Galleria,
Block B1
Tel. 772-628
8am–11pm daily
Balinese and western-style café. Pleasant and airy. Full bar/wine.
Rp12,000
◑

MEI YAN CHINESE RESTAURANT
Grand Bali Hyatt, Nusa Dua
Tel. 771-234 ext 8390
6 pm–10.30 pm
Lovely building in the style of an old Shanghai tea house; authentic Cantonese cuisine (Hong Kong chef).
Rp45,000
★ ⑪

PJ's
Four Seasons Resort
Jimbaran Bay
Tel. 771-288
11am–10pm.
Seafood, on the beach. Casual, excellent.
Rp35,000
★ ⑪ ⤼

THE RESTAURANT
Amanusa, Nusa Dua
Tel. 772-333
Northern Italian cuisine (Italian chef). Setting is elegant and spare. Dinner only. Two courses Rp65,000; three courses Rp80,000
★ ⑪ ⤼

SALSA VERDE
Grand Bali Hyatt, Nusa Dua
Tel. 771-234 ext 8310
6am–11pm
Open-air Italian restaurant by the pool on the beach. Casual chic.
Rp25,000
◑ ⤼

THE TERRACE
Amanusa, Nusa Dua
Tel. 772-333
All-day dining; Thai and Western. Evenings Thai and Indonesian cuisine. Indonesian menu of the day is Rp30,000. Thai specialty dishes.
Rp20,000
★ ◑ ⤼

ACCOMMODATION

Note: The five-star hotels offer similar services: rooms with AC, IDD phones, satellite TV, in-house video, and the usual amenities. All have several categories of rooms from standard/deluxe to VIP suites. All are on the beach, have at least one swimming pool, water sports, tennis courts, fitness center, and spas, gardens, cultural performances, tours and travel services, shops, banks, postal services, beauty shops, childcare facilities, clinics, and in-house doctors. All have 24-hour room service and/or 24-hour
coffeeshops, one or more fine restaurants, beachside casual restaurants and bars, "fun pubs" or discos. Many arrange Balinese-style weddings.*

AMANUSA
Nusa Dua
P.O. Box 33, Nusa Dua
Tel. 772-333
Fax 772-335
Small, secluded luxury hotel overlooking the sea and golf course. Architecture is handsomely austere. Sophisticated restaurants; genial first-class hospitality. This is becoming a very special place.
US$330–770/£220–514
★ ⌂ ▭ ⤼ ⌂ ⊶ ⌔ ☎

BALI CLIFF RESORT
Ungasan, Nusa Dua
P.O. Box 90
Nusa Dua, Bali 80363
Tel. 771-992
Fax 771-993
Typical 5-star resort, dramatically situated 250 feet above the Indian Ocean. The view is entirely blue, and the lagoon pool at the cliff's edge really seems to disappear into the sky.
US$170-2000/
£114–1334 . *No charge for children under eighteen occupying same room as parents.*
⌂ ▭ ⤼ ⌂ ⊶ ⌔ ♫ ⑪ ☎ ⊶

BALI HILTON INTERNATIONAL
P.O. Box 46, Nusa Dua
80361
Tel. 771-102/12
Fax 771-616
Resort glamor on a grand scale. Offers "Wa No Kutsurogi", a service catering to the special needs and high standards of Japanese travelers. The VIP suite is a small palace with large swimming pool and private ballroom.
US$150–2000/
£100–1334
⌂ ▭ ⤼ ⌂ ⊶ ⌔ ♫
▭ ☎ ⊶

BALI INTER-CONTINENTAL RESORT
Jimbaran Bay
P.O. Box 35, Nusa Dua
Tel. 755-055
Fax 755-056
Huge, imposingly grand, with the best beach frontage in Bali. Helicopter pad. Good Japanese restaurant. Asian swank.
US$165–1800/£110–2100. *Children under fourteen free of charge.*
⌂ ▭ ⌂ ⌔ ♫ □
☎ ⊶

BALI ROYAL
Jl. Pratama, Tanjung Benoa, Nusa Dua
Tel. 771-039
Fax 771-885
Luxury suites and bungalows on the beach; associated with Clark Hatch Sports Club and Bali Golf and Country Club. Austrian owned and managed; spacious rooms and lovely gardens.
US$140–180/£94–120, *includes airport transport.*
⌂ ▭ ⤼ ⌂ ⌔ □
☎

CLUB MED BALI
P.O. Box 7, Nusa Dua
Tel. 771-521/3
Fax 771-831
Club Med's unique style of hospitality offers a team of energetic, young European and Indonesian staff to entertain guests and help them to entertain themselves. Complete sports facilities include seven 24-hour tennis courts, archery range, and a six-hole golf course. Circus School with trapeze and high wire. Excellent childcare programs. Rates upon inquiry, include activities fees and meals at all three restaurants.
⌂ ▭ ⤼ ⌂ ⊶ ⌔
♫ ⊶

FOUR SEASONS RESORT BALI
Jimbaran Bay
Tel. 771-288
Fax 771-280/81
An architectural delight. The rooms are actually townhouses with private walled compounds enclosing three pavilions and a dip-pool looking out into the bay. The pavilions are built on Balinese principles and the layout is like a Mediterranean village. Beautiful gardens,

excellent restaurants, first-rate staff. Remarkable combination of spaciousness and privacy.
Rates: $275–1500/£184–1000. No charge for children under twelve occupying same villa as parents.
🏠 ☐ � 🏠 🍴 ♫
☐ ☎ 🛏

GRAND HYATT BALI
P.O. Box 53, Nusa Dua
Tel. 771-234
Fax 771-084
Hats off to the architects for hiding 750 rooms in a four-"village" layout over gardens of meandering pools and lagoons; the Chinese and Japanese restaurants are quietly elegant buildings. Central "night market" has shops and food stalls. Atmosphere is spacious, relaxing, and fun. Fine collection of Indonesian art and antiques distributed throughout the resort. Six swimming pools, one with a 165-foot water slide. Great restaurants. Regency Club. Highly recommended for couples, families, and VIPs. US$170–2000/ £114–1334. Children under eighteen free in same room as parents.
🏠 ☐ ⚗ 🏠 🍴 ♫
☐ ☎ 🛏

KERATON COTTAGES
Jimbaran Bay
P.O. Box 2023, Kuta
Tel. 753-991
Fax 753-881
Luxury rooms and suites in two-story beach "cottages"; three restaurants, three bars, tennis court, fishing, outrigger sailing. Substantial architecture in rich gardens. Secure. Excellent beach. Caters to upmarket package tourism on a comfortable and quiet scale.
US$110–400/£74–267. No charge for children under fourteen sharing room with parents.
🏠 ☐ 🏠 ♫ ☐ ☎

MELIA BALI SOL
P.O.Box 1048, Nusa Dua
Tel. 771-510
Fax 771-360

Managed by the Spanish hotel chain Melia-Sol and catering to Spaniards. Specializes in Balinese-style weddings and honeymoon packages. Beautiful gardens; huge ornamental swimming pool. No smoking sections on the beach and poolside. Undergoing gradual refurbishment.
US$180–1000/ £120–667
🏠 ☐ ⚗ 🏠 ♫ ☐
☎ 🛏

NUSA DUA BEACH HOTEL
P.O.Box 1028, Denpasar
Tel. 771-210
Fax 771-229
The first hotel built in Nusa Dua (1983). Its baroque entrance and decor are touted as a "showcase of Balinese arts and architecture". Undergoing massive refurbishment. Main attraction is the Nusa Dua Spa with state-of-the-art fitness center.
US$150–1200/ £100–800
🏠 ☐ 🏠 🍴 ♫ ☐
☎ 🛏

PANSEA PURI BALI
Jl. Uluwatu, Jimbaran Bay
Tel. 752-605
Fax 752-220
Luxury rooms and bungalows on great beach; two restaurants, bar; tennis court, windsurfing. Beachside bungalows in a grove of trees. Low-key, romantic. Pleasant staff.
US$130–$190/ £87–127, including charges, sports facilities, and half-board (breakfast and buffet/set dinner). $22/£15 supplement for sea view. Children three to eleven $22/£15.
🏠 🏠 🍴

PURI JOMA
Jl. Pratama, Tanjung Benoa, Nusa Dua
Tel./Fax 771-526
Ten rooms in five Balinese-style bungalows on the beach; AC, hot water. Pleasant small hotel managed by the owner.

US$55/£37, extra bed $10/£7
🏠 🏠 🍴 ☎

PUTRI BALI HOTEL
P.O. Box 1, Nusa Dua
Tel. 771-020
Fax 771-139
Owned and managed by an Indonesian government corporation, and one of the earliest hotels opened in Nusa Dua. Public areas are a bit odd and dreary, but the staff is gracious, and the beach cottages are a bargain ($165/£110). Best beach in Nusa Dua, especially at low tide. Very high guest loyalty among older middle Europeans.
US$125–550/£84–367
🏠 ☐ 🏠 🍴 ♫ ☐
☎ 🛏

SHERATON LAGOON NUSA DUA BEACH RESORT
P.O. Box 77, Nusa Dua
Tel. 771-327/8
Fax 771-326
Good 5-star family hotel. Relatively small and recently built hotel emphasizing personal service and touches of luxury. 24-hour butler service. Huge complimentary breakfast buffet. Swimmable lagoons with sandy shore access. Shares signing privileges with Nusa Indah resort next door. The casual beachside restaurant has a salad bar, fresh seafood, sandwiches on homemade bread.
US$180–1800/ £120–1200. No charge for children under seventeen occupying same room as parents.
🏠 ☐ 🏠 🍴 ♫ ☐
☎ 🛏

SHERATON NUSA INDAH BEACH RESORT
P.O. Box 36, Nusa Dua
Tel. 771-906
Fax 771-908
Attached to the Bali International Convention Centre, and the public spaces share its city glamor. The resort becomes more casual the closer one goes to the beach. Huge swimming pool with hidden cove and waterfall. Excellent

Balinese/seafood restaurant beachside and good Japanese restaurant with teppanyaki bar.
US$150–1200/ £100–800
🏠 ☐ 🏠 🍴 ♫ ☐
☎ 🛏

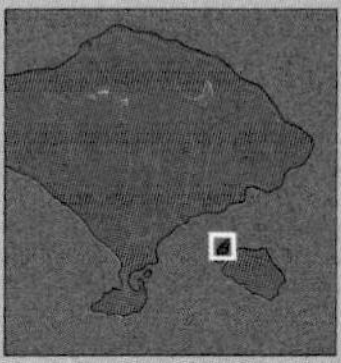

SISTER ISLANDS

The nearby islands of Nusa Penida, Nusa Ceningan, and Nusa Lembongan are not really set up for tourism ▲ 280. People go there primarily to surf, scuba dive, or snorkel. There are no facilities on Nusa Ceningan, only a losmen or two on Nusa Penida and no restaurants, and a few homestays on Nusa Lembongan. New facilities are being developed, the best at Mushroom Beach, on the western part of the island.

ACCOMMODATION

AGUNG
Nusa Lembongan
Thatch-roofed bungalows, some with private mandi. Good restaurant.
US$5–10/£4–7
🏠

MAIN SKI INN
Nusa Lembongan
Duplex bungalows.
US$5–10/£4–7
🏠

NUSA LEMBONGAN BUNGALOWS
Booking office: Jl. Pantai Legian, Kuta
Tel.753-071/5, 751-1665
Transport provided from hotel to Nusa Lembongan bungalows. Two-story bungalows with living rooms and spacious bathrooms. Pleasant and clean. Breakfast included.
US$15/£10.
🏠

◆ Notes

APPENDICES

◆ ESSENTIAL READING ◆

◆J. L. SWELLENGREBEL, W. VAN HOEVE (ed.), *Bali: Studies in Life, Thought, and Ritual* and *Further Studies in Life, Thought, and Ritual*, The Hague, 1960/1969.
◆ BLAIR (L. AND L.): *Ring of Fire: Exploring the Last Remote Places of the World*, Bantam Books, New York, 1988.
◆ COVARRUBIAS (M.): *Island of Bali*, Alfred A. Knopf Inc., New York, 1937 (Oxford University Press, 1972).
◆ EISEMAN (F.): *Bali Sekala & Niskala: Vol. I: Essays on Religion, Ritual, and Art. Vol. II: Essays on Society, Tradition, and Craft*, Periplus Editions HK Ltd, 1989/1990.
◆ KRAUSE (G.): *Bali: Volk, Land, Tänze, Feste, Tempel*, Müeller, München, 1926.
◆ LUERAS (L.): AND LLOYD (I.): *Bali: The Ultimate Island*, St. Martin's Press, New York, 1987.
◆ PICARD (M.) AND BASSET (C.): *Bali: L'ordre cosmique et la quotidiennete*, Editions Autrement, No. 66, Paris, 1993.
◆ RAMSEYER (U.): *The Art and Culture of Bali*, Oxford University Press, Singapore, 1986.
◆ VICKERS (Adrian): *Bali: A Paradise Created*, Penguin, 1989.

◆ ARCHITECTURE ◆

◆ JAMES (J.): "Sacred Geometry on the Island of Bali", *Journal of the Royal Asiatic Society*, 1973.
◆ JIWA (I. B. Ny): *Kamus Bali Indonesia: bidang istilah arsitektur tradisional Bali*, Upada Sastra, Denpasar, 1992.
◆ TONJAYA (I Ny. Gd. Bandesa K.): *Lintasan Asta Kosali*, Penerbit & Toko Buku Ria, Denpasar, 1982.
◆ WIJAYA (M.): *Balinese Architecture: towards an encyclopedia*, privately printed, Sanur, 1984.

◆ ARTS ◆

◆ BANDEM (I Made) AND DE BOER (F.): *Kaja and Kelod: Balinese Dance in Transition*, Oxford University Press, Kuala Lumpur,1981.
◆ DE ZOETE (B.) AND SPIES (W.): *Dance and Drama in Bali*, Harper and Brothers Publishers, New York, 1939.
◆ DJELANTIK (Dr A. A. Made): *Balinese Painting*, Oxford University Press, Singapore, 1986.
◆ HAUSER-SCHÄUBLIN (B.), NABHOLZ-KARTASCHOFF (M.-T.), AND RAMSEYER (U.) *Textiles in Bali*, Periplus Editions HK Ltd., 1991.
◆ HINZLER (H.I.R.): *Bima Swarga in Balinese Wayang*, Martinus Nijhoff, The Hague, 1981.
◆ HITCHCOCK (M.): *Indonesian Textiles*, Periplus Editions HK Ltd., 1991.
◆ HOBART (A.): *Dancing Shadows of Bali*, KPI, London, 1987.
◆ HOLT (C.): *Art in Indonesia, Continuity and Change*, Cornell University Press, 1967.
◆ KAM (G.): *Perceptions of Paradise, Images of Bali in the Arts*, Yayasan Dharma Seni Museum Neka, Bali, 1993.
◆ *Neka Museum: Guide to the Painting Collection*, The Neka Museum, Ubud, Bali, 1986.
◆ PUCCI (I.): *The Epic of Life, A Balinese Journey of the Soul*, Alfred Van de Mark Editions, New York, 1985.
◆ RAMSEYER (U.): *Balinese Textiles*, Periplus Editions HK Ltd., 1991.
◆ RAMSEYER (U.): *Clothing, Ritual and Society in Tengenan Pegringsingan (Bali)*, Verhandlungen der Naturforschenden Gesellschaft in Basel, Bd. 95, 1984.
◆ RHODIUS, (H.): AND DARLING (J.): *Walter Spies and Balinese Art*, Terra, Zutphen, 1980.
◆ Rhodius (H.), *Schönheit und Reichtum des Lebens: Walter Spies (Maler und Musiker auf Bali 1895-1942): eine Autobiographie in Briefen mit erganzenden Erinnerungen, gesammelt und hrsg. von Hans Rhodius*, Boucher, Den Haag, 1964.
◆ TENZER (M.): *Balinese Music*, Periplus Editions HK Ltd., 1991.
◆ WALKER (B.) AND HELMI (R.): *Bali Style*, Times Editions, Singapore, 1994.
◆ ZURBUCHEN (M.): *The Language of Balinese Shadow Theatre*, Princeton University Press, Princeton, 1987.

◆ GUIDES ◆

◆ *Bali: Island of the Gods*, ed. Eric Oey, Periplus Editions HK Ltd, 1994.
◆ DALTON (B.): *Bali Handbook*, Moon Publications, Inc., Chico, California, 1989.
◆ WHEELER (T.) AND LYON (J.) *Bali & Lombok*, Lonely Planet Publications, Hawthorn, Victoria, Australia, 1992.

◆ HISTORY ◆

◆ ANAK AGUNG KTUT AGUNG, *Kupu Kupu Kuning yang Terbang di Selat Lombok: Lintasan Sejarah Kerajaan Karangasem (1661-1950)*, Upada Sastra, Denpasar, 1991.
◆ ANUG AGUNG GEDE AGUNG: *Bali in the 19th Century*, Yayasan Obor Indonesia, Jakarta, 1991. English trans. by Rochmulyati Hamzah of *Bali pada Abab XIX*, Gadjah Mada University Press, Yogyakarta, 1989.
◆ GEERTZ (C.): *Negara: The Theatre State in Nineteenth Century Bali*, Princeton University Press, 1980.
◆ HANNA (W.): *Bali Profile: people, events, circumstances (1001-1976)*, Rumah Budaya Banda Naira, Moluccas, 1990.
◆ KEMPERS, (B.): *Monumental Bali*, Periplus Editions HK Ltd., 1991.
◆ MAS MUTERINI PUTRA (NY. I G.A.): *Peranan Pura Ulun Batur bagi Umat Hindu*, Yayasan Dharma Sarathi, Jakarta, 1989.
◆ NYOKA: *Sejarah Bali*, Penerbit & Toko Buku Ria, Denpasar, 1990.
◆ RAFFLES (T.): *History of Java*, Oxford University Press, 1817.
◆ SCHULTE-NORDHOLDT (H.): *Bali: Colonial Conceptions and Political Change 1700-1940. From Shifting Hierarchies to "Fixed Order"*, Comparative Asian Studies Program 15,

Rotterdam, 1986.
◆ SCHULTE (N.): "The Mads Lange Connection: A Danish Trader on Bali in the Middle of the 19th Century", *Indonesia* 32, 1981.
◆ SOEBANDI (KETUT): *Sejarah Pembangunan Pura-Pura di Bali*, Kayumas, Denpasar, 1983.
◆ SUTABA (I Made): *Prasejarah Bali*, Yayasan Purbakala Bali, Denpasar, 1980.
◆ VAN DER KRAAN (A.): *Lombok: Conquest, Colonialization and Underdevelopment, 1870-1940*, Heinemann, Singapore, 1980.
◆ VAN HOEVELL (W. Van): *De Eerst Schipvaart der Nederlanders naar Oost-Indie onder Cornelis de Houtman, 1595-1597*, The Hague, 1929.
◆ WORSLEY (P.): *Babad Buleleng*, Martinus Nijhoff, The Hague, 1972.
◆ ANON.: "Short account of the island of Bali", *Singapore Chronicle*, 1840.

◆ LITERATURE ◆

◆ BAUM (V.): *A tale from Bali*, Oxford University Press, 1973. English trans. by Basil Creighton of *Liebe und Tod auf Bali*, Querido, Amsterdam, 1937.
◆ I GUSTI BAGUS SUGRIWA: *Dwijendra Tatwa*, Upada Sastra, Denpasar, 1993.
◆ NIEUWENKAMP, (W.O.J.): *Zwerftochten op Bali*, Elsevier, Amsterdam, 1910.
◆ ZOETMULDER, (P.J.): *Kalangwan: A Survey of Old Javanese Literature*, The Hague, 1974.

◆ NATURE ◆

◆ DHARMA (A.P.): *Indonesian Medicinal Plants*, Balai Pustaka, Jakarta, 1987.
◆ EISEMAN (F. AND M.): *Flowers of Bali*, Periplus Editions HK Ltd, 1988.
◆ EISEMAN (F. AND M.): *Fruits of Bali*, Periplus Editions HK Ltd, 1988.
◆ LANSING, (S.): *Priests and Programmers: Technologies of Power in the Engineered Landscape of Bali*, Princeton University Press, 1991.
◆ MACKINNON (J.): *Field Guide to the Birds of Java and Bali*, Gadjah Mada University Press, Yogyakarta, 1988.
◆ MASON (V.): *Birds of Bali*, Periplus Editions HK Ltd, 1989.
◆ RISMUNANDAR: *Rempah-Rempah: komoditi ekspor Indonesia*, Sinar Baru, Bandung, 1988.
◆ WALLACE (A.): *The Malay Archipelago*, London, 1898.
◆ WHITTEN (T. and J.): *Wild Indonesia*, New Holland, London, 1992.
◆ ZAENURI AL YUSAK (K.H.A.): *Resep Obat-Obat Kuno*, (n/p), 1986.

◆ SOCIETY AND RELIGION ◆

◆ BRINKGREVE (F.) AND FOX (D.): *Offerings: the Ritual Art of Bali*, Image Network Indonesia, Sanur, 1992.
◆ GEERTZ (C. AND H.): *Kinship in Bali*, University of Chicago Press, Chicago, 1975.
◆ HOOYKAAS (C.): *RELIGION IN BALI*, E. J. Brill, Leiden, 1973.
◆ MERSHON (K.): *Seven Plus Seven: Mysterious Life-Rituals in Bali*, Vantage Press, New York, 1971.
◆ PICARD (M.): *Bali: Tourisme Culturel et culture touristique*, L'Harmattan, Paris, 1992.
◆ SCHAAREMAN (D.): *Tatulingga: Tradition and Continuity. An Investigation in Ritual and Social Organization in Bali*, Wepf & Co. AG Verlag, Basel, 1986.
◆ *State and Society in Bali*, ed. Hildred Geertz, KITLV Press, Leiden, 1991.
◆ WARREN (C.): *Adat and Dinas: Balinese Communites in the Indonesian State*, Oxford University Press, Singapore, 1993.

ACKNOWLEDGMENTS

We would like to thank the following publishers or copyright-holders for permission to reproduce the quotations on pages 122–36.
◆ SAMUEL PURCHAS: *Hakluytus Posthumous or Purchas His Pilgrimes*, as quoted in *The anthropological romance of Bali 1597-1972*, James A. Boon, Cambridge University Press, 1977.
◆ JUSTUS HEURNIUS, "Schriftleluck Rapport over Ende En Bali", 1638, as translated by Adrian Vickers.
◆ FRANÇOIS VALENTIJN, *Oud En Nieuw Oost Indien* , Dordrecht, 1726, as translated by Adrian Vickers.
◆ R. T. FRIEDERICH, "Voorlopig Verslag Van Het Eiland Bali", *Verhandelingen Bataviaasch Genootschap 23*, 1850, as translated by Alfons van der Kraan, "Human Sacrifice in Bali: Sources, Notes and Commentary", *Indonesia* 40 (October 1985).
◆ J. H. MOOR, *Notices of the Indian Archipelago*, 1837, reproduced by permission of Frank Cass & Co. Ltd., London.
◆ HICKMAN POWELL, *The Last Paradise*, Jonathan Cape, London, 1930.
◆ MIGUEL COVARRUBIAS, *Island of Bali*, Alfred A. Knopf Inc., New York, 1937 (Oxford University Press, 1972).
◆ FRANK CLUNE, *To the Isles of Spice with Frank Clune*, Angus and Robertson Publishers, New South Wales, 1940.
◆ COLIN MCPHEE, *A House in Bali*, Day, New York, 1946 (Oxford University Press, 1986).
◆ JOHN COAST, *Dancing Out of Bali*, London, 1954.
◆ ANNA MATHEWS, *The Night of Purnama*, Jonathan Cape, London, 1965.
◆ INEZ BARANAY, *The Saddest Pleasure*, Angus & Robertson Publishers, New South Wales, 1989.
◆ DIANA DARLING, *The Painted Alphabet*, Copyright 1992 by Diana Darling. Reprinted by permission of Houghton Mifflin Co. All rights reserved.
◆ A. A. PANJI TISNA, *Ni Rawit, Seller of Soules*, Balai Pustaka, Jakarta, 1935. Translated by Thomas M. Hunter, Jr.
◆ I GUSTI PUTU ARYA TIRTAWIRYA, "Grandmother", *Sands of White, Sands of the Sea*, Balai Pustaka, Jakarta, 1973. Translated by Thomas M. Hunter, Jr.

◆ LIST OF ILLUSTRATIONS

We have not been able to trace the heirs or publishers of certain documents. An account is being held open for them at our offices.

INDEX

◆ INDEX

Page numbers in bold refer to the Practical information section, pages 281–339.

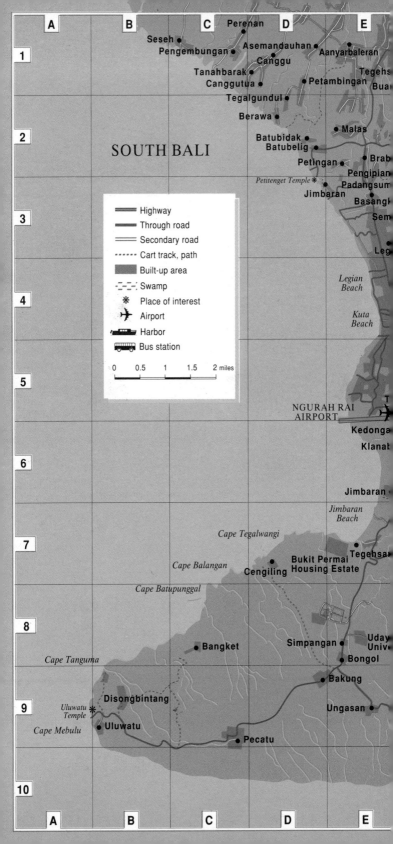

SOUTH BALI

Legend

- Highway
- Through road
- Secondary road
- Cart track, path
- Built-up area
- Swamp
- * Place of interest
- ✈ Airport
- 🚌 Harbor
- 🚌 Bus station

0   0.5   1   1.5   2 miles

Grid references (columns A–E, rows 1–10):

Perenan
Seseh
Pengembungan
Asemandauhan
Canggu
Aanyarbaleran
Tanahbarak
Petambingan
Tegehs
Canggutua
Bua
Tegalgundul
Berawa
Malas
Batubidak
Batubelig
Petingan
Brab
Pengipian
Petitenget Temple *
Padangsum
Jimbaran
Basangl
Sem
Leg
Legian
Beach
Kuta
Beach
NGURAH RAI
AIRPORT
Kedonga
Klanab
Jimbaran
Jimbaran
Beach
Cape Tegalwangi
Cape Balangan
Bukit Permai
Housing Estate
Cengiling
Tegehsa
Cape Batupunggal
Bangket
Simpangan
Uday
Univ
Bongol
Cape Tanguma
Bakung
Disongbintang
Ungasan
Uluwatu
Temple *
Uluwatu
Cape Mebulu
Pecatu